Early Intervention
in Transition

EARLY
INTERVENTION
———— IN TRANSITION

**Current Perspectives on Programs
for Handicapped Children**

Edited by KOFI MARFO

New York
Westport, Connecticut
London

Library of Congress Cataloging-in-Publication Data

Early intervention in transition : current perspectives on programs
  for handicapped children / edited by Kofi Marfo.
       p.   cm.
    Includes bibliographical references and indexes.
    ISBN 0–275–93470–5 (alk. paper)
    1. Handicapped children—Services for.   2. Handicapped children—
Services for—United States.   3. Early childhood education.
4. Early childhood education—United States.   I. Marfo, Kofi.
HV888.E16   1991
362.4'083—dc20   91–15312

British Library Cataloguing in Publication Data is available.

Library of Congress Catalog Card Number: 91–15312
ISBN: 0–275–93470–5

First published in 1991

Praeger Publishers, One Madison Avenue, New York, NY 10010
An imprint of Greenwood Publishing Group, Inc.

Printed in the United States of America

The paper used in this book complies with the
Permanent Paper Standard issued by the National
Information Standards Organization (Z39.48–1984).

10 9 8 7 6 5 4 3 2 1

To Rose and the girls,
Amma Obeaa and Nana Ampoma,
and to another very special person—
Eno (Mother) Abenaa Obeaa

Contents

Preface

Within the relatively short history of the early intervention movement
in the United States, we have witnessed many notable developments.
The last two decades have been marked by rapid expansion in services
for children with developmental disabilities. Research activity on programs for these children and their families has increasingly taken on
an identity of its own, having been closely intertwined with research
on services for socioculturally disadvantaged populations for a better
part of the history of the field. Traditional approaches to the design
and delivery of services are currently being reexamined in light of newly
emerging theoretical perspectives in the primary disciplines that inform
the field. Some of these changing perspectives have influenced early
intervention practice by first shaping social policy. The directions for
early intervention set forth in Public Law 99–457 provide a good illustration of this development. Equally noteworthy are the conceptual
and methodological shifts that are beginning to occur in the area of
efficacy research.

In any field, it takes time for conceptual and philosophical shifts to
fully manifest themselves so that researchers and practitioners alike
can draw readily on the new ideas to further advance the field and
extend existing applications. Periodic state-of-the-art publications,
such as this one, can help bridge the time lag between the emergence
of new perspectives and their applications to service delivery. In the
hope of fulfilling this role, the present volume was developed to inform
early intervention professionals about some of the key transitions cur-

rently taking place in the field, not only in the United States but also in other industrialized countries.

The division of the book into two parts reflects the two-pronged strategy adopted to accomplish the objective stated above. The first strategy was to invite scholars whose work depicts some of the changing perspectives in the field to address specific transitional themes. The seven chapters in Part I deal with these themes. Chapter 1, by Marfo and Cook, sets the stage for the more focused discussions that follow; it provides a general overview of major trends and issues in the areas of theory and efficacy research. Marfo and Cook identify two key trends in early intervention theory: (a) the emergence of developmental frameworks that make way for formulations of a more comprehensive theoretical rationale for early intervention with handicapped children, and (b) the development of theory-driven early intervention programs focusing specifically on parent-child interaction. In the second area, the authors summarize some of the concerns expressed frequently in the literature about past research and discuss several developments that illustrate the growing maturity in the way early intervention efficacy is conceptualized. They conclude the section with suggestions for further enhancing the quality of efficacy research.

The remaining six chapters in Part I address three major transitional themes: etiology-specific intervention programming (Chapters 2 and 3), family-focused intervention (Chapters 4 and 5), and interaction-focused intervention (Chapters 6 and 7). In Chapter 2, Hodapp and Dykens make a strong case for greater attention to the development of etiology-specific early intervention strategies, while recognizing that general, noncategorical techniques will always have a place in early intervention work because of the many common developmental attributes shared by all children. In developing their rationale for an etiology-specific approach, Hodapp and Dykens draw on a convergence of insights from several areas of research. First, they cite the phenomenal advances that biomedical research has made in the subtyping and early diagnosis of a wide range of handicapping conditions. Second, they refer to the continuing progress behavioral researchers are making in identifying the unique developmental and learning attributes that accompany specific disabilities. Finally, they point to evidence from family-dynamics research indicating that the reactions of parents and other family members to the handicapped child vary significantly as a function of the etiology and severity of the handicapping condition.

Chapter 3, also on the subject of etiology-specific early intervention, is a more focused examination of why children with Down syndrome are not likely to benefit substantially from omnibus early intervention curricula that are applied indiscriminately to clinically heterogeneous groups of children. Gibson suggests that part of the reason for the poor outcomes of early intervention services for children with Down syndrome is that past efforts have largely failed "to build on the specific reflexive, neuromotor, sensory, and pre-cognitive growth profiles of the syndrome" (p. 83). Through an extensive review of research on the developmental deficits and strengths associated with the syndrome, Gibson establishes a compelling rationale for a syndrome-specific approach to intervention—one that is also sensitive to individual differences within the syndrome. The attention that Gibson pays to life beyond the early childhood years in his review of the literature underscores his position that such intervention should be both intensive and life-span oriented. One significant implication of his analysis, although not discussed explicitly in the chapter, is that programs targeting children with Down syndrome need to be founded on multidisciplinary models that allow for a stronger integration of biomedical and psychoeducational strategies.

The transition from child-focused to family-focused approaches to early intervention programming is perhaps one of the more noticeable trends in the field. In Chapter 4, Simeonsson and Bailey trace some of the theoretical origins of the family focus in early intervention work with handicapped children, describing their own efforts in the development, implementation, and validation of one of the better-known family-focused models in the early intervention field today. In particular, they show how their original model has been revised through insights gained from their preliminary work. In discussing the implications of their model, Simeonsson and Bailey raise a number of challenges that need to be addressed: the need for program sensitivity to ethnic and cultural variation; the need for a new cadre of intervention workers capable of assessing family needs, working collaboratively with families to set goals, and communicating effectively with families; and the need for more comprehensive professional development curriculum models to facilitate the transition to family-focused intervention.

In Chapter 5, Barrera, too, discusses the theoretical underpinnings of her transactional model of early intervention and describes extensively the various components of the intervention process. The description reveals a rich blending of a multidisciplinary team approach, a family-focused service delivery system, and an infant curriculum model. Until recently, the model had been validated largely with low-birth-weight infants and their families. In this chapter, Barrera describes the process of applying the model to families with children who have confirmed developmental disabilities or who are at risk for developmental delay because of a poor parenting environment. From the validation data gathered on 119 infants participating in the program,

Barrera examines the question of whether intervention outcomes vary (a) for different categories of disabled children, and (b) as a function of the timing of enrollment.

The third major transitional theme covered in this book pertains to the growing popularity of interaction-focused early intervention strategies, the central features of which are introduced in Chapter 1. Chapters 6 and 7 in Part I address, at a conceptual and methodological level, some of the critical issues that this emerging approach raises. In Chapter 6, McCollum appraises this new approach through a review and analysis of research on interaction coaching. Following a review of the theoretical rationales and assumptions underpinning interaction-focused intervention, she attempts to paint a composite picture of the interaction coaching literature by synthesizing information on such common themes as the goals, content, procedures, and outcomes of coaching. McCollum offers a number of very useful suggestions for fine-tuning research methods and extending current research questions to more adequately assess the viability and long-term developmental outcomes of interaction coaching. She concludes the chapter with a provocative discussion of the extent to which interaction coaching efforts to date can be said to be conceptually compatible with the spirit of the family-focused orientation to early intervention.

In Chapter 7, Marfo identifies research on maternal directiveness in interactions with handicapped children as one of the major forces providing the impetus for interaction-focused intervention, presenting an in-depth critical analysis of this research. He argues that problems in the conceptualization and empirical study of directiveness have placed severe limitations on the extent to which we can translate existing findings into intervention practice. He challenges the conventional view of directiveness as a negative interactional style, pointing out conceptual beliefs and methodological practices that have served to perpetuate this negative connotation. Marfo cautions that the indiscriminate application of strategies for reducing directiveness to all mothers of handicapped children could be potentially counterproductive for some dyads. Several suggestions for refining the research on maternal directiveness are made, in the hope that future studies will produce more enlightening insights and yield clearer directions for intervention.

The second strategy adopted to accomplish the book's mission was to invite scholars from the United States and three other industrialized countries who are active in the early intervention field to prepare accounts of the field in their respective countries. The four chapters in Part II present descriptions and discussions of the development and current status of early intervention services in the United States (Summers and Innocenti), Canada (Marfo), Australia (Hayes), and the United

Kingdom (Sturmey). While these chapters reveal obvious differences in the extent of coverage of specific issues and in the format of presentation, authors were asked to follow a set of guidelines to permit a comparative study of policies and practices in the four countries. In each chapter an attempt is made to undertake the following tasks:

1. Trace the development of early intervention services, noting significant scientific, socioeconomic, and political forces shaping the development process.
2. Identify significant shifts or trends in conceptualization, service delivery, funding, curriculum development, staff preparation, and evaluation.
3. Identify the major research issues, synthesize available research on major themes, and highlight exemplary theoretical and empirical initiatives.
4. Identify current and future challenges, offering directions on how such challenges may be met.

A reading of these four chapters reveals the remarkable influence that forces in the United States have had on research and practice in the three other countries. In their respective chapters on Canada and Australia, Marfo and Hayes comment on the blessings as well as the curses that go with such influence. While this influence has created many similarities in service delivery and in research focus across the four countries, there are also marked differences. For example, Sturmey's chapter reveals that in the United Kingdom, the interaction-focused approach to early intervention remains relatively unknown; in contrast, this approach is already becoming firmly established in the United States and Canada, and in Australia the "milieu approach" described by Hayes signals a trend in this direction. On the policy front, the United States and the United Kingdom have in common the existence of national legislative provisions that have ensured nationwide accessibility to services, whereas in Canada and Australia the absence of a national agenda continues to foster regional imbalances in the availability of services.

The reader will also find interesting differences in what the authors perceive to be major accomplishments, current challenges, and future directions in the field in their respective countries. For example, Summers and Innocenti consider issues pertaining to the quality of efficacy and cost-effectiveness research to be key challenges in the United States, whereas Marfo suggests that the major challenges for Canada include the need for a national policy, provincial and federal support for research, and mechanisms for nationwide dissemination of existing knowledge. Funding for both research and program delivery is a major issue for Australia, but Hayes also underscores the importance of addressing the twin geographic problem of distance and isolation in the development of delivery models. Finally, in the United Kingdom, the absence of a strong research base for the country's dominant approach to early intervention—the Portage Model—is a major concern.

As early intervention services become firmly established around the globe, the cross-national comparative study of delivery systems, programming approaches, and research foci will likely become an exciting area of scholarship within the field. It is my fervent hope that the insights presented in the international perspectives section of this volume will take us one step closer to the formal launching of this specialty area.

Acknowledgments

I wish to thank my contributing authors for agreeing to participate in the mission of the volume and for their remarkable cooperation throughout the editorial process. I owe a special debt of gratitude to Patti Fleck, my dedicated and indefatigable research assistant, for her thorough proofreading of most of the chapters and for her assistance with indexing. I am thankful also to the following individuals: Associate Dean Leo Anglin and Joanne Uslick for their kind permission to let several of the chapters be typed at the Bureau of Research and Training Services; Janie Knight at the dean's office for saving me much precious time by scanning several of the chapters on her computer; Madelyn Thomas and Shirley Smith of the Department of Educational Psychology and Leadership Studies for typing portions of the manuscript; and Patti Koch for assistance with the indexing.

Finally, I salute my beloved family who, willingly as well as under duress, provided release time from my family responsibilities to complete this project. They are equal contributors to this volume by sacrifice!

I

THEMATIC ISSUES

1

Overview of Trends and Issues in Early Intervention Theory and Research

Kofi Marfo and Christine Cook

Phenomenal transitions are occurring in the field of early intervention. Over the last twenty years, multidisciplinary perspectives have received greater emphasis, and the intervention process itself has increasingly come to be viewed as encompassing a broader variety of services, models, and strategies for addressing both the developmental needs of handicapped children and the psychological well-being of family members. Increased public support, in some cases backed by national legislation (e.g., in the United States and in the United Kingdom), has resulted in dramatic expansion of services. As many of the chapters in this volume reveal, a great deal of rethinking is going on in the field regarding how best to develop and deliver programs. At the same time, the debate over (a) the theoretical foundations of early intervention and (b) the status of efficacy research appears to be intensifying.

In this chapter, we attempt to provide an overview of major trends and issues pertaining to theory and research in this field. The chapter is divided into two main sections: (a) trends and issues relating to theory, and (b) trends and issues in efficacy research. Two themes are addressed in the first section. The first pertains to the theoretical rationale for early intervention, while the second deals with trends in the development of theory-driven intervention frameworks. Given the multidisciplinary nature of the field, it is useful to point out that the issues addressed in this chapter mainly relate to the role of early intervention in handicapped children's behavioral development from the points of view of developmental psychology and early childhood special education.

TRENDS AND ISSUES RELATING TO THEORY

One of the long-standing concerns in the early intervention field is that much of intervention work has been atheoretical. In the 1970s, there was a vigorous debate over the theoretical foundations of early intervention programs. However, as the early intervention movement became widespread around the world and gained legislative support in some countries, the controversy surrounding its theoretical grounds faded naturally into the background. Early intervention programs continued to proliferate in the virtual absence of systematic theory building to guide practice. In recent years, the field has begun to witness a return to theoretical concerns (see Brownell & Strauss, 1985; Dunst, 1986; Marfo, 1991; Odom, Yoder, & Hill, 1988; Ramey & Suarez, 1985). Admittedly, some of the concerns that are currently being expressed over the theoretical bases of early intervention are different in certain regards from those that confronted the early intervention movement during its formative years. For example, while the early concerns tended to focus more on the validity of the *primacy of early experience* theory as the central rationale for early intervention, current concerns are addressing the link between theory and practice. Nevertheless, issues relating to the theoretical rationale for early intervention services are as valid today as they were twenty years ago.

In this section we examine a number of issues relating to the role and status of theory in early intervention work with handicapped children and their families. The discussion will focus on two central themes. First, we will examine trends and issues pertaining to the formulation of a theoretical rationale for early intervention. We will then review the trend toward extending the focus of early intervention beyond the traditional skill-teaching paradigm, paying particular attention to selected exemplary theory-driven approaches targeted toward handicapped infants and toddlers.

Rationale for Early Intervention

When early intervention programs for handicapped infants and young children emerged in the early 1970s, they were essentially premised on extrapolations of the same conceptual and theoretical formulations that had served as the catalyst for the proliferation of programs for disadvantaged children. As Caldwell (1970) indicates in her classic review, the theoretical rationale for early intervention grew out of an extensive body of literature (from both infra-human and human research) demonstrating the importance of early experience for later development. It is this literature that Hunt (1961) and Bloom (1964) used as the basis for their conceptual analyses that stressed the first few years of life as the most opportune period in which to stimulate children's development. The ideas contained in these two influential books, and the additional research they spawned, were to find practical expression in the widespread acceptance of infant and preschool programs as a viable strategy for addressing the developmental and educational needs of environmentally disadvantaged children.

However, the pendulum began to swing against the *primacy of early experience* view amidst (a) the growing popularity of methodological articles faulting much of the infra-human studies that supported the importance of early experience, (b) the emergence of the first negative appraisals of Head Start programs (Jensen, 1969; Westinghouse Learning Corporation, 1969), and (c) the appearance of critical reviews of Bloom's position (A. D. Clarke, 1978; McCall, 1977). The attacks on the theoretical foundations of early intervention had begun.

Contributing in no small measure to early intervention's theoretical vulnerability was the fact that no effort had as yet been made to formulate a more comprehensive theoretical rationale that went beyond the basic belief that what occurred in the early years were of critical importance to later development. Thus, the entire theoretical edifice of early intervention hinged tenuously upon speculations about the importance of the *timing* of intervention rather than on formulations regarding the actual mechanisms of developmental change and how these mechanisms interacted with timing to produce specific outcomes.

Over the past decade and a half, several theoretical frameworks describing the mechanisms of development and developmental change have emerged in the literature. These frameworks have contributed significant insights into behavioral development, provided important directions for developmental interventions in general, and have thus set the stage for more comprehensive conceptualizations of the rationale for early intervention with atypically developing children. Among these formulations are Urie Bronfenbrenner's ecological systems theory (Bronfenbrenner, 1979, 1989), Arnold Sameroff's transactional model (Sameroff, 1975, 1980; Sameroff & Chandler, 1975; Sameroff & Fiese, 1990), and Reuven Feuerstein's theory of structural cognitive modifiability (Feuerstein, Rand, Hoffman, & Miller, 1980). The three frameworks have at least two attributes in common: (1) they all view human development as a transactional process, and (2) each of the theories has drawn extensively from the literature on atypically developing or developmentally at-risk children. The essential features of these frameworks and the ways in which they contribute to the rationale for early intervention with handicapped children are examined below.

Development as a transactional process. The common thread in Sa-meroff's and Bronfenbrenner's frameworks is the proposition that nei-ther biological-constitutional factors underlying the uniqueness of individuals nor the experiential-environmental contexts of develop-ment are the sole determinants of developmental outcomes. In both the original and more recent formulations of Bronfenbrenner's ecological systems theory, the processes and outcomes of development are seen to occur as a joint function of factors pertaining to the person and the environment. Bronfenbrenner goes beyond a static, additive model of person-environment interaction to emphasize the dynamic nature of person-environment transactions, such that at any given time specific characteristics of the person and the environment are deemed to be both "products and producers of development" (Bronfenbrenner, 1989, p. 191).

Environments do not affect a person independently of his/her char-acteristics; depending upon the individual characteristics of the person, particular environmental conditions produce different developmental outcomes. In the same vein, characteristics of the person do not produce developmental outcomes independently of the environment. Bronfen-brenner illustrates these principles with the following observations taken from a thirty-year-old Scottish study in which Drillien (1957, 1964) examined the developmental sequelae associated with prema-turity.

Responsive maternal care can substantially reduce the severity of psychological problems associated with low birth weight among socioeconomically deprived families, and can subsequently reduce the number of low-birth-weight children experiencing any serious difficulty. (p. 199)

Living organisms have the capacity, and indeed the active disposition, to heal themselves over time. . . . In sum, significant resources for counteracting effects of prenatal handicaps exist both on the side of the environment and of the organism itself. (p. 198)

The first of the two observations above essentially echoes the central empirical observation underlying Sameroff's transactional model, which was developed in reaction to the prevailing main-effect model for predicting long-term developmental outcomes. The defining attrib-ute of main-effect developmental models is that they tend to view in isolation the contributions that the child and his/her environment make to long-term developmental outcomes. For example, much of the re-search assessing the effects of biological risk conditions (i.e., *repro-ductive casualty*) on development, prior to Sameroff's work, failed to consider the moderating role of the child's experiential and socioeco-nomic environment.

From an empirical point of view, support for the main-effect model tended to come largely from confounded retrospective studies in which most of the children with the biological risk conditions studied appeared also to have come from poorer socioeconomic backgrounds (see Passamanick & Knobloch, 1966, for a synthesis of aspects of this research). A totally different picture emerged from prospective studies of children with such *reproductive casualties* as anoxia, prematurity, and perinatal complications. As Sameroff (1980) observed,

> Whenever a perinatal risk factor was hypothesized to be related to later dysfunction, prospective studies found no greater incidence of disorder in the risk population than in control populations without the risk factor. Whether the risk was related to preterm birth, low birthweight, anoxia, or neurological signs, few causal chains were found when appropriate control populations were studied. (p. 344).

This observation led Sameroff and Chandler to conclude that "even if one continues to believe that a continuum of reproductive casualty exists, its importance pales in comparison to the massive influences of socio-economic factors on both prenatal and postnatal development" (1975, p. 238).

The transactional model perhaps provides one of the strongest grounds for the optimism that underlies early intervention programs for handicapped children and their families. According to this view of development, "although reproductive casualties may play an initiating role in the production of later problems, it is the caretaking environment that will determine the ultimate outcome" (Sameroff, 1975, p. 274). Thus, the long-term developmental outcomes for children who manifest problems of a biological or constitutional nature can be understood more completely only in relation to a "continuum of caretaking casualty." At the extreme positive end of this continuum, it is conceivable that a supportive and ameliorative caretaking environment can even eliminate the deleterious behavioral effects of some kinds of biological insult, whereas on the extreme negative end, a deficient caretaking environment can indeed aggravate the effects of early biological insult. Early interventionists need to realize that the extent to which the caretaking environment can mitigate the long-term developmental effects of a handicapping condition depends very much on the exact nature and severity of the handicap.

The transactional model also provides some basis for addressing the "naive environmentalism" criticism of early intervention practice. Some critics have charged that early intervention is founded on the assumption that infant development is influenced more by environmental factors than by biological or genetic factors (Brownell & Strauss,

1985). This may be a valid criticism when we consider that the enthusiasm of some zealous early interventionists sometimes fails to acknowledge the limitations imposed by constitutional factors.
Nevertheless, this rather inaccurate depiction of the basis for early
intervention work stems in large part from the absence of clearly artic-
ulated theoretical rationales in which the relative contributions and
limitations of various mechanisms of development are specified. The
transactional principle that development is influenced by a complex,
continuous, and dynamic interaction between biological and experiential factors is fundamental to the conceptualization of early intervention. It must be pointed out, however, that any form of behavioral
intervention, whether carried out early or later in life, seeks to improve
the development of human competence by taking advantage of the
portion of the developmental equation that is more easily susceptible
to manipulation. This is what early intervention is about, and is what
differentiates the early intervention stance from the naive environmentalism position inherent in J. B. Watson's comment of 1935 that he could
turn any child into any number of outcomes if he could control his/
her rearing environments (cf. Brownell & Strauss, 1985).

Not only is the transactional model optimistic, but it provides a framework for conceptualizing the intervention process. For example, the
view of the caretaking environment-child relationship as a "continual
interplay between a changing child and a changing environment" (Sameroff, 1980, p. 345) suggests that intervention activities need to be
constantly modulated to reflect the progressions of change occurring
within the child, within the caretaking environment, and within the
caretaking environment-child relationship.

*Feuerstein's theory of structural cognitive modifiability as a specific
formulation of the Transactional Principle.* The transactional model,
as presented above, addresses developmental outcomes in general,
without any specific formulations about how changes occur within
different developmental domains. Domain-specific theories of development have the potential to make more substantial contributions to
programming with handicapped children than general developmental
models. One such domain-specific theory has been formulated by the
Israeli psychologist Reuven Feuerstein. While the theory has more direct relevance for work with children with mental retardation or general
delays of a cognitive nature, principles derived from it can be applied
to a much broader population of atypically developing children.

Feuerstein's *theory of structural cognitive modifiability* states that
"changes of a structural nature that can alter the course and direction
of cognitive development" (Feuerstein, Rand, Hoffman, & Miller, 1980,
p. 9) can be effected through systematic and consistent mediation.
Feuerstein contrasts structural changes with specific changes in an in-

dividual's repertoire of skills (such as the acquisition of a particular strategy for searching for a hidden object) that result from exposure to a given set of experiences. "Structural changes ... refer not to isolated events but to the organism's manner of interacting with, acting on, and responding to, sources of information" (p. 9). The ultimate manifestation of structural cognitive change is receptivity and sensitivity to internal and external sources of stimulation.

The extent to which mentally retarded and developmentally delayed children can be said to be susceptible to structural cognitive modifiability, even in the face of genetic and other constitutional factors, can be found in Feuerstein's characterization of the determinants of retarded cognitive performance. He distinguishes between two determinants: *distal* and *proximal*. Factors that are traditionally considered the causes of mild mental retardation and developmental delay—such as polygenic inheritance, biological insult associated with teratogenic and other noxious agents, and early environmental deprivation—are classified as *distal* etiologic factors. These factors are labeled distal because, in the words of Feuerstein and his associates, they "neither directly nor inevitably cause" retarded performance (p. 17). The immediate or *proximal* determinant of retarded performance is a lack of[1] or reduced exposure to mediated learning experience (MLE). MLE is defined as the process by which environmentally emitted stimuli "are transformed by a 'mediating' agent, usually a parent, sibling, or other caregiver," who, "guided by his (her) intentions, culture, and emotional investment, selects and organizes the world of stimuli for the child" (p. 16).

According to this framework, children with mental retardation and developmental delays, like nonhandicapped and culturally disadvantaged children, are highly susceptible to structural cognitive modifiability. The so-called distal factors, traditionally considered the primary cause of mild mental retardation or developmental delay, are not deemed to constitute a significant hinderance or limit to modifiability as long as the quality of MLE is high and "except in the most severe instance of genetic and organic impairment" (p. 9).

At face value, the claim that the so-called distal factors "neither directly nor inevitably cause retardation" departs radically from conventional wisdom in the field and may even sound untenable. It is possible, however, to reconcile conventional wisdom and Feuerstein's perspective by viewing MLE as moderating the *expression* of polygenic inheritance or the developmental manifestations of biological insult. In other words, polygenic inheritance and biological insults of a pre-, peri-, and postnatal environmental nature can be a necessary and sufficient cause of retarded cognitive performance, if these forces are not countered effectively through high-quality MLE. In a sense, then, as radical as Feuerstein's theory may sound, it really represents a more specific formulation of the transactional view of development.

Recast in transactional terms, the theory states that the long-term developmental manifestations of either polygenic predisposition to low cognitive functioning or biological insult can only be understood in relation to a continuum of MLE. In the best of scenarios, an extremely high-quality MLE can conceivably nullify or abate the effects of these distal factors, and in the worst situation, a deficient MLE can aggravate the effects of these determinants. This view certainly offers further theoretical grounding for the emergent *interaction-focused* approach to early intervention. It suggests that one way to reduce the impact of disability and enhance the handicapped child's developmental competence is to offer the significant adults in the child's life (i.e., parents in the case of infants and toddlers, and parents and teachers in the case of preschool and school-age children) support in the development of effective mediational skills. In fact, in the United States, some interventionists are beginning to apply the theory of mediated learning experience to the development of interaction-focused early intervention programs (Kahn, 1990).

Handicapped children and the importance of the early years. The frameworks examined above speak only indirectly to the issue of the timing of intervention, yet any formulation of a theoretical rationale for early intervention must formally address the importance of the early years. Initial propositions regarding the special importance of the early years were premised on the notion of the plasticity of central nervous system (CNS) development and on the relative contributions to CNS development of early versus later experiences. Over the past two decades, these propositions have been both vehemently criticized (Brownell & Strauss, 1985; Clarke & Clarke, 1976a, 1976b, 1979) and ardently defended (Anastasiow, 1986b, 1990; Wachs & Gruen, 1982). The emerging consensus is that while greater attention needs to be paid to the issues of continuity and developmental experiences occurring later in life, the early years are still of especial importance in children's development (Guralnick & Bennett, 1987).

From a neurobiological perspective, Anastasiow (1990) has recently synthesized some evidence demonstrating the role of early facilitative environments in the amelioration of risk factors associated with brain activity and other constitutional problems. For the most part, however, within the developmental disabilities field, the trend in conceptualizations of the importance of the early years appears to be shifting away from the traditional invocation of theoretical and empirical arguments regarding critical periods in CNS development. A more functional view of the rationale for facilitating the establishment and continued nurturance of optimal environment-child behavior transactions at the earliest possible time is emerging. Part of the rationale is tied to the stark reality that handicapping conditions have the tendency to constrain or cause disturbances in the development of those early behavioral and sensory competencies upon which optimal transactions with the worlds of objects and persons are founded. Delayed or atypical behavioral development in turn affects the interactional styles of significant others in ways that serve to further deprive the child of developmentally appropriate experiences. Logically, since these difficulties begin to emerge in the early years, when the foundations of behavioral development are being laid, it only makes sense that intervention should begin early as well.

The parent-child interaction literature provides compelling evidence in support of this perspective. It is widely acknowledged in the developmental literature that early parent-child interaction processes play a central role in mediating children's development of social, linguistic, and cognitive competence. The quality of parent-child interactions, however, depends as much on the child's input as it does on the parent's. Evidence from a variety of investigations suggests that the interactions of parents with their handicapped children tend to be much less optimal than parental interactions with nonhandicapped children (see syntheses of this research by Field, 1980; Marfo, 1984; Richard, 1986; Rogers, 1988). Part of the reason is that various child-related developmental and interactional characteristics associated with specific handicaps do make the task of providing a stimulating and developmentally enhancing caretaking environment a challenging one. But the causal links to interactional difficulties do not always originate from the child. The perceptions and emotions that the birth of a handicapped child engenders within the family can also negatively affect the quality of caregiver interactions (Emde & Brown, 1978; Hodapp, 1988; Wasserman & Allen, 1985), touching off a potential cycle of disruptive interactions in some dyads.

The psychological needs of parents within the broader context of their caretaking role provide an equally good reason for intervening early. While the levels of stress associated with parenting a handicapped child may vary across handicapping conditions and across families, the need for some form of assistance in coping with the challenges that rearing a handicapped child presents is very real for many families. The support received from an intervention program can be most valuable especially when such stress stems from uncertainty about what parenting behaviors are appropriate or what the developmental needs of a handicapped child are. Sometimes such support may only serve to build parenting confidence, restore or enhance self-esteem, and foster family well-being; the important point, nevertheless, is that providing these psychological resources early in the parenting process can set the stage for a healthy and developmentally enhancing relationship.

From the foregoing analysis, one of the main goals of early intervention is to counter the potential deleterious effects of primary handicapping conditions by facilitating early behavioral development. To accomplish this objective, the needs of both child and parents/family are emphasized equally. The ecological focus that the preceding discussion implies is particularly noteworthy. By targeting not just the child but the transactions between the child and his/her social-experiential environment, intervention programs should help set in motion mechanisms within the child's own developmental ecology that can be expected to continuously fuel optimal development within the limits imposed by disability. This is not to suggest in any way that providing early intervention services will remove the need for future services. Many handicapped children and their families need continued support past the preschool years. Indeed, part of the ultimate goal of early intervention programs is to promote continuity in the accessing of a broad range of multidisciplinary services by families of handicapped children.

Trends in the Development of Theory-Driven Intervention Frameworks

Relatively speaking, there is little doubt that phenomenal advances have been made in the application of theoretical principles to the design and delivery of early intervention programs over the past twenty years. A great deal of progress has also been made in the development of theoretical guidelines for delineating the components and phases of the intervention process and for translating initial assessment information into program goals, instructional activities, and evaluation procedures (see Bricker & Veltman, 1990). In spite of these acknowledged strengths, there is a great deal of room for improving the marriage between theory and practice in the field.

For many years, early intervention programming for handicapped children has been driven vaguely by general developmental models emphasizing the acquisition of sequenced, age-appropriate skills within the various developmental domains (see Berkeley & Ludlow, 1989, for a critical evaluation of the traditional developmental model) . Didactic instruction of the handicapped child aimed at fostering timely acquisition of normative skills, often with a parent as the instructor, remains the principal hallmark of many intervention programs (see Peterson, 1987). Instead of using theoretical frameworks that show how specific practices produce particular outcomes for individual clients, many programs are characterized by a "global experiential approach" (to borrow the terminology of Bricker & Veltman, 1990) and are driven more by the availability of packaged curricular and assessment materials on the market. This unfortunate state of affairs must certainly be one of the reasons why the efficacy of early intervention has been difficult to establish.

One indication of the transitions within the field in recent years is that we are beginning to witness the emergence of theory-driven intervention models that are conceptualized in a manner that makes it possible to empirically assess the relationship between specific inputs (independent variables) and specific outcomes. The examples we have selected to illustrate this transition are mainly programs addressing the developmental needs of handicapped *infants and toddlers* within the broader context of the family ecology. Representing the growing influence of ecological, transactional, and family-systems perspectives on human development, these models are extending the focus of early intervention significantly beyond the traditional skill-teaching emphasis.

Two such emerging approaches, the *family-focused* and the *inter-action-focused* models of intervention, are illustrated below. In one sense the second model can be subsumed under the first. For example, Simeonsson and Bailey (Chapter 4; see also Bailey et al., 1986) have conceptualized family-focused intervention much more broadly to include interventions into the parent-child interaction process. However, there are self-contained interaction-focused intervention programs that do not necessarily address the broader needs of the family at large (Mahoney, 1988a; Mahoney & Powell, 1988). For this reason the two will be presented as separate perspectives.

Family-focused and social support intervention models. The family-focused intervention model and the transactional model of intervention described by Simeonsson and Bailey (Chapter 4) and Barrera (Chapter 5) are good examples of this emerging orientation. Carl Dunst and his associates have also developed a family systems intervention model based on the conceptualized influences that both formal and informal social support networks have on parental health and well-being, family functioning, parent-child interactional styles, and child behavior and development (see Dunst & Trivette, 1988a, 1988b, 1990). Supporting, strengthening, and empowering families of handicapped children are the cornerstones of social support intervention. Having thoroughly identified the family's needs and resources (both within and outside the family), the role of the interventionist is to help the family mobilize these resources to meet the identified needs.

While the definition of early intervention underlying the model (see Dunst, 1986) is so broad as to encompass most services that early intervention programs make available to families with a handicapped child, the research of Dunst and his associates has focused on (1) identifying how specific aspects of social support impact family and child functioning, (2) the conditions under which the provision of support makes a positive impact, and (3) mechanisms for identifying which supports are most needed by families in intervention. For example, Dunst and his colleagues have found that the kinds of supports that contribute most positively to family functioning are those that families themselves identify as needed, not those that are generically hypothesized, *a priori*, to be valuable or necessary for families with a handicapped child. This finding accounts for their emphasis on needs-based family systems assessment (see Dunst & Trivette, 1990).

Apart from specifying the philosphical and conceptual bases of social support interventions (see Dunst & Trivette, 1987, 1990), Dunst has paid significant attention to employing rigorous methodological and analytical tools to assess the impact of social support networks and social support interventions on various dimensions of parent, family, and child functioning (for a summary of aspects of this research, see Dunst & Trivette, 1988a).

Interaction-focused intervention models. Another significant development in the field is the emergence of theory-driven *interaction-focused* early intervention programs. These are programs that target the parent-child interaction process. So far, much of this work has been limited to the mother-infant/toddler dyad. The relative strengths of interaction-focused interventions over the didactic, skill-teaching approach have been discussed extensively by Affleck, McGrade, Mc-Queeny, and Allen (1982). Two of these programs are reviewed briefly here. In Chapter 6, McCollum provides a more extensive review and analysis of intervention efforts targeting the parent-child interaction process.

Mahoney's Transactional Intervention Program (TRIP). The TRIP was designed to enhance the motivation and development of handicapped infants and toddlers by focusing intervention on the quality of interaction between these children and their caregivers. Underlying the TRIP (Mahoney, 1988a; Mahoney & Powell, 1986, 1988) is a transactional view of human development, with particular emphasis on the important role of parental interactional style in children's cognitive, linguistic, and socioemotional development. The program itself was the product of a systematic line of enquiry designed to ascertain which specific features of parental interactional style are most or least facilitative of children's development (Mahoney, 1988a, 1988b; Mahoney, Finger, & Powell, 1985; Mahoney & Robenalt, 1986). This line of enquiry revealed a profile of developmentally enhancing maternal interactional style that was characterized by high degrees of acceptance and responsiveness

to child-initiated behavior and low degrees of instruction and directiveness. Consequently, the intervention program addresses these attributes of interaction.

The program comprises two main instructional paradigms: *turntaking* and *interactive match*. The turntaking component of the program
has a twofold objective: (a) to promote balanced interaction between
parent and child, and (b) to increase parental responsiveness to the
child, while decreasing directiveness. The interactive match component is premised on the view that how actively children participate in
the interaction is a function of the degree of compatibility between
parent and child behavior. For this reason, the primary goal of the
second paradigm is to get parents to match their behaviors to the child's
interactional style, current interests, developmental level, and information-processing capabilities (Mahoney, 1988a; Mahoney & Powell,
1988).

Evidence presented by Mahoney and his associates (Mahoney, 1988a;
Mahoney & Powell, 1988) indicates that not only can parental interactional style be modified through this form of intervention but that
such modification does result in positive changes in handicapped children's rate of cognitive and language development. The results of similar forms of intervention corroborate aspects of Mahoney's findings.
The TRIP approach is very much like the *conversational model* of
language intervention, as is reflected in the work of MacDonald and
his associates in the United States (MacDonald & Gillette, 1984, 1988)
and Girolametto and associates in Canada (Girolametto, 1988; Girolametto, Greenberg, & Manolson, 1986; Tannock, Girolametto, & Siegel,
1988).

Girolametto's (1988) intervention study involving preschool-age developmentally delayed children produced observable differences in the
interactional skills of experimental and control dyads. However, unlike
Mahoney's findings, the improved quality of interaction in Girolametto's experimental families did not produce corresponding increases in
children's linguistic competence as measured by mean length of utterance or by receptive and expressive language skills. In another study
employing the conversational model, Tannock, Girolametto, and Siegel
(1988) reported somewhat similar results: greater responsiveness and
reduced directiveness on the part of experimental mothers were not
accompanied by superior linguistic skills in their children.

Bromwich's 'Mutual Enjoyment' Model. In the 1970s, Rose Bromwich
and her associates with the UCLA Infant Studies Project were among
the first to propose interaction-focused early intervention as a more
appropriate alternative to the dominant skill-teaching approach, especially for infants. Bromwich (1977) suggested that instead of training
parents to teach sequentially ordered skills in the various develop-

mental domains to their infants, early interventionists should work with parents to increase "(1) awareness of their infant's sensory tolerance and temperamental organization, (2) enjoyment of their infant and their sensitive responsiveness to all his or her communications, and (3) ability to anticipate changes in behaviors likely to occur in the child's early development" (p. 81). Underlying Bromwich's (1976) model were three basic assumptions. First, infant-mother interaction is a truly reciprocal process in which the behavior of each affects the other's responses. Second, a mutually satisfying relationship between mother and infant is a key prerequisite to optimal child development. Finally, as a mother experiences her infant's increasing responsiveness to her interactional strategies, she gains competence and confidence as a primary agent of change for her infant and thus becomes less dependent upon the intervention of a professional. This independence is deemed to be the utlimate key to the intervention program's long-term developmental outcomes for the child.

The intervention process itself is structured around a progression of six maternal behaviors (Bromwich, 1976; see also Marfo, 1984). The first three levels of the progression are primarily affective in nature, reflecting a strong belief that the parent-child interaction process must be mutually satisfying if it is to serve as the cornerstone for facilitating the child's development. They include the mother's (1) capacity to enjoy her infant, (2) sensitivity to and ability to read the infant's cues, and (3) ability to engage in the kind of quality interactions that enable the infant to develop attachment and early communication skills. The three upper levels of the progression, which pertain more directly to skills in identifying and providing a broad range of age-appropriate cognitive growth-enhancing experiences in a variety of contexts, are stressed only after a firm affective foundation has been laid.

Unfortunately, while Bromwich's model has been acclaimed widely in the literature as a promising approach to early intervention (Affleck, McGrade, McQueeney, & Allen, 1982; Marfo, 1984; Zigler & Hodapp, 1986), there is not much substantive data base beyond the clinical case reports appearing in Bromwich (1981) upon which to assess the effectiveness of the model. However, some supportive data are beginning to emerge from the work of other researchers who have been using similar models in more recent years. For example, using a single-subject design, McCollum (1984) demonstrated the effectiveness of a Social Interaction Assessment and Intervention (SIAI) model in changing the interactions of dyads with a variety of interactive problems. Like Bromwich's approach, a key feature of the SIAI model is the establishment of "maximum enjoyment for both partners by helping the caregiver adjust his/her own interactive style to the particular interactive needs of the baby" (McCollum, 1984, p. 303-4). Parental impressions data reported by Rose and Calhoun (1990) provide additional indication of the promise of this approach. One of the components of the Charlotte Circle Project (Rose & Calhoun, 1990) is a *social reciprocity* model for enhancing parent-child interaction. Although the model does not appear to draw directly from the work of Bromwich, the caregiver's attainment of mutually satisfying social interactions with the child is one of the major goals of the intervention.

It appears from the foregoing review of the family-focused and interaction-focused approaches that one significant challenge lies in the ability of their proponents to demonstrate how the positive changes observed in the quality of dyadic interactions or in the dynamics of family functioning translate ultimately into child developmental gains. Other equally important challenges to the interaction-focused approach, in particular, are discussed in Chapter 6.

TRENDS AND ISSUES IN EFFICACY RESEARCH

The past decade has witnessed several indicators of the coming of age of early intervention efficacy research. In this section we examine three of these indicators, noting their significance for continued growth in the field. They are: (1) the increased recognition of the limitations of extrapolating findings from research with other populations, (2) the remarkable ascendancy of critical analysis within the field, and (3) the diminishing importance of the traditional global efficacy question. In addition to these three themes, we provide a summary of specific directions for the future, based on the insights that we have gained from past efficacy research. Summers and Innocenti address additional issues pertaining to the status of efficacy research in Chapter 8, on early intervention in the United States.

Increased Recognition of the Limitations of Extrapolating Findings from Research with Other Populations

For years, many of the claims regarding factors associated with the efficacy of early intervention services for handicapped children and their families were based on findings extrapolated from the literature on early intervention with environmentally at-risk or culturally disadvantaged children. This was understandable, given that early intervention services for handicapped children grew out of a tradition of services for disadvantaged children. However, such extrapolated knowledge had limited value because of the phenomenal differences in the developmental characteristics and needs of the two populations of children.

One significant indicator of the remarkable progress that has been made in the subfield of early intervention with handicapped children is that over the past decade efforts to understand the factors that are related to the effectiveness of early intervention with handicapped children and their families have been increasingly based on analyses of research focusing specifically on this population. The early intervention literature is now replete with an impressive number of reviews concentrating particularly on efficacy research involving handicapped infants and young children (Bricker, 1985; Bricker, Bailey, & Bruder, 1984; Bricker & Kaminski, 1986; Casto & Mastropieri, 1986; Dunst, 1986; Dunst & Rheingrover, 1981; Dunst, Snyder, & Mankinen, 1987; Gibson & Fields, 1984; Gibson & Harris, 1988; Guralnick & Bennett, 1987; Marfo & Kysela, 1985; Shonkoff & Hauser-Cram, 1987; Simeonsson, Cooper, & Scheiner, 1982). With the number of studies reviewed reaching as high as 57 in one analysis (Dunst & Rheingrover, 1981), it is now possible not only to appraise programs for handicapped children on their own merit but also to enhance the quality of services for handicapped children drawing upon a directly relevant and pertinent knowledge base.

The Ascendancy of Critical Analysis within the Field

One of the remarkable accomplishments of the past decade is that the uncritical acceptance of the complacent and self-serving tradition of efficacy research that characterized the early years has given way to a phenomenal concern for critical "self-analysis and reflection" among early intervention researchers. It is a credit to the field that a substantial proportion of the most poignant reviews of the efficacy literature has been undertaken by leading proponents of early intervention services for handicapped children.

It is fair to point out, however, that even in the wake of this shift toward increased critical analysis, both liberal and conservative positions are identifiable. There are those who take the view that notwithstanding the numerous methodological problems identified by reviewers, the efficacy of early intervention services is very well established in the literature (Anastasiow, 1986a; Barrera, Chapter 5; Guralnick & Bricker, 1987). The opposing, more conservative view is that much of the evidence in support of efficacy is based on research that is so methodologically flawed that the scientific basis for efficacy claims is at best shaky (Dunst, 1986; Farran, 1990; Gibson & Fields, 1984; Gibson & Harris, 1988). Our purpose in this section is not to adjudicate, one way or the other, between these two viewpoints. However, because one of our primary objectives is to identify ways of strengthening early intervention research through analyses of past shortcomings, we take the more conservative viewpoint.

The key work on thorough methodological analyses of efficacy research in which handicapped children are the primary target population is that of Carl Dunst and his associates (Dunst, 1986; Dunst &
Rheingrover, 1981). Dunst (1986) reviewed a total of fifty-seven studies,
including the forty-nine reviewed with Rheingrover in 1981. He found
that 82% of the studies (forty-seven out of fifty-seven) were so methodologically flawed that their findings were essentially uninterpretable.
Of the ten studies employing reasonably rigorous designs, only three
reported clearly positive findings in support of the efficacy of early
intervention (these three studies represent only 5% of all the studies
reviewed by Dunst). It is this kind of finding that underlies the more
conservative viewpoint that our current knowledge regarding the efficacy of early intervention for handicapped children is based on rather
weak scientific evidence.

There is increasing support for this conservative viewpoint in the
literature, but as implied earlier, there is also a fair amount of resistance
to this conclusion. One basis for this resistance is the misconception
that the absence of convincing evidence in support of efficacy implies
that early intervention does not work. There is no basis, however, for
this inference. The conclusion drawn by Dunst and his associates is
indeed a double-edged sword; that is, there is neither convincing evidence in support of efficacy nor evidence to suggest that early intervention does not work. It cannot be overemphasized that the absence
of strong evidence in support of efficacy reflects the complexity of the
conceptual and methodological issues associated with early intervention efficacy research. At worst, the finding is more an indictment of
the quality of evaluation research in the field of early intervention than
of the value of early intervention per se (Dunst, 1986; Marfo, Browne,
Gallant, Smyth, & Corbett, 1989).

Are we to conclude, then, that the last quarter century or so of efficacy
research constitutes a wasted effort? Not really. We owe our current
insights to work carried out over the last several decades. However, we
need to continue our efforts to identify why exactly past efforts have
not paid off in the way that they should have. The challenge of charting
a better future for efficacy research requires that researchers in this field
continue the critical and thorough examination of past efforts and practices.

Guralnick (1989) has aptly characterized all the efficacy research
conducted up to about the mid–1980s as *first generation efficacy research*, providing explanations as to why this body of information failed
to provide the exemplary data base necessary to address some of today's
burning questions. For example, Guralnick explains that the quality of
evaluation efforts was negatively affected by two important factors: (1)
the reality of having to struggle "to balance intervention and evaluation

in a context of limited resources and experience" and (2) "the rapid development of new curricula and teaching techniques, along with demands for staff training" (p. 2).

While these explanations are valid, it is important to point out other, more serious problems that contributed to the current status of first generation efficacy research. Any attempt to understand the contributions of past research must take into consideration the *zeitgeist* that spawned most of that research. Traditionally, two related objectives— one, relatively more scientific in nature, and the other more political— have been associated with early intervention efficacy research. The scientific objective finds expression in the need to generate data that will lead to the development of more effective models and, hence, to the improvement of the quality of intervention. The political objective, on the other hand, finds expression in the perceived obligation to demonstrate to funders and policy makers that continued fiscal support and possible expansion of services are justified.

One stark reality is that first generation efficacy research fell victim to the politicization of scientific enquiry; the scientific objective of efficacy research was often overpowered by the politics of human-services funding appropriation. As long as scientists and policy makers alike tied continued funding and expansion of services to the results of efficacy research, the risk that such research would become biased toward producing supportive evidence was bound to increase. Dunst's (1986) review presents a strong case that most efficacy claims in existing research have no strong scientific basis when the studies making such claims are analyzed critically in terms of the quality of design and data analyses.

A related point that White and Casto (1989) have alluded to is that the early intervention movement was founded on optimism. As they point out:

Those concerned about the welfare of young children tend to be optimists, and, consequently, often interpret data more optimistically than deserved. Indeed, many of the statements that are made about early intervention efficacy have been based more on optimism than [on] fact. (p. 15)

Our own contention, however, is that the tendency toward more liberal interpretations of efficacy research was itself a product of an era in which the justification for continued funding of intervention programs was perceived to hinge on supportive scientific evidence. Support for this characterization of the *zeitgeist* of first generation efficacy research can be found in the hostile reactions that greeted studies reporting negative efficacy findings. The Piper and Pless (1980) study, which found no support for the efficacy of early intervention with Down syndrome children, is perhaps the most frequently criticized efficacy study on record. While some of the criticisms of this study are valid, each of those criticisms (see Bricker, Carlson, & Schwarz, 1981) applies equally to most of the studies reporting positive results. In fact, the Piper and Pless study remains one of the better scientifically designed studies in the literature. As Carr (1985) points out, the Piper and Pless study is almost unique in its employment of blind assessment to ensure that results were not biased by knowledge of which children were in the intervention or control group. Thus, the notoriety the authors of this study have gained appears to stem mainly from their bold reporting of their unpleasant findings.

If the foregoing historical analysis is accurate, one principal shift in philosophical orientation must take place for researchers to address questions that have greater relevance for improving the quality and coverage of early intervention services. We need to view efficacy research less as the basis for determining whether early intervention services should be provided for handicapped children and their families and more as a tool for identifying variables and mechanisms for fine-tuning specific programs and for enriching early intervention services in general (Farran, 1990; Shore, 1981; White & Casto, 1989).

There is some suggestion that the tendency to let efficacy research, rather than social conscience and humanistic values, determine the provision of services is characteristically American (see Anastasiow, 1986a; Shore, 1981). Fortunately, the United States seems to have caught up with its European counterparts in this regard. The days when the survival or expansion of early intervention services seemed (or was perceived) to hinge on the outcomes of efficacy research appear to be coming to an end. Through Public Law 94–142, and its subsequent amendments, in particular Public Law 99–457, early intervention services have become an established integral part of publicly supported human services. Although there are some who continue to see a need to gather efficacy data to "justify continued financial support for existing and expanded services" (Guralnick, 1989, p. 2), this pivotal development in legislation of early intervention services very much diminishes the political significance of the traditional efficacy question.

The Diminishing Importance of the Global Efficacy Question

A third notable indicator of progress in early intervention research is the increased interest in going beyond the rather global traditional efficacy question, *Does early intervention work?* to examine the relative importance of specific dimensions of the intervention process. At this stage, however, with very few exceptions (Brassel, 1977; Bricker & Dow,

1980; Dunst, Trivette, & Cross, 1986; Marfo, 1990a), this objective has been pursued largely through secondary analyses and syntheses of existing research rather than through componential analysis at the level of individual empirical studies.

Through descriptive summaries, traditional integrative reviews (Farran, 1990; Marfo & Kysela, 1985; Simeonsson, Cooper, & Scheiner, 1982) have provided composite pictures of some of the variables acknowledged conceptually to be critically related to efficacy—for example, what percentage of programs employed *parental involvement*, the average *age of children at entry* into intervention, variations in the *duration and/or intensity* of programs, the degree of *structure* in the curriculum, and the variety of *settings* in which intervention has occurred. Contemporary meta-analytic studies (Casto & Mastropieri, 1986; Shonkoff & Hauser-Cram, 1987; White & Casto, 1985) have taken traditional secondary analysis one step further by assessing statistically the impact of these variables on intervention outcomes. The application of the technique of meta-analysis to early intervention efficacy research can perhaps be seen as marking the formal beginning of a systematic effort to understand the variety of factors that influence the differential effectiveness of programs.

So far, however, the findings from these meta-analytic studies have been rather equivocal. For example, the studies conducted at the Utah State Early Intervention Research Institute (EIRI) have reported the following: (a) while parents can be effective intervenors, "they are probably not essential to intervention success" because "those intervention programs which utilize parents are not more effective than those which do not" (Casto & Mastropieri, 1986, p. 421); (b) contrary to the conventional belief that earlier exposure to intervention is better, it appears that for handicapped children later exposure is associated with better outcomes; (c) more structured programs are only marginally superior to less structured programs; and (d) "longer, more intense programs are associated with intervention effectiveness" (p. 422). Thus, according to this analysis, only one of the four traditionally acclaimed critical variables in intervention is clearly associated with successful outcomes.

As can be expected, these findings have generated a heated debate in which both specific characteristics of the Casto and Mastropieri analysis and the meta-analytic technique in general have been questioned. More important, however, a meta-analytic study of a subset of the EIRI data by Shonkoff and Hauser-Cram (1987) has produced contradictory findings. First, the analysis revealed that "programs that planned extensive parent involvement showed significantly greater effects than those with little or no planned parent participation" (p. 653). Second, Shonkoff and Hauser-Cram found a differential effect of age at entry as a function of severity of handicap. Mildly impaired infants enrolled in intervention prior to age six months made better gains than more severely handicapped children, who appeared to "have a constant rate of improvement regardless of their age at program entry" (p. 654). Third, programs employing structured curricula produced better child outcomes than those with no structured curricula. Intriguingly, on the only variable that the Casto and Mastropieri analysis found to be associated with program effectiveness—that is, duration of service as an index of program intensity—the Shonkoff and Hauser-Cram analysis did not find a significant effect.

While these starkly conflicting findings can be explained away partially by differences in the specific types of studies included in the two analyses, they raise a number of issues with significant implications for future research. Specific concerns with handling and interpretation of data in the Casto and Mastropieri analysis have been discussed in critiques that immediately followed the publication of that paper. For these critiques and the original authors' reactions to them, the interested reader is referred to Volume 53 (November, 1986) of Exceptional Children (Dunst & Snyder, 1986; Casto & Mastropieri, 1986; Strain & Smith, 1986). For our purposes, it is sufficient to point out that even if a specific meta-analysis is carried out soundly, its findings are only as valid as the individual studies upon which it is based.

As we point out elsewhere in this chapter, there seems to be a general consensus that most of the first generation efficacy studies are scientifically weak in design and analysis. From this perspective, the Casto and Mastropieri (1986) and the Shonkoff and Hauser-Cram (1987) studies can best be seen as first generation early intervention meta-analytic studies. By sensitizing us to some of the critical considerations that influence the validity and practical usefulness of this technique, these two studies should serve to whet our appetite for even more elegant meta-analyses in the future. For example, given some of our current conceptual beliefs regarding individual differences and the differential responsivity of specific categories of handicapped children to different intervention approaches, meta-analytic studies that ensure greater specificity in target populations and intervention approaches may yield more valuable insights than those that encompass a broad array of handicapping conditions and a hodgepodge of intervention approaches.

In terms of a fundamental direction for future research, perhaps the best place to assess the effect of these so-called critical variables on early intervention outcomes is at the level of individual primary empirical studies. It is important for individual efficacy studies to perform the kinds of componential analysis necessary to determine the relative significance of such factors as parental involvement, age at entry, degree of structure, intervention setting, and the direct target of the intervention (child, parent, child and parent, or family). Studies of this nature are bound to be richer inputs for future meta-analytic studies.

There is a remarkable consensus in the literature that second generation efficacy research must be driven by more specific, individual-variation-oriented questions. A representative sample of such questions include the following: What type of intervention is best with which children? (White & Casto, 1989); What mechanisms determine or influence the outcomes of intervention? (Marfo et al., 1989); What dimensions of early intervention are related to changes on different outcome measures? (Dunst, 1986); and How should services be delivered, with what materials, and in what settings? (Anastasiow, 1986a).

Improving Efficacy Research: Some Specific Future Directions

In examining previous reviews of the efficacy literature, we identified five recurring themes about which reviewers frequently expressed concerns and/or made recommendations for future research. In this section, we present these themes and provide supporting arguments to reiterate their importance.

The need for clear specification of intervention procedures and more thorough descriptions of client characteristics. As a label, *early intervention* does not refer to a uniform set of procedures that all interventionists employ; rather it is a generic concept that encapsules a wide variety of educational, psychological, medical, and other therapeutic programs and services. Not only do programs exist in different forms, but within programs, specific strategies and targets can vary for subgroups of clients (Hauser-Cram, 1990; Odom, Yoder, & Hill, 1988; White, Bush, & Casto, 1985). For this reason, it is imperative that reports of efficacy research provide thorough descriptions of the specific intervention program studied and of the variations in the application of particular procedures. Similarly, because clients who receive early intervention services vary widely in child characteristics (including the etiology and severity of handicap), in family demographic attributes (including family socioeconomic status, parental education levels, parental age, number of siblings), and in the quality of the immediate caretaking environment, it is crucial that efficacy studies provide reasonably extensive documentation of sample characteristics.

Unfortunately, among the most frequently mentioned deficiencies in extant efficacy research is the absence of adequate descriptions of specific intervention activities and characteristics of the recipients of the intervention (Bricker & Kaminski, 1986; Dunst, 1986; Farran, 1990; Guralnick, 1988; Shonkoff & Hauser-Cram, 1987). Conceptually, we expect differences in child attributes and family circumstances to influence outcomes because no single intervention approach or program is appropriate for every child and family. This serious lapse in previous research needs to be rectified in future efforts, as it places severe limitations on the usefulness of the findings generated to date.

The need to assess intervention outcomes more broadly. Although the facilitation of child developmental progress appears to be the central goal of most intervention programs, analyses of early intervention practices reveal attention to several other important goals as well. Marfo and Kysela (1985) identified four other goals of intervention based on their analyses of three distinct intervention models (the parent therapy, parent-training/infant curriculum, and the parent-child interaction models). These goals were: (a) to help parents overcome feelings of confusion, uncertainty, guilt, or fear associated with the birth and parenting of a handicapped child; (b) to help parents understand the handicapping condition and its implications and to prepare them to accept the responsibility of assisting in planning and implementing ameliorative program activities; (c) to prevent possible disruption of normal mutually reinforcing parent-child interaction by training parents to be sensitive and responsive in ways that enhance reciprocal interactions; and (d) to assist families with handicapped children in accessing relevant community services.

With the increasing impact of the social systems and ecological perspectives on the design and analysis of early intervention, other equally important goals relating to personal well-being and coping, family integrity, and parental expectations have been highlighted by Dunst and his associates (1986). Yet, as Shonkoff and Hauser-Cram (1987) point out, "Despite the growing acceptance of a family-oriented approach to early intervention services, measures of family functioning have been neglected in virtually all outcome studies" (p. 655).

In light of this broad range of goals, most of the critical reviews of efficacy research have deplored the overwhelming tendency to judge efficacy solely on the basis of indices of child developmental progress (Dunst, 1986; Marfo & Kysela, 1985; Simeonsson, Cooper, & Scheiner, 1982; Shonkoff & Hauser-Cram, 1987). Some may argue, perhaps legitimately, that all other goals of intervention are secondary to the enhancement of child developmental progress because they pertain largely to variables that mediate child developmental outcomes. However, even this argument does not negate the importance of including measures of these mediator variables in efficacy evaluations. On the contrary, Marfo and Kysela (1985) have provided grounds for emphasizing this class of outcome measures. They argue that it is perhaps unrealistic to expect dramatic gains in development as a function of intervention, which spans a relatively brief period in the child's life, especially in the case of more severely handicapped children. Immediate program impact, they argue, is much more likely to be noticed in relation to the mediator variables: parental attitudes, expectations, interactional strategies, instructional competence, coping skills, and utilization of relevant support services. To the extent that desirable changes for these variables can be expected to foreshadow long-term child developmental benefits, it is axiomatic that outcome measures relating to the variables receive greater attention, especially in short-term efficacy studies.

It is also important to note that even within the focus of child developmental progress, greater emphasis has been placed on cognitive gains than on gains in other developmental domains. Concern over this narrow focus has its history in debates on the efficacy of early intervention with disadvantaged children (see Zigler and Balla, 1982; Zigler and Berman, 1983; Zigler & Trickett, 1978). That it remains an issue in the literature on handicapped children today (see Dunst, 1986; Shonkoff & Hauser-Cram, 1987) is perhaps an indication of how little researchers have learned from previous analyses. In his foreword to Meisels and Shonkoff's *Handbook of Early Childhood Intervention*, Zigler (1990) summed up the limitations of the narrow focus on cognitive outcomes as follows:

We must consider the child as more than a walking cognitive system, for cognitive ability alone will not dictate how well the child will function in our world.... The aim, therefore, of intervention efforts must be to affect positively all aspects of the child's development (p. xii).

Dimensions of children's development that need to be assessed more systematically include social competence, emotional development, physical health and well-being, and motivation. In paying greater attention to a broader-based assessment of child developmental outcomes, however, we should also heed Dunst's advice that rather than take the "shotgun approach" of merely measuring everything, we should "be more specific about predictions regarding what dimensions of intervention are likely to impact upon what dimensions of child performance" (Dunst, 1986, p. 128). Thus, it is the goals and targets we set for clients that should determine which kinds of measures are to be included in the outcome evaluation.

The role of process measures in outcome evaluations. The efficacy of a program is determined not merely on the basis of outcome measures but also on the basis of the *relationship* between process and outcome measures. For this reason, the collection of process data is as important in program evaluation as the collection of outcome data (Marfo & Kysela, 1985). Efficacy claims, whether they are negative or positive, imply that the program was implemented with sufficient effort to warrant the expectation of particular outcomes (Hughes, Cordray, & Spiker, 1981; Marfo & Kysela, 1985). In addition to their lack of detailed descriptions of programs, most efficacy reports do not include measures of the implementation process. For example, of the twenty studies reviewed by Marfo & Kysela (1985), only two (Bricker & Dow, 1980; Hayden & Haring, 1977) involved the collection of some form of process data. Bricker and Dow measured the degree of parental participation in intervention activities, while Hayden and Haring recorded classroom observations to monitor the extent to which the intervention procedures in a center-based program were being employed.

There are at least three good reasons why early intervention researchers cannot take the implementation process for granted. First, there is not always a good match between a program's conceptual model and its field implementation (Hauser-Cram, 1990), and therefore evaluators need to demonstrate through the collection of process data the extent to which programs were implemented as planned: there is no point in being concerned about program impact unless it can be shown that a program was delivered to a reasonable degree of expectation. Second, the absence of process data constrains interpretation of results, often forcing the researcher to resort to speculative explanations (see Marfo & Kysela, 1985, for an illustration). In situations when statistical analyses indicate that treatment has failed, process data become especially crucial because they can provide the basis for ascertaining the extent to which the treatment failure may be related to conceptual, implementation, or methodological problems (Weiss, 1972). Third, the absence of process data that are accompanied by thorough descriptions of implementation procedures constrains replicability and, thus, slows down the progress that can be made in the field.

Chapter 5 provides an example of a subset of process measures that can be included in an evaluation: duration of treatment, number of home visits, duration of home visits, and the extent to which visits focused on the child, parent, home, or all three. Additional variables that may be considered include measures of the extent of parental commitment to program routines, proportion of program components actually covered, indices of the match between planned and implemented activities, and so on. It must be stressed, however, that once taken, these measures should not be analyzed in isolation; rather, their usefulness lies in examining how they relate to outcomes.

The need for greater program and population specificity. Categorical early intervention programming is the exception rather than the rule; most programs serve children with a broad range of handicapping conditions (Bricker & Kaminski, 1986; Shonkoff & Hauser-Cram, 1987). This situation is partly the result of the philosophy of noncategorical special education, which became a dominant tradition in the 1970s. However, it is also partly a reflection of practicalities of the real world; with the exception of a few specialized programs with a strong research mission, the distribution of handicapping conditions in the populations served by most intervention programs is determined solely by prevalence patterns within the communities served by the programs.

While the noncategorical service delivery model has its advantages (see Bricker & Kaminski, 1986), it presents serious challenges to efficacy research. Much of our current knowledge of the efficacy of early intervention with handicapped children is based on research that typically pools outcomes across children with a broad range of handicapping conditions, making it extremely difficult to determine the extent to which different categories of children benefit from various types of programming. One of the findings of the Shonkoff and Hauser-Cram (1987) meta-analysis underscores how misleading global efficacy statements can be. These researchers found that programs serving heterogeneous groups of handicapped children produced an effect size as large as 0.94, compared to effect sizes of 0.42 and 0.11 for programs that exclusively targeted mentally retarded and orthopedically handicapped children, respectively. This kind of analysis, which is rarely done in primary efficacy studies, illustrates that efficacy data taken for heterogeneous samples severely mask the differential impact of programs for different categories of children. One unfortunate consequence of this masking is the potential fostering and perpetuation of unrealistically high expectations regarding the benefits of intervention for children in certain disability groups.

The above revelation has significant implications for the conduct of secondary analyses of the efficacy literature as well. Reviews of the literature, whether they are of the traditional descriptive or more contemporary meta-analytic type, can yield misleading results if they lump together studies done on a wide range of handicapped and at-risk groups. Fortunately, over the past few years, reviewers have become increasingly sensitive to the need for more focused analyses of intervention outcomes—a sensitivity that is reflected in two distinct classes of reviews. The first consists of reviews that focus solely on one relatively homogeneous etiological group. Representative examples include reviews concentrating on Down syndrome (Carr, 1985; Gibson, Chapter 3; Gibson & Fields, 1984; Gibson & Harris, 1988), motor handicaps (Harris, 1987), autism (Simeonsson, Olley, & Rosenthal, 1987), visual impairment (Olson, 1987), hearing impairment (Meadow-Orlans, 1987), and language and communication disorders (Snyder-McLean & Mc-Lean, 1987).

While dealing with a more heterogeneous group, the second class consists of reviews that include differential analyses of relatively homogeneous subgroups. For example, the Guralnick and Bricker (1987) traditional integrative review focused broadly on children with cognitive and general developmental delays; however, separate analyses and syntheses were done for the ten studies reporting outcomes for Down syndrome children and for the fourteen reporting outcomes for children with other biologically based delays. Similarly, although the Shonkoff and Hauser-Cram (1987) meta-analytic review was based on a highly heterogeneous group of handicapping conditions, efforts were made to tease out differential effects for relatively homogencous subgroups.

As we move into a new era of programming and efficacy research, serious consideration must be given to the study of more focused intervention strategies targeted toward more specific groups. In this volume, both Gibson (Chapter 3; see also Gibson & Harris, 1988) and Hodapp and Dykens (Chapter 2) have put forward strong arguments in support of etiology-specific intervention programming. This approach should lead naturally to increased etiology-specific efficacy studies. We must clarify that our support for etiology-specific programming and evaluation is not necessarily an advocacy for categorical specialization of early intervention programs. We believe that programs serving heterogeneous populations will continue to be the norm. However, these programs should be more sensitive to the differential needs of the various etiological groups served. Similarly, efficacy studies of such programs need to be etiology-sensitive enough to permit the discerning of differential outcomes.

It is also important to point out that etiological subgrouping is only one way of studying the differential impact of programs. Indeed, Hauser-Cram (1990) has suggested that using functional status as the basis for subgrouping may be a better approach. From a programming point of view, however, etiological subgrouping is probably the natural first step; much of our existing knowledge about the developmental and learning attributes of handicapped children is organized along the lines of diagnostic rather than functional categories. At any rate, at the evaluation level, we ought to be thinking not about unidimensional approaches to subgrouping but rather about more complex approaches, such as examining differential impact for varying levels of functional status across different etiological groups.

The need to pay greater attention to individual differences. Besides the growing emphasis on etiology-specific intervention programming and efficacy research, the importance of paying greater attention to the differential impact of intervention activities for individual children and their families is also receiving increased attention in the literature

(Dunst, 1986; Halpern, 1984; Marfo & Kysela, 1985; Shonkoff & Hauser-Cram, 1987). The essence of this concern is captured quite aptly in the following appraisal by Shonkoff and Hauser-Cram (1987):

The critical research problem currently facing the field of early intervention is to understand the differential impacts specific kinds of services have on infants and families depending upon the nature of the child's adaptive capacities and disabilities as well as upon the characteristics of the family. In a field that emphasizes the importance of individual differences, and recognizes the limitations of a "one-size-fits-all" service model, there is a critical need for greater understanding of interactions among child, family, and service variables. (p. 656)

Early intervention efficacy research has been plagued by what Kiesler (1966), in his critical analysis of psychotherapy research, referred to as *uniformity assumption myths*. Of these myths, the two that are most closely pertinent to the discussion here are (1) that clients enter (or can be selected to enter) intervention with the same characteristics, and (2) that different intervenors or therapists operating within the same program implement intervention activities in the same way. A third myth that can safely be grouped with Kiesler's uniformity myths has recently been raised by Dunst (1986), namely, that early intervention has homogeneous effects. The analysis of individual variation in efficacy research is a rare exercise, but the few studies that have paid attention to differential program impact suggest that the outcomes of early intervention are not homogeneous; rather they vary for any child and family as a function of such factors as the child's level of functioning at program entry (Brassel, 1977; Bricker & Dow, 1980; Dunst, Trivette, & Cross, 1986; Marfo, 1990a), the child's handicapping condition (Shonkoff & Hauser-Cram, 1987), and parental expectations about the child's development (Marfo, 1990a).

In earlier sections of this chapter, we have shown that there is already a conceptual shift toward efficacy research that concerns itself more with differential programming and differential outcomes for subgroups of handicapped children. As the new era of efficacy research dawns, the analysis of differential impact at the individual child and family level should be high on the agenda.

CONCLUDING REMARKS

While noting many areas where progress has been made, this chapter also identifies areas where much remains to be done. The need for comprehensive formulations of the theoretical rationale for early intervention remains a paramount concern. To be complete, such formulations should not only address the importance of the timing of intervention but also (a) the mechanisms by which developmental change occurs, and (b) the manner in which the timing of intervention interacts with various mechanisms of developmental change to produce specific intervention outcomes. It is our view that the transactional and ecological systems models of development reviewed in this chapter provide some of the vital raw material needed to formulate a comprehensive rationale for early intervention with handicapped and developmentally delayed children.

With regard to the emergence of family- and interaction-focused intervention models, the marriage that these models are initating between theory and practice constitutes a noteworthy trend; however, this promising trend comes with its own challenges. Principal among these is the importance of demonstrating the superiority of the interaction-focused or social support models of intervention over traditional didactic models. Ultimately, judgments about the usefulness of these emerging models will rest not only on how much family well-being they engender but also on how much child developmental progress they promote. The question as to whether these "newer" approaches should preclude skill-teaching altogether also needs to be addressed. This is certainly one area where the proverbial danger of throwing the baby out with the bath water appears real.

Finally, we would like to add to the summary of recommendations for future efficacy research one admonition that has received relatively little attention in the literature (see Dunst, 1986; Marfo & Dinero, in press). Despite the progress made toward enhancing the empirical quality and theoretical soundness of efficacy research, we continue to conceptualize the early intervention process as if it operates in a vacuum and is, therefore, the sole independent variable responsible for child developmental and other outcomes. With very few exceptions (Brassel, 1977; Bricker & Dow, 1980), evaluators of early intervention programs have generally not given serious consideration to nonprogram variables that may either influence children's development directly or mediate the program's impact on target children and their families. Instead, it has often been assumed that whatever changes occur in the recipients of intervention during the period of involvement are due exclusively to the intervention process. Pre-experimental studies employing one-group pretest-posttest designs are most guilty of this assumption, but, generally speaking, not even the best true experimental studies in the literature can escape this criticism. It is rarely the case that even true experimental studies institute controls beyond the diagnostic category of the child.

As early intervention scholars anticipate the second generation of efficacy research, it is axiomatic that the viability and effectiveness of the intervention process be considered in relation to a wide range of nonprogram variables. Although an intervention program may have several components (e.g., cognitive, language, social, motor, family psychological support, etc), it is only one of many variables with potential influence on child development or family functioning. Complicating the issue further is that the various factors that impinge on child and family functioning often work in a complex interactive fashion rather than in a unidimensional manner. The quest for a proper understanding of the mechanisms that determine intervention outcomes must, therefore, be a search for the way and manner in which nonprogram variables interact with intervention variables to produce specific outcomes. Illustrative models and analytic tools for ascertaining early intervention outcomes in relation to the contributions of various classes of nonprogram variables (e.g., child, family demography, family ecology, and nonprogram auxiliary services) have been presented by Dunst (1986) and Marfo and Dinero (in press).

To end on an optimistic note, there are clear indications that the field is already primed for the kind of comprehensive evaluation research advocated here. The basis for this optimism can be found in the work of several leaders in the field. For example, the family-focused intervention model which Simeonsson and Bailey discuss in Chapter 4 specifies, under the follow-up assessment phase, several of the variables that have traditionally not been considered adequately in efficacy studies. Guralnick's (1989) three-dimensional matrix organizational framework for designing and analyzing early intervention efficacy research, while requiring extension to include other nonprogram variables, provides an exemplary direction for the future. Finally, by offering us regression models for teasing out the contributions of a broad range of program and nonprogram variables to intervention outcomes, Dunst (1986) has provided some of the methodological tools needed to move efficacy research to a new plane.

NOTE

1. As Marfo (1991) points out, it may be a bit simplistic to construe MLE as a phenomenon that is either present or absent. To the extent that every human child begins life in a social context, the earliest and most fundamental being the infant-caregiver relationship, MLE is universally available to all humans. However, the quality of the MLE to which individuals are exposed varies. It is more appropriate, then, to view MLE on a continuum of quality rather than as a bipolar construct.

REFERENCES

Affleck, G., McGrade, B. J., McQueeney, M., & Allen, D. (1982). Promise of relationship-focused early intervention in developmental disabilities. *Journal of Special Education, 16*, 413-430.

Anastasiow, N. J. (1986a). The research base for early intervention. *Journal of the Division for Early Childhood, 10,* 99-105.

Anastasiow, N. J. (1986b). The case for early experience. In D. Tamir, A. Russell, & T. B. Brazelton (Eds.), *Intervention and stimulation in infant development* (pp. 1-16). Tel Aviv, Israel: Freund Publishers.

Anastasiow, N. J. (1990). Implications of the neurobiological model for early intervention. In S. J. Meisels & J. P. Shonkoff (Eds.), *Handbook of early childhood intervention* (pp. 196-216). New York: Cambridge University Press.

Bailey, D. B., Simeonsson, R. J., Winton, P. J., Huntington, G. S., Comfort, M., Isbell, P., O'Donnell, K. J., & Helm, J. M. (1986). Family-focused intervention: A functional model for planning, implementing, and evaluating individualized family services in early intervention. *Journal of the Division for Early Childhood, 10,* 156-171.

Berger, J., & Cunningham, C. C. (1983). Development of early vocal behaviors and interactions in Down syndrome and nonhandicapped infant-mother pairs. *Developmental Psychology, 19,* 322-331.

Berkeley, T. R., & Ludlow, B. L. (1989). Toward a reconceptualization of the developmental model. *Topics in Early Childhood Special Education, 9*(3), 51-66.

Bloom, B. S. (1964). *Stability and change in human characteristics.* New York: Wiley.

Brassel, W. R. (1977). Intervention with handicapped infants: Correlates of progress. *Mental Retardation, 15* (August), 18-22.

Bricker, D. (1985). The effectiveness of early intervention with handicapped and medically at-risk infants. *Journal of Children in Contemporary Society, 17*(1), 51-65.

Bricker, D., Bailey, E., & Bruder, M. B. (1984). The efficacy of early intervention and the handicapped child. In M. Wolraich & D. Routh (Eds.), *Advances in developmental and behavioral pediatrics,* Vol. 5 (pp. 373-423). Greenwich, CT: JAI Press.

Bricker, D., Carlson, L., & Schwarz, R. (1981). A discussion of early intervention for infants with Down syndrome. *Pediatrics, 67,* 45-46.

Bricker, D., & Dow, M. (1980). Early intervention with the young severely handicapped child. *Journal of the Association for the Severely Handicapped, 5,* 130-142.

Bricker, D., & Kaminski, R. (1986). Intervention programs for severely handicapped infants and children. In L. Bickman & D. L. Weatherford (Eds.), *Evaluating early intervention programs for severely handicapped children and their families* (pp. 51-75). Austin, TX: Pro-Ed.

Bricker, D., & Veltman, M. (1990). Early intervention programs: Child-focused approaches. In S. J. Meisels & J. P. Shonkoff (Eds.), *Handbook of early childhood intervention* (pp. 373-399). New York: Cambridge University Press.

Bromwich, R. M. (1976). Focus on maternal behavior in infant intervention. *American Journal of Orthopsychiatry, 46,* 439-446.

Bromwich, R. M. (1977). Stimulation in the first year of life? A perspective on infant development. *Young Children,* (January), 71-82.

Bromwich, R. M. (1981). *Working with parents and infants: An interactional approach*. Baltimore: University Park Press.

Bronfenbrenner, U. (1979). *The ecology of human development*. Cambridge, MA: Harvard University Press.

Bronfenbrenner, U. (1989). Ecological systems theory. In R. Vasta (Ed.), *Six theories of child development: Revised formulations and current issues* Vol. 6 of Annals of Child Development (pp. 187-219). Greenwich, CT: JAI Press.

Brownell, C. A., & Strauss, M. S. (1985). Infant stimulation and development: Conceptual and empirical considerations. *Journal of Children in Contemporary Society, 17*(1), 109-130.

Caldwell, B. M. (1970). The rationale for early intervention. *Exceptional Children, 36*, 717-726.

Carr, L. (1985). The development of intelligence. In D. Lane & B. Stratford (Eds.), *Current approaches to Down's syndrome* (pp. 167-186). New York: Praeger.

Casto, G., & Mastropieri, M. A. (1986). The efficacy of early intervention programs: A meta-analysis. *Exceptional Children, 52*, 417-424.

Clarke, A. D. (1978). Predicting human development. *Bulletin of the British Psychological Society, 31*, 249-258.

Clarke, A. D., & Clarke, A. M. (1976a). The formative years. In A. D. Clarke & A. M. Clarke (Eds.), *Early experience: Myth and evidence* (pp. 3-24). London: Open Books.

Clarke, A. M., & Clarke, A. D. B. (1976b). Some contrived experiments. In A. D. Clarke & A. M. Clarke (Eds.), *Early experience: Myth and evidence* (pp. 213-228). London: Open Books.

Clarke, A., & Clarke, A. (1979). Early experience: Its limited effect upon late development. In D. Shaffer & J. Dunn (Eds.), *The first year of life* (pp. 135-151). New York: Wiley.

Drillien, C. M. (1957). The social and economic factors affecting the incidence of premature birth. *Journal of Obstetrical Gynaecology, British Empire, 64*, 161-184.

Drillien, C. M. (1964). *The growth and development of the prematurely born infant*. Edinburgh and London: E. & S. Livingston Ltd.

Dunst, C. J. (1986). Overview of the efficacy of early intervention programs. In L. Bickman & D. L. Weatherford (Eds.), *Evaluating early intervention programs for severely handicapped children and their families* (pp. 79-147). Austin, TX: Pro-Ed.

Dunst, C. J., & Rheingrover, R. (1981). An analysis of the efficacy of infant intervention programs with organically handicapped children. *Evaluation and Program Planning, 4*, 287-323.

Dunst, C. J., & Snyder, S. W. (1986). A critique of the Utah State University early intervention meta-analysis research. *Exceptional Children, 53*, 269-276.

Dunst, C. J., Snyder, S. W., & Mankinen, M. (1987). Efficacy of early intervention. In M. C. Wang, M. C. Reynolds, & H. J. Walberg (Eds.), *Handbook of special education: Volume 3* (pp. 259-294). New York: Pergamon.

Dunst, C. J., & Trivette, C. M. (1987). Enabling and empowering families: Conceptual and intervention issues. School Psychology Review, 16, 443-456.

Dunst, C. J., & Trivette, C. M. (1988a). Determinants of parent and child interactive behavior. In K. Marfo (Ed.), Parent-child interaction and developmental disabilities: Theory, research, and intervention (pp. 3-31). New York: Praeger.

Dunst, C. J., & Trivette, C. M. (1988b). A family systems model of early intervention with handicapped and developmentally at-risk children. In D. Powell (Ed.), Parent education as early childhood intervention: Emerging directions in theory, research, and practice (pp. 131-180). New York: Ablex.

Dunst, C. J., & Trivette, C. M. (1990). Assessment of social support in early intervention programs. In S. J. Meisels & J. P. Shonkoff (Eds.), Handbook of early childhood intervention (pp. 326-349). New York: Cambridge University Press.

Dunst, C. J., Trivette, C. M., & Cross, A. H. (1986). Mediating influences of social support: Personal, family, and child outcomes. American Journal of Mental Deficiency, 90, 403-417.

Emde, R., & Brown, C. (1978). Adaptation to the birth of a Down syndrome infant: Grieving and maternal attachment. Journal of the American Academy of Child Psychiatry, 17, 299-323.

Farran, D. C. (1990). Effects of intervention with disadvantaged and disabled children: A decade review. In S. J. Meisels & J. P. Shonkoff (Eds.), Handbook of early childhood intervention (pp. 501-539). New York: Cambridge University Press.

Feuerstein, R., Rand, Y., Hoffman, M. B., & Miller, R. (1980). Instrumental enrichment: An intervention program for cognitive modifiability. Baltimore: University Park Press.

Field, T. (1980). Interactions of high-risk infants: Qualitative and quantitative differences. In S. B. Sawin, R. C. Hawkins, L. O. Walker, & J. H. Penticuff (Eds.), Exceptional infant (Vol. 4): Psychosocial risks in infant-environment transactions (pp. 120-143). New York: Brunner/Mazel.

Gibson, D., & Fields, D. L. (1984). Early infant stimulation programs for children with Down's syndrome: A review of effectiveness. In M. Wolraich & D. Routh (Eds.), Advances in developmental and behavioral pediatrics, Vol. 5 (pp. 331-371). Greenwich, CT: JAI Press.

Gibson, D., & Harris, A. (1988). Aggregated early intervention effects for Down's syndrome persons: Patterning and longevity of benefits. Journal of Mental Deficiency Research, 32, 1-17.

Girolametto, L. E. (1988). Developing dialogue skills: The effects of a conversational model of language intervention. In K. Marfo (Ed.), Parent-child interaction and developmental disabilities: Theory, research, and intervention (pp. 145-162). New York: Praeger.

Girolametto, L. E., Greenberg, J., & Manolson, A. (1986). Developing dialogue skills: The Hanen early language parent program. Seminars in Speech and Language, 7, 367-382.

Guralnick, M. J. (1988). Efficacy research in early childhood intervention programs. In S. L. Odom & M. B. Karnes (Eds.), Early intervention for infants

    and children with handicaps: An empirical base (pp. 75-88). Baltimore:
    Paul H. Brookes.
Guralnick, M. J. (1989). Recent developments in early intervention efficacy
    research: Implications for family involvement. *Topics in Early Child-
    hood Special Education, 9*(3), 1-17.
Guralnick, M. J., & Bennett, F. C. (1987). A framework for early intervention.
    In M. J. Guralnick & F. C. Bennett (Eds.), *The effectiveness of early in-
    tervention for at-risk and handicapped children* (pp. 3-29). Orlando:
    Academic Press.
Guralnick, M. J., & Bricker, D. (1987). The effectiveness of early intervention
    for children with cognitive and general developmental delays. In M. J.
    Guralnick & F. C. Bennett (Eds.), *The effectiveness of early intervention
    for at-risk and handicapped children* (pp. 115-173). Orlando: Academic
    Press.
Halpern, R. (1984). Lack of effects of home-based early intervention? Some
    possible explanation. *American Journal of Orthopsychiatry, 54*, 33-42.
Harris, S. R. (1987). Early intervention for children with motor handicaps. In
    M. J. Guralnick & F. C. Bennett (Eds.), *The effectiveness of early inter-
    vention for at-risk and handicapped children* (pp. 175-212). Orlando:
    Academic Press.
Hauser-Cram, P. (1990). Designing meaningful evaluations of early intervention
    services. In S. J. Meisels & J. P. Shonkoff (Eds.), *Handbook of early child-
    hood intervention* (pp. 583-602). New York: Cambridge University Press.
Hayden, A. H., & Haring, N. G. (1977). The acceleration and maintenance of
    developmental gains in Down syndrome school-age children. In P. Mit-
    tler (Ed.), *Research to practice in mental retardation, Vol. 1: Care and
    education* (pp. 129-141). Baltimore: University Park Press.
Hodapp, R. M. (1988). The role of maternal emotions and perceptions in in-
    teractions with young handicapped children. In K. Marfo (Ed.), *Parent-
    child interaction and developmental disabilities: Theory, research, and
    intervention* (pp. 32-46). New York: Praeger.
Hughes, S. L., Cordray, D. S., & Spiker, V. A. (1981). Combining process with
    impact evaluation. In R. F. Conner (Ed.), *Methodological advances in
    evaluation research* (pp. 109-125). Beverly Hills, CA: Sage.
Hunt, J. M. (1961). *Intelligence and experience.* New York: Ronald Press.
Jensen, A. R. (1969). How much can we boost intelligence and academic
    achievement? *Harvard Educational Review, 39*, 1-123.
Kahn, R. (1990, May). *The mediation of learning experiences: An early inter-
    vention approach for facilitating cognitive and socioemotional devel-
    opment.* Round table presentation made at the 20th Anniversary
    Symposium of the Jean Piaget Society, Philadelphia.
Kiesler, D. J. (1966). Some myths about psychotherapy research and the search
    for a paradigm. *Psychological Bulletin, 65* (2), 110-136.
MacDonald, J. D., & Gillette, Y. (1984). Conversation engineering: A pragmatic
    approach to early social competence. *Seminars in Speech and Language,
    5*, 171-183.
MacDonald, J. D., & Gillette, Y. (1988). Communicating partners: A conversa-
    tional model for building parent-child relationships with handicapped

children. In K. Marfo (Ed.), *Parent-child interaction and developmental disabilities: Theory, research, and intervention* (pp. 220-241). New York: Praeger.

Mahoney, G. (1988a). Enhancing the developmental competence of handicapped infants. In K. Marfo (Ed.), *Parent-child interaction and developmental disabilities: Theory, research, and intervention* (pp. 203-219). New York: Praeger.

Mahoney, G. (1988b). Maternal communication style with mentally retarded children. *American Journal on Mental Retardation, 92,* 352-359.

Mahoney, G., Finger, I., & Powell, A. (1985). Relationship of maternal behavioral style to the development of organically impaired mentally retarded infants. *American Journal on Mental Retardation, 90,* 296-302.

Mahoney, G., & Powell, A. (1986). *The Transactional Intervention Program: Teacher's Guide.* Farmington, CT: Pediatric Research and Training Center.

Mahoney, G., & Powell, A. (1988). Modifying parent-child interaction: Enhancing the development of handicapped children. *Journal of Special Education, 22,* 82-96.

Mahoney, G., & Robenalt, K. (1986). A comparison of conversational patterns between mothers and their Down syndrome and normal infants. *Journal of the Division for Early Childhood, 10,* 172-180.

Marfo, K. (1984). Interactions between mothers and their mentally retarded children: Integration of research findings. *Journal of Applied Developmental Psychology, 5,* 45-69.

Marfo, K. (1990a, April). *Correlates and predictors of child developmental progress and parental satisfaction in an early intervention program.* Paper presented at the Annual Meeting of the American Educational Research Association, Boston.

Marfo, K. (1990b). Maternal directiveness in interactions with mentally handicapped children: An analytical commentary. *Journal of Child Psychology and Psychiatry, 31,* 531-549.

Marfo, K. (1991). Forging competence in developmentally delayed children: Grounds for optimism, directions for intervention. In W. A. Rhodes & W. Brown (Eds.), *Why some children succeed despite the odds* (pp. 107–129). New York: Praeger.

Marfo, K., Browne, N., Gallant, D., Smyth, R., & Corbett, A. (1989). *Child, program, and family ecological variables in early intervention.* Unpublished manuscript, Department of Educational Psychology and Leadership Studies, Kent State University.

Marfo, K., & Dinero, T. E. (in press). Assessing early intervention outcomes: Beyond program variables. *International Journal of Disability, Development and Education.*

Marfo, K., & Kysela, G. M. (1985). Early intervention with mentally handicapped children: A critical appraisal of applied research. *Journal of Pediatric Psychology, 10,* 305-324.

McCall, R. (1977). Challenge to a science of developmental psychology. *Child Development, 48,* 333-344.

McCollum, J. A. (1984). Social interaction between parents and babies: Validation of an intervention procedure. *Child: Care, Health and Development, 10*, 301-315.

Meadow-Orlans, K. P. (1987). An analysis of the effectiveness of early intervention programs for hearing-impaired children. In M. J. Guralnick & F. C. Bennett (Eds.), *The effectiveness of early intervention for at-risk and handicapped children* (pp. 325-362). Orlando: Academic Press.

Odom, S. L., Yoder, P., & Hill, G. (1988). Developmental intervention for infants with handicaps: Purposes and programs. *Journal of Special Education, 22*, 11-24.

Olson, M. (1987). Early intervention for children with visual impairments. In M. J. Guralnick & F. C. Bennett (Eds.), *The effectiveness of early intervention for at-risk and handicapped children* (pp. 297-324). Orlando: Academic Press.

Passamanick, B., & Knobloch, H. (1966). Retrospective studies on the epidemiology of reproductive casualty: Old and new. *Merrill-Palmer Quarterly, 12*, 7-26.

Peterson, N. L. (1987). *Early intervention for handicapped and at-risk children: An introduction to early childhood special education.* Denver: Love Publishing Co.

Piper, M. C., & Pless, I. B. (1980). Early intervention for infants with Down syndrome. *Pediatrics, 65*, 463-468.

Ramey, C. T., & Suarez, T. M. (1985). Early intervention and the early experience paradigm: Toward a better framework for social policy. *Journal of Children in Contemporary Society, 17*(1), 3-13.

Richard, N. B. (1986). Interaction between mothers and infants with Down syndrome: Infant characteristics. *Topics in Early Childhood Special Education, 6*(3), 54-71.

Rogers, S. J. (1988). Characteristics of social interactions between mothers and their disabled infants: A review. *Child: Care, Health and Development, 14*, 301-317.

Rose, T. L., & Calhoun, M. L. (1990). The Charlotte Circle Project: A program for infants and toddlers with severe/profound disabilities. *Journal of Early Intervention, 14*, 175-185.

Sameroff, A. J. (1975). Early influences on development: Fact or fancy? *Merrill-Palmer Quarterly, 21*, 267-294.

Sameroff, A. J. (1980). Issues in early reproductive and caretaking risk: Review and current status. In D. B. Sawin, R. C. Hawkins, II, L. O. Walker, & J. H. Penticuff (Eds.), *Exceptional infant, volume 4: Psychosocial risk in infant-environment transactions* (pp. 343-359). New York: Brunner/Mazel.

Sameroff, A. J., & Chandler, M. J. (1975). Reproductive risk and the continuum of caretaking casualty. In F. D. Horowitz, M. Hetherington, S. Scarr-Salapatek, & G. Siegel (Eds.), *Review of child development research*, Volume 4 (pp. 187-224). Chicago: University of Chicago Press.

Sameroff, A. J., & Fiese, B. H. (1990). Transactional regulation and early intervention. In S. J. Meisels & J. P. Shonkoff (Eds.), *Handbook of early childhood intervention* (pp. 119-149). New York: Cambridge University Press.

Shonkoff, J. P., & Hauser-Cram, P. (1987). Early intervention for disabled infants and their families: A quantitative analysis. *Pediatrics, 80*, 650-658.

Shore, M. F. (1981). Marking time in the land of plenty: Reflections on mental health in the United States. *American Journal of Orthopsychiatry, 51,* 391-402.

Simeonsson, R. J., Cooper, D. H., & Scheiner, A. P. (1982). A review and analysis of the effectiveness of early intervention programs. *Pediatrics, 69,* 635-641.

Simeonsson, R. J., Olley, J. G., & Rosenthal, S. (1987). Early intervention for children with autism. In M. J. Guralnick & F. C. Bennett (Eds.), *The effectiveness of early intervention for at-risk and handicapped children* (pp. 275-296). Orlando: Academic Press.

Snyder-McLean, L., & McLean, J. E. (1987). Effectiveness of early intervention for children with language and communication disorders. In M. J. Guralnick & F. C. Bennett (Eds.), *The effectiveness of early intervention for at-risk and handicapped children* (pp. 213-274). Orlando: Academic Press.

Strain, P. S., & Smith, B. J. (1986). A counter-interpretation of early intervention effects: A response to Casto and Mastropieri. *Exceptional Children, 53,* 260-265.

Tannock, R., Girolametto, L., & Siegel, L. (1988, August). *Efficacy of a conversational model of language intervention: Preliminary findings.* Paper presented at the 8th Congress of the International Association for the Scientific Study of Mental Deficiency, Dublin, Ireland.

Wachs, T. D., & Gruen, G. E. (1982). *Early experience and human development* New York: Plenum.

Wasserman, G., & Allen, R. (1985). Maternal withdrawal from handicapped toddlers. *Journal of Child Psychology and Psychiatry, 26,* 381-387.

Weiss, C. H. (1972). *Evaluation research.* Englewood Cliffs, NJ: Prentice-Hall.

Westinghouse Learning Corporation. (1969). *The impact of Head Start: An evaluation of the effects of Head Start on children's cognitive and affective development* (Report to the Office of Economic Opportunity). Washington, D.C.: Clearinghouse for Federal Scientific and Technical Information.

White, K. R., Bush, D. W., & Casto, G. (1985). Learning from reviews of early intervention efficacy. *Journal of Special Education, 19,* 417-428.

White, K. R., & Casto, G. (1985). An integrative review of early intervention efficacy studies with at-risk children: Implications for the handicapped. *Analysis and Intervention in Developmental Disabilities, 5,* 177-201.

White, K. R., & Casto, G. (1989). What is known about early intervention. In C. Tingey (Ed.), *Implementing early intervention* (pp. 3-20). Baltimore: Paul H. Brookes.

Zigler, E. F. (1990). Foreword to S. J. Meisels & J. P. Shonkoff (Eds.), *Handbook of early childhood intervention* (pp. ix-xiv). New York: Cambridge University Press.

Zigler, E., & Balla, D. (1982). Selecting outcome variables in evaluations of early childhood special education programs. *Topics in Early Childhood Special Education, 1*(4), 11-22.

Zigler, E., & Berman, W. (1983). Discerning the future of early childhood interventions. *American Psychologist, 38,* 894-906.

Zigler, E., & Hodapp, R. M. (1986). *Understanding mental retardation*. New York: Cambridge University Press.

Zigler, E., & Trickett, P. K. (1978). IQ, social competence, and evaluation of early childhood intervention programs. *American Psychologist, 33,* 789-798.

Toward an Etiology-Specific Strategy of Early Intervention with Handicapped Children

Robert M. Hodapp and Elisabeth M. Dykens

Due to advances in both the behavioral and biomedical sciences, knowledge of mental retardation has greatly increased over the past thirty years. From the discovery of the exact cause of Down syndrome in 1959 to the recent explorations of fragile X syndrome, Prader-Willi Syndrome, and other disorders, the field is examining different types of retardation and specifying the characteristic behaviors of each group in cognition, language, and social adaptation. Grossman (1983) notes that there are now over 200 identified causes of mental retardation. While we do not yet fully understand behavioral functioning in every etiological group, data are accumulating on at least some of these disorders.

To date, however, little of this information has affected practices within the early intervention field. Although some programs have tailored their interventions specifically for children with Down syndrome, autism, or sensory impairments, most programs are not etiologically based. This lack of attention to etiology was understandable in earlier years, when only a small set of disabilities (e.g., Down syndrome, prematurity, microcephaly) could be accurately diagnosed during infancy. In contrast, recent work has yielded more accurate and earlier diagnoses for a variety of etiological groups.

The changing ability to diagnose during the early childhood years is probably best exemplified by the case of fragile X syndrome. Fragile X syndrome is an X-linked disorder thought to be the second most prevalent genetic cause of mental retardation, accounting for 2 to 7 percent of all retarded males (although females can also be affected). Diagnoses can now be performed in early infancy and, in some cases, even in utero (Murphy, Watson, Kidd, & Breg, 1986). Such early diagnoses are particularly interesting, given the fact that fragile X syndrome is a disorder that was not even discovered until twenty years ago.

In addition to diagnostic concerns, a second reason for the lack of attention to etiology involves the history of behavioral research in mental retardation. The majority of behavioral studies continues to segment research groups by level of functioning, not by cause of retardation. Researchers compare the functioning of mildly retarded children to nonretarded children of comparable chronological or mental ages, or profoundly retarded children to those with severe or moderate levels of impairment. Such studies attempt to document deficits in functioning that are common to profoundly, severely, moderately, or mildly retarded groups. It is implicitly denied that individuals of the same level of impairment who have different etiologies might differ from one another.

However, this inattention to etiology, while widespread, does not apply to the entire mental retardation field. Although most etiological work has focused on genetic, epidemiologic, and biomedical aspects, some researchers have also examined the developmental and behavioral profiles of such groups as Down syndrome (Cicchetti & Beeghly, 1990; Gibson, 1978, and Chapter 3 of this volume), autism (Cohen & Donnellan, 1987), fragile X syndrome (Dykens & Leckman, 1990), and Prader-Willi Syndrome (Taylor & Caldwell, 1988). These efforts are in many cases just beginning, but they do provide the foundation for an etiology-based approach to early intervention.

Yet the practice of ignoring etiology in mental retardation work has been challenged historically by those adhering to the "two-group approach" to mental retardation. As originally proposed by Zigler (1967, 1969), the mentally retarded population can be divided into two distinct groups, those showing no clear organic etiology for their retardation and those whose retardation has a specific, organic etiology. The retardation of the first group, thought to comprise from one-half to three-quarters of all retarded persons (Zigler & Hodapp, 1986), has been given a variety of labels: cultural-familial retardation, familial retardation, nonorganic retardation, retardation due to environmental deprivation, even "garden variety" retardation. As differences in these names suggest, we do not yet know what causes retardation in this group. Causes may involve polygenic factors (receiving fewer genes for high intelligence from one's parents), environmental deprivation, an undiscovered genetic defect, or some combination of these factors.

Whatever the cause of familial retardation, Zigler proposed that intellectual functioning in this group is not qualitatively different from lower intelligence across the distribution of IQ. Thus, a person with familial retardation who has an IQ of 65 differs from the person with an IQ of 85 for the same reasons that a person with an IQ of 100 differs from the person with an IQ of 120. Such differences must in some sense be organically based, but the factors causing retardation in this group are the same as those (unspecified) factors that cause any person of nonretarded intelligence to have lower intelligence compared to another nonretarded person.

A second group, the so-called organically retarded population, does show clear organic cause for their retardation. This cause may be prenatal, perinatal, or postnatal in origin. Prenatal causes include all of the genetic syndromes, as well as rubella, thalidomide, and other disorders caused by infections, diseases, or harmful events during pregnancy. Perinatal causes include prematurity, anoxia, and other birth-related disorders, while postnatal causes include head trauma, meningitis, and other disorders during the childhood years. In each case, there is a clear organic cause for the retardation.

In part because individuals with familial retardation are not qualitatively different from persons of average intelligence, Zigler (1969) hypothesized that the developmental approach to mental retardation should be limited only to this first group of retarded individuals. He therefore proposed that familial retarded children develop as nonretarded children do in that both groups progress along the same sequences of development. For example, familial retarded children should progress in order through Piagetian cognitive stages and substages, through the early stages of language, and so on. Any set of developments that shows a single, universal, and invariant sequence in nonretarded development should be traversed in identical order by familial retarded children. This prediction, called the similar sequence hypothesis, has generally been borne out for familial retarded children (Weisz & Zigler, 1979).

A second prediction was that familial retarded children should show the same coherence of development across different domains of functioning as do groups of nonretarded children. This prediction, called the similar structure hypothesis, is operationally demonstrated when familial retarded children perform identically on cognitive-linguistic tasks as nonretarded children of the same mental ages. Although this prediction has held true for a large number of Piagetian tasks (Weisz, Yeates, & Zigler, 1982), its status is not so clear for at least some information-processing tasks (see Mundy & Kasari, 1990, and Weisz, 1990, for discussions).

Familial retarded children, then, are those retarded individuals who show no clear organic etiology to their mental retardation. They do not appear to be qualitatively different from nonretarded persons, and their development seems to occur in the same way that development in nonretarded children occurs. These children therefore would seem amenable to interventions that follow normative sequences in cognition, language, and other areas in which universal sequences of development occur.

Although Zigler did not specifically apply a developmental perspective to the second group of retarded individuals, those with organic retardation, later workers have attempted to apply the findings, theories, and approaches of normal development to retarded persons with organic retardation (Cicchetti & Pogge-Hesse, 1982; Hodapp & Zigler, 1990). In particular, several studies have found that the similar sequence hypothesis is applicable even for organically retarded children: virtually all organically retarded children progress through the same stages of development in the same order as do nonretarded children. For example, Dunst (1990) has noted that in infancy Down syndrome children progress along Piagetian sensorimotor stages in object permanence, means-ends, symbolic uses, and other sensorimotor domains. The early language development of Down syndrome children also occurs along sequences identical to those shown by nonretarded children (Beeghly & Cicchetti, 1987; Fowler, 1990). Children with other types of organic retardation are similarly thought to develop along normal sequences of development (Weisz & Zigler, 1979).

Despite these similarities in the ordering of development between organically retarded and nonretarded children, the structures of intelligence may be different for organically retarded children. When matched by mental age to nonretarded children, organically retarded children perform worse on Piagetian tasks of sensorimotor, preoperational, and concrete operational functioning (Weisz, Yeates, & Zigler, 1982). We will return to this issue later, but suffice it to say now that a "general" developmental approach is applicable to familial retarded children and is at least partially applicable to organically retarded children.

In recent work, Burack, Hodapp, and Zigler (1988) have emphasized the need to further delineate organic mental retardation into groups based on the individual's specific etiology of retardation. For example, different types of organically retarded children seem to show different trajectories of cognitive development, a finding with important implications for the timing of intervention efforts. Down syndrome children slow down in cognitive development as they get older; indeed, they may be "losing ground" at several transition points where the nature of the developmental tasks facing the child changes qualitatively (e.g., the child's entry into language, shown by Dunst, 1988). In contrast, retarded children with cerebral palsy seem relatively steady in their developmental trajectories over time (Cruickshank, Hallahan, & Bice,

1976; Klapper & Birch, 1967), whereas boys with fragile X syndrome may show slowed intellectual development beginning in the pubertal years (Dykens et al., 1989). Similarly, different types of organic retardation show different characteristic strengths and weaknesses, a topic to which we will return in the next section. Burack, Hodapp, and Zigler (1988) support the use in behavioral research of etiology-based research groups, noting that etiologically homogeneous groupings allow for more fine-grained research and intervention efforts.

If we base intervention strategies on these emerging research findings, the problem becomes one of joining the general and the specific in early intervention work. A general developmental approach employs universal sequences, structures, and environments and applies them to all handicapped children, regardless of etiology. It is, then, a "general" strategy that is used with all retarded children. Thus, as we will detail later, sequences, structures, and environments that mirror those of nonretarded children have been used in intervention programs for children with handicaps.

At the same time, if we advocate an etiology-based approach to early intervention, then each retarded group should be intervened with differently. Specific interventions based on the particular etiology of the child will be necessary. Intervention programs for children with Down syndrome will differ from those for children with fragile X syndrome or other disabilities. Each disability condition will receive a program of intervention at least partly specific to the child's etiology.

Thus, there is an emerging tension in early intervention work between general approaches based on commonalities between retarded and nonretarded children and specific approaches based on different trajectories and profiles that vary across specific etiological groups. This tension between the general and the specific in early intervention work is the focus of this chapter. Although we conclude the chapter with a model for reconciling these two approaches, we will first provide details about how specific etiological groups differ from one another and why a specific, etiology-based intervention strategy might prove useful. This section is followed by an expanded discussion of general developmental theory, after which we attempt to join these two approaches.

THE "SPECIFIC" IN EARLY INTERVENTION WORK: DIFFERENTIATING AMONG DIFFERENT ETIOLOGICAL GROUPS

Etiology-Specific Strengths and Weaknesses

The most important way that various etiological groups differ is in their particular behavioral profiles. As previously mentioned, there is a small but growing body of work showing that the specific areas of behavioral strengths and weaknesses vary in each of several etiological groups. This is not to say that our knowledge of etiologically based differences is complete, or that every etiological group differs from every other group in every domain. These findings are provided only to indicate that there now seem to be enough differences across diverse etiological groups to warrant specific, etiologically based intervention strategies in a number of areas.

Compare, for example, the intellectual strengths and weaknesses of two groups of children, those with fragile X syndrome and those with Down syndrome. In a study using an intelligence test based on styles of information processing (Kaufman Assessment Battery for Children, or K-ABC; Kaufman & Kaufman, 1983), Dykens, Hodapp, and Leckman (1987) found that males with fragile X syndrome had particular difficulties in sequential processing tasks, that is, those tasks requiring short-term memory in the recall or reproduction of a series of items in serial or temporal order. Performance on other tasks was much less impaired in these children. In particular, males with fragile X syndrome performed relatively better on tasks of general achievement and of simultaneous processing (i.e., tasks requiring integrative, frequently spatial approaches to problem solving). Furthermore, among the various tests of sequential processing, performance on a subtest requiring the reproduction of a series of motor movements (the Hand Movements subtest) was particularly delayed, a weakness even when compared to the child's performance on other subtests of sequential processing.

Findings from these males with fragile X syndrome contrast markedly with those from studies examining children with Down syndrome. Pueschel, Gallagher, Zartler, and Pezzullo (1987) found no differences between sequential and simultaneous processing for Down syndrome children. Indeed, the single highest subtest for Down syndrome children was the Hand Movements subtest, which had been the most depressed area of functioning for boys with fragile X syndrome. Although few studies have directly compared functioning in Down syndrome versus fragile X syndrome groups, those few that have are replicating this difference in intellectual strengths and weaknesses (Hodapp et al., 1990).

Such differences in strengths and weaknesses across different etiological groups are not limited to the domain of intelligence. In particular, language skills seem to vary in different etiological groups. In a comparison of Down syndrome and fragile X syndrome children, for example, Wolf-Schein and her colleagues (1987) found that speech characteristics such as jargon, perseveration, echolalia, and inappropriate and tangential language were more apparent in the fragile X group. Other studies comparing several aspects of language and communication in children with fragile X syndrome, autism, and Down syndrome are producing similar findings concerning particular areas of strengths and weaknesses (Ferrier, 1987).

Although etiological comparisons are in many instances only beginning, their implications are important for intervention work. For example, several studies have noted that the language of Down syndrome children is below their functioning in other areas (Cornwell & Birch, 1969; Gibson, 1978). Grammatical development in this group is both delayed compared to nonretarded children at similar levels of cognitive ability and variable in rate of development once these children do begin to acquire grammatical forms and concepts (Beeghly & Cicchetti, 1987; Fowler, 1990). In an effort to foster their linguistic abilities, Down syndrome children in some intervention programs are taught sign language. The findings from the K-ABC's Hand Movements subtest (Pueschel, Gallagher, Zartler, & Pezzulo, 1987) seem to support this strategy, as it may be that Down syndrome children are better able to sequence behaviors that are motoric as opposed to vocal. In contrast, introducing sign language to boys with fragile X syndrome, a group that is particularly deficient in motor imitation skills, is likely to meet with only limited success. Although these intervention suggestions have not yet been tested, such specific recommendations become possible only after we identify the strengths and weaknesses of individual etiological groups.

Different Reactions of Parents and Families

It may also be the case that different types of handicap lead to different reactions from parents and other family members. In pioneering work in the early 1960s, Solnit and Stark (1961) noted that mothers of children with many different types of handicaps underwent a process of "mourning" the birth of the idealized, perfect infant. Partly as a result of such work, researchers and interventionists have been accustomed to thinking of all parents of handicapped children in the same way. Each parent with a handicapped child, the argument goes, has concerns and reactions that are similar, if not identical, to those of all other parents of handicapped children. Thus, recent investigations of whether maternal reactions are "stage-like" generally do not distinguish between reactions to children of varying types of handicaps (Blacher, 1984).

However, parents of children with different types of handicaps do appear to differ in their reactions to their offspring. Comparing mothers of Down syndrome and autistic children, Holroyd and MacArthur (1976) found that mothers of children with autism demonstrated much greater levels of familial and personal disruption and distress than did mothers of children with Down syndrome. Similarly, Goldberg, Marcovitch, MacGregor, and Lojkasek (1986) have recently found that mothers of children with retardation of unknown etiology show much more guilt and distress than mothers of children with Down syndrome or neurological impairments. In both studies, it emerged that parents were helped by possessing a clear and unambiguous reason for the child's retardation. In contrast, a cause that is uncertain (as in autism) or undetermined (as in retardation of unknown etiology) leads to greater levels of parental guilt and familial stress.

Even when a clear cause is present, however, parents may experience emotional ups and downs in reaction to aspects of the child's particular etiology. Emde and Brown (1978) noted that mothers of Down syndrome infants experienced several emotional setbacks over the first year of the baby's life. The first came at birth, when parents were told of the child's condition. But then, following a period of relative parental calm, a second wave of depression arose at approximately four months. It was primarily at this time that the parents realized the child's permanent and lifelong problems, as the child only inconsistently smiled and laughed during social interactions.

In contrast to findings on mothers of Down syndrome babies, Fraiberg (1974, 1977) noted that maternal reactions to blind babies followed their own, unique patterns, as increased levels of maternal concern were caused by delays in attachment and other developments related to vision. She found that mothers often reacted to the lack of facial expression and eye-to-eye contact of blind infants by feeling that these babies were unresponsive and depressed. Mothers needed to be taught to look to the baby's hands, as opposed to his or her face and eyes, in order to correctly "read" their infants. Describing the approach of her staff, Fraiberg (1974) noted:

We became "hand watchers" as a staff. . . . When we examined mother-child reciprocity, we looked at the mother's face and the baby's hands. (The baby's face told us little.) When we studied investment in a toy or toy preference, we looked at the baby's hands. When we examined emotional reactions to momentary separation from the mother, or toy loss, we looked at the hands. (p. 225)

These differences in maternal responses to Down syndrome and blind infants illustrate but a few of the issues causing emotional reactions to different types of young, handicapped children. Other issues that warrant consideration in tailoring intervention programs include the educational level of the parents and the family's socioeconomic status (SES) and cultural background. For example, although there is little research on the impact of SES, some reports indicate that SES has less effect on family distress and disruption than the specific handicaps and functioning of the child (Korn, Chess, & Fernandez, 1978). In addition, interventionists need to assess the impact that handicaps in several family members may have on family functioning. For example, approximately one-third of the females that carry and transmit the chromosomal marker for fragile X syndrome are themselves mildly to moderately intellectually impaired and may be at particular risk for certain psychiatric disorders (Fishburn, Turner, Daniel, & Brookwell, 1983; Reiss et al., 1988). In addition to these maternal vulnerabilities, this genetically transmitted disorder may result in considerable variability in its expression in children. Thus, one or more sons may or may not have fragile X syndrome, and daughters who carry the marker may or may not be mildly affected. This variability of impairment among family members is a critical component in assessing the intervention needs of these families.

Clearly, interventionists must alter the type and intensity of their efforts in accordance with family need, degree of impairment in affected members, and the emotional reactions that parents experience toward their children at various stages of development. The best intervention programs are those that target the child's specific handicapping conditions as well as the family's responses to these conditions over time.

THE "GENERAL" IN EARLY INTERVENTION WORK: ASPECTS OF DEVELOPMENT THAT APPLY TO ALL HANDICAPPED CHILDREN

In contrast to the etiology-specific characteristics described above, there are several aspects of normal development that apply to all retarded persons. These aspects include similar sequences in several domains, similar cross-domain relationships, and similar themes about what constitute developmentally appropriate environments. These aspects of general development, and their implications for early intervention work, are described below.

Similar Sequences of Development

As mentioned in the introduction, all retarded children seem to progress through universal stages of development in orderings that are identical to those of nonretarded children. Indeed, the idea of sequential development is the hallmark of most developmental models for either nonretarded or retarded populations (Cicchetti & Pogge-Hesse, 1982; Zigler & Hodapp, 1986).

There are at least three possible explanations for why such universal orderings might occur, especially in the early years. First, early development seems to be more canalized, or biologically driven, than are many aspects of later development (Scarr-Salapatek, 1975; McCall, 1981). This process of "unfolding" in early development, while delayed in children with various types of handicaps, nevertheless continues along identical species-specific pathways for all children. Second, logic demands that certain developments occur before others. Children are likely to uncover an object hidden under one cloth before being able to uncover an object hidden under two or more cloths, or to develop two separate behaviors (visually tracking a moving object; reaching out for a stationary object) before coordinating these behaviors into one combined action (tracking and reaching out for a moving object). Third, there are certain intrinsically human characteristics that help order development. From birth on, novel events are noticed first, before old or customary activities. As a result, toddlers speak about the "here and now" in their earliest language (Brown, 1973). For each of these reasons, all children—those with handicaps and those without—proceed through identical, universal stages of development, particularly in the sensorimotor period (Hodapp, 1990).

Universal sequences are the most important of the "general" aspects of development that are applicable to children with diverse handicaps. Sequences in early cognitive development, in early communication and language, and in other areas are now being incorporated into developmental work. Indeed, we can think of universal sequences as providing the "staged curriculum" (Kaye, 1982) along which early interventionists can proceed in fostering development in children with handicaps.

A good example of this type of sequence—and its use in intervention work—occurs in the development of early communicative abilities. Nonretarded one-year-olds request adult attention, make demands, and give comments, but they communicate to request information only at later ages (Halliday, 1975). Similarly, in their two-word speech, children talk about actors, actions, and objects, whereas talk of past or future events is acquired later (Bloom, 1970; Schlesinger, 1971). The grammatical morphemes of English are also developed in set order, with the acquisition of the present progressive "-ing" before the prepositions "in" and "on," which in turn develop before plurals, the irregular past tense ("went" instead of "goed"), and possessives (Brown, 1973). Intervention curricula have been developed based on these invariant sequences in the pragmatic, semantic, and grammatic aspects of language (MacDonald & Blott, 1974; McLean & Snyder-McLean, 1978). If all retarded children develop along similar sequences as nonretarded children, then a general developmental approach can be used for all.

Similar Cross-Domain Relations

Zigler's original similar structure hypothesis stated that when matched by overall mental age (MA), familial retarded children function at a level equivalent to that of nonretarded children on cognitive and linguistic tasks. Similar structures have been found for familial retarded children on a variety of Piagetian tasks, although the evidence is equivocal for some information-processing tasks. In contrast, as predicted by Zigler (1969), similar structures of development have generally not been found for children with different types of organic retardation, many of which have their own particular, etiology-based strengths and weaknesses (see previous section).

To many, the lack of similar structures in organically retarded populations has led to an emphasis on examining cross-domain relations primarily in familial (and not organically) retarded populations (Weisz, 1990). These workers feel that a more "conservative" application of developmental principles seems warranted: if organically retarded children perform below MA-matched nonretarded children, then little information about cross-domain relations can be applied from nonretarded to organically retarded populations.

Although organically retarded children do not possess structures of intelligence that are similar to those of their nonretarded peers, we nevertheless feel that cross-domain information can be applied from nonretarded to all types of retarded populations. Indeed, even for non-retarded children, researchers increasingly reject the view that development is organized "horizontally," that all developments in diverse domains are at identical levels (as predicted by Piaget and other stage theorists; Kessen, 1962). As Flavell (1982) notes, individual nonretarded children are not equivalent across all domains of functioning, and the search for strengths and weaknesses is important in nonretarded as well as in retarded children.

This is not to say that development is totally unorganized across domains. In particular, there may be smaller, more circumscribed areas of organization that can be helpful in early intervention work with all types of retarded individuals. Bates and her colleagues (1979) have identified "local homologies," in which two or more individual achievements reflect a single underlying concept (see also Mundy, Seibert, & Hogan, 1984). For example, McCune-Nicholich and Bruskin (1982) have found a strong relationship between levels of early language and levels of symbolic play in nonretarded children. Children in the prelinguistic stage mouth or bang objects, whereas those who utter only one-word sentences engage in single-schemed play (e.g., combing a doll's hair). In contrast, children who are beginning to engage in two-word utterances combine simple schemes such as feeding a doll, then grooming it. This relationship has also been discovered in children with Down syndrome (Beeghly & Cicchetti, 1987) and those with autism (Mundy, Sigman, Ungerer, & Sherman, 1987). Thus, there appears to be ample evidence of a "true" connection across two different domains of functioning.

Local homologies and other cross-domain relations are especially helpful for early intervention work. It now seems possible to foster development of specific underlying schemes through a variety of complementary strategies. The early interventionist can foster language through linguistic tasks or through symbolic play, and he or she can aid the development of object permanence by hiding objects, by having the mother leave the room (as in the Strange Situation), or by engaging in peek-a-boo and other hiding games (Hodapp & Goldfield, 1983). Dunst's (1980) modification of the Uzgiris-Hunt scales also follows this logic: in order to make these Piagetian-based scales easier to administer to physically handicapped children, he has added items that require different behaviors, but which, nevertheless, measure identical underlying concepts. The goal throughout is to foster development of a single concept through behaviors and activities that cross the usual domains of functioning.

Similar Themes of Developmentally Appropriate Interaction

A final aspect of general applicability in the developmental approach involves strategies of interaction between adults and children. Although strategies will need to be modified based on characteristics of the child, there are certain types of behaviors that most interventionists would agree are developmentally appropriate for all children, regardless of disability.

The first interactive theme is that the behavior of the adult must, in fact, be "developmentally appropriate" for the child. Called by many names, appropriate maternal interactive behavior is that which is "in synch" with the child. In social interaction with two- to four-month-old infants, mothers match the number and intensity of their interactive behaviors to the activity level of the child, increasing behavior when the child is actively engaged and slowing or stopping behavior when the child requires a rest (Brazelton, Koslowski, & Main, 1974; Stern, 1974). In mother-infant games at the end of the first year, mothers adjust their level of behaviors based on the child's level of abilities, both from month-to-month and within a single interactive session (Hodapp, Goldfield, & Boyatzis, 1984). Similarly, mothers of children who are beginning to enter language shorten their speech, emphasize and repeat key words, and in other ways simplify the language they provide for their children (Rondal, 1985; Snow, 1972). Throughout the early years, then, mothers match their level of interaction to the child's level of ability in any number of ways.

At the same time, mothers do not simply match the child's level; they also foster the child's development. Throughout infancy, mothers react to infant behavior "as if" it were intentional (Clark, 1979), thereby providing behavioral expectations that infants will eventually fulfill. Similarly, in infant games, mothers more often request high-level behaviors once the child has shown a preliminary ability to engage in these behaviors (Hodapp, Goldfield, & Boyatzis, 1984). In addition, by keeping the child attentive, providing appropriate contextual support, and breaking the task down into its component parts, mothers help infants to perform behaviors that children are unable to do on their own until later ages (Wertsch, 1985; Vygotsky, 1978). In each of these ways, mothers "pull" the child along in what has been called the scaffolding, tutoring, or apprenticing of early development (Bruner, 1982; Kaye, 1982).

Granted, the ideas of matching and of scaffolding are general concepts that must be modified for specific children and specific etiological groups. Still, a sense of which behaviors are developmentally appropriate is an important addition to early intervention work, one that applies equally well for children with a variety of specific disabilities.

JOINING THE "SPECIFIC" AND THE "GENERAL" IN EARLY INTERVENTION WORK

From the two preceding sections, it becomes clear that there are both specific and general aspects to early intervention. Children with different etiologies have different strengths and weaknesses, different modalities in which they perceive information, and even different parental and familial characteristics. Yet there remain several general aspects to the early intervention enterprise, as all children traverse identical sequences of development, show similar cross-domain relations, and respond to the same types of developmentally appropriate behaviors and parental interactions.

The task now becomes one of joining the specific and the general, of respecting those aspects of the child that are etiology-specific while at the same time capitalizing on aspects of development that are general to all children. This task is made more difficult because we are still in the early stages of learning about development in many etiological groups.

The strategy we propose might best be illustrated by a model of the "fit" between the child and the environment. This model owes much to Hunt's (1961) "problem of the match" between child and environment, Chess and Thomas's (1984) idea of the "goodness of fit" between parent and child in terms of behavior disorder, and other models of person-environment interactions. Here, however, we combine general aspects of child development with specific aspects of the child's etiology in the same way as general styles of clothing are produced in various sizes. The garment is roughly the same for all individuals—indeed, if style and color are the same, we speak of wearing the "same clothes" as another. But the size is adjusted to better fit the particular individual.

Etiology-specific characteristics are akin to clothing of different sizes in that they approximate, but do not achieve, a perfect fit. Only clothing that is individually tailored *exactly* fits a particular person, yet people of identical sizes are similar enough in body type that a large improvement is attained over no sizing whatsoever. Thus, while two or more children who have Down syndrome, or fragile X syndrome, or any other disorder will differ widely from one another, there are certain etiology-specific characteristics that make useful an intervention strategy that is at least partly based on etiology. At the same time, the general developmental approach—the style and design of a program—can still be followed in early intervention efforts.

A few examples might serve to make more concrete this joining of the general and the specific in early intervention work. Males with fragile X syndrome are better at tasks requiring simultaneous as opposed to sequential processing (Dykens, Hodapp, & Leckman, 1987). It might help, therefore, to first present the entire task to the child, and to employ visual aids and other "holistic devices," before breaking the task down into smaller, discrete steps. Presentation of the whole before the parts runs counter to many behaviorist intervention strategies but, at least with this population, might be a more beneficial strategy.

Similarly, we now know that children with Down syndrome are relatively less impaired in linguistic pragmatics (i.e., the use of language) than in the grammar of language (Beeghly & Cicchetti, 1987; Leifer & Lewis, 1984). If so, intervention programs that are largely pragmatically based might be helpful for Down syndrome children, whereas identical interventions might be less effective in populations in which the social aspects of language are particularly delayed—for example, autistic children (Wetherby, 1986). In addition, as in deaf children, etiology-specific difficulties in speech production are currently leading to greater use of sign language with Down syndrome children.

Many of these ideas focus on the development of underlying concepts as opposed to the performance of individual behaviors. It may not be important whether the child develops oral language or sign language, or is given one as opposed to another specific task in object permanence or other areas, as long as the skill itself is developed. This focus on the underlying meaning of behavior, while often associated with the developmental approach (Hodapp, Burack, & Zigler, 1990), allows for the use of very different strategies that tap identical underlying concepts. To the developmentally oriented worker, it is the concept, not the behavior, that is most important in terms of linguistic or cognitive development.

In terms of parents and families, it is also important to employ general developmental findings (e.g., maternal mourning; transactional model) that are then modified based on the specific problems of the child. It may well be that all parents of handicapped children experience similar stresses from raising a handicapped child, but these concerns may be exacerbated by having a child about whom the cause of disability is unknown (Goldberg, Marcovitch, MacGregor, & Lojkasek, 1986; Holroyd & MacArthur, 1976). Similarly, different milestones may cause more or less concern for parents of children with different disabilities. Our own preliminary work finds that mothers of cerebral palsy children are more concerned about motor milestones (e.g., walking), whereas those with Down syndrome are more concerned about cognitive-linguistic developments (e.g., first words). While not surprising, information of this sort helps the early interventionist to understand and partially predict the timing and areas in which parents might require increased support. The joining of general and specific aspects in early intervention work will not be easy. We continue to know little about functioning in many specific disorders, and, frequently, specific diagnoses are not given to children in the early years. If current trends hold, however, specific diagnoses will be provided to increasing numbers of children at earlier and earlier ages. Increasingly, an etiology-based approach to intervention will become possible, as programs join general developmental principles to individual etiological characteristics. It is our hope that such a joining of the general and the specific in early intervention work will allow for more fine-grained, focused, and effective programs of intervention for young children with handicaps.

ACKNOWLEDGMENTS

The writing of this chapter was supported by program project grant HD 03008 from the U.S. National Institutes of Child Health and Human Development and a grant from the Joseph P. Kennedy, Jr., Foundation.

REFERENCES

Bates, E., Benigni, L., Bretherton, I., Camaioni, I., & Volterra, V. (1979). *The emergence of symbols: Cognition and communication in infancy.* New York: Academic Press.

Beeghly, M., & Cicchetti, D. (1987). An organizational approach to symbolic development in children with Down syndrome. In D. Cicchetti & M. Beeghly (Eds.), Symbolic development in atypical children. New directions for child development (No. 36) (pp. 5-29). San Francisco: Jossey-Bass.

Blacher, J. (1984). Sequential stages of parental adjustment to the birth of a child with handicaps: Fact or artifact? Mental Retardation, 22, 55-68.

Bloom, L. (1970). Language development: Form and function in emerging grammars. Cambridge, MA: MIT Press.

Brazelton, T. B., Koslowski, B., & Main, M. (1974). The origins of reciprocity: The early mother-infant interaction. In M. Lewis & L. A. Rosenblum (Eds.), The effect of the infant on its caregiver (pp. 49-76). New York: Wiley.

Brown, R. (1973). A first language. Cambridge, MA: Harvard University Press.

Bruner, J. (1982). The organization of action and the nature of adult-infant transaction. In E. Z. Tronick (Ed.), Social interchange in infancy (pp. 23-35). Baltimore: University Park Press.

Burack, J. A., Hodapp, R. M., & Zigler, E. (1988). Issues in the classification of mental retardation: Differentiating among organic etiologies. Journal of Child Psychology and Psychiatry, 29, 765-779.

Chess, S., & Thomas, A. (1984). Origins and evolution of behavior disorder. New York: Brunner/Mazel.

Cicchetti, D., & Beeghly, M. (Eds.). (1990). Children with Down syndrome: A developmental perspective. New York: Cambridge University Press.

Cicchetti, D., & Pogge-Hesse, P. (1982). Possible contributions of the study of organically retarded persons to developmental theory. In E. Zigler & D. Balla (Eds.), Mental retardation: The developmental-difference controversy (pp. 277-318). Hillsdale, NJ: Erlbaum.

Clark, R. (1979). The transition from action to gesture. In A. Locke (Ed.), Action, gesture, symbol (pp. 231-260). New York: Academic Press.

Cohen, D. & Donnellan, A. (Eds.). (1987). Autism and pervasive developmental disorders. New York: John Wiley & Sons.

Cornwell, A., & Birch, H. (1969). Psychological and social development in home-reared children with Down syndrome (mongolism). American Journal of Mental Deficiency, 74, 341-350.

Cruickshank, W., Hallahan, D., & Bice, H. (1976). The evaluation of intelligence. In W. Cruickshank (Ed.), Cerebral palsy: A developmental disability (3rd ed.) (pp. 87-114). Syracuse, NY: Syracuse University Press.

Dunst, C. J. (1980). A clinical and educational manual for use with the Uzgiris-Hunt Scales of Infant Development. Baltimore: University Park Press.

Dunst, C. J. (1988). Stage transitioning in the sensorimotor development of Down syndrome infants. Journal of Mental Deficiency Research, 32, 405-410.

Dunst, C. J. (1990). Sensorimotor development of infants with Down syndrome. In D. Cicchetti & M. Beeghly (Eds.), Children with Down syndrome: A developmental perspective (pp. 180-230). New York: Cambridge University Press.

Dykens, E. M., Hodapp, R. M., & Leckman, J. F. (1987). Strengths and weaknesses in the intellectual functioning of males with fragile X syndrome. *American Journal of Mental Deficiency, 92,* 234-236.

Dykens, E. M., Hodapp, R. M., Ort, S. I., Finucane, B., Shapiro, L., & Leckman, J. F. (1989). The trajectory of cognitive development in males with fragile X syndrome. *Journal of the American Academy of Child and Adolescent Psychiatry, 28,* 422-426.

Dykens, E. M., & Leckman, J. F. (1990). Developmental issues in fragile X syndrome. In R. M. Hodapp, J. A. Burack, & E. Zigler (Eds.), *Issues in the developmental approach to mental retardation* (pp. 226-245). New York: Cambridge University Press.

Emde, R., & Brown, C. (1978). Adaptation to the birth of a Down syndrome infant. Grieving and maternal attachment. *Journal of the American Academy of Child Psychiatry, 17,* 299-323.

Ferrier, L. (1987). *A comparative study of the conversational skills of fragile X, autistic, and Down syndrome individuals.* Unpublished doctoral dissertation, Boston University (Dissertations Abstracts International, # DA8715419).

Fishburn, J., Turner, G., Daniel, A., & Brookwell, R. (1983). The diagnosis and frequency of X-linked conditions in a cohort of moderately impaired males with affected brothers. *American Journal of Medical Genetics, 14,* 713-724.

Flavell, J. (1982). Structures, stages, and sequences in cognitive development. In D. Harris (Ed.), *The concept of development. The Minnesota Symposia on Child Psychology, Vol. 15* (pp. 1-28). Hillsdale, NJ: Erlbaum.

Fowler, A. (1990). The development of language structure in children with Down syndrome. In D. Cicchetti & M. Beeghly (Eds.), *Children with Down syndrome: A developmental perspective* (pp. 302-328). New York: Cambridge University Press.

Fraiberg, S. (1974). Blind infants and their mothers: An examination of the sign system. In M. Lewis & L. A. Rosenblum (Eds.), *The effect of the infant on its caregiver* (pp. 215-232). New York: John Wiley & Sons.

Fraiberg, S. (1977). *Insights from the blind.* New York: Basic Books.

Gibson, D. (1978). *Down syndrome: The psychology of mongolism.* Cambridge England: Cambridge University Press.

Goldberg, S., Marcovitch, S., MacGregor, D., & Lojkasek, M. (1986, August). *Developmental delay, etiology unknown: Problems for parents.* Paper presented to the convention of the Canadian Psychological Association, Toronto, Canada.

Grossman, H. (Ed.). (1983). *Classification in mental retardation* (3rd ed.). Washington, D.C.: American Association on Mental Retardation.

Halliday, M.A.K. (1975). Learning how to mean. In E. Lenneberg & E. Lenneberg (Eds.), *Foundations of language development: A multi-disciplinary approach, Vol. 1* (pp. 240-264). New York: Academic Press.

Hodapp, R. M. (1990). One road or many? Issues in the similar sequence hypothesis. In R. M. Hodapp, J. A. Burack, & E. Zigler (Eds.), *Issues in the developmental approach to mental retardation* (pp. 49-70). New York: Cambridge University Press.

Hodapp, R. M., Burack, J. A., & Zigler, E. (1990). The developmental perspective in the field of mental retardation. In R. M. Hodapp, J. A. Burack, & E. Zigler (Eds.), *Issues in the developmental approach to mental retardation* (pp. 3-26). New York: Cambridge University Press.

Hodapp, R. M., & Goldfield, E. C. (1983). The use of mother-infant games as therapy with delayed children. *Early Child Development and Care, 13,* 27-32.

Hodapp, R. M., Goldfield, E. C., & Boyatzis, C. J. (1984). The use and effectiveness of maternal scaffolding in mother-infant games. *Child Development, 55,* 772-781.

Hodapp, R. M., Leckman, J. F., Dykens, E. M., Sparrow, S. S., Zelinsky, D. G., & Ort, S. I. (1990). *Cognitive profiles in children with fragile X syndrome, Down syndrome, and nonspecific mental retardation.* Unpublished manuscript, Psychology Department, Yale University, New Haven, CT.

Hodapp, R. M., & Zigler, E. (1990). Applying the developmental perspective to individuals with Down syndrome. In D. Cicchetti & M. Beeghly (Eds.), *Children with Down syndrome: A developmental perspective* (pp. 1-28). New York: Cambridge University Press.

Holroyd, J., & MacArthur, D. (1976). Mental retardation and stress on parents: A contrast between Down syndrome and childhood autism. *American Journal of Mental Deficiency, 80,* 431-436.

Hunt, J. M. (1961). *Intelligence and experience.* New York: Ronald Press.

Kaufman, A., & Kaufman, N. (1983). *Kaufman Assessment Battery for Children (K-ABC).* Circle Pines, MN: American Guidance Service.

Kaye, K. (1982). *The mental and social life of babies.* Chicago: University of Chicago Press.

Kessen, W. (1962). Stage and structure in the study of children. In W. Kessen & C. Kuhlman (Eds.), *Thought in the young child. Monographs of the Society for Research in Child Development, 27,* 53-70.

Klapper, Z., & Birch, H. (1967). A fourteen year follow-up study of cerebral palsy: Intellectual change and stability. *American Journal of Orthopsychiatry, 3,* 540-547.

Korn, S., Chess, S., & Fernandez, P. (1978). The impact of children's physical handicaps on marital quality and family interaction. In R. M. Lerner & G. B. Spanier (Eds.), *Child influences on marital and family interaction: A life-span perspective* (pp. 299-326). New York: Academic Press.

Leifer, J., & Lewis, M. (1984). Acquisition of conversational response skills by young Down syndrome and nonretarded young children. *American Journal of Mental Deficiency, 88,* 610-618.

MacDonald, J., & Blott, J. (1974). Environmental language intervention: A rationale for diagnostic and training strategy through rules, context, and generalization. *Journal of Speech and Hearing Disorders, 39,* 395-415.

McCall, R. B. (1981). Nature-nurture and the two realms of development: A proposed integration with respect to mental development. *Child Development, 52,* 1-12.

McCune-Nicholich, L., & Bruskin, C. (1982). Combinatorial competency in symbolic play and language. In D. Pepler & K. Rubin (Eds.), *The play of children* (pp. 30-45). New York: Karger.

McLean, J., & Snyder-McLean, L. (1978). *A transactional approach to early language training*. Columbus, OH: Merrill.

Mundy, P., & Kasari, C. (1990). The similar structure hypothesis and differential rate hypothesis in mental retardation. In R. M. Hodapp, J. A. Burack, & E. Zigler (Eds.), *Issues in the developmental approach to mental retardation* (pp. 71-92). New York: Cambridge University Press.

Mundy, P., Seibert, J., & Hogan, A. (1984). The relationship between sensorimotor and early communication abilities in developmentally delayed children. *Merrill-Palmer Quarterly, 30*, 33-48.

Mundy, P., Sigman, M., Ungerer, J., & Sherman, T. (1987). Nonverbal communication and play correlates of language development in autistic children. *Journal of Autism and Developmental Disorders, 17*, 349-364.

Murphy, P., Watson, M., Kidd, K., & Breg, W. R. (1986). Molecular approaches to carrier detection and prenatal diagnosis of the fragile X syndrome. *Pediatric Research, 20*, 269A.

Pueschel, S., Gallagher, P., Zartler, A., & Pezzullo, J. (1987). Cognitive and learning processes in children with Down syndrome. *Research in Developmental Disabilities, 8*, 21-37.

Reiss, S., Hagerman, R., Vinogradov, S., Abrams, M., & King, R. (1988). Psychiatric disability in female carriers of the fragile X chromosome. *Archives of General Psychiatry, 45*, 25-30.

Rondal, J. (1985). *Adult-child interaction and the process of language acquisition*. New York: Praeger.

Scarr-Salapatek, S. (1975). An evolutionary perspective on infant intelligence: Species patterns and individual variations. In M. Lewis (Ed.), *Origins of intelligence* (pp. 165-197). New York: Plenum.

Schlesinger, I. (1971). Production of utterances in language acquisition. In D. Slobin (Ed.), *The ontogenesis of grammar* (pp. 62-102). New York: Academic Press.

Snow, C. (1972). Mother's speech to children learning language. *Child Development, 43*, 549-565.

Solnit, A., & Stark, M. (1961). Mourning and the birth of a defective child. *The Psychoanalytic Study of the Child, 16*, 523-537.

Stern, D. (1974). Mother and infant at play: The dyadic interaction involving facial, vocal, and gaze behaviors. In M. Lewis & L. A. Rosenblum (Eds.), *The effect of the infant on its caregiver* (pp. 187-213). New York: Wiley.

Taylor, R., & Caldwell, M. (Eds.). (1988). *Prader-Willi Syndrome: Selected research and management issues*. New York: Springer-Verlag.

Vygotsky, L. S. (1978). *Mind in society*. Cambridge, MA: MIT Press.

Weisz, J. (1990). Cultural-familial mental retardation: A developmental perspective on cognitive performance and "helpless" behavior. In R. M. Hodapp, J. A. Burack, & E. Zigler (Eds.), *Issues in the developmental approach to mental retardation* (pp. 137-168). New York: Cambridge University Press.

Weisz, J., Yeates, K., & Zigler, E. (1982). Piagetian evidence and the developmental-difference controversy. In E. Zigler & D. Balla (Eds.), *Mental retardation: The developmental-difference controversy* (pp. 213-276). Hillsdale, NJ: Erlbaum.

Weisz, J., & Zigler, E. (1979). Cognitive development in retarded and nonretarded persons: Piagetian tests of the similar sequence hypothesis. *Psychological Bulletin, 86,* 831-851.

Wertsch, J. (1985). *Vygotsky and the social formation of mind.* Cambridge, MA: Harvard University Press.

Wetherby, A. M. (1986). Ontogeny of communicative functions in autism. *Journal of Autism and Developmental Disabilities, 16,* 295-316.

Wolf-Schein, E., Sudhalter, V., Cohen, I., Fish, G., Hanson, D., Pfadt, A., Hagerman, R., Jenkins, E., & Brown, W. T. (1987). Speech-language and fragile X syndrome: Initial findings. *Journal of the American Speech-Language Hearing Association (ASHA), 29,* 35-38.

Zigler, E. (1967). Familial mental retardation: A continuing dilemma. *Science, 155,* 292-298.

Zigler, E. (1969). Developmental versus difference theories of mental retardation and the problem of motivation. *American Journal of Mental Deficiency, 73,* 536-566.

Zigler, E., & Hodapp, R. M. (1986). *Understanding mental retardation.* New York: Cambridge University Press.

3

Down Syndrome and Cognitive Enhancement: Not Like the Others

David Gibson

Mankind owes to the child the best it has to give.
U.N. Declaration

In the beginning, the single most marketable objective of early intervention (EI)/infant stimulation (Infant-Stim) programs was to enhance intelligence for the at-risk, disadvantaged, and damaged child. The promise, an extrapolation from traditional child development theory, attracted large-scale public funding and mission-oriented proponents of cognitive salvation through early behavioral treatments. The apparent benefits of these EI demonstration projects for the Down syndrome (DS) child to date are short-term developmental gains, often impressive, but not convincing signs of durable advances in the domains of cognition and communication (Gibson & Fields, 1984). The aggregated outcomes of twenty-one adjudicated EI program accountability reports for DS children in the open literature (Gibson & Harris, 1988) indicate consensus for durable growth in finer coordination and early self-help skills, over similar subjects not exposed to special remedial intervention. Gains in DQ/IQ scores were also evident but fleeting, the by-product of the eye-hand-skills task demand of most infant developmental schedules. There was sparse evidence of the lasting effects of Infant-Stim on gross motor, cognitive, or linguistic development (Gibson & Harris, 1988). These outcomes are consistent with the Piper, Goselin, Gendron, and Mazer (1986) longitudinal study of the growth profile of thirty-two DS infants exposed to EI programming. Most stable

over time were eye-hand and personal-social performance gains on the
Griffiths Scale (Griffiths, 1970). Fewest benefits were recorded for the
locomotor and speech-hearing test items. Other critical appraisals of
collective EI program outcomes include those by Harris (1981), Cunningham (1983, 1986), Dunst (1985), Sloper, Glenn, and Cunningham
(1986), and Weisenfeld (1987).

Given the collapse of the original intellectualization objectives of
early intervention for DS children, the rush was on to elevate secondary
program gains to the status of original good intentions. Some of these
are ingenious, and all are worthy if somewhat belated. Examples include a schedule of maturational intervention goals (Buckley & Sacks,
1987), a functional model of effects assessment (Simeonsson, Huntington, & Short, 1982), a social systems benefits model (Dunst, 1985; Zigler
& Berman, 1983), an ecological enhancement approach (Bronfenbrenner, 1979; Marfo & Kysela, 1985) and a personal-life satisfactions outcome criterion set (Landesman, 1986). The diffusion of expectations
regarding the benefits of EI programs has the additional convenient
effect of rendering the objective study of program accountability nearly
impossible—a potential disservice to the DS child, the parent, and the
taxpayer.

The position taken in the present chapter is that the expulsion of
cognitive training, as central to EI program design, is premature. The
DS child has, after all, been the target of omnibus intervention curricula
applied indiscriminately to clinically and etiologically heterogeneous
subject groups. An alternative treatment approach, the time for which
has perhaps come, is that EI prescriptions be made responsive to both
individual and group differences in growth potential—a recognition,
finally, that the DS child is genetically, structurally, neurophysiologi-
cally, and behaviorally distinct in many ways from other causal categories of mental handicap. It is increasingly acknowledged that EI
treatments should be harmonized to the specific needs of the DS child
(Burack, Hodapp, & Zigler, 1988; Gibson, 1989; Gunn & Berry, 1989;
Ottenbacher, 1989; Spitz, 1986; White & Casto, 1985). To meet these
needs it will be necessary to (a) chart the ways in which the DS individual is developmentally different from others in cognitive and related
potentials, and (b) point the way to EI program approaches and content
based on the biobehavioral particulars of the syndrome.

MAPPING COGNITIVE PROCESS: MENTAL TEST
SCATTER AND PROFILE EVIDENCE

The Early Work

First attempts to discover psychometric signature patterns for the DS
child depended on the venerable Binet scales. Later research employed

the Wechsler (WISC), the ITPA, the Purdue Perceptual-Motor Survey, the Uzgiris and Hunt Scale, and the Kaufman Assessment Battery, among the many (Gibson, 1978). The fruits of these studies, while sparking little interest among the designers of EI programs for the DS child, have given valuable direction to present-day experimental research on cognitive processing styles associated with the syndrome. It will be useful at the outset to determine the extent of agreement among mental test findings respecting a characteristic cognitive configuration for the DS child and adult.

Brousseau and Brainerd (1928) analyzed Binet item scatter for DS subjects and concluded that the subjects could readily identify and name items but failed on subtest material calling for sequencing and relating strategies. Pototzky and Grigg (1942) identified a deficiency in number skills at below-age-level expectation. Kostrzewski (1965) confirmed the markedly deficient number sense for the DS subjects and noted, additionally, a particular inability to multiply. Even for the least retarded DS child, the arithmetic subtest of the WISC was the most depressed of the cognitive items (Rosencrans, 1971). These essentially symbol-management inadequacies have been attributed to attention deficit, immature cross-modal transfer facility for especially the auditory-perceptual loop, and reduced abstraction potential—more so than for other mentally retarded (MR) subjects at similar mental age (MA) levels.

Wallin (1944) had previously extended the hope that DS individuals can overcome the symbolization facility shortfall when meaningful, relevant attention-holding demands were made in the educational process. Under these conditions, some DS students could read at a better level than their overall MA score would predict. The new skill proved ephemeral, however, leading Wallin to conclude that the reading performance had been built on a "mechanics of word calling" that was largely devoid of comprehension. Wallin attributes this minor savant-like skill to relatively superior rote memory and unimpaired cross-modality function of the visual-motor circuitry. Rollin (1946) noted that the impulsivity of the DS youngster interferes with comprehension but not, evidently, with simple storage functions—an explanation of sorts for the Wallin finding.

Consistency of Cognitive Profiles Over Time

There is useful agreement that the typical Binet-derived cognitive profile of the DS child has significant forecast value for cognitive patterning displayed (on average) by older DS subjects. For the less retarded DS population, Stickland (1954) confirmed that peaks in Binet test scatter indicated comparatively superior memory capacity in interaction with extent of memory training. At the same time, abstract and conceptual vocabulary exhibited progressive growth deceleration into adulthood. On this point, Lyle (1959) concluded that DS subjects of all ages were simply less verbal than other MA-matched MR subjects. McNeill (1955) and Stedman and Eichorn (1964) identified eye-hand skills as best in relation to mental age, whereas test demand for symbolization was most deficient. Cornwell (1974) confirmed a satisfactory accretion of rote skills but little advance over time in the conceptual and integrative domains of cognitive processing. Examining the full range of Binet test content, Nakamura (1965) discovered that of sixty test items, DS subjects were inferior at repeating digits but were able to surpass MR control subjects in performance on form board, block bridging, and circle drawing tasks. This ability configuration indicates continuing expressive language deficit and relative superiority for spatial-motor and eye-hand tasks. Overall, older DS individuals displayed best performance potentials involving rote memory, finer coordination, visual-motor input-output loops, and nonconceptual learning styles.

Current Research

More recent biobehavioral studies have gained in reliability by the use of larger samples, MA-matched comparison groups, and a more critical approach to interpretation of results. These recent findings have tended to support and elaborate the earlier research. For example, using Binet items with 754 DS subjects and controls, Silverstein, Legutki, Friedman, and Takayama (1982) found specific deficiencies for comprehension, judgment, and reasoning facility and more advanced status over non-DS MR control subjects for test items having figural content. This aspect of visual-motor ability was seen earlier to be a comparative cognitive strength for the syndrome. McDade and Adler (1980) previously noted that DS subjects have particular cognitive process limitations for the storage and retrieval functions in the auditory mode but only a storage deficit for visually presented information. Visual information retrieval is evidently more efficient for DS subjects than for non-DS MR controls.

This peculiarity of information processing will require further examination in view of the Anwar and Hermelin (1979) report that spatial orientation is more readily upset by intervening motor tasks than is the case for comparable non-DS samples of MR subjects. For now, though, the Silverstein, Legutki, Friedman, and Takayama (1982) study provides the most apparently useful material for the purpose of program design. Their central thesis is that DS children excel, comparatively, on tasks having a common spatial-motor dimension. The non-DS sample excel on test items having semantic content, those involving social judgment, and on general comprehension items. In practical terms, DS individuals more readily respond to visual direction, whereas non-DS MR control subjects react more effectively to verbal directions.

Of central concern for cognitive systems intervention purposes is the seeming paucity of DS subjects' judgment and reasoning facility relative to their MA and the tendency for these eclipsed potentials to retreat further as age advances. Seyfort and Spreen's (1979) finding that DS individuals do comparatively well on the motor aspects of mental test performance but lack the facility to plan strategies that would permit them to execute tasks through to completion might explain the general deceleration of cognitive development with advancing age.

Relative superiority with visual-motor mental test content does not necessarily promise superior spatial performance in the other sensory or expressive channels. Indeed, Share (1975) found that DS persons exhibit poor overall management of spatial relationships. For instance, O'Connor and Hermelin (1961) found tactile shape and stereognostic recognition to be slower than for non-DS MR control subjects (e.g., to handle an object "unseen" and then be required to draw it). Ongoing experimental research in this subarea will be evaluated in a following section.

Modern Special Abilities Testing Elaborates Old Findings

Because the relatively consistent cognitive picture for the syndrome to date is chiefly a product of one test, the Binet, and given the limited potential of this test for qualitative analyses, it is essential that further support be sought based on more specialized cognitive measures.

Using the Bender-Gestalt test, Rosencrans (1971) found his DS subjects to be perseverative, to experience directional difficulty, and to exhibit poor visual-perceptual organization, distraction, and attention disorder. These deficiencies are more often associated with right hemisphere disturbance. Bilovsky and Share (1965) applied the Illinois Test of Psycholinguistic Ability (ITPA) to DS subjects who proved to be advanced in visual decoding (identifying what they see with minimum verbal involvement) and depressed for auditory-vocal encoding and decoding. Associated with this test profile was a low intrasubject variability, which is suggestive of the syndrome specificity of the cognitive profile. Motor encoding and visual decoding were most advanced. These strengths are among the essential working components of learning by imitation or modeling.

On the negative side, significant neuropsychological deficits for DS subjects over controls was proposed by Neeman (1971) to include visual acuity, threshold for speech, reaction time (response to pictures), brightness discrimination, and aspects of kinesthetic bilateral responding. Certain of these areas are, however, subject to medical intervention.

Cunningham and McArthur (1981) detected a 75-percent conductive hearing loss in DS persons, often overlooked in cursory examination, but which could explain part of the much-claimed auditory-motor circuit limitation.

Exploring Information Strategies for the Syndrome

The increasing specialization of cognitive measures has afforded opportunities for more differentiated mapping of information-processing strategies among the many categories of mental handicap. A key current research issue is the extent to which the various causal groups of MR subjects use sequential cognitive processes over successive processing of mental inputs. The identification of etiologically distinctive information-processing styles will facilitate the design of potentially more functional early intervention programs geared both to the unique needs of MR individuals and to the collective needs of etiological categories.

From Bilovsky and Share in 1965 to Snart, O'Grady, and Das in 1982, the most striking deficit of information-processing performance for DS subjects has been with auditory sequential memory and the speed at which auditory information is processed (Lincoln, Courchesne, Kelman, & Galambos, 1985). Das, Kirby, and Jarman (1979) proposed that successive coding skills underpin language production, while simultaneous coding facility is essential both to planning and to developing higher-level thought processes. Unfortunately, DS subjects are weaker than other comparable MR subjects in both simultaneous and successive coding (Snart, O'Grady, & Das, 1982), although Hartley (1982) reported that DS subjects nevertheless score lower on measures of successive than on simultaneous mental tasks. She attributes this departure from the expected finding for those of subnormal intelligence (Jensen, 1969) to an anomaly in the hemispherical localization of speech for DS persons that implicates the right lobe. The validity and implications of this pioneer proposal will require further study.

Pueschel, Gallagher, Carter, and Pezzullo (1987) inspected cognitive and learning tactics in DS children, employing the Kaufman Assessment Battery for Children. They documented a significant difference between DS children and their normal siblings for sequential versus simultaneous styles of information processing. The DS members were most delayed developmentally for number recall (the auditory-vocal channel again) and word order (an auditory-motor channeling task). Performance engaging visual-vocal and visual-motor loops were less affected. In contrast, siblings achieved best with auditory over visual modes of information processing. Pueschel and his associates recommend that:

Teaching strategies should capitalize on DS children's strengths and should focus on visual-vocal and visual-motor processing modalities in remediation ... (and that) increasing emphasis on auditory teaching strategies may lead to frustration in the child and may impede academic progress. (p. 35)

The observation is not new, but neither has it been tested in the classroom. Rohr and Burr (1978) had recorded the lower than expected verbal-auditory abilities of DS children and supposed the deficit to be some amalgam of a more primary developmental shortfall of successive coding ability, auditory processing lag, and indigent verbal outputs. Also implicated is a possibly defective rehearsal mechanism and a reduced capacity to store information, the latter handicap being ascribed to poor language skills. Rohr and Burr concluded that information-processing difficulties peculiar to DS children are mainly a function of slow auditory processing levels. The outcome can be a failure to build more complex and stable stimulus traces (Ellis, 1963) appropriate for mental age and, consequently, impeded cognitive development. Successful remedial intervention will be a particular challenge for the future.

Finally, Pueschel and his collegues (1987) have presented a maturational-biochemical paradigm for the origins of the cognitive anomalies frequently associated with DS individuals. They proposed that:

Myelination of nerve fibres occurs for specific neuronal tissue at different times in the development of the central nervous system. It is known that nerve fibres of auditory associations are myelinated late during development when increased peroxidative damage may occur. Thus selective perturbation of oxygen-free radical metabolism will affect adversely myelin formation in nerve tracts concerned with auditory processing. (p. 33)

Support for the explanation is available from the auditory evoked potential literature (Lincoln, Courchesne, Kelman, & Galambos, 1985). As well, poor muscle tone in DS infants is known to be a powerful predictor of later rate of motor and language skill acquisition and of mental functioning overall (Pueschel, 1984).

Stability of the Proposed Cognitive Profile for DS Adults

Psychometric profile studies of the DS adult support the continuity of the already suggested cognitive profile for the syndrome, with modification in the form of a smoothing of the profile peaks as age advances. Accordingly, Lott (1982) found memory for recent events and short-term visual retention to be among the first signs of intellectual decline for DS adults past age thirty-five. Emery (1984) detected decline with age on memory and linguistic tasks. Wisniewski (1985) claimed that memory loss in the visual modality, when succeeded by reduced learning capacity, was likely to be a preeminent indicator of early dementia for the syndrome. Older DS persons were depicted by Kolata (1985) as functioning more poorly on tests of visual memory and attention as MA scores declined.

For Thase and associates (Thase, Liss, Smeltzer, & Maloon, 1982; Thase, Tigner, Smeltzer, & Liss, 1984), problems with digit span, visual memory, and object naming tasks were most prominent among the cognitive functions that differentiated aging DS adults from MR control subjects. Also implicated was an age-graded paucity of short-term storage ability and declining capacity for processing auditory information. These erosions of the classical cognitive profile were thought to account for the increasing verbal difficulty experienced by DS adults as they aged, especially as reflected in their declining ability to process lexical information. Hewitt and Jancar (1986) similarly observed the diminution of an already limited capacity for auditory processing as having serious consequences for the retention of verbal facility. Most recently, Shapiro, Haxby, Grady, and Duara (1987) have recorded significant alterations in language function, visual-spatial ability, attention, and memory as age advances.

Evidently, not only do the strongest components of the early mature cognitive profile for the syndrome (visual retention, aspects of memory, naming skills) show most rapid decline with aging, but the initially weak elements of the cognitive profile simply "bottom-out" with advancing age (especially the auditory and linguistic test items). The overall result will be a still recognizable DS cognitive profile, if somewhat attenuated. This configuration of decay, presumed to signal premature aging and risk of early amentia, is not typical of the normal aging population where memory loss and disorientation are among the first signs of senile dementia (Miniszek, 1983).

A follow-up of comparative WISC subtest profiles for DS and brain-damaged MR adults over time provides preliminary evidence (a) for the relative stability of cognitive patterning with DS subjects well into adulthood, and (b) of cognitive aspects of the syndrome most likely to provide a marker for impending senile dementia (Gibson, Groeneweg, Berry, & Harris, 1988). The high degree of age constancy in the test profile items for the DS adults, viewed against the caprice of test scatter for non-DS brain-damaged subjects, is depicted in Figures 3.1 and 3.2. It can be seen that the DS cohort exhibited relatively little age-related decay of test content having a high loading for short- and long-term visual memory and visual-motor coordination facility. Of special interest, though, is the rapid decline with age of Block Design scores for the DS subjects; this finding is consistent with Fuld's (1984) report that individuals who are prone to Alzheimer's disease in the general pop-

Figure 3.1
WISC-R Subtest Profile for Down Syndrome Adults

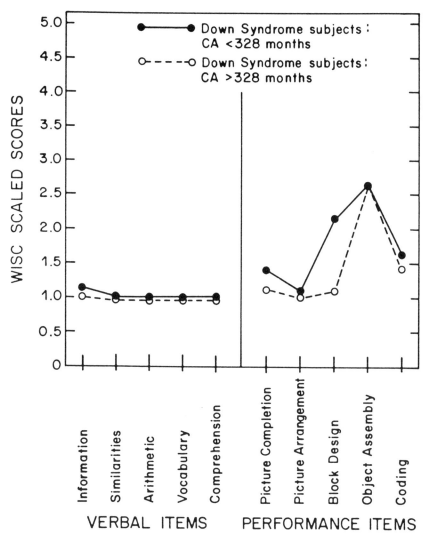

ulation fail especially to complete the Block Design subtest (see also Brinkman & Braun, 1984). This subtest is claimed to require the perceptual representation of "wholes" in terms of their constituent parts. As such, it is a fundamental ingredient of conceptualization and one that is evidently poorly represented in the cognitive catalogue of the typical DS individual (Kaufman, 1979). Given the culture-free and factorially specific quality of this cognitive ability (Glasser & Zimmerman,

Figure 3.2
WISC-R Subtest Profile for Non-DS Brain-Damaged Adults

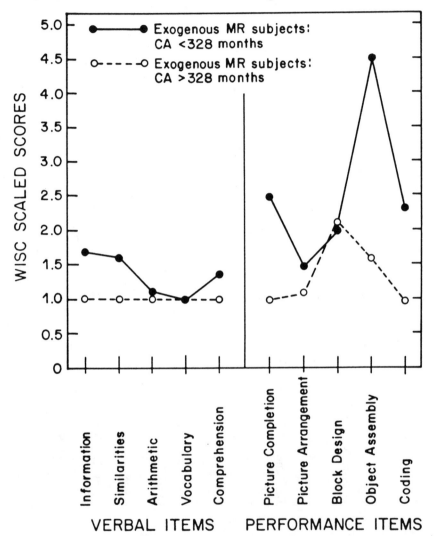

1967), and its superior status as a measure of general intelligence (Guilford & Merrifield, 1960), it will be essential to attempt to build early remediation programs around advancing perceptual organization and spatial visualization. Among the potential effects of such remediation might be improved adult judgment facility and a deferral of the onset of amentia to later ages.

MAPPING COGNITIVE PROCESS: EXPERIMENTAL STUDIES OF THE CONSTITUENCIES OF INFORMATION PROCESSING

Perception and the Sensory Modalities

Perception involving all sensory modes appears to be qualitatively and developmentally different for DS children, compared with other MA-matched MR children and CA- (chronological age) or MA-matched normal subjects. In the realm of visual perception, Anwar (1983) suggests that even by age six months DS infants show different preferences for attention to visual stimuli than do normal infants. They will fix on a single aspect of an image, whereas normal infants engage a broader scanning process and, unlike the DS infant, do not avoid complex patterns. In the same vein, Loveland (1987) found DS and other children to differ in number and types of exploratory behaviors—such as in a mirror task—independent of mental or chronological age. Richard (1986), too, mentions differences between DS and normal infants in gaze patterns and in the coordination of gesture, gaze, and vocalization. Stratford (1985) observes that DS subjects fixate on parts rather than on "wholes," especially if there is a degree of complexity in the stimulus presentation. As if especially attracted to "good form," they tend to organize visually presented material by giving increased symmetry to it when required to copy. As perceptual complexity increased, information overload occurred, presumably related to limited short-term memory.

Cunningham (1974) offers an attentional inflexibility hypothesis for DS persons that might help to simplify the foregoing findings. He has demonstrated that when requiring DS subjects to shift attention from one visual aspect of a task to another, they become confused, for example, when the size and complexity of the design card increase in tandem. Ordinarily, the extra cue would aid in problem solving. Yet the response of DS subjects to distraction is unique; these subjects increase their rate of work to task while also increasing their error rate. Where the task demand is reasonable, and the distraction is in a different modality than that engaged for task management, the result could be to facilitate task completion, a positive gain derived from a cross-modal transfer deficit. Stratford and Ching (1983) add a "drive" element to the explanation. These authors required DS subjects to tap out the beat while listening to a rhythm. Subjects performed at a complexity level similar to that of MA-matched normal children and superior to non-DS MR children, indicating an ability potential that could advance cognitive status.

Experimental psychologists have tested the auditory-motor channeling difficulty alleged by psychometric researchers to be characteristic of DS persons, but the results have been mixed. Zekulin, Gibson, Mosley, and Brown (1974), while finding no clear support for a specific auditory-motor performance deficit, did find evidence of a greater susceptibility of the auditory modality to distraction—whether or not the distraction was meaningful (patterned). An inhibitory deficit explanation is offered. In support of a more centralist explanation, Lincoln and his associates (1985), using event-related brain potentials and reaction times, claimed that DS subjects process auditory information more slowly than do CA- and MA-matched control samples. The DS group also differed in scalp distribution of amplitude of brain potentials, which could not be explained simply as maturational delay. Rather, these researchers attribute the auditory input limitations to neurofibrillary tangles in the hippocampus, to loss of pyramidal neurons (as in Alzheimer's disease), and to abnormalities of the dendrite spines in the hippocampal region. The extent of auditory-motor channeling difficulty could provide yet another predictor of risk for early senile dementia for the syndrome.

The Primitive Sensory Modalities and Functional Uniqueness

Anwar (1981, 1983) claims that a critical developmental risk for DS infants and children is their failure to develop viable sensorimotor and visual schema. They have fewer eye movements, in part a function of hypotonic musculature and an indolent arousal/activation system. Consequently, they do not develop effective scanning strategies as readily as age and general developmental status would forecast. So the DS child has ongoing frustrations in linking visual and motor outputs, excepting early eye-hand coordination facility. The deficit has implications for competent visually guided reaching, for age-appropriate exploratory behavior, and for attention-span maintenance as a foundation for later associative-type learning. Yet DS children can "generate accurate movements to special location on the basis of their internal kinesthetic or proprioceptive feedback only" (Anwar, 1981, p. 127), thus providing a further design opportunity for an early intervention curriculum.

Cerebral Specialization is Different?

Anderson and Barry (1975, cited in Zekulin-Hartley, 1981), Reinhart (1974), and Zekulin-Hartley (1981) report that DS children have a left-ear advantage for processing linguistic stimuli, whereas most other MR children and normal control subjects exhibit the expected right-ear advantage. It is proposed that the right hemisphere (left ear) is not as efficient with language processing as is the left. Implicated is a centrally mediated communication/processing deficit more pronounced for the DS subject than for other MR etiological groups. The Zekulin-Hartley experiments have been supported by Pipe (1983), who places speech perception in the right hemisphere for DS subjects. The work of Elliot, Weeks, and Elliot (1987), however, is only indirectly supportive. Their conjecture is that DS children are simply less well lateralized than are many other MR and normal children. The previously mentioned preference of DS children for perceptual symmetry could, as well, be a result of simple delay of cerebral specialization, as might be the relative inability of DS subjects to manage sequential linguistic tasks. The greater success of DS subjects with simultaneous linguistic tasks is nevertheless better understood, at this time, in terms of the Hartley (1982) model.

Supportive of neither the lateralization delay nor the reversed cerebral specialization hypotheses is evidence by Kerr and Blais (1987) that DS subjects have particular difficulty exploiting directional probability information to the same extent as comparable non-DS MR subjects. They attribute the persistent difference, despite improvement of the DS cohort with practice, to an unspecified central processing limitation. The most recent work on the matter by Pipe (1988) explores the proposition that atypical cerebral dominance is related causally to a generalized cognitive defect in DS subjects. The hypothesis owes much to Berman's (1971) viewpoint. Pipe concludes that despite the dichotic listening evidence reviewed, it is premature to claim that left-hemisphere dysfunction plays a major role in explaining singular cognitive deficits ascribed to the syndrome. Furthermore, it is said that attempts to advance cerebral lateralization will not aid cognitive and speech development or that the withholding of age-appropriate bilateral activities will not strengthen cerebral hemispherical specialization for DS children. Regardless, Kerr and Blais (1985, 1987) were able to achieve a significant improvement in the use of directional probability information in cognitive processing by DS subjects. A less fragmented research approach is clearly warranted.

Evidence of a Distinctive Pattern of Motor Impairment

The small cerebellum and hypotonic musculature of the DS child implicates a motor defect over and above that shown by most non-DS MR individuals of comparable general functioning (Anwar, 1981; Pueschel, 1984). The behavioral research findings are supportive. Frith and Frith (1974) exposed DS, normal, and non-DS subnormal persons to simple finger-tapping tasks and discovered that only the DS subjects failed to show improvement over time. The failure implicates both raw motor-system deficit and motor-sequencing deficit. Furthermore, there is a comparative inferiority of DS subjects over MR control subjects for general coordination (Carr, 1970), balance (Butterworth & Ciccehetti, 1978), reaction time (Berkson, 1960), stereognostic discrimination (O'Connor & Hermelin, 1961), and rapid motor sequencing (Seyfort & Spreen, 1979). More recently, Henderson and collegues (1981, cited in Kerr & Blais, 1985) have recorded relatively depressed motor performance for DS subjects on ten of twelve motor tasks of the Cratty Test of Gross Motor Performance (Cratty, 1969). Subjects performed much more slowly overall and could not exercise sufficient balance to complete many tasks. Motor Scale scores correlated .77 with mental age, suggesting a link with cognitive capacity in the nature of limited motor-sequencing facility.

Potentials for Memory Function in Down Syndrome as Special

Memory and mimicry facility was viewed by early clinicians as a special or savant talent (Wood, 1909; Wallin, 1949), even though Tennies (1943) had found no transfer of memory or mimicry skill for educational purpose. Oster (1953) was the first to differentiate strength of memory potential by sensory modality. Visual recall for persons and situations was regarded as comparatively strong, whereas auditory-verbal recall (for messages or a shopping list) was considered wanting. Sinson and Wetherick (1973) added that DS persons, on average, have especially poor memory for color and good memory for form when compared with other classes of MR individuals.

Modern experimental findings acknowledge, however, that memory facility for DS individuals is not a homogeneous entity to be declared uniformly ahead or behind in the developmental timetable in relation to other clinical populations. For example, McDade and Adler (1980) found short-term memory function for auditorially presented information to be appropriate for MA, both in the storage (input) and retrieval (output) phases. Visually presented material was associated with a storage deficit only. Impoverished auditory/sequencing memory and superior recall for auditory items of the ITPA and the WISC were also reported by Marcell and Armstrong (1982) and Marcell and Weeks (1988). These results included a possible special facility for echoic memory affiliated with visual stimulation, a finding that would require validation against MR controls. Using such controls, MacKenzie and Hulme (1987) were able to demonstrate that DS subjects perform no less well on auditory/sequencing tasks (digit span) than do MR controls and differ from controls only in exhibiting much less performance variability as a group.

Turning to spatial memory in general, DS adults (with a mean IQ of

47) were found to be especially inferior on recall of spatial material than were non-DS controls (Ellis, Woodley-Zanthos, & Dulaney, 1989). Recall skill was unrelated to IQ level. The explanation is that "memory for location is mediated by more primitive brain mechanisms that are less vulnerable to pathological insult than are those responsible for effortless processing" (p. 525). The distinction appears to be that *recall* of spatial material is much more deficient than for the *simple location and relocation* of such material, on which DS subjects tend to perform close to the level of college students. This phenomenon deserves further research.

Addressing the particular deficiency of auditory-sequential cognitive processing, Varnhagen, Das, and Varnhagen (1987) concluded that DS individuals have a special problem with short-term storage and retrieval of lexical information as well as syndrome-specific limitations in accessing long-term memory for lexical material. The operable result is impoverished verbal memory, impaired verbal problem solving, and poor language comprehension or production. They favor a general information/processing deficit as mediational, the supposition being that the route to communication-skills training is by early and direct cognitive intervention. The expectation that language can be directly "taught" in the usual ways, and as urged by the plethora of handy little training manuals for parents and teachers of DS children, is likely therefore to be unmet.

An inventory of cognitive and associated features of the DS child is presented in tables 3.1 and 3.2. The few apparent contradictions in terminology between tables and text are mostly a matter of semantics, a product of how the independent variable has been specified across related experimental studies.

IMPLICATIONS FOR EARLY COGNITIVE INTERVENTION TAILORED TO THE "GIVENS" OF THE SYNDROME

The Infant and Preschooler

Consumers of standard infant schedules are often pleasantly surprised at test results of DS neonates that fall close to or within the normal range of development. The practiced clinical eye is not deceived. As far back as 1946 Benda had cataloged the many and unique pathologies of the DS infant, ranging from the skeletal-motor to the endocrinal and behavioral. Engler (1949) closely followed with his detailed description of the many anomalies that seemed peculiar to the syndrome. A good deal more is now known, sufficient to provide the biopathological evidence needed to derive special programs of behavioral intervention for the syndrome.

Table 3.1

Cognitive and Associated Developmental Vulnerabilities Claimed to be Characteristic of the Down Syndrome Child[1]

Behavioral pattern in infancy
- weak and/or delayed tonic neck, post-ural and other reflexes
- depressed gross motor function
- less reactive eye movement and limited scan radius
- reduced brightness and olfactory discrimination
- comparatively limited initial tactile, stereognostic and kinesthetic recognition ability

Memory functioning in early childhood
- relatively limited verbal memory: attributed to (1) diminished auditory sequencing facility, and (2) defective rehearsal mechanisms
- poor recall for spatial events
- poor memory for colors

Properties of attention and distraction
- impulsive responding
- characteristically slow reaction times
- low arousal/activation thresholds
- motivation difficult to sustain and easily distracted
- directionality confusion and relatively delayed lateralization
- error perseveration in problem-solving

Properties of cross-modal functioning
- relatively reduced auditory-motor and auditory-verbal performance
- especially limited coding of auditory material
- inferior management of spatial material except directly in the visual modality

Vulnerability of cognitive growth
- restricted mental sequencing facility, more or less through all sensory channels
- reduced facility for encoding simultaneous information
- slow information processing speed
- an especially restricted time perspective in planning/problem
- delayed development of the perception of patterns or 'wholes' from parts
- deficient judgement, comprehension and reasoning facility in relation to mental age
- limited facility for symbol material management and power of abstraction in relation to mental age; poor number skills, especially multiplication, in relation to mental age

Cognitive limitations implicating speech development
- deficient coding for word order
- more marked delay in connecting words with their use and meaning; versus simple word naming
- centrally mediated language comprehension deficiency
- unique structural handicaps associated with speech development

---

1.These developmental anomalies are more often seen among DS children than among most other etiological categories of mental retardation of comparable general mental age levels. Particular developmental delays and disorders, fully understood, provide an opportunity for more highly focused and effective remediation.

Table 3.2
Cognitive and Associated Developmental "Assets" Claimed for the Down Syndrome Child and Youth[1]

Relatively unimpaired for:

Sensorimotor function

- close to normal eye-hand skill and finer coordination
- superior motor imitation and social modelling propensities
- superior gestural communication
- relatively superior motor encoding
- relatively effective with spatial-motor tasks

Memory functioning

- stronger than expected rote naming facility and general rote memory
- relatively good memory for form
- 'special' facility for echoic memory in a visual stimulation context
- adept at the relocation of spatial material
- can comparatively easily replicate rhythm or pattern of beat

Cognitive function in the visual mode

- attracted to the symmetry of shapes and objects
- exploration most effective in the visual mode
- superior visual identification (coding) vis a vis the auditory channel
- relatively strong figural content learning (non-symbolic)
- superior performance through the visual-motor and visual-verbal circuits
- comparatively stronger coding of successive versus simultaneous information

---

1.The foregoing developmental/behavioral characteristics tend to be more prominent among Down Syndrome children than among most other categories of mental retardation. These relative strengths should generate leverage for learning when incorporated into special remediation programs.

Among the first to recognize the palliative opportunities associated with the maturational shortfall of the DS infant were de Coriat, Theslenco, and Waksman (1967) of the Argentine. These pioneers understood that the developmentally inappropriate advance and recession of various reflexes for the DS infant and child could distort the nurtural environment. The weak oral reflexes that control *search, suck, and swallow* activity are delayed. Poor muscle tone is an additional contributing factor. Taken together, the result can be reduced mother-infant bonding, too early weaning, and compensatory mouth sounds and facial grimacing that further distance mother from child and the DS child from the community. Communication competency, too, is off to a bad start. The postural reflexes, especially the tonic neck reflex, is feeble in most DS infants. A weak tonic neck reflex can inhibit breathing and normal exploratory drive and thus result in increase in hand use. The latter is complicated by a deficient grasp reflex. The developmental problem is compounded further by a delayed parachute reflex that retards straightening of the back to support sitting or hitching activity. With straightening and walking now delayed, the DS infant risks the further loss of care-agent stimulation, the opportunity to maneuver more effectively in a widening environment, and the impetus needed for communication growth.

De Coriat and his associates stimulated the oral search reflex prior to nursing and used a soother to elicit the sucking reflex and strengthen the lips' orbicular muscles, initially to prevent tongue protrusion and tongue sucking. The tonic neck reflex was stimulated by regular head and neck exercises. A program of head and neck control exercises in neonates is offered by Satterfield and Yasumura (1987). In this program, grasping is encouraged by the use of high-sensory-impact play materials, the limbs are stimulated preparatory to walking, and eye-following drills are practiced. Developmental gains were abundant, but subject loss was high during the demonstration treatment period. The durability and leverage value of these gains is therefore uncertain. What the demonstration program teaches is the promise of a multidisciplinary, biobehavioral approach to Infant-Stim, whatever the disorder.

It has been long known that advancing finer motor or eye-hand capability enhances growth in early self-help skills for DS children (Kralovich, 1959; Fisher, Share, & Koch, 1964). Unfortunately, the developmental advantage can be short-lived (Dicks-Mireaux, 1966) unless the DS child is in an ongoing intervention program that includes the precognitive components of training (Piaget, 1954). Similarly, Dunst and Rheingrover (1983) have confirmed that relatively advanced sensorimotor (more varied and differentiated) behavior is tied to a facility for gestural and vocal imitation with DS subjects. It is suggested that a social/imitation model of instruction could advance impulse self-control. Also offered is the suggestion that the wider-than-expected range of sensorimotor expression, even though transitory, could be harnessed at critical times for the promotion of cognitive growth from Stage 5 to Stage 6. The effectiveness of motor-based imitation training for the expansion of essentially cognitive exploratory activity for DS children has been illustrated by Shimada (1988).

Esenther (1984) builds on Pueschels's (1984) statistical evidence that muscle tone predicts mental, motor, language, and social development in DS children, as well as even the ability of parents to cope. Esenther proposes intensive exercises in reaching and banging to hasten motor manipulation and to extend attention span and the range of exploration. The latter activity is an elemental form of information gathering and is, therefore, precognitive in nature. Haley (1987) finds that hypotonia-related postural difficulty in DS individuals is especially pronounced, in particular, the ability to maintain body equilibrium. The sequencing of postural development is evidently different for DS infants. Appropriate exercises in equilibrium and balance are urged from a very early age. Harris (1981) says of DS infants:

Specific neurodevelopmental techniques used to increase postural tone included joint approximation through the spine and extremities, bouncing, tapping and resistance to movement (Semans, 1967). Righting, equilibrium and protective responses were facilitated in prone and supine for the younger infants, and in quadrupeds, sitting and standing for the older ones. Developmentally appropriate movement patterns were shaped and facilitated after the activities to increase postural tone. They included pivoting in prone, rolling prone to supine and supine to prone progression on abdomen, reciprocal creeping, and moving into and out of the sitting position during trunk rotation. (p. 479-480)

Past infancy and into the preschool period, the DS child advances with help through the sensorimotor stages of growth to face the difficulties of direct conceptual training. Morss (1985), for example, presents a hidden-object task and reports comparatively poor performance for DS children. Training to task was helpful, but the DS child appeared unable to consolidate these gains, a problem, collectively, of attention disorder, imitation learning without comprehension, poor short-term memory, and a defect of arousal-state maintenance. Training to the performance norm required suitably small task steps within highly structured practice sessions. These observations are supported by Wishart (1986, 1987), who agreed that each repeat trial was, in a sense, a relearning experience and that DS children do not respond well to generic teaching techniques and teaching environments, at least for purposes of early cognitive intervention. While Morss has effectively discounted "over-learning" as a training technique suited to the DS child, the possibility needs more study.

Not unlike Wishart's results, Mervis and Cardoso-Martins (1984) claimed success in training for Piagetian Stage 6 sensorimotor skills but found a failure in DS children to subsequently and spontaneously use these skills. Pasnak and Pasnak (1987) provided eight months of training to six DS children but achieved only Piagetian Stage 5 precognitive functioning. What is possibly happening is the emergence of the first signs of the cognitive developmental wall (Gibson, 1966), where conceptualization, memory facility, and drive-maintenance decelerate, thereby failing to meet the hopes of parents and teachers produced by much stronger-earlier sensorimotor development of the typical DS child. Among promising new approaches to breaching the developmental wall into effective conceptual learning (Hartley, 1986; Hill & McCune-Nicolich, 1981; Retveld, 1983) is to train preschoolers to scan alternatives to task completion by improving combinational free (play) activity. Such activity is a precursor to acquiring grouping, relating, and comparing skills—the vital ingredients of effective information processing and problem solving in both the academic and practical worlds.

Another avenue to the maintenance of precognitive and cognitive system gains is through understanding the possibly different nature of attention and reaction time (RT) in DS children. Reaction time has been widely reported as slower for DS subjects than for control subjects, except in response to visual signals (Gibson, 1978). The deficiency is attributed to a reduced cerebellum, poor muscle tension, sensory system immaturity, and delayed development of motor set. The consequences for psychological growth must surely involve impoverished cognitive development. Attention disorder can, in turn, be a product of eye muscle hypotonia, faulty auditory channeling, defects in the inhibitory mechanisms, and limitations in comprehension (Gibson, 1978). Central to both areas of handicap are cardiovascular system (CVS) anomalies that are associated with autonomic nervous system (ANS) function, weaker drive levels, and an unreliable attention span. These, too, have implications for cognitive development. Not to be overlooked is that CVS limitations are responsive to medical intervention (Zausmer, Pueschel, & Shea, 1972).

Fehr (1976) has suggested that if the spontaneous fluctuations of the ANS can be manipulated, discrimination response capacity for DS individuals, on average, is likely to improve. Untreated, the ANS lability characteristic of the DS child leads to increasingly limited participation in sustained activity and, at other times, to bouts of unproductive impulsivity. Ordinarily, the resulting attention disorder would be managed by building distraction controllers into the intervention program. Marcell, Harvey, and Cothran (1988), using sixteen DS subjects and MR control subjects, reduced visual and auditory distractions but failed to improve short-term auditory memory for the DS group. Other prospects for remedial intervention are (a) to increase the intensity and duration of stimulus conditions to elicit richer responses, (b) to program appropriate lateralization training at appropriate ages, (c) to "drive" attention by hinging precognitive learning exercises to motor activity, especially motor activity having an impulsivity element, and (d) to identify and manage the characteristic resistance of DS children to respond in formal learning sets. On the last point, the tendency of DS children of all ages to be heavily dependent on caregivers, and be especially sensitive to affectional cues, furnishes a useful device for attention training, with the prospect of enhancing the transition from precognitive to durable cognitive status. What appears to matter is that the cognitive intervention curricula for the young DS child be designed to express more precisely what we know about the biobehavorial nature of the syndrome.

The Older Down Syndrome Child

The objectives of precognitive training for the DS child are to build the infrastructure for the development of effective information-processing skills. The failure of existing EI programs to yield durable cognitive gains (Spitz, 1986) is especially evident in the characteristic deceleration of DS children's intellectual development by early adolescence. This is not surprising, given the distinctive maturational timetable of the syndrome and the failure of popular EI programs to exploit these distinctions. For older DS children, there is a growing expectation that syndrome-appropriate cognitive strategies can also be invented to cement early developmental gains and to inhibit later intellectual deceleration among DS adolescents and adults. The following experimental research holds out that hope.

Varnhagen, Das, and Varnhagen (1987) have contended that verbal growth lag is a product of limited memory for sequential order, which leads the DS child to impoverished language comprehension and production—essentially a limitation of cognitive growth. On the other hand, Ellis, Woodley-Zanthos, and Dulaney (1989) report that DS subjects remember spatial locations as well as normal subjects do, despite IQ differences. Thus, DS youth can be trained to get to work and school unaided, and to remember the location of tools and belongings. Notwithstanding, short-term memory span can be progressively impaired as a consequence of limited speech use, especially speech output at speeds that would facilitate "rehearsal" for storage (MacKenzie & Hulme, 1987). Short-term memory functions "as a working memory system responsible for the storage and manipulation of material during the performance of other cognitive tasks such as reasoning, reading or mental arithmetic" (MacKenzie & Hulme, 1987, p. 318). If the objective is to advance the DS child in short-term-memory status and in verbal skills, these being reciprocal growth processes, then special instructional methods are needed that tie memory training to speech acquisition. One approach is to exploit a more intact spatial memory apparatus and on a life-span basis (Rondal, 1988).

Other facets of developmental shortfall, more noticeable as DS children age, include the proposed hemispherical differences in the way they process linguistic stimuli. While simple delay in rate of lateralization appears to be culpable, possibly switched hemispherical specialization for speech remains a promising area for future EI program research (Zekulin-Hartley, 1981). The expectation is that most DS individuals will display specific deficits on tasks requiring *both* the perception and production of speech. Pending further investigation, the present evidence supports strengthening unilateral and later bilateral motor function, and initiating earlier treatment for hypotonia and the control of attention. Subsequent training in speech would exploit the visual-spatial modality and correct the all too common structural defects associated with speech for the syndrome.

Included among the special learning difficulties faced by the older DS child is a limited facility for the transfer of learning, a low-level capacity for the generalization of what is learned, and deficient incidental learning (Stratford, 1985). Accordingly, when teaching, it is advisable to limit stimulus complexity to prevent confusion resulting from stimulus overload. Only later in the intervention process is the simultaneous manipulation of two or more stimulus dimensions likely to be profitable. Evidence of the characteristic stages of readiness for cognitive enhancement is essential to successful programming, as is the need to cope remedially with the particular difficulty that DS children experience in inhibiting auditory distraction. At the end of the cognitive enhancement trail is likely to be a firmer foundation for language acquisition and practical problem-solving facility.

Finally, Anwar's work (1981) with the more primitive modalities indicates that strengthening motor competence for even older DS children begins with proprioceptive and kinesthetic systems training. One result of this type of early intervention is to increase the chances of effective visual-motor system integration. Cognitive status should improve accordingly. For instance, enhanced proprioceptive feedback can be achieved by excluding visual feedback from the learning experience (e.g., tracing an imbedded figure under hand covers). Strengthening the primitive feedback systems provides an impetus to advancing the precognitive motor schema, the effects of which will transfer to the visual ocular-motor system. Vestibular stimulation is known to escalate ocular-motor pursuit movements in the newborn, and proprioceptive feedback in the absence of vision is readily managed by DS children. Thus, writing and copying skills might improve where visual feedback to the hand is prevented. Visual scanning exercises could start with the tracing of imbedded shapes to build on the apparently effective coding facility of DS children for proprioceptive and kinesthetic information processing. Higher-level sensory modality development should benefit from such intervention. Anwar's proprioceptive training approach to advancing visual learning for DS persons is both novel and reflective of the neurophysiology of the syndrome. Moreover, since the visual-motor circuit is relatively more intact than the auditory-motor or verbal circuits, reinforcement of the former through practice should be a program priority (Frith & Frith, 1974).

CONCLUSION

Among the reasons for the unsatisfactory benefits record of EI programs designed to enhance the intellectual development of the DS child and adult are (a) the failure of past demonstration projects to build on the specific reflexive, neuromotor, sensory and precognitive growth profiles of the syndrome, and (b) the unrealistic expectation that durable cognitive advances can be earned in short-lived generic stimulation programs applied willy-nilly during early childhood. Yet Casey, Jones, Kugles, and Walkins found (1988) that DS children in mainstreamed primary school achieved higher numeracy, language comprehension, and MA levels than did "congruent" DS students in special schools. One explanation is that an open or general academic program will likely accommodate more varied learning styles and needs and thus do less harm to the DS student than a highly structured special MR training program will that is not built on ability/disability configurations particular to individuals with the syndrome. Contemporary research findings now suggest that cognitive intervention should be special, intensive, of life-span duration (Berry, Groeneweg, Gibson, & Brown, 1984), and fully integrated with the structural and arousal properties of the disorder.

The immediate practical implications are that the cognitive and allied abilities profiles of DS children and adults are sufficiently unique developmentally to justify construction of (a) a cognitive/arousal resources diagnostic schedule for the syndrome, and, based on this instrument, (b) a life-span intervention program engineered to work with the cognitive idiosyncrasies of the disorder, while respecting within-syndrome variability. Otherwise, U.S. Public Law 99–457, which authorizes EI programs to be implemented by the 1990-91 school year, will continue to fail the intellectual promise of the Down syndrome child and citizen.

REFERENCES

Anwar, F. (1981). Motor function in Down syndrome. In N. R. Ellis (Ed.), *International review of research in mental retardation*, Volume 10 (pp. 107-138). New York: Academic Press.

Anwar, F. (1983). The role of sensory modality for the reproduction of shape by the severely retarded. *British Journal of Developmental Psychology*, 1(4), 317-327.

Anwar, R., & Hermelin, B. (1979). Kinesthetic movement after-effects in children with Down syndrome. *Journal of Mental Deficiency Research*, 23, 287-297.

Benda, C. E. (1946). *Mongolism and cretinism*. New York: Grune & Stratton.

Berkson, G. (1960). An analysis of reaction time in normal and mentally deficient young mongoloids III: Variation of stimulus and response complexity. *Journal of Mental Deficiency Research, 4,* 69-77.

Berman, A. (1971). The problem of assessing cerebral dominance and its relation to intelligence. *Cortex, 7,* 372-386.

Berry, P,. Groeneweg, G., Gibson, D., & Brown, R. I. (1984). Mental development in Down syndrome adults. *American Journal of Mental Deficiency, 89,* 252-256.

Bilovsky, D., & Share, J. (1965). The ITPA and Down syndrome: An exploratory study. *American Journal of Mental Deficiency, 70,* 78-82.

Brinkman, S. D., & Braun, P. (1984). Classification of dementia patients by the WAIS profile related to central cholinergic deficiencies. *Journal of Clinical Neuropsychology, 6,* 393-400.

Bronfenbrenner, U. (1979). *The ecology of human development.* Cambridge, MA: Harvard University Press.

Brousseau, K., & Brainerd, M. G. (1928). *Mongolism: A study of the physical and mental characteristics of mongoloid imbeciles.* Baltimore: Williams & Wilkins.

Buckley, S., & Sacks, B. (1987). *The adolescent with Down syndrome: Life for the teenager and for the family.* Portsmouth: Down syndrome Trust.

Burack, J. A., Hodapp, R. M., & Zigler, E. (1988). Issues in the classification of mental retardation: Differentiating among organic etiologies. *Journal of Child Psychology and Psychiatry and Allied Disciplines, 29,* 765-779.

Butterworth, G., & Cicchetti, D. (1978). Visual calibration of posture in normal and motor retarded Down syndrome infants. *Perception, 7,* 513-525.

Carr, J. (1970). Mental and motor development in young mongol children. *Journal of Mental Deficiency Research, 14,* 205-220.

Casey, W., Jones, D., Kugles, B. & Walkins, B., (1988). Integration of Down syndrome children in primary school: A longitudinal study of cognitive development and academic attainments. *British Journal of Educational Psychology, 58,* 279-286.

Cornwell, A. C. (1974). Development of language abstraction and numerical concept formation in Down syndrome children. *American Journal of Mental Deficiency, 79,* 179-190.

Cratty, B. J. (1969). *Motor activity and the education of retardates.* Philadelphia: Lea & Febigerr.

Cunningham, C. C. (1974). *Visual discrimination in the mentally handicapped.* Manchester, NH: Hester Adrian Research Centre, University of Manchester.

Cunningham, C. C. (1983). *Early development and its facilitation in infants with Down syndrome.* Final Report, Part 1 to DHSS. London: HMSO.

Cunningham, C. C. (1986, May). *Early intervention in Down syndrome.* Paper presented at the Royal Society of Medicine Conference on Prevention of Mental Handicap: A World View, London, England.

Cunningham, C. C., & McArthur, K. (1981). Hearing loss and treatment in young Down syndrome children. *Child: Care, Health, and Development, 7,* 357-374.

Das, J. P., Kirby, J., & Jarman, R. F. (1979). *Simultaneous and successive cognitive processes.* New York: Academic Press.

de Coriat, L. F., Theslenco, L., & Waksman, J. (1967). The effects of psychomotor stimulation on the IQ of young children with trisomy–21. *Proceedings of the First Congress of the International Association for the Scientific Study of Mental Deficiency* (pp. 377-385). Surrey, England: Michael Jackson Publishing Co.

Dicks-Mireaux, M. J. (1966). Development of intelligence of children with Down syndrome. Preliminary report. *Journal of Mental Deficiency Research, 10,* 89-93.

Dunst, C. J. (1985). Rethinking early intervention. *Analysis and Intervention in Developmental Disabilities, 5,* 165-201.

Dunst, C. J., & Rheingrover, R. M. (1983). Structural characteristics of sensorimotor development in individuals with Down syndrome. *Journal of Mental Deficiency Research, 27,* 11-22.

Elliot, D., Weeks, D. J., & Elliot, C. L. (1987). Cerebral specialization in individuals with Down syndrome. *American Journal of Mental Deficiency, 92,* 263-271.

Ellis, N. R. (1963). The stimulus trace and behavioral inadequacy. In N. R. Ellis (Ed.), *Handbook of mental deficiency: Psychological theory and research* (pp. 134-158). New York: McGraw-Hill.

Ellis, N. R., Woodley-Zanthos, P., & Dulaney, C. R. (1989). Memory for spatial location in children, adults and mentally retarded persons. *American Journal on Mental Retardation, 93,* 521-527.

Emery, O. B. (1984, August). *Cognitive functioning and Alzheimer's Disease.* Paper presented at the Annual Meeting of the American Psychological Association, Toronto, Canada.

Engler, M. (1949). *Mongolism.* Bristol, England: John Wright & Sons.

Esenther, S. E. (1984). Developmental coaching of the Down syndrome infant. *American Journal of Occupational Therapy, 38,* 440-445.

Fehr, F. S. (1976). Psychophysiological studies of Down syndrome children and the effects of environmental enrichment. In R. Karrer (Ed.), *Developmental psychophysiology of mental retardation* (pp. 219-246). Springfield, IL: C. C. Thomas.

Fisher, K., Share, J., & Koch, R. (1964). Adaptation of Gesell developmental scales for evaluation of development in children with Down syndrome. *Journal of Mental Deficiency, 68,* 642-646.

Frith, U., & Frith, C. D. (1974). Specific motor disabilities in Down syndrome. *Journal of Child Psychology and Psychiatry and Allied Disciplines, 15,* 292-301.

Fuld, P. A. (1984). Test profiles of cholinergic dysfunction of Alzheimer's-type dementia. *Journal of Clinical Neuropsychology, 6,* 380-392.

Gibson, D. (1966). Early developmental staging as a prophecy index in Down syndrome. *American Journal of Mental Deficiency, 70,* 825-828.

Gibson, D. (1978). *Down syndrome.* London: Cambridge University Press.

Gibson, D. (1989). The potential of syndrome-specific research for more effective assessment and psycho-educational intervention. Comments of Gunn and Berry. *European Journal of Psychology of Education, 4,* 247-249.

Gibson, D., & Fields, D.L. (1984). Early infant stimulation programs for children with Down syndrome: A review of effectiveness. In M. L. Wolraich & D. K. Routh (Eds.), *Advances in developmental and behavioral pediatrics*, Volume. 5 (pp. 331-371). Greenwich, Conn: JAI Press.

Gibson, D., Groeneweg, G., Berry, P., & Harris, A. (1988). Age and pattern of intellectual decline among Down syndrome and other mentally retarded adults. *International Journal of Rehabilitation Research, 11*, 45-47.

Gibson, D., & Harris, A. (1988). Aggregated early intervention effects for Down syndrome persons: Patterning and longevity of benefits. *Journal of Mental Deficiency Research, 32*, 1-17.

Glasser, A. J., & Zimmerman, I. L. (1967). *Clinical interpretation of the Wechsler Intelligence Scale for Children*. New York: Grune & Stratton.

Griffiths, R. (1970). *The abilities of young children*. Somerset, England: Young & Son.

Guilford, J. P., & Merrifield, P. R. (1960). *The structure-of-intellect model: Its uses and implications*. Report from the Psychological Laboratory (No. 24), University of Southern California.

Gunn, P., & Berry, P. (1989). Education of infants with Down syndrome. *European Journal of Psychology of Education, 4*, 235-246.

Haley, S. M. (1987). Sequence of development of postural reactions by infants with Down syndrome. *Developmental Medicine and Child Neurology, 29*, 674-679.

Harris, S. R. (1981). Effects of neurodevelopmental therapy on motor performance of infants with Down syndrome. *Developmental Medicine and Child Neurology, 23*, 477-483.

Hartley, X. Y. (1982). Receptive language processing of Down syndrome children. *Journal of Mental Deficiency Research, 26*, 263-269.

Hartley, X. Y. (1986). A summary of recent research into the development of children with Down syndrome. *Journal of Mental Deficiency Research, 30*, 1-14.

Hewitt, K. E. & Jancar, J. (1986). Psychological and clinical aspects of aging in Down syndrome. In J. M. Berg (Ed.), *Science and service in mental retardation* (370-379). London: Methuen.

Hill, P. M., & McCune-Nicholch, L. (1981). Pretend play and patterns of cognition in Down syndrome children. *Child Development, 52*, 611-617.

Jensen, A. R. (1969). How much can we boost IQ and scholastic achievement? *Harvard Educational Review, 39*, 1-123.

Kaufman, A. S. (1979). *Intelligence testing with the WISC-R*. New York: Wiley.

Kerr, R., & Blais, C. (1985). Motor skill acquisition by individuals with Down syndrome. *American Journal of Mental Deficiency, 90*, 313-318.

Kerr, R., & Blais, C. (1987). Down syndrome and extended practice of a complex motor task. *American Journal of Mental Deficiency, 91*, 591-597.

Kolata, G. (1985). Down syndrome-Alzheimer's linked. *Science, 230*, 1152-1153.

Kostrzewski, J. (1965). The dynamics of intellectual and social development in Down syndrome: Results of experimental investigation. *Rocznike: Filozo Ficzne, 13*(4), 5-32.

Kralovich, A. M. (1959). A study of performance differences on the Cattell infant intelligence scale between matched groups of organic and mongoloid subjects. *Journal of Clinical Psychology, 15,* 198-199.

Landesman, S. (1986). Quality of life and personal life satisfactions: Definition and measurement issues. *Mental Retardation, 24,* 141-143.

Lincoln, A. J., Courchesne, E., Kelman, B. A., & Galambos, R. (1985). Neuropsychological correlatest of information-processing by children with Down syndrome. *American Journal of Mental Deficiency, 89,* 403-414.

Lott, I. T. (1982). Down syndrome, aging and Alzheimer's disease: A clinical review. *Annals of the New York Academy of Sciences, 396,* 15-27.

Loveland, K. A. (1987). Behavior of young children with Down syndrome before the mirror: Exploration. *Child Development, 58,* 768-778.

Lyle, J. G. (1959). The effect of an institution environment upon the verbal development of imbecile children: I. Verbal intelligence. *Journal of Mental Deficiency Research, 3,* 122-128.

MacKenzie, S., & Hulme, C. (1987). Memory span development in Down syndrome, severely subnormal and normal subjects. *Cognitive Neuropsychology, 4,* 303-319.

Marcell, M. M., & Armstrong, V. (1982). Auditory and visual sequential memory of Down syndrome and non-retarded children. *American Journal of Mental Deficiency, 87,* 86-95.

Marcell, M. M., Harvey, C. F., & Cothran, L. P. (1988). An attempt to improve auditory short-term memory in Down syndrome individuals through reducing distractions. *Research in Developmental Disabilities, 9,* 405-417.

Marcell, M. M., & Weeks, S. L. (1988). Short-term memory difficulties and Down syndrome. *Journal of Mental Deficiency Research, 32,* 153-162.

Marfo, K., & Kysela, G. M. (1985). Early intervention with mentally handicapped children: A critical appraisal of applied research. *Journal of Pediatric Psychology, 10,* 305-324.

McDade, H. L., & Adler, S. (1980). Down syndrome and short-term memory impairment: A storage or retrieval deficit? *American Journal of Mental Deficiency, 84,* 561-567.

McNeill, W. D. (1955). Developmental patterns of mongoloid children: A study of certain aspects of their growth and development. *Dissertation Abstracts, 15,* 86-87.

Mervis, C. B. & Cardoso-Martins, C. (1984). Transition from sensorimotor Stage 5 to Stage 6 by Down syndrome children: A response to Gibson. *American Journal of Mental Deficiency, 89,* 99-102.

Miniszek, N. A. (1983). Development of Alzheimer's disease in Down syndrome individuals. *American Journal of Mental Deficiency, 87,* 377-385.

Morss, J. R. (1985). Early cognitive development: Difference or delay? In D. Lane & B. Strattford (Eds.), *Current approaches to Down syndrome* (pp. 242-259). London: Cassell; New York: Praeger.

Nakamura, H. (1965). An enquiry into systematic differences in the abilities of institutionalized adult mongoloids. *American Journal of Mental Deficiency, 69,* 661-665.

Neeman, R. L. (1971). Perceptual-motor attributes of mental retardates: A factor analytic study. *Perceptual and Motor Skills, 33,* 927-934.

O'Connor, N., & Hermelin, B. (1961). Visual and stereognostic shape recognition in normal children and mongol and non-mongol imbeciles. *Journal of Mental Deficiency Research, 5*, 63-66.

Oster, J. (1953). *Mongolism.* Copenhagen: Danish Science Press.

Ottenbacher, K. J. (1989). Statistical conclusion validity of early intervention research with handicapped children. *Exceptional Children, 55*, 534-540.

Pasnak, C. F., & Pasnak, R. (1987). Accelerated development of object permanence in Down syndrome infants. *Child: Care, Health, and Development, 13*, 247-255.

Piaget, J. (1954). *The construction of reality in the child.* New York: Basic Books.

Pipe, M. E. (1983). Dichotic-listening performance following auditory discrimination training in Down syndrome and developmentally retarded children. *Cortex, 19*, 481-491.

Pipe, M. E. (1988). Atypical laterality and retardation. *Psychological Bulletin, 104*, 343-347.

Piper, M. C., Gosselin, C., Gendron, M., & Mazer, B. (1986). Developmental profile of Down syndrome infants receiving early intervention. *Child: Care, Health, and Development, 12*, 183-194.

Pototzky, C., & Grigg, A. E. (1942). A reversion of the prognosis in mongolism. *American Journal of Orthopsychiatry, 12*, 503.

Pueschel, S. M. (Ed.). (1984). *The young child with Down Syndrome.* New York: Human Sciences Press.

Pueschel, S. M., Gallagher, P. L., Carter, A. S., & Pezzullo, J. C. (1987). Cognitive and learning processes in children with Down syndrome. *Research in Developmental Disabilities, 8*, 21-37.

Reinhart, C. (1974). *The cerebral lateralization of speech processes in Down syndrome and normal individuals.* Unpublished masters' thesis, University of Saskatchewan, Canada.

Retveld, C. M. (1983). The training of choice behaviours in Down syndrome and nonretarded pre-school children. *Australia and New Zealand Journal of Developmental Disabilities, 9*, 75-83.

Richard, N. B. (1986). Interaction between mothers and infants with Down syndrome: Infant characteristics. *Topics in Early Childhood Special Education. 6*, 54-71.

Rohr, A., & Burr, D. B. (1978). Etiological differences in pattern of psycholinguistic development of children of IQ 30–60. *American Journal of Mental Deficiency, 82*, 549-553.

Rollin, H. R. (1946). Personality in mongolism with special reference to the incidence of catatonic psychosis. *American Journal of Mental Deficiency, 76*, 291-294.

Rondal, J. A. (1988). Language development in Down syndrome: A life-span perspective. *International Journal of Behavioral Development, 11*, 21-36.

Rosencrans, C. J. (1971). A longitudinal study of exceptional cognitive development in a partial translocation Down syndrome child. *American Journal of Mental Deficiency, 76*, 291-294.

Satterfield, M. J., & Yasumura, K. (1987). Facilitating the high risk neonate's head control: Effects of teaching method on mother's performance. *International Journal of Rehabilitation Research, 10*, 55-62.

Seyfort, B., & Spreen, O. (1979). Two-plated tapping performance by Down syndrome and non-Down syndrome retardates. *Journal of Child Psychology, 20*, 351-355.

Shapiro, M. B., Haxby, J. V., Grady, C. L., & Duara, R. (1987). Decline in cerebral glucose utilization and cognitive function with aging in Down syndrome. *Journal of Neurology, Neurosurgery and Psychiatry, 50*, 766-774.

Share, J. B. (1975). Developmental progress in Down syndrome. In R. Koch & F. F. de la Cruz (Eds.), *Down syndrome (mongolism): Research, prevention and management* (pp. 78-86). New York: Brunner/Mazel.

Shimada, S. (1988). Comparison of structured modeling and mother-child play settings on the development of pretend actions in young children with Down syndrome. *RIEEC Report* No. 37, 65-71.

Silverstein, A. B., Legutki, G., Friedman, S. L., & Takayama, D. L. (1982). Performance of Down syndrome individuals on the Stanford-Binet Intelligence Scale. *American Journal of Mental Deficiency, 86*, 548-551.

Simeonsson, R. J., Huntington, G. S., & Short, R. J. (1982). Individual differences and goals: An approach to the evaluation of child progress. *Topics in Early Childhood Special Education, 1*, 71-80.

Sinson, J., & Wetherick, N. E. (1973). Short-term retention of color and shape information in mongol and other severely subnormal children. *Journal of Mental Deficiency Research, 17*, 177-182.

Sloper, P., Glenn, S. M., & Cunningham, C. C. (1986). The effect of intensity of training on sensorimotor development in infants with Down syndrome. *Journal of Mental Deficiency Research, 30*, 752-760.

Snart, F., O'Grady, M., & Das, J. P. (1982). Cognitive processing by subgroups of moderately mentally retarded children. *American Journal of Mental Deficiency, 86*, 465-472.

Spitz, H. H. (1986). *The raising of intelligence*. Hillside, NJ: Erlbaum.

Stedman, D. J., & Eichorn, D. H. (1964). A comparison of the growth and development of institutionalized and home-reared mongoloids during infancy and early childhood. *American Journal of Mental Deficiency, 69*, 391-401.

Stickland, C. A. (1954). Two mongoloids of unusually high mental status. *British Journal of Medical Psychology, 27*, 80-83.

Stratford, B. (1985). Learning and knowing: The education of Down syndrome children. In D. Lane & B. Stratford (Eds.), *Current approaches to Down syndrome* (pp. 149-166). London: Cassell; New York: Praeger.

Stratford, B., & Ching, Y.Y.E. (1983). Rhythm and time in the perception of Down syndrome children. *Journal of Mental Deficiency Research, 27*, 23.

Tennies, L. G. (1943). Some comments on the mongoloids. *American Journal of Mental Deficiency, 48*, 46-48.

Thase, M. E., Liss, L., Smeltzer, D., & Maloon, J. (1982). Clinical evaluation of dementia in Down syndrome: A preliminary report. *Journal of Mental Deficiency Research, 26*, 239.

Thase, M. E., Tigner, R., Smeltzer, D., & Liss, L. (1984). Age-related neuropsychological deficits in Down syndrome. *Biological Psychiatry, 19*, 571-585.

Varnhagen, C. K., Das, J. P., & Varnhagen, S. (1987). Auditory and visual memory span: Cognitive processing by TMR individuals with Down syndrome or other etiologies. *American Journal of Mental Deficiency, 91*, 398-405.

Wallin, J.E.W. (1944). Mongolism among school children. *American Journal of Orthopsychiatry, 14*, 104.

Wallin, J.E.W. (1949). *Children with mental and physical handicaps.* New York: Prentice Hall.

Weisenfeld, R. B. (1987). Functionality in the IEP's of children with Down syndrome. *Mental Retardation, 25*, 281-286.

White, K. R., & Casto, G. (1985). An integrative review of early intervention efficacy studies with at-risk children: Implications for the handicapped. *Analysis and Intervention in Developmental Disabilities, 5*, 177-201.

Wishart, J. G. (1986). The effects of step-by-step training on cognitive performance in infants with Down syndrome. *Journal of Mental Deficiency Research, 30*, 233-250.

Wishart, J. G. (1987). Performance of young nonretarded children and children with Down syndrome on Piagetian infant search tasks. *American Journal of Mental Deficiency, 92*, 169-177.

Wisniewski, K. E. (1985). Alzheimer's disease in Down syndrome: Clinicopathologic Studies. *Neurology, 35*, 957-961.

Wood, J. (1909). *Mongolian imbecility.* Melbourne: Australian Medical Congress.

Zausmer, E., Pueschel, S. M., & Shea, A. (1972). A sensori-motor stimulation program for the young child with Down syndrome. *MCH Exchange, 2*, 1.

Zekulin, X. Y., Gibson, D., Mosley, J. L., & Brown, R. I. (1974). Auditory-motor channeling in Down syndrome subjects. *American Journal of Mental Deficiency, 78*, 571-577.

Zekulin-Hartley, X. Y. (1981). Hemispherical asymmetry in Down syndrome children. *Canadian Journal of Behavioral Science, 13*, 210-217.

Zigler, E., & Berman, W. (1983). Discerning the future of early childhood intervention. *American Psychologist, 38*, 894-906.

4

Family-Focused Intervention: Clinical, Training, and Research Implications

Rune J. Simeonsson and Donald B. Bailey, Jr.

Early intervention programs for infants and preschoolers with handicaps are currently encouraged to be more family-focused in their approach to service delivery. What factors have contributed to this shift in orientation? As initial reviews of the early intervention efficacy literature raised concerns about the lack of strong evidence for intervention effectiveness (Dunst & Rheingrover, 1981; Simeonsson, Cooper, & Scheiner, 1982), professionals began to ask questions about the fundamental purposes of early intervention programs. Although early intervention services are established and offered because infants and preschoolers have, or are at risk for, handicapping conditions, increasingly it has become accepted that a fundamental purpose of early intervention is to support the families of children with at-risk or handicapping conditions. A second factor was increased recognition that infant development could best be understood and stimulated in the family context. Grounded in an ecological orientation to early intervention (Bronfenbrenner, 1979), professionals began to view the child as embedded within the family and to recognize that "any reasonable intervention with a handicapped child involves an entrance into a family system" (Trout & Foley, 1989, p. 61). A third factor was the recognition that the family was a legitimate and appropriate recipient of early intervention services in its own right. The birth of a chronically ill or handicapped child often creates unique needs for families, some of which can be supported in the context of early intervention. Included among these may be needs for information, training, support, child care, community service, case management, or financial assistance. A final factor built on the transactional model of child and family outcome (Sameroff, 1975) assumes that child and family interactions are reciprocal and continuously serve to influence each other over time. The focus of intervention, then, cannot be the child in isolation from the caregiving context.

The trend toward the increased family focus in early intervention is reflected in the provisions of Public Law 99–457 as well as throughout the professional literature. The law requires early intervention programs serving infants and toddlers with handicaps to write an Individualized Family Service Plan (IFSP), which is to include, if the family so desires, a documentation of family strengths and needs, a specification of major family outcomes, a description of the services to be provided to the family, and the name of a case manager who is to assist the family in implementing the plan and coordinating services. Zigler and Black (1989) characterize this trend as a family-support movement, the ultimate goal of which is "to enable families to be independent by developing their own informal support networks" (p. 11). Other labels have been used to describe this orientation in the context of early intervention, including parent empowerment (Dunst, 1985; Dunst, Trivette, & Deal, 1988), family-focused intervention (Bailey et al., 1986), and family-centered care (Shelton, Jeppson, & Johnson, 1987). Characteristics that can be seen as common to all have been summarized as follows by Brewer, McPherson, Magrab, and Hutchins (1989):

Family-centered care is the focus of a philosophy of care in which the pivotal role of the family is recognized and respected in the lives of children with special health needs. Within this philosophy is the idea that families should be supported in their natural care-giving and decision-making roles by building on their unique strengths as people and families. In this philosophy, patterns of living in the home and in the community are promoted; parents and professionals are seen as equals in a partnership committed to the development of optimal quality in the delivery of all levels of health care. To achieve this, elements of family-centered care and community-based care must be carefully interwoven into a full and effective coordination of the care of all children with special health needs. (p. 1055)

Although the philosophical roots of the family-focused approach to early intervention are now becoming well established, data regarding its implementation are scant. The purpose of this chapter is to describe the development and implementation of a specific model of family-focused intervention (Bailey et al., 1986). Findings from the development and research activities of that effort provide a broad basis for the identification of implications for clinical practice, personnel preparation, and research.

CONTEXT AND PURPOSE OF THE FAMILIES PROJECT

In the early 1980s, the importance of a family focus in early intervention was increasingly recognized. Implementing that focus, however, was difficult for many programs because of a limited understanding of the role of families in early intervention and a lack of functional measures and models to guide family-focused practices. At that time, the family was still viewed as an extension of the professional, and a primary goal of early intervention was to train parents to effectively teach and provide therapy for their children. Although parent support groups and parent meetings were made available, it was clear that early intervention assumed a limited role for family involvement.

The FAMILIES project, a component of the Carolina Institute for Research on Early Education of the Handicapped at the University of North Carolina, was initiated in 1982 in order to study families of young children with handicaps participating in early intervention programs, and to explore models and procedures that might assist early intervention programs in building a family-focused approach to services. The project had the following primary objectives:

1. Determine the current status of research on home-based intervention with handicapped infants and their families.
2. Identify or develop measures to document child and family variables in early intervention.
3. Establish an initial battery of measures for infants with handicaps and their families served by home-based intervention teams.
4. Obtain repeated measures of children and families in early intervention.
5. Analyze factors contributing to child and family change in early intervention.
6. Evaluate findings to identify both conceptual and practical implications for an intervention base.
7. Develop a comprehensive model for family-focused intervention.
8. Implement an intervention phase of family-focused intervention.
9. Evaluate the effects of family-focused intervention.

The scope of the research in the FAMILIES project was conceptualized in two major phases. The first phase was designed to develop a literature and research base on dimensions of child and family functioning in early intervention that could be readily assessed in the context of a state-wide home-based intervention network. The second phase built on the findings of the first phase and resulted in the development and application of a family-focused model of early intervention.

Phase I: Literature Review and Assessment Study

Phase I of the FAMILIES project involved two primary activities. First, a series of reviews of research and practice with families in early intervention was completed. Second, a longitudinal descriptive study of families was conducted.

Literature reviews. In order to understand the complex issues surrounding a family focus in early intervention, a review of pertinent research and practice was undertaken. Early intervention studies that focused on families as targets of intervention or reported changes in families on at least one outcome measure (Bailey & Simeonsson, 1986) were reviewed. A limited number of studies were found. Only a few, however, incorporated adequate research designs; most focused on parent training programs. Although most studies reported effectiveness in terms of improved parent teaching or interaction skills, other family outcomes were rarely documented. Furthermore, essential family characteristics, such as cultural diversity, economic status, perceived locus of control, and family preferences and needs for service, were seldom taken into account in the study design or service delivery. It seemed clear from that review that expanded efforts were needed to define the goals of a family-focused approach to service, to identify and describe effective service models, and to identify family characteristics that would call for individualized approaches to services.

A second review focused on siblings of children with handicaps (Simeonsson & Bailey, 1986). This review was undertaken in part because of a recognition that "family-focused" had been historically defined as "mother-focused" early intervention. This review indicated that siblings of young children with handicaps do indeed have special needs; however, a consistent and predictable pattern was not evident from the literature. Thus the need for an individualized approach to families and family members was further reinforced.

A third review focused specifically on home-based intervention services for young children with handicaps and their families (Bailey & Simeonsson, 1988a). Home-based programs were found to vary widely in the nature and focus of services. Almost all, however, stressed the importance of a family-centered approach to intervention. Research outcomes reported were variable, but a major finding was that few studies incorporated a broad array of family outcome measures, with most focusing on improvement in parent teaching skills or on child progress.

In a summary of critical issues underlying research and intervention with families of young children with handicaps (Bailey & Simeonsson, 1984), six needs were identified and discussed that appeared to be fundamental to both research and services with families:

1. The need for a defensible rationale for family involvement, consistent with both research and practice;
2. the need for caution in defining desired family outcomes;
3. the need to view families from a developmental perspective;
4. the need to view families within ecological contexts;
5. the need to account for variability in family composition or structure when conducting research and intervention with families; and
6. the need for an adequate system for assessing family needs. (p. 39)

The most striking and consistent finding emerging from the literature reviews was the fundamental principle that family adaptation to a young child with handicaps is a highly individualized experience. Much of the earlier research had focused on a deficit model and stressed pathological aspects of family functioning rather than adaptive and constructive dimensions. It was concluded that (a) more information was needed about families and their unique patterns of adaptation, and (b) the field needed functional models for planning, implementing, and evaluating a family focus in early intervention. The first of these conclusions served as the stimulus for a descriptive study of families and infants receiving early intervention services.

Descriptive assessments. The state-wide home-based infant intervention network in North Carolina served as the context for a descriptive study of families and children. Three rounds of assessments were conducted at six-month intervals, beginning in the fall of 1983. The first round of data collection yielded data received from 200 families and twenty-two programs.

The children initially had a mean age of twenty-one months (SD = 12.5 months). They had a wide range of handicapping conditions; the average child had a developmental quotient of fifty-six. Sixty percent were boys. Approximately 30% came from minority families, mostly black. Nearly 60% were from the lower two strata of Hollingshead's index of socioeconomic status. Approximately two-thirds of the parents were married.

A comprehensive battery of information was gathered on child status (development, behavior, temperament); family functioning (home environment, social support, perceived stress, parent-child interaction, locus of control); and intervention (job satisfaction, interventionist priorities for services, home visit information, and monthly contacts). Data on a restricted set of variables were collected for the initial families during a second round of data collection, beginning in April 1984. Full data were collected in thirty-five additional families at this time. A third set of data, including all families and utilizing all measures, was collected in the fall of 1984. Results from the three rounds of data collection in the assessment study were analyzed in a number of specific investigations with the findings presented at conferences and prepared for publication. Selected findings are presented in this summary.

A consistent finding in research with handicapped infants and their mothers has been that maternal involvement is affected by characteristics of the child. Typically, the focus of much of the research has been on molecular aspects of behavior between mother and child. The use of the Parent/Caregiver Involvement Scale (PCIS) (Farran, Kasari, Comfort, & Jay, 1986) has provided an opportunity to examine broader aspects of the mother's involvement as it may be affected by the characteristics of the child. The PCIS documents the amount, quality, and appropriateness of caregiver behavior in eleven domains, including teaching, verbal and physical involvement, play, and equipment. After documenting the reliability of the in-home observations and ratings of mother-child interaction, 176 mother-child pairs were studied. Three characteristics of the child—severity of the handicap, temperament type, and interactive style— accounted for as much as 15% of the quality of maternal involvement and almost 19% of the appropriateness of that involvement (Huntington, Simeonsson, Bailey, & Comfort, 1987). The mothers of children rated as "difficult" or "slow-to-warm up" were rated lower on the measures of quality and appropriateness of interaction. In addition, when the effect of maternal characteristics was examined, maternal philosophy, as measured by the mother's locus of control (Nowicki & Duke, 1974), was found to be the most powerful single predictor of maternal involvement with infant.

The dimensions of parental involvement were further explored in a study of twenty-four families, in which the play and caregiving roles of mothers and fathers were compared using PCIS and other measures (Comfort, 1986). The results revealed similarity between mothers and fathers in the quantity, quality, appropriateness, and affective climate of caregiving and involvement in play. Both parents expressed a desire for greater involvement of the father. The findings were interpreted as evidence for increased flexibility and interchangeability of parental roles in the care of young at-risk or handicapped children.

In another study, the concept of goodness-of-fit was applied to the conceptualization and analysis of variables associated with caregiving behavior. Child, maternal, and support variables discriminated high and low levels of the quality and appropriateness of caregiving involvement as measured on the PCIS. Our findings indicated that an index of maternal and child characteristics, and measures of maternal locus of control (LOC), child temperament, and social support, contributed to the correct classification of 77% of mothers into high versus low involvement groups (Simeonsson, Bailey, Huntington, & Comfort, 1986). In a follow-up analysis, the initial child and family variables were examined in terms of predicting subsequent assessment of maternal caregiving involvement. The results were consistent with predictions of the concurrent maternal behavior. The finding illustrated the applicability of the goodness-of-fit concept and provided support for the efforts designed to maximize the fit between child, family, and environmental variables in early intervention.

Maternal involvement behavior was compared in adolescent and adult mothers for a subset of the larger sample (Helm, Comfort, Bailey, & Simeonsson, 1990). Consistent with the literature describing behaviors of mothers with their normally developing children, adult mothers were more verbal, more responsively contingent, and provided a more positive affective climate than adolescent mothers. Both maternal LOC and social support predicted aspects of adolescent maternal behavior, while only LOC predicted adult maternal behavior. For a subset of the subjects, both LOC and social support were found to be signifigant predictors of maternal behavior six months later. These results support an ecological view of family functioning and suggest that programs working with the families of handicapped and at risk preschoolers need to develop strategies aimed at the broader context in which children grow and develop.

Another example of data from this initial effort was an examination of the temperament of Down syndrome toddlers (Huntington & Simeonsson, 1987). Temperament subscale profiles of sixty-four toddlers with Down syndrome were compared to those of their nonhandicapped peers. The one- to two-year-old youngsters with Down syndrome were comparable to the nonhandicapped group on all subscales, while the two- to three-year-old children with Down syndrome were rated by their parents as slightly less persistent and requiring somewhat more stimulation to elicit a response than their nonhandicapped counterparts. In the area of temperament type, the most striking difference was in the finding of twice as many children with Down syndrome who received a rating of "slow-to/warm-up" as children in the nonhandicapped sample. Overall, however, the results indicated that toddlers with Down syndrome were generally similar to their nonhandicapped peers in terms of temperamental characteristics.

In addition to these published results, the data also were examined in a number of other ways, existing programs were reviewed, and meetings were held with professionals and parents. The goal of these activities was to define and clarify the need for a family focus in early intervention and to identify characteristics of an effective model of family-focused services. The need for an increased family focus was evident in our data documenting the influence of children's behavioral characteristics on maternal behavior and the substantial number of families who felt that they were not able to exert significant control over life events. On a survey of family needs, families reported a wide variety of needs that were occasioned by the birth of their child with a handicap but that were not directly related to child-focused treatments. Included among those expressed were needs relating to information, support, child care, and financial assistance.

The variability observed in family needs, family characteristics, child needs, and child characteristics was impressive. Although we found some relationships among selected child and family variables, it became clear that family needs are determined by a complex interaction of family and child skills, values, resources, and style. To offer a single program of family services clearly would not meet the diverse needs of families nor would it serve to reinforce and support family strengths and resources. It became clear that an individualized approach to documenting family needs and resources was essential in order to provide relevant and useful services.

It also became apparent that implementing a family focus would be a challenge for many early intervention professionals. Although most endorsed a family-centered philosophy, lack of agreement on the specifics of that philosophy or how to implement it served as major barriers to change. In spite of an agency regulation requiring at least one family goal for each individualized plan, it was found that this actually occurred for only about 20% of the families served. Thus, three priority areas emerged: (a) a functional model was needed for planning, implementing, and evaluating a family focus; (b) functional and nonintrusive assessment procedures were needed to facilitate the application of such a model; and (c) in-service training and support would be needed to implement such a model.

Phase 2: Model Development and Implementation

The second phase of the FAMILIES project was devoted to developing and field testing a functional model for assessing family needs, specifying family goals, implementing family services, and evaluating effectiveness. A six-step model, depicted in Figure 4.1, was developed (Bailey et al., 1986) for intervention planning, based on the goodness-of-fit concept described in the longitudinal research of Thomas and Chess (1977). The fundamental premise of the model was that the professional's task is to optimize the "fit" between the family, child, and community services. Four specific goals of the model were to (a) help families cope with the demands of caring for their child with a handicap, (b) help families grow in their understanding of their child, (c) promote satisfying and facilitative parent-child interactions, and (d) preserve and reinforce the dignity and sense of control of families. Appropriate assessment, effective communication skills, and collabo-

Figure 4.1
Family-Focused Intervention Model (Initial)

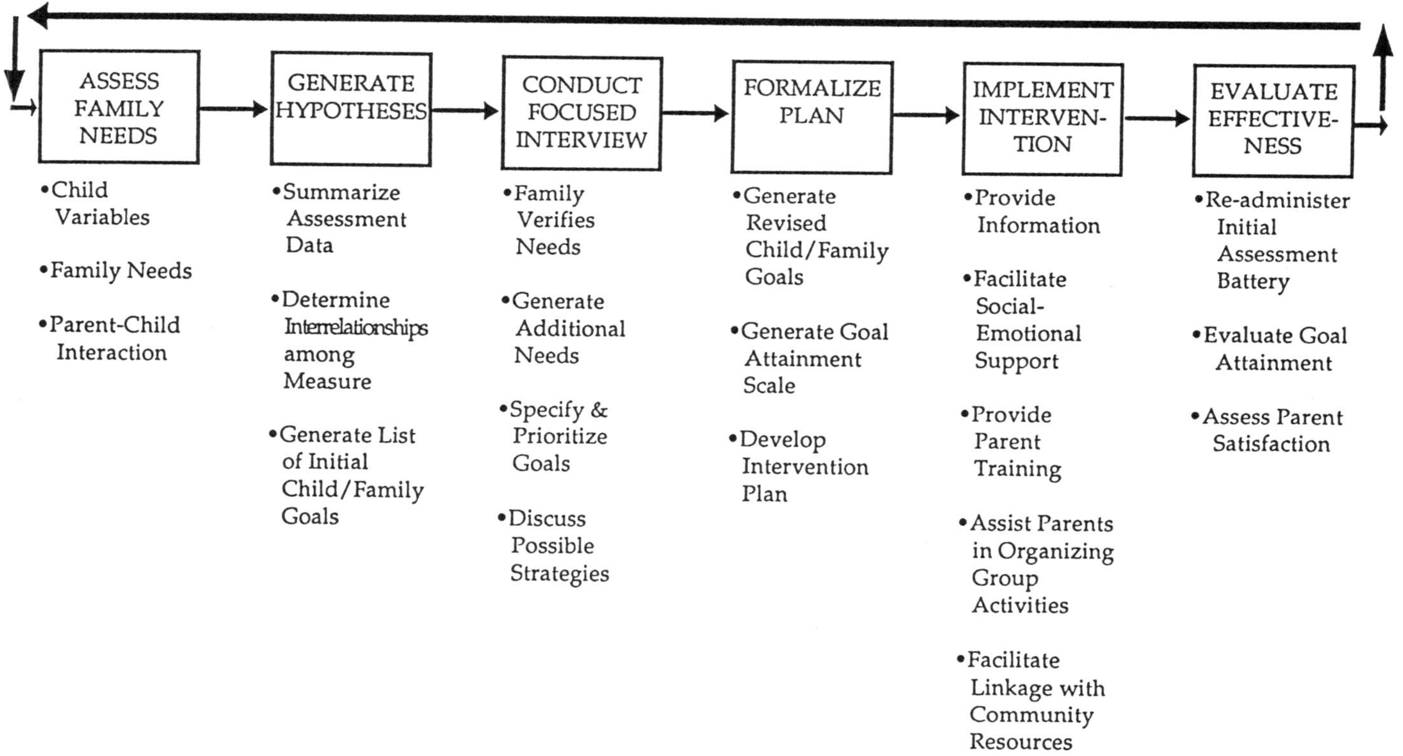

rative goal/setting strategies formed the basic methods of implementing the model (Bailey, 1987). In the process of developing the model, an assessment tool—the Family Needs Survey (Bailey & Simeonsson, 1988b)—and a framework for conducting effective interviews with families (Winton & Bailey, 1988) were created.

In order to field-test the model, twenty-nine home-based interventionists received a three-day in-service training program designed to provide a theoretical framework for working with families and to teach skills in assessing family needs, communicating with families, and generating family goals.

The workshop, described by Bailey and his colleagues., (1988), included approximately nine hours of training in four domains of family assessment: child characteristics likely to influence family functioning, critical events, parent-child interactions, and family needs. Approximately seven hours were devoted to training in interviewing and communicating effectively with parents. Finally, approximately 2 hours were devoted to operationalizing family goals and writing goals in the Goal Attainment Scaling format (Kiresuk & Sherman, 1968). In each section, training activities included presentations, videotapes, and practical activities.

Following the training, the interventionists implemented the model with forty-eight families in their programs. The average age of the children was fourteen months, most were moderately or severely handicapped, and approximately half were from low SES families. Outcomes were examined in terms of goals established, sources of goals, and goal attainment. The first finding was that the interventionists with training wrote more family goals than did interventionists without training (Bailey et al., 1988). Furthermore, it was found that the focused interview with families (Winton & Bailey, 1988) significantly affected the final written goals, in that many goals were modified, deleted, or added to those developed on the basis of assessment data alone. Of the original goals, 29% were modified or deleted after the focused interview, and thirty-two new goals were added. Of the final goals, 28% were affected in some fashion by the focused interview. In the assessment area, it was found that the Family Needs Survey provided an efficient and comprehensive way to assess family needs from the perspective of the parents of the handicapped infant (Bailey & Simeonsson, 1988c). While there was some variability between mothers and fathers in perceived needs, most parents expressed common needs, with particular emphasis on the need for information. In the area of infant assessment, it was also found that the characteristics of infants with handicaps could be assessed in a functional manner with the Carolina Record of Individual Behavior (CRIB) (Simeonsson, 1979). Such assessment highlighted individual differences and remained stable across a six-month period.

With regard to outcome documentation, the use of the Goal Attainment Scaling procedure revealed that after training, approximately 60% of the goals were written for children, and 40% were written for families (Simeonsson, Bailey, Huntington, & Brandon, 1991). An analysis of initial and final status revealed that approximately two-thirds of all goals met or exceeded expected levels. An impressive finding from these data was that family goals were as readily achieved as child goals. The attainment of goals was also found to correspond with changes in pre-post measures of family adaptation in the form of lower scores on measures of family needs and impacts. These findings illustrate the fact that family intervention can be individualized and that planned goals can be achieved for infants with handicaps and their families.

Finally, we examined the Family Needs Survey in greater detail to document its utility in family assessment (Bailey & Simeonsson, 1988c). The instrument provided useful information, serving as a primary source for more than two-thirds of the family goals identified. Some differences were observed in the responses of mothers and fathers, providing evidence of the need for individualized and multifaceted approaches to assessment and service planning. The stability of family needs was evident in moderately high correlations observed over a six-month interval. We also found that an open-ended question included in the Family Needs Survey provided substantial additional information that would not have been obtained from the structured items alone. In a recent study (Bailey & Blasco, 1990), it was found that parents were very positive about the instrument as a vehicle for sharing their needs with professionals, a finding that was consistent across socioeconomic groups and for both white and minority-group parents.

Several outcomes were noted, however, that led to a revision of the intervention model. The revised model, reported by Bailey and Simeonsson (1988b), is displayed in Figure 4.2 and reflects three major changes. First, it became clear that the initial battery of measures was time consuming and not always related to the needs of the individual family. The number of initial measures to be completed was reduced, viewing the initial assessment phase as a screening process to be followed by interviews or discussions with families and further assessments, if deemed appropriate. Second, it was clear that the importance of assessing family characteristics, including strengths that might mediate family adaptation, should be recognized in the model. Finally, the team meeting was added to reflect the importance of an interdisciplinary approach to planning and also to show that the meeting was different and separate from the family-focused interview.

Although Figures 4.1 and 4.2 imply that the process is a linear one, the circular and variable nature of family-focused services must be emphasized. In practice, professionals constantly meet with families

Figure 4.2
Family-Focused Intervention Model (Revised)

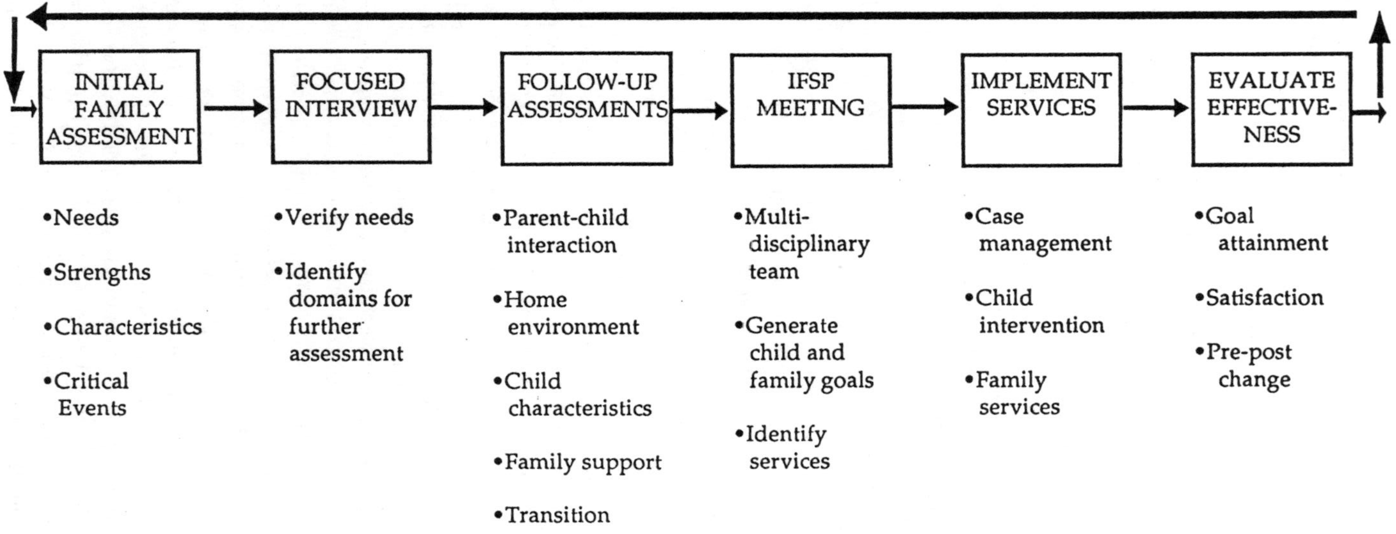

to negotiate priorities for goals and services. Inevitably, these interactions are transactional in nature, with each party influencing and being influenced by the other.

IMPLICATIONS FOR PRACTICE, PERSONNEL PREPARATION, AND RESEARCH

The FAMILIES project, like the broader family support movement, was based on the assumption that a family focus is an important principle in early intervention. Findings from the assessment and clinical trial phases of the research program yield implications for practice, professional training, and research. Regarding clinical practice, evidence was provided that: (a) a comprehensive approach to assessment is needed that incorporates, at a minimum, assessment of the child, the family, and the nature of the interaction between the child and family; (b) family characteristics in the form of needs and strengths can and should be assessed in a systematic manner; (c) child characteristics need to be taken into account as variables mediating caregiver behavior; (d) a focused interview is an important aspect of family assessment, as it encourages a collaborative role for parents in the identification and prioritization of goals; and (e) planned intervention goals can be achieved and documented.

This evidence is supportive of the central premise of individualized services in early intervention as embodied in the requirements of Public Law 99–457 for the IFSP. While the premise for individualization of services is clear, the implementation of that premise has varied considerably depending in no small part upon the philosophical framework, priorities, and resources of a particular program. Representative of such variability are a transactional approach to home intervention (Barrera, Chapter 5; Barrera & Rosenbaum, 1986); an approach that fosters the enablement and empowerment of families (Dunst, Trivette & Deal, 1988); a systems approach defined in terms of resources, life cycles, functions, and interactions of the family (Turnbull & Turnbull, 1986), and a goodness-of-fit conceptualization of concordance between abilities and demands (Bailey & Simeonsson, 1988b). Each of these approaches differs in the specifics of underlying assumptions, assessment, and nature of intervention. But a common theme can be identified in the promotion of an active role for families, which recognizes their unique needs and characteristics. The very nature of this variability calls for family-centered services, that can accommodate qualitatively different levels of involvement by the family. In recognition of the fact that the level of involvement by families in early intervention is not static and unidirectional, any framework must take into account its dynamic nature and the nature of the investment made by interventionists. To this end, we have drawn from a model in family-centered medical care to define levels of involvement ranging from elective non-involvement to involvement that seeks psychological change at the family or personnel level (Simeonsson & Bailey, 1990). The mutually determined nature of involvement should thus involve sensitivity to cultural, ethnic, and other individual differences in families in the work of the interventionist and reflect "a delicate balance, the worker taking a casework attitude, but using therapeutic skills" (Kraemer, 1987, p. 210).

Taken collectively, the findings of the FAMILIES project also support the fact that most early interventionists lack formal training in family assessment and intervention (Bailey, 1988). The results emphasize the value of training early interventionists to assess family needs, communicate with families, and develop family goals. As a result of our in-service training, interventionists made significant modifications in planning and prioritizing goals for families.

In a subsequent study, however, interventionists who conducted family interviews after in-service training reported that many topics emerged in the interviews on which they were uncertain of how to respond (Winton & Bailey, 1990). It is unlikely that skills related to communicating with families, collaborative goal setting, and conflict resolution can be taught in one or two workshops. As programs continue to become more family-focused, ongoing support and assistance will likely be needed.

The family-focused intervention model calls for training of interventionists in using systematic and comprehensive assessment information, specifying objectives, and developing individualized intervention plans for families. The implications are for skills training as well as philosophical orientation. With regard to skills training, the focus is likely to be on priorities in assessment, developing IFSPs, implementing interventions, and case management. The form for such training can be met by in-service and continuing education of interventionists who desire to upgrade skills to meet changing work demands. From a philosophical perspective, however, it must be recognized that for many professionals, a family orientation requires a significant shift in their approach to service delivery. A change of such magnitude will likely be difficult for some, and undoubtedly will demand extensive and on-going support.

The focus for the long-range picture needs to be on addressing the conceptual, research, and policy needs of the field. Addressing these needs will require changes in preprofessional training programs involving disciplinary as well as interdisciplinary efforts. Of particular importance here will be the acquisition of knowledge bases pertaining to typical and atypical development of infants and children, family development and functioning, and models for interdisciplinary team work. In a recent national survey of training programs across eight disciplines, however, it was found that many professionals receive very little training in working with families (Bailey, Simeonsson, Yoder, & Huntington, 1990). Curricula and faculty training will likely be needed before substantial changes in preservice training programs can be achieved.

With regard to research, a number of implications emerges from the project findings. While concerns about the efficacy of early intervention continue, the nature of questions about the variables in early intervention has become more precise (Simeonsson, 1985). One important implication for research is the need for further studies of variables that contribute to an effective matching of family needs with interventions. In a recent review of twenty research studies in which family outcomes were documented, Heinicke, Beckwith, and Thompson (1988) found that most studies reported significant family effects. The magnitude and direction of effects were not influenced by target group or type of intervention. Frequent and sustained services emerged as factors most associated with significant effects in families.

Drawing on the goodness-of-fit conceptual framework used in this project, however, there may also be specific characteristics of the intervention and the interventionist that may account for the different outcomes for families whose children have handicaps. For example, Affleck and associates (1989) found that the effects of a hospital-to-home transition program for mothers of high-risk infants varied significantly depending upon the mother's perceived need for support. Mothers who perceived a need for support reported a greater sense of competence, control, and responsiveness as a result of the program. On the other hand, mothers who did not perceive the need for support but who were given the services anyway reported feeling less competent and less in control as a result of the program. This finding points to the need for services to be matched to the needs and preferences of families and for research that provides guidance in how to optimize this goodness of fit. It may be appropriate to examine how implementation procedures influence family-focused intervention. Of particular research interest is the investigation of the relationship between intervention activities and family outcome; that is, how does the process of implementation of planned intervention influence the attainment of expected goals? The continued search for answers to questions of this nature is important to the refinement of early intervention as a timely and effective endeavor for families with handicapped infants.

ACKNOWLEDGMENTS

The FAMILIES project was funded from 1982 to 1987 by Contract No. 300–820–0366 from the Special Education Program, Office of Special Education and Rehabilitative Services, U.S. Department of Education. Appreciation is expressed to Gail Huntington, Pam Winton, Karen O'Donnell, Marilee Comfort, Trish Isbell, James Helm, and Ed Arndt for their contributions to the FAMILIES project.

REFERENCES

Affleck, G., Tennen, H., Rowe, J., Roscher, B., & Walker, L. (1989). Effects of formal support on mothers' adaptation to the hospital-to-home transition of high-risk children: The benefits and costs of helping. *Child Development, 60,* 488-501.

Bailey, D. B. (1987). Collaborative goal setting with families: Resolving differences in values and priorities for services. *Topics in Early Childhood Special Education, 7*(2), 59-71.

Bailey, D. B. (1988). Issues and directions in preparing professionals to work with young handicapped children and their families. In J. J. Gallagher, R. M. Clifford, & P. Trohanis (Eds.), *Policy implementation and Public Law 99–457: Planning for young children with special needs* (pp. 97-132). Baltimore: Paul H. Brookes.

Bailey, D. B., & Blasco, P. M. (1990). Parents' perspectives on a written survey of family needs. *Journal of Early Intervention, 14,* 196-203.

Bailey, D. B., & Simeonsson, R. J. (1984). Critical issues underlying research and intervention with families of young handicapped children. *Journal of the Division for Early Childhood, 9,* 38-48.

Bailey, D. B., & Simeonsson, R. J. (1986). Design issues in family impact evaluation. In L. Bickman & D. L. Weatherford (Eds.), *Evaluating early intervention programs for severely handicapped children and their families* (pp. 209-230). Austin, TX: Pro-Ed.

Bailey, D. B., & Simeonsson, R. J. (1988a). Home based early intervention. In S. L. Odom & M. B. Karnes (Eds.), *Early intervention for infants and children with handicaps: An empirical base* (pp. 199-215). Baltimore: Paul H. Brookes.

Bailey, D. B., & Simeonsson, R. J. (1988b). *Family assessment in early intervention.* Columbus, OH: Merrill.

Bailey, D. B., & Simeonsson, R. J. (1988c). Assessing the needs of families with handicapped infants. *Journal of Special Education, 22,* 117-127.

Bailey, D. B., Simeonsson, R. J., Isbell, P., Huntington, G. S., Winton, P. J., Comfort, M., & Helm, J. M. (1988). In-service training in family assessment and goal setting for early interventionists: Outcomes and issues. *Journal of the Division for Early Childhood, 12,* 126-136.

Bailey, D. B., Simeonsson, R. J., Winton, P. J., Huntington, G. S., Comfort, M., Isbell, P., O'Donnell, K. & Helm, J. M. (1986). Family-focused intervention: A functional model for planning, implementing and evaluating individualized family services in early intervention. *Journal of the Division for Early Childhood, 10*(2), 156-171.

Bailey, D. B., Simeonsson, R. J., Yoder, D. E., & Huntington, G. S. (1990). Infant personnel preparation across eight disciplines: An integrative analysis. *Exceptional Children, 57*, 26-35.

Barrera, M., & Rosenbaum, P. (1986). The transactional model of early home intervention. *Infant Mental Health Journal, 7*(2), 112-131.

Brewer, E. J., McPherson, M., Magrab, P. R., & Hutchins, V. C. (1989). Family-centered, community-based coordinated care for children with special health care needs. *Pediatrics, 83*, 1055-1060.

Bronfenbrenner, U. (1979). *The ecology of human development: Experiments by nature and design.* Cambridge, MA: Harvard University Press.

Comfort, M. (1986). *Parental involvement in play interaction and caregiving roles in families with young handicapped children: A comparison of father and mother.* Unpublished doctoral dissertation, University of North Carolina, Chapel Hill.

Dunst, C. J. (1985). Rethinking early intervention. *Analysis and Intervention in Developmental Disabilities, 5*, 165-210.

Dunst, C., & Rheingrover, R. (1981). An analysis of the efficacy of infant intervention programs with organically handicapped children. *Evaluation and Program Planning, 4*, 287-323.

Dunst, C. J., Trivette, C. M., & Deal, A. G. (1988). *Enabling and empowering families: Principles and guidelines for practices.* Cambridge, MA: Brookline Books.

Farran, D., Kasari, C., Comfort, M., & Jay, S. (1986). *Parent/Caregiver Interaction Scale training manual.* Unpublished manual, Frank Porter Graham Child Development Center, University of North Carolina, Chapel Hill.

Heinicke, C. M., Beckwith, L., & Thompson, A. (1988). Early intervention in the family system: A framework and review. *Infant Mental Health Journal, 9*, 111-141.

Helm, J. M., Comfort, M., Bailey, D. B. & Simeonsson, R. J. (1990). Adolescent and adult mothers of handicapped children: Maternal involvement in play. *Family Relations, 39*, 432-437.

Huntington, G. S. & Simeonsson, R. J. (1987). Down syndrome and toddler temperament. *Child: Care, Health, and Development, 13*, 1-11.

Huntington, G. S., Simeonsson, R. J., Bailey, D. B., & Comfort, M. (1987). Handicapped child characteristics and maternal involvement. *Journal of Reproductive and Infant Psychology, 5*, 105-118.

Kiresuk, T., & Sherman, R. (1968). Goal attainment scaling: A general method for evaluating comprehensive community mental health programs. *Community Mental Health Journal, 4*, 443-453.

Kraemer, S. (1987). Working with parents: Casework or psychotherapy? *Journal of Child Psychology and Psychiatry, 28*, 207-213.

Nowicki, S., & Duke M. P. (1974). A locus-of-control scale for college as well as non-college adults. *Journal of Personality Assessment, 38*, 136-137.

Sameroff, A. (1975). Early influences on development: Fact or fancy. *Merrill-Palmer Quarterly, 21*, 267-294.

Shelton, T. L., Jeppson, E. S., & Johnson, B. H. (1987). *Family-centered care for children with special health needs.* Washington, D.C.: Association for the Care of Children's Health.

Simeonsson, R. J. (1979). *Carolina Record of Individual Behavior*. Unpublished instrument, University of North Carolina, Chapel Hill.

Simeonsson, R. J. (1985). Efficacy of early intervention: Issues and evidence. *Analysis and Intervention in Development Disabilities, 5*, 203-209.

Simeonsson, R. J., & Bailey, D. B. (1986). Siblings of handicapped children. In J. J. Gallagher & P. Vietze (Eds.), *Families of handicapped persons* (pp. 67-77). Baltimore: Paul H. Brookes.

Simeonsson, R. J., & Bailey, D. B. (1990). Family dimensions in early intervention. In J. J. Meisels & J. P. Shonkoff (Eds.), *Handbook of early childhood intervention* (pp. 428-444). New York: Cambridge University Press.

Simeonsson, R. J., Bailey, D. B., Huntington, G. S., & Brandon, L. (1991). Scaling and attainment of goals in family-focused intervention. *Community Mental Health Journal, 27*, 77-83.

Simeonsson, R. J., Bailey, D. B., Huntington, G. S., & Comfort, M. (1986). Testing the concept of goodness of fit in early intervention. *Infant Mental Health Journal, 7*(1), 81-93

Simeonsson, R. J., Cooper, D. H., & Scheiner, A. P. (1982). A review and analysis of the effectiveness of early intervention programs. *Pediatrics, 69*, 635-641.

Thomas, A., & Chess, S. (1977). *Temperament and development*. New York: Brunner/Mazel.

Trout, M., & Foley, G. (1989). Working with the families of handicapped infants and toddlers. *Topics in Language Disorders, 10*(1), 57-67.

Turnbull, A. P., & Turnbull, H. R. (1986). *Families, professionals and exceptionality*. Columbus, OH: Merrill.

Winton, P. J., & Bailey, D. B. (1988). The family-focused interview: A collaborative mechanism for family assessment and goal setting. *Journal of the Division for Early Childhood, 12*, 195-207.

Winton, P. J., & Bailey, D. B. (1990). Early intervention training related to family interviewing. *Topics in Early Childhood Special Education, 10*(1), 50-62.

Zigler, E., & Black, K. B. (1989). America's family support movement: Strengths and limitations. *American Journal of Orthopsychiatry, 59*, 6-19.

5

The Transactional Model of Early Home Intervention: Application With Developmentally Delayed Children and Their Families

Maria E. Barrera

The main purpose of this chapter is to describe the transactional model of early home intervention (TMEHI), its operationalization within an intervention program (the Infant-Parent Program), and its empirical validation with developmentally delayed infants and their families. When the model was first developed ten years ago (see Barrera & Rosenbaum, 1986), it incorporated developmental knowledge (particularly of infant competencies and parent-infant interaction), empirical knowledge gained in the field of early intervention, knowledge of behavior analysis applied to child rearing, and knowledge of adult educational strategies. Since then, the model has become more refined as a result of its application to a wider diversity of infants and their families, greater understanding of cognitive problem-solving strategies applied to parenting, and the incorporation of the ecological and family/social systems perspectives on human development. These developments have necessitated a formal revision of the model.

The TMEHI has been evaluated for low-birth-weight infants and their families with some promising results (Barrera, Rosenbaum, & Cunningham, 1986; Barrera, Cunningham, & Rosenbaum, 1986), including positive intervention effects at a five-year follow-up (Barrera, Doucet, & Kitching, 1990). In this chapter some evaluation results from application of the model to developmentally delayed infants and their families are presented for two reasons. First, the heterogeneity of this population provides a good medium for applying the model. Second, although the effectiveness of early intervention with developmentally delayed infants has been demonstrated in previous research (for excellent reviews and analyses of the literature, see Dunst & Rheingrover, 1981; Guralnick & Bricker, 1987; Harris, 1987; Marfo & Cook, Chapter 1 Marfo & Kysela, 1985; Shonkoff & Hauser-Cram, 1987; Simeonsson, Cooper, & Scheiner, 1982), specific questions about early intervention with this population still need to be addressed: Is the impact of early intervention the same with all developmentally delayed infants? What is the optimal age of enrollment? What is the relationship between severity of delay and impact of intervention?

Before describing the model, definitions of early intervention and developmental delay and a brief discussion of severity of delay and age of enrollment are necessary.

Early Intervention

Traditionally, the term "early intervention" has been used to describe external manipulations of environmental events in the form of enrichment, education, and physical or psychotherapeutic input, with the objective of maximizing the infant's potential. The infant in that context was considered the target of the intervention. In the TMEHI, early intervention is defined as the combination of enrichment, education, and psychosocial support within the ecological context of the community and the family. The objective in this model is to maximize the development of *both* infants and parents, and to promote positive parent-infant interactions. Thus, the infant-parent dyad, rather than either the infant or the parent singly, is considered the target of the intervention.

Developmentally Delayed Infants

The label "developmental delay" is used in this chapter in a broad, generic sense. From this generic use, developmentally delayed children constitute a highly heterogeneous group, both in terms of etiology and rate of development. For example, Denhoff (1981) described developmentally delayed infants from the United Cerebral Palsy Association's (UCPA) collaborative study (n = 1,000) from five centers in the United States, as follows: 6% were considered emotionally deprived, 84% "high risk," and only 10% developmentally disabled. Of the latter, 50% were considered to have a spectrum of the cerebral palsies, 15% had sensory or multihandicaps, 10% had Down syndrome, and 25% had minor neurological dysfunction.

Developmentally delayed children may show significant delays in multiple aspects of cognitive, motor, communication, language, and socioemotional development. Some tend to reach developmental milestones similar to those of nondelayed children but at a much slower rate. Many severely delayed children, however, may never reach some developmental milestones, such as walking or toilet training. The actual rate of attaining milestones, limits on development, and other characteristics vary depending on the nature and severity of the disabling condition, the nature and quality of the home and familial environment over time, and the complex interaction between these factors.

Operationally, developmental delay is defined in this chapter as a score of less than eighty-five on the Bayley Mental Scale. To address the problem of heterogeneity within the population, evaluation data on six subgroups of developmentally delayed infants are examined in the context of developmental gain at the end of intervention.

It is estimated that only a minority of children diagnosed as disabled show clearly identifiable impairments at birth (Hayden & Haring, 1976). Most have a less obvious disability that may not be detected until after the first year, when developmental milestones fail to occur. Mildly delayed children who are actually identified as so in infancy are likely to have some clear biological basis for their delays. Other milder disabilities may be transient (Allen, 1987). Thus, it is reasonable to assume that in most cases, the earlier the identification, the more obvious and possibly more severe the problem is. Clearly, these differences in the patterns of identification associated with the severity of delay have important implications for the planning of intervention programs and for the evaluation of their effectiveness.

With regard to age of enrollment, less recent reviews of the early intervention literature by Bronfenbrenner (1975) and Tjossem (1976) suggested that early enrollment is associated with greater effectiveness. The evidence since these reviews has not been convincing. There is controversy regarding how early developmentally delayed children should be enrolled in an intervention program. Age of enrollment varies widely across studies, partly because of the issue of identification mentioned above, and partly because of the nature of the programs themselves. Simeonsson, Cooper, and Scheiner (1982) identified the age range at enrollment across twenty-seven studies to be 2.5 months to more than 6 years. Casto and Mastropieri (1986) found that although twenty-six of twenty-seven studies reviewed concluded that "earlier is better," critical analysis of intervention effects showed that with handicapped children early enrollment was not necessarily better. In contrast, Shonkoff and Hauser-Cram (1987) found greater effects for children who were enrolled at a younger age. The wide variability in age of enrollment is problematic, as age of identification or entry into treatment can in themselves be markers of severity of disability. Given the controversy noted here, age of the infant at enrollment is also examined in relation to outcomes.

RATIONALE OF THE TMEHI

Historically, four main issues in the early intervention field motivated the development of the TMEHI. These issues pertain to (a) conceptual models, (b) the role of parents, (c) the role of staff, and (d) the setting of the intervention.

Conceptual Model

Early intervention programs in the 1960s were based mainly on the environmental deprivation model, developed from empirical research with animals (Denenberg, 1969) and clinical observations of deprived young children in orphanages (Spitz, 1945). Based on the deprivation model, intervention programs assumed that extra environmental stimulation would prevent developmental problems, or would ameliorate or arrest further delay in the case of infants already showing delay in their development. Most of the programs developed in the 1960s and 1970s focused on the developmental needs of the infant only. They were aimed at maximizing developmental potential either through direct hands-on therapy by a professional, or through parent training, or both. This trend is reflected in reviews of early studies: 81% of the studies reviewed by Simeonsson, Cooper, and Scheiner (1982) provided programming for children based on concepts of child development.

It became evident that early intervention programs generally overlooked many important components of the intervention process, such as the child's level of competence; the contribution of the child's personal and biological characteristics to his/her own development; parental competence and the active role parents play in the intervention process; the dynamic relationship between the child's development and his/her environment, particularly between parent and child; and the dynamic relationships within the family and between the family and the community (the ecological context).

A different approach to intervention began to emerge in the late 1970s and early 1980s, focusing on the parent-infant interaction rather than on the infant alone (Affleck, McGrade, McQueeney, & Allen, 1982; Allen, 1987; Barrera & Rosenbaum, 1986; Bromwich, 1981; Bromwich & Parmelee, 1979; Fraiberg, 1975, 1977). This relationship-focused approach advocates flexible, individually tailored programming that responds to the specialized needs of the child and the family. It promotes reciprocity in the parent-infant interaction, partnership between parent and professional, and parental competence. It regards the parent-infant interaction "as the basis from which mutual enjoyment, parenting skills, and the child's social, linguistic, and cognitive competencies develop" (Affleck, McGrade, McQueeney, & Allen, 1982, p. 259). Bromwich (1981), and Barrera and Rosenbaum (1986) applied this approach to parents and their biologically at-risk infants; Fraiberg (1975) applied a similar interactive approach to families with blind young children; and Affleck and associates (1982) applied it to parents and their infants with severe perinatal complications or genetic disorders associated with developmental delay.

A more recent intervention model based on this approach has been developed by Dunst and his associates (Dunst, 1985; Dunst & Trivette, 1988; Dunst, Trivette, & Deal, 1988). As its name indicates, the focus of Dunst's family (social) systems model is the family, not just the child, and its main objectives are to strengthen family functioning, to promote development in all family members, and to empower families to mobilize their resources to make the social system work for them, as they take control over their own lives. Perhaps the most important element of this model is the application of the empowerment concept as defined by Rappaport (1981) and others. According to Dunst and Trivette (1988), parental empowerment culminates in parents acquiring a sense of control necessary for parenting and managing family affairs. Empowered parents assume responsibility for changes in their children's behavior.

As a relationship-focused model, the TMEHI identifies parent-infant interaction in the context of the family as the target of the intervention (Barrera & Rosenbaum, 1986). Similar to Dunst's model, the TMEHI has incorporated family systems principles, the objective being to strengthen and empower families in managing their own affairs. Thus, if parents need assistance with their developmentally delayed children, it is critical that the assistance is provided, but *how* it is provided is even more important. Hence, a clear definition of the roles of the parent, the professional, and the parent-professional relationship is essential to understand how parents are empowered.

The Role of the Parent

The state-of-the-art reviews by Bronfenbrenner (1975) and Tjossem (1976) indicated that one of the shortcomings of early intervention programs in the 1960s and early 1970s was the limited, if any, parental involvement in the intervention process. Since then, most programs have included various degrees of parental involvement. Simeonsson, Cooper, and Scheiner (1982) found that 70% of the twenty-seven programs reviewed indicated parental involvement, with 58% reporting some form of parental support or training. Casto & Mastropieri (1986) concluded from their meta-analysis of intervention studies that parental involvement was not necessary. In contrast, the Shonkoff and Hauser-Cram (1987) meta-analysis found that programs that planned extensive parent involvement produced greater effects of intervention, and that if the program focused on both parent and child the results were more successful.

Although the nature of parental involvement has varied greatly over time and across programs, for the most part parents have played a mainly instrumental role in the implementation of the intervention. Specifically, parental involvement has been primarily as "trainees" who observe the "experts" handling their baby and subsequently try to reproduce the observed activity. The exceptions are found in programs based on the relationship-focused or family/social systems models. If the focus of the intervention changes, so does the role of the parent. However, the full impact of early intervention can only be achieved when parents become active not only in the implementation but in the decision making as well. Moreover, parents' needs, within the family context and the home environment, along with the child's needs, must become intervention targets.

Not only are the needs and characteristics of children different but the needs and characteristics of parents and families are also quite diverse. With regard to parental needs, the birth of a developmentally delayed infant can have a severe emotional impact on parents' psychosocial well-being, as well as on the entire family. Evidence is beginning to appear on the impact on siblings of having a handicapped child in the family (Ballard, Maloney, Shank, & Hollister, 1984). Parents need assistance in coping with the instrumental and emotional burden of having a handicapped child. Moreover, parents must become active partners in the intervention process if they are to carry the responsibility of parenting their disabled children.

A final note on parental involvement has to do with gender. Typically, parental involvement and training have been aimed at the mother, as mothers in our society have been the primary caretakers. This traditional role is gradually changing as fathers become more involved in caretaking activities. Therefore, in the implementation of the TMEHI, special efforts are made to reach not only mothers but fathers, when available, in the context of the entire family.

The Role of the Professional

In traditional intervention programs staff have usually acted as the expert professionals who teach and train parents to become teachers and therapists for their own children. As a result, the relationship of parents to professionals has been that of subordinates who are told what to do. This approach undermines parents' confidence in their parenting role—particularly when the intervention setting is the home, where parents greet the professional in their own territory. Bromwich

(1981) provides great insights into how to relate with parents respectfully, emphasizing the basic practice of reciprocity in relationships and acknowledging parental competence and partnership with the professional.

As the role of parents in the intervention process changes, so should the role of the staff. The establishment of an active partnership between parents and professionals is essential. In this partnership, the decisions regarding the needs of the child and his/her family, as well as the implementation of intervention strategies, are ultimately left to parents, who are assisted by the professionals. Affleck and his associates' consultation program for parents of handicapped infants (1982) and Dunst's social systems approach to early intervention (Dunst, 1985; Dunst & Trivette, 1988; Dunst, Trivette, & Deal, 1988) provide good examples of the changing role of early intervention staff. In an intervention program based on the TMEHI the professional and parents share decision making and work in partnership.

Setting of Intervention

Most programs for developmentally delayed infants that began in the 1960s were center-based, as they followed the model of enrichment programs for disadvantaged young children. In the 1970s, however, Bronfenbrenner's ecologically based intervention model influenced the field of early intervention throughout North America. Home-based early intervention became widely accepted, with most programs having a combination of both. For example, Simeonsson, Cooper and Scheiner (1982) found that 44% of programs offered a combination of home- and center-based intervention, 26% offered home-based only, and 11% offered center-based only.

There are advantages and disadvantages of home- and center-based intervention. Some of the merits and difficulties with home-based intervention have been eloquently stated by Halpern (1984):

Home-based early intervention is in some ways inherently nonstandardized and idiosyncratic. In most programs, the home visitor enters into a young family's life, begins to assemble a portrait of strengths and stresses, attempts to respond to immediate parental concerns, and usually adapts whatever infant stimulation agenda he or she has to what is being learned about a family's needs.

This flexibility and responsiveness, along with the long-term, sustaining nature of support provided, constitute the unique strengths of home visiting programs. In addition, these features allow the home visitor to observe the constraints to adequate child development in a particular family in a manner not accessible to other service providers. Nonetheless, when home visitors respond to unique problems and stresses, they are likely to produce unique outcomes. Thus some parents benefit most in ability to manage infant feeding, others in ability to identify and respond to infant cues, others in provision of a safe and stimulating physical environment, others in their general ability to cope with day-to-day household problems, still others in their personal sense of efficacy. These are all important influences on parent-child interaction, but as different families benefit in different domains, havoc is wreaked on research designs seeking group difference in central tendency scores, especially in studies starting with relatively small samples in the first place. (p. 217)

In terms of effectiveness, Shonkoff and Hauser-Cram (1987) found no significant differences between programs with home- versus center-based intervention, even though home-based programs started six months earlier. However, this analysis was based on child outcomes only. If early home intervention should have an ecological base, clearly its effectiveness must be assessed using measures of the ecological context as well. Although the evidence is inconclusive regarding the effectiveness of either setting, a flexible combination of home- and center-based intervention may provide the most effective help, as the alternatives may better address the needs of both the child and the family. The decision regarding the intervention setting should be made jointly by parents and professionals.

THEORETICAL INFLUENCES ON THE TMEHI

Developmental Relationships Theory

The concept of reciprocal, bidirectional influences between the child and the environment has been popularized by Bell (1968), but it was also inherent in Piaget's theory through the ideas of accommodation and assimilation. Bell reexamined the socialization literature, in which parents were thought to be the primary determinants of the young child's social behavior, and concluded that as the child's social behavior is influenced by the parents, the parents' rearing practices are influenced by the child from birth.

The concept of bidirectionality was expanded later by Sameroff and Chandler (1975) in their transactional model of development. They concluded that the evidence on early influences on development emphasizes the importance of caretaking factors as well as the child's unique behavioral and physical characteristics in developmental outcome. They recognized the importance of the reciprocal interaction between the infant and the caretaking environment and adopted the term "transaction," which was defined by the continuous and dynamic transformations that occur between two individuals as they interact with each other over time.

The relationship between a mother and her preterm infant provides a good example of transactions. Typically, in the early months of the infant's life, the mother works very hard to get her child's attention, with little response in return. As the small baby's health improves and the central nervous system matures, the infant gradually becomes more responsive to the mother's efforts. The mother, in turn, modifies her style to allow the baby gradually to play a more active role in their interactions. In cases in which this developmental/transactional process does not take place, disrupted mother-infant interactions are observed.

In the TMEHI the parent-infant dyad is considered the unit of intervention in which reciprocal influences are ongoing over time, for enjoyment and learning. Both parent and child are conceptualized to be in continuous/dynamic change as they develop, but they are also viewed as active and competent participants in their own learning and development. On this basis, an important objective of early intervention is to optimize or foster harmonious reciprocal and mutually enjoyable parent-infant interactions. It is assumed that through the interaction process infants will learn to act on the environment and to predict it, which, in turn, will foster competence, self-confidence, and trust in others—the basis of mental health. Similarly, it is assumed that parents will learn to read, respond to, and predict their child's behavior through interactions that consequently will foster parental competence and self-confidence.

Ecology of Human Development

In addition to the strong developmental/relationship base of the model, Bronfenbrenner's (1975, 1979) ecology of human development theory influenced the transactional model of early intervention. Bronfenbrenner has suggested that for early intervention to be effective, all elements of the child's environment need to work in concert. Borrowing also from Piagetian theory of cognitive development, Bronfenbrenner postulated that both the child and his/her ecological context accommodate to one another over time, and that the child actively participates in the construction of reality or the knowledge of his/her ecological setting.

In his book *The Ecology of Human Development*, Bronfenbrenner (1979) developed an ecological systems theory of different orders of influence to explain the development of the child, similar in some ways to the family systems theory pioneered by Minuchin (1974). However, in Bronfenbrenner's theory, the child, not the entire family, is treated in relation to the broader ecological system. He acknowledged the influence of the larger social setting on the developing child and the interconnectedness of community life.

Presumably, the ecological setting (home environment, family members) goes through transitions as well, to accommodate to the child's new skills and to adjust parental expectations. Bronfenbrenner, however, does not see families as dynamic ecological systems exhibiting a wide range of needs and strengths interconnected with the larger system, the community.

Family/Social Systems Theory

Minuchin's (1974) family systems theory shaped the prevailing psychiatric focus on the individual in clinical practice. Minuchin saw the family as the interactional system in which the symptomatic behavior of children is embedded. Like Bronfenbrenner, Minuchin utilized the Piagetian concepts of accommodation and assimilation to explain how the family and its subsystems change. He also used the terms "boundaries" "and" "hierarchies" to explain how change and information are regulated from one subsystem to another. For example, open boundaries would facilitate development by allowing interactions among family members to occur. Through accommodation to internal and external stresses, assimilation of general family patterns, and membership in subsystems such as relationships with the mother or father, children develop a sense of belonging.

In the TMEHI the parent-infant unit is considered a system within a larger ecological context or system composed of various subsystems: the family unit (parents and siblings), the extended family (grandparents and other relatives), friends, and community organizations (church, schools, health, social and recreational centers). These systems are all interconnected and therefore cannot be ignored when addressing the specific needs of delayed or at-risk infants.

Taking the parent-infant dyad, the ecological context, and the family relational systems concepts together, another objective of the TMEHI is to foster open communication and mutual positive interaction across the subsystems, from the parent-child system to other family members, friends, and the community at large. Specifically, considering the needs of a developmentally delayed infant and his/her parent(s), the TMEHI promotes enabling parents to mobilize their own internal or personal resources, their child's strengths and competencies, and the strengths and needs of external resources within their family and community. Moreover, the family, with its unique cultural background, available resources, and needs, should dictate where, when, and what areas of identified needs should be addressed in early intervention.

COMPONENTS OF THE MODEL

The major components of the model are: (a) the recipients, (b) needs assessment, (c) educational strategies, (d) therapeutic strategies and curriculum, and (e) evaluation. Each of these is described briefly.

The Recipients

Within the TMEHI the recipient of intervention is the parent-child dyad in the context of the family and the community. As such, the model addresses all of the following: (a) the child's developmental needs and competencies; (b) parents' need to develop adequate skills and confidence in their various roles; (c) the family as a unit with its needs, strengths, and cultural background; (d) the unique characteristics of the home environment (economic, educational); (e) the complex transactions (interactions over time) among the family members; (f) the complex transactions between the family unit and the extended family and friends; (g) the transactions between the family and the community; and (h) the transactions between parents, other members of the family, and the intervention staff.

Although the scope of the TMEHI is quite wide, decision making regarding the setting of priorities and the selection of needs to be addressed is a critical first step in the intervention process. The decision-making step involves close collaboration between the staff and parents. The following components will describe the steps leading to decision making.

Needs Assessment

Any intervention must be preceded by a needs assessment. This intervention model makes a comprehensive developmental/ecological/family assessment essential in order to identify individual, dyadic, and family needs and strengths. While needs are prioritized, strengths serve as the basis for building competence and confidence. Assessment is based on verbal reports by parents and other relevant individuals, on direct observation of parent-child behaviors and interactions within and outside of their natural context of the home environment, and on developmental examination.

Educational Strategies

The therapeutic/educational components are interwoven, as the model of intervention addresses provision of information, training, and psychosocial support. This is best exemplified in the problem-solving training that is described below. For clarity, however, these components are described separately. Specifically, the educational strategies are divided into two sections, one that discusses general educational strategies and the other that refers to specific parenting skills and infants' developmental needs.

Didactic strategies. Since parents differ in their level of motivation to become involved in an intervention program—and in their skills, personality, and belief system regarding child rearing—a variety of didactic strategies are included in this model. These range from direct instruction (in which the parent is a passive recipient of information), to demonstration, modeling, role playing, prompting, and suggesting (in which parents play an active role with direct or indirect guidance), to simply guiding parental observations to foster self-directed/self-motivated learning and information sharing. All through this continuum, a Socratic questioning technique is utilized, reinforced with support for self-direction.

The self-motivated learning approach used within the model is based on the McMaster model of education, in which it is assumed that the learner is interested in learning, is able to direct his/her own learning, and plays an active role throughout the learning process with the guidance of a tutor (Hamilton, 1976; Neufeld & Barrows, 1974). Self-motivated learning is considered the optimal strategy for teaching parenting skills, problem solving, and identification of needs and strengths. Self-motivated learning empowers parents as it makes them independent of professionals, gives them full control of their family affairs, and strengthens their confidence in their own skills.

Developmental curriculum. Although in the TMEHI the target of intervention is the parent-child dyad, the educational strategies of the model were designed with the parent in mind as mediator of the environment for the young child, and thus as recipient of the intervention. However, it is recognized that the child plays an active role in the transactions with parents and others and in his/her development. Therefore, development of specific parenting skills is based on the child's developmental level, needs, temperamental style; the nature of the parent-child interaction; and on parental knowledge, experience, temperamental style, and needs.

The actual implementation of the intervention takes into account how active both parent and child are in their mutual transactions. The degree of active involvement may depend on a variety of factors: temperamental differences; the child's developmental level; parental ambivalence toward the child; or a combination of many factors, including unidentified ones. One of the goals of the intervention is to assist parents in synchronizing their activity level to that of their child, based on the child's developmental level. For that purpose, the *Curriculum Manual of Developmental Activities for Teaching Parents and Infants* (Barrera et al., 1984) was developed. This curriculum manual was designed as a guide to enable parents and professionals working with young developmentally delayed children to tailor individual program plans with active parent-child participation. The use of this manual requires an initial thorough assessment of the child, the home environment, and the relationship between child and parent, to determine developmental level in every area of development in addition to strengths and weaknesses of the environment. This information serves as the basis for selecting specific developmental activities.

The actual *curriculum* is organized under the following sections, based on the sequence of normal child development during the first two years of life: perceptual-cognitive, communication/socioemotional, fine and gross motor, and self-help skills. There are approximately 400 developmental activities, and each stresses the active interaction between parent and child, the interrelationship and interdependence between the various developmental areas. Activities within each section are grouped by trimesters of functional age in months: 0–3, 3–6, 6–9, 9–12, 12–18, and 18–24. Functional age is defined as the expected age during which a specific skill is observed in the average child.

Therapeutic Strategies

The therapeutic strategies refer to three areas of socioemotional support for parents and families: (a) socioemotional support and counseling; (b) parent-infant psychotherapy; and (c) problem-solving training.

Socioemotional support and counseling. This is support provided to parents who may be experiencing personal or interpersonal conflict in relation to any one or more of the following: circumstances surrounding the birth of the child, the baby's condition, or other life events. Empathetic listening, assistance in identifying parental needs (as well as those of the family and child), prioritizing those needs, and generating ways to address them are part of the support. The type of resources offered to parents depends on the nature, severity, and complexity of the needs. The needs may be addressed solely within the Infant-Parent Program or by the program in collaboration with other community services.

Parent-infant psychotherapy. The basic approach consists of encouraging parents to engage in behaviors that facilitate initiation and maintainance of social interaction with their baby, for example, holding the baby face-to-face to maximize eye contact, vocalizing, and smiling. Parents are coached to respond to their baby's cues and to observe the baby's reactions in order to learn to modulate their own behavior, a method similar to Fraiberg's (1977) technique.

Problem-solving training. Problem-solving techniques have been used educationally and therapeutically in a variety of ways. In the TMEHI, problem solving is the basis of the intervention relationship with parents. Through problem-solving training, parents develop cognitive-behavioral strategies to solve any identified problem. This parental problem-solving approach is modeled partly on cognitive behavior principles (Beck, 1976) similar to Jacobson's approach to marital therapy (Jacobson & Gurman, 1986), and partly on the problem-solving model of education adopted at the McMaster University Medical School.

Problem-solving training alone applied to parenting has been used with some success with physically abusive and neglectful parents (Dawson, de Armas, McGrath, & Kelly, 1986; Hansen et al., 1989; MacMillan, Guevremont, & Hansen, 1988). Typically, training has consisted of a set number of sessions of problem solving over hypothetical vignettes of problem situations where, through modeling and prompting, generation of alternative solutions is accomplished. In the TMEHI the actual problem-solving steps are:

1. Identify the problem(s) or need(s) of the child, parent, and family by actually listing them. This process facilitates a more objective approach to problem solving.

2. Select one problem at a time to deal with, based on parental/child needs and priorities.

3. Define the problem, identifying its components, as in the following examples: behavioral (e.g., prerequisite behavioral repertoire of the child or the parent), cognitive (e.g., Is the child or parent ready for the task? Is basic knowledge in place?), emotional (e.g., how parent feels about it), social (e.g., What are the family supports? Can others help?), situational/physical (e.g., family has no car, apartment is too small).

4. Identify possible solutions. List ways in which the need can be met, analyzing each of the components.

5. Select the solution that is most likely to succeed and hence enhance parental self-confidence and sense of competence.

6. Implement and assess effectiveness of the solution.

Evaluation

There are some difficulties in doing evaluation research with developmentally delayed infants. Ethical considerations and economic constraints are some of these difficulties. However, other variables have also contributed to the difficulties in evaluating intervention effectiveness, the heterogeneous nature of this group being one of them. For example, neuromotor deficits are often highly individualized, making it difficult to obtain matched control subjects (Denhoff, 1981).

Notwithstanding these problems, evaluation research is an integral part of the TMEHI. The empirical section of this chapter illustrates some of the key variables that receive strong attention under the evaluation component of the model.

IMPLEMENTATION OF THE TMEHI: THE INFANT-PARENT PROGRAM

The main objectives of the Infant-Parent Program are (a) to help parents to develop effective ways of relating with their infants, (b) to foster maximum developmental potential, (c) to promote reciprocal parent-infant interactions, and (d) to enable parents to develop confidence in their parenting role and skills. In the following sections, the main components of the program and of the intervention process are described briefly under the following headings: the staff, staff training and support; program stages; program coordination process; other services; and program evaluation.

The Staff, Staff Training and Support

The program staff consists of a multidisciplinary team to provide comprehensive assessment, treatment, and consultation services to families. The team consists of a program director, a program coordinator, infant-parent therapists, a psychologist, pediatricians, a psychometrist, a social worker, and a speech pathologist. Other services—for example, audiology, nutrition, and physio/occupational therapy—are also available to families who need them from other programs within the hospital.

The infant-parent therapist (IPT) works directly and regularly with parents, infants, and their families, whereas the rest of the staff may see the family periodically for assessments and recommendations or may play a consultative role. Although all members of the team are trained on the basic philosophy of the intervention, training of the IPT is particularly intense given the nature of the job.

The IPT is trained to observe parental patterns of responsivity, (as described by Bell and Ainsworth, 1972), including predictability during parent-infant interactions, and to recognize potential problems, for example, timing of responding, tone of utterances, and pauses between utterances. The IPT is also trained to identify potential family difficulties, for example, behavior problems with older siblings, or marital discord. These observations are used to foster parental self-awareness of the problem, to define the problem, and to come up with alternative solutions in the manner described in previous sections.

Throughout the intervention process the role of the IPT varies, depending on the identified needs and parental resources; however, the following key components of the IPT's role must be emphasized: as facilitator (with access to resources/services and training in problem solving); as resource for information about child development or community resources; and as case manager, working in collaboration with parents to maintain regular contact with all professionals who aid the family, and to keep track of their services without taking over the parental right of decision making.

Recognizing that the ultimate objective is to assist parents in becoming managers of the services provided to their children, the IPT does not do for the parents but assists parents in doing things for themselves. For example, if parents are unclear about specific recommendations given by another professional, parents are assisted in identifying and writing down the questions and are encouraged to contact the professional themselves.

An area that has been given very little attention in the early intervention field is the impact on the frontline staff of working with families who have developmentally delayed infants. Clinical experience suggests that direct support to staff by peers and supervisors is essential in maintaining a healthy approach to working with these families. Often times the family's pain is difficult to bear; other times the parents' difficulty in accepting their disabled infant may manifest in anger toward those professionals they encounter. Staff must have the opportunity to discuss their own feelings in a supportive environment. In the Infant-Parent Program, emotional support is provided on a personal basis by the supervisor and can be initiated either by the supervisor herself or by the therapist. This is an important aspect of intervention maintenance, as staff may find it difficult to cope with others' needs when their own needs are not met. Emotional support is provided also through case reviews where each therapist shares concerns and personal frustrations, in addition to information regarding intervention progress.

Program Stages

Intake process. Upon referral to the program by a physician or other health professional, detailed information regarding the following is obtained, by phone or in person, from the referral source and the parents: the reason(s) for referral, family demography, child and family characteristics, and other professional services being received. This information is gathered by the program coordinator, who then presents it at the intake meeting for discussion and decision making regarding the appropriateness of the referral.

Assessment stage. Initial assessments include clinic-based developmental pediatric assessment and home psychosocial assessment for all cases. Audiology, social work, speech/communication, and physio/occupational therapy assessments may be followed for some cases, if necessary. Developmental pediatric assessments are done by pediatricians specializing in developmental disabilities.

The psychosocial assessment is completed by the psychometrist in the family home, with the child, parents, and other members of the family often present. The objective of the home assessment is twofold: to provide an objective evaluation of developmental progress and of the caretaking environment, and to provide the data base for program evaluation. The home assessment identifies general areas of concern and strength regarding the child's development, the parent-child interaction, the physical environment, and the family in general. The following instruments are utilized for this assessment: the Bayley Mental and Motor Scales (Bayley, 1969), the Home Observation for Measurement of the Environment (HOME: Caldwell, 1978), the Infant and Toddler Temperament Questionnaires (Carey & McDevitt, 1978; McDevitt & Carey, 1978), the Minnesota Child Development Inventory (Ireton & Thwing, 1974), the Minnesota Infant Development Inventory (Ireton & Thwing, 1980), and the Parenting Stress Index (Abidin, 1983).

In addition, observations of parent-infant interaction are recorded during free play, and ratings of family support are obtained using a scale adapted from Dunst, Trivette, and Deal (1988). Home assessment is repeated at regular intervals, depending on the child's age at referral. The minimum number of assessments for all clients is two, at entry and at exit.

Intervention treatment. The main form of intervention consists of regular home visits for one to two hours by an IPT, weekly, every other week, or monthly, depending on the progress made by the parents and child. The objectives of the first home intervention visits include the following: (a) to develop rapport and a trusting relationship with the family; (b) to learn more about the family's cultural values, parenting styles, and family resources; (c) to determine specific strengths and needs of the child, the parents, and the family; (d) to examine the nature of the parent-infant interaction; and (e) to develop a collaborative working relationship with parents in which the parents feel that they have control over the decision making. Subsequently, in partnership with parents, goals and objectives of the intervention are identified in relation to the child, the home environment, and the parent-child interaction. For each visit, the IPT prepares a tentative program plan and writes a brief home report describing what actually happened during the visit.

To monitor the child's development, the IPT administers the Infant-Parent Program Developmental Checklist. Parents are updated regularly about the child's performance on this instrument. The checklist is a useful tool for assisting parents to develop and maintain realistic expectations about their child, while setting up the home environment to promote optimal development.

As part of the intervention process evaluation, the IPT keeps an ongoing record of contacts with the family or other professionals involved. Record is also kept of the focus of each home visit: the proportion of time during the visit spent on issues related to the child alone, the parent alone, the parent-child, the family as a whole, the physical environment, or community resources. Finally, at the end of the intervention, the IPT completes a treatment summary that includes information such as months of treatment, number of home visits, cancelations, and so on.[1]

Program Management Process

After referral, families are first contacted by phone by the program coordinator to confirm their awareness of and reason for the referral, to determine their interest in the program, and to arrange a home visit to complete the intake information-gathering process described above. Subsequently, a visit to the clinic is arranged for pediatric examination, and a visit or two to the home is scheduled for the standard psychosocial assessment. When the initial assessments are completed, the family may be assigned to an IPT, who becomes the family's primary contact.

From program entry to termination, the coordinator of the program monitors the services provided to the families and organizes initial review and discharge case conferences with the multidisciplinary team. During these conferences intervention services are integrated and additional recommendations for parents may be discussed. These recommendations are usually presented to parents by the IPT, who will assist parents in the decision-making process through the problem-solving strategies previously described.

Review of cases is done with the multidisciplinary team every other month for supervision, consultation, information sharing, and coordination of services. In addition, meetings with the supervisor regarding individual cases are initiated by either the IPT or the supervisor for additional supervision and support.

As the child approaches two years of age, preparation for discharge begins. This consists of exploring community resources that may be useful for the family and the child, making the necessary referrals, and assisting the family to set priorities regarding alternative programs and services suitable to their needs. At this stage in the intervention process, usually parents already have a network of support systems through their extended family, friends, or community services. The mobilization of this network is essential in supporting parents during the transition from the program to other services. The coordination of internal and external agency services is carefully organized through collaborative work by the coordinator and the IPT.

Other Services

Various forms of additional services for families are provided through the program. These include a toy and equipment lending library and a book library with a selection for parents on child development, parenting, specific handicaps, behavior management, and so on. Throughout the year, therapeutic and educational parent groups are offered as an alternative to individual family home intervention, and special recreational events are organized for the families in the program, with transportation provided when needed. During the summer, parent groups are also available and involve organized recreational outings and educational groups that focus on topics chosen by parents.

Program Evaluation

Evaluation includes the following: standardized pre- and post-intervention developmental measures, and for children aged less than twelve months, review assessments performed by the psychometrist; intervention process evaluation based on the IPTs' reports; and consumer perception/satisfaction, measured at the end of the intervention using a Parent Satisfaction Questionnaire developed by the Infant-Parent Program staff.

EMPIRICAL EVIDENCE ON DEVELOPMENTALLY DELAYED INFANTS AND THEIR PARENTS

In this section some empirical evidence from the application of the TMEHI with developmentally delayed infants and their parents is presented. Given that there is consensus in the literature that most early intervention approaches result in some benefits for delayed infants, we were concerned not with the global efficacy question but with the following two specific questions: (a) Is the impact of the TMEHI approach to early intervention the same for all categories of developmentally delayed infants? and (b) Is early enrollment better?

Although the model and its program evaluation include outcome measures that focus on the parent-child dyad and on the parent and child individually, in this chapter only child developmental and home environmental outcomes are reported. Specifically, the rate of development of delayed infants who were enrolled in the program is described, along with changes in their caretaking environment. The last section of the results examines what combination of variables—child, home environment, and treatment process—best predicts developmental outcome and changes in the home environment at the end of intervention.

Subjects

There were 119 infants who obtained a score of less than eighty-five on the Bayley Mental Scale at program entry. They represented a widely heterogeneous group of infants referred to the program between 1979 and 1988. Infants had had at least an initial and an upon-discharge psychometric assessment and were living at home with their families. Of the 119 infants, 57 (48%) obtained a score below fifty; 34 (29%) between fifty and sixty-nine, and 28 (24%) between seventy and eighty-five. Thus, 77% of the infants were considered to have mild to severe delay in their development at the time of referral. Based mainly on the etiology associated with the delay, the following six subgroups were formed:

1. *Environmental risk (ENV)*: Twenty-seven apparently biologically intact infants who were born to parents with identified poor parenting skills or extreme inexperience, including parents with mental illness or mental retardation.

2. *Prematurity (PREM)*: Seventeen infants whose delay was attributed to complications of prematurity (e.g., gestational age of less than thirty-seven weeks, birth weight of less than 2500g): bronchopulmonary dysplasia, apnea, seizures, ventricular hemorrhages, and the like.

3. *Down syndrome (DS)*: Sixteen infants who were diagnosed as having Down syndrome.

4. *Physical handicaps (PH)*: Twenty-one infants who exhibited various degrees of motor impairments (mainly of the cerebral palsies) or sensory impairments as the primary problem. This group included three legally blind babies and one with severe hearing loss.

5. *Multihandicaps (MH)*: Twenty-seven infants with identified severe delay in more than one developmental area—motor, perceptual, or cognitive—typically associated with established neurological impairment. This group included one autistic infant and five with rare congenital syndromes that are associated with severe retardation.

Table 5.1
Demographic Characteristics of the Six Subgroups of Developmentally Delayed Infants

Parameters	ENV	PREM	DS	GDUR	PH	MH
N	27	17	16	11	21	27
Infant Age						
Entry $\underline{M}$	14	9	7	14	13	12
	(5.8)[1]	(2.4)	(4.4)	(4.7)	(5.2)	(4.8)
Exit $\underline{M}$	24	20	24	24	24	23
	(2.0)	(3.0)	(1.1)	(0.8)	(2.2)	(2.2)
% Males	70	76	38	73	33	70
Mother's						
Age $\underline{M}$	26	30	30	31	27	29
	(5.2)	(6.1)	(7.4)	(2.1)	(5.2)	(7.2)
Father's						
Age $\underline{M}$	31	34	32	31	30	31
	(7.0)	(6.5)	(7.3)	(4.9)	(6.1)	(6.6)
Marital Status						
% Married	30	76	36	43	44	74
SES[2] $\underline{M}$	6	4	3	5	4	4
	(.94)	(1.6)	(1.6)	(1.3)	(1.6)	(1.4)

1. Standard deviations are in brackets.
2. On a scale of 1 to 6, 6 represents low socioeconomic status and 1 represents high socioeconomic status.

6. *General delay for unknown reasons (GDUR)*: Eleven infants who had been diagnosed as developmentally delayed but for whom no major biological or environmental concerns had been identified. This group included a child experiencing kidney dysfunction.

Table 5.1 presents the demographic characteristics of the six subgroups of delayed infants and their families. Except for the infants with Down syndrome, whose mean age at referral was seven months, most of the other infants were referred at about their first birthday: 45%

Table 5.2

Number of Infants at Each Age of Referral (in months) by the Six Subgroups

Age	Total	ENV	PREM	DS	GDUR	PH	MH
Prior to 6 Months	25	33	4	8	1	4	5
6 to 12 Months	41	10	11	6	2	3	9
Over 12 Months	53	14	2	2	8	14	13

of the infants were referred after their first year of life; 34% between six and twelve months; and only 21% were referred before six months of age. Table 5.2 presents the age of referral by diagnostic subgroups.

Outcome Measures

Although we are using a variety of measures to evaluate the program, as indicated above, only data from the Bayley scales, the HOME inventory, and the treatment process are presented here. The treatment process variables were duration of treatment (in months), number of home visits, mean duration of home visits (in minutes), focus of the home visit (i.e., whether on the needs of the child, the parents, the family, or on all three), and number of external agencies involved with the family. These treatment variables are first described for each of the subgroups, and subsequently included in a multiple regression analysis in order to examine outcomes in relation to the actual treatment.

Data Analysis

The results from the Bayley Scales are presented as standard mental scores (MDI), standard motor scores (PDI), developmental age (based on the mental raw scores), and relative developmental gain (RDG). RDG is a ratio that takes into account months of treatment, and is computed as follows: mental developmental age at exit minus mental developmental age at entry, divided by months of treatment. The lower the ratio the smaller the developmental gain. This ratio has been used by Marfo and his associates (1988), but Marfo (1990) now considers it an index of the rate of development during intervention (RDI). ANOVAs were run on the MDI, PDI, and RDG, while a MANOVA was performed on the HOME subscales.

Table 5.3
Treatment Information

Parameters	ENV	PREM	DS	GDUR	PH	MULTI
Duration of Treatment (months)	10 (5.5)[1]	13 (3.9)	17 (4.7)	9 (3.4)	10 (4.7)	11 (4.9)
No. of Home Visits	22 (11.1)	20 (8.8)	29 (13)	20 (8.6)	23 (8.6)	23 (2.2)
Duration of Home Visit (mins.)	99 (19)	102 (22)	103 (16)	100 (20)	106 (26)	87 (10)
Focus of Home Visit (%)[2]						
CHILD	9	30	28	25	25	26
PARENT	28	28	10	16	29	26
HOME	4	5	7	10	7	9
ALL THREE	58	37	54	48	38	38
No. of Agencies involved[3]	2 (1.6)	1 (1)	1 (.8)	1 (1.3)	2 (1.2)	3 (1.9)

1. Standard deviations are in brackets.
2. Percent based on group data.
3. Other than the services in the hospital.

Finally, multiple regression analyses were run to determine the predictors of (a) development and (b) the caretaking environment at two years. These predictors were chosen from the treatment process data, child developmental data, and the HOME scores.

RESULTS

Treatment Process Data

Table 5.3 presents treatment information on the six subgroups of families. Except for the families with Down syndrome infants, who had longer involvement and more visits, the average treatment duration was approximately twelve months, and the average number of home treatment visits was twenty-one. As far as the duration of the home visits was concerned, it appeared that the groups were consistent at approximately 1.5 hours per visit.

Data on the focus of the home visits yielded some interesting findings:

for the environmentally at-risk families the focus on the child alone was 9%, whereas for the other groups it was approximately 25% to 30%. Families with multihandicapped infants were involved with more agencies than any other group, followed by families with physically handicapped and environmentally at-risk infants. These variables were included in the multiple regression analyses reported later in this section.

Developmental Data

Mental and motor scores. A 2 (time) x 6 (diagnostic group) ANOVA on the MDI scores yielded significant diagnostic group $(F_{(5,113)} = 10.89, p < .001)$ and time of assessment $(F_{(1,113)} = 11.30, p < .001)$ main effects, and a group x time interaction effect $(F_{(5,113)} = 3.85, p < .003)$. These significant effects are depicted in Figure 5.1. Although the groups differed in their scores, and an overall increment was observed in the before and after comparison, some groups increased their scores whereas others actually showed a decrement. At entry, the environmentally at-risk and premature infants obtained mental scores at about the same level as the scores of the infants with Down syndrome (between fifty and fifty-five).

At exit, the scores of the infants with Down syndrome showed a slight decrement, whereas those of the environmentally at-risk and premature infants showed a significant increment $(p < .05)$. Another interesting pattern is seen in the mental scores of the physically handicapped infants, compared with those of the multihandicapped. Whereas both groups showed a severe delay at entry, the physically handicapped infants showed a significant increment $(p < .05)$ in their scores by the end of the intervention, but the multihandicapped infants experienced a slight decrement. A similar pattern is seen in the motor scores, although the decrement in the scores of the infants with Down syndrome and those with multihandicaps was much greater.

Developmental age: In contrast to the standard scores, estimates of mental developmental age showed improvements in all the subgroups (see Figure 5.2). On the other hand, if we look at the developmental gap (the difference between chronological age and developmental age), the picture appears somewhat disappointing. The multihandicapped infants showed the greatest gap both at entry and at exit. While infants with Down syndrome showed the smallest gap at entry, the gap had increased by 3.5 months at exit. In fact, except for the premature infants, whose gap decreased by the end of intervention, the gap between chronological and developmental age increased in all the other groups. In the case of the premature infants, chronological age was not corrected

Figure 5.1
Bayley Mental (MDI) and Motor (PDI) Scores at Entry and Exit for the Six Subgroups of Infants

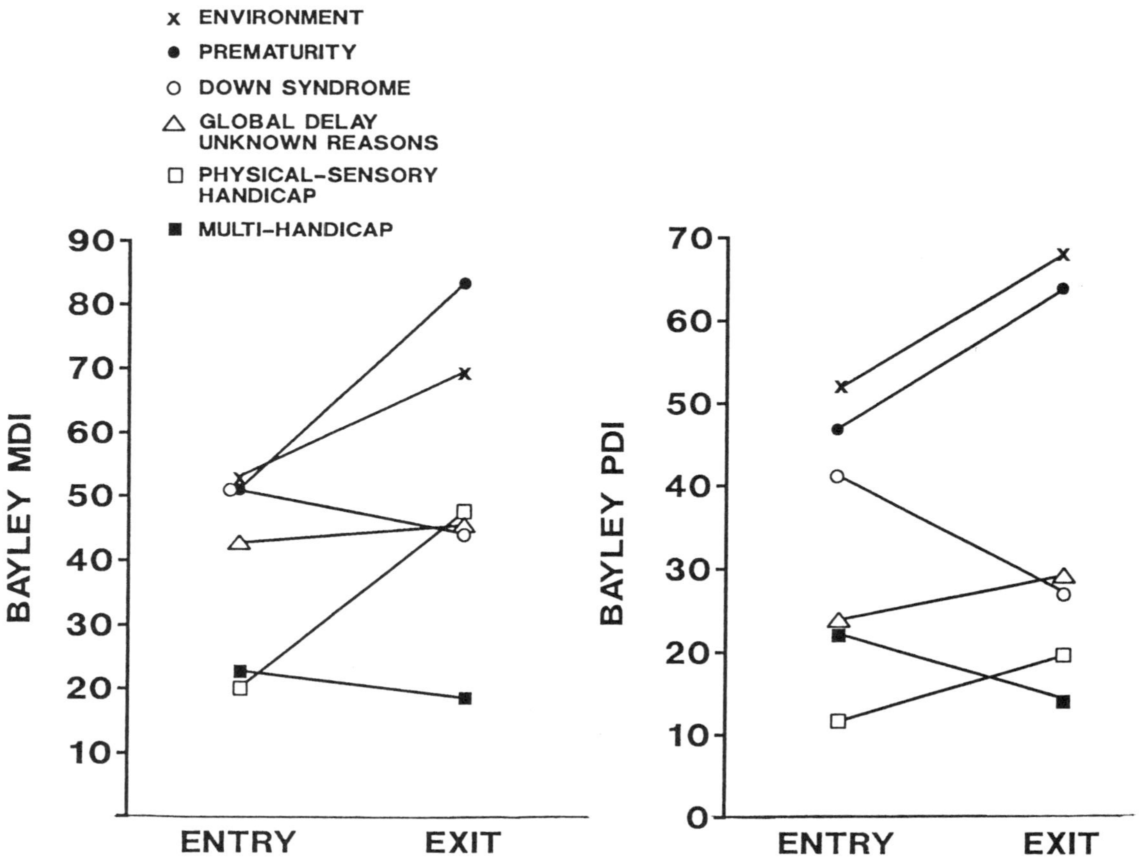

Figure 5.2
Developmental Age (Based on the Bayley Mental Scale) and Chronological Age at Entry and Exit
for the Six Subgroups of Infants

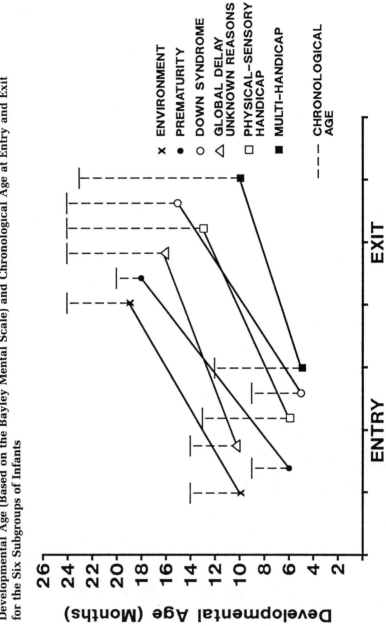

for prematurity; thus, the decrement in the gap may partially reflect greater maturity of their central nervous system.

Relative developmental gain: A one-way ANOVA comparing the six groups indicated a significant difference ($F_{(5,113)}$ = 4.93, p < .001). The environmentally at-risk and premature infants showed the greatest gain (.92 and .93, respectively), followed by the GDUR (.76), the PH (.68), the DS (.62), and the MH (.38) groups. Figure 5.3 shows these results.

Changes in the Caretaking Environment

The total scores on the HOME inventory, as a measure of the caretaking environment for developmentally delayed infants, showed that, except for the environmentally at-risk infants, at entry all groups scored in the upper 25% and remained there at exit.

A 2 × 6 ANOVA using the total HOME scores yielded significant differences between the diagnostic groups ($F_{(5,113)}$ = 19.90, p < .001), pre- and post-program assessment ($F_{(1,113)}$ = 7.27, p < .005), and a significant interaction between the two variables ($F_{(5,113)}$ = 4.07, p < .002). Post-hoc analysis of the group effect revealed significant differences between the ENV group and each of the other groups (Tukey, p < .05). Analysis of the interaction effect indicated a significant difference between the ENV group and each of the other groups at entry, and a significant difference between the ENV and the PREM groups at exit (Scheffe, p < .05). Except for the scores of the ENV group, which were mainly in the twenty-fifth percentile, the scores of the other groups, particularly those of the GDUR, may reflect a ceiling effect. Figure 5.4 presents these findings.

Analyses of the HOME subcategories indicated significant group differences in all the subcategories (all F values were significant at p < .001). Improvement in the scores was obtained in emotional responsivity ($F_{(1,116)}$ = 13.94, p < .001), provision of materials ($F_{(1,116)}$ = 75.87, p < .0001), and opportunities for variety in stimulation ($F_{(1,116)}$ = 15.24, p < .001). A significant interaction between the two variables was found in maternal involvement and is shown in Figure 5.5. Maternal involvement increased significantly (p < .05) in the environmentally at-risk group, and in the physically handicapped and multihandicapped groups, which were those with the lower scores at entry.

Age at Entry and Changes in Developmental Scores

A 2 (time) × 3 (age at entry) ANOVA was performed for the mental scores and the motor scores. The mental scores yielded significant main effects for age ($F_{(2,116)}$ = 3.19, p < .045) and time of assessment ($F_{(1,116)}$ = 10.03, p < .002). Analysis of the main effect for age indicated a

Figure 5.3
Relative Development Gain (or Rate of Development During Intervention, for the Six Subgroups of Infants

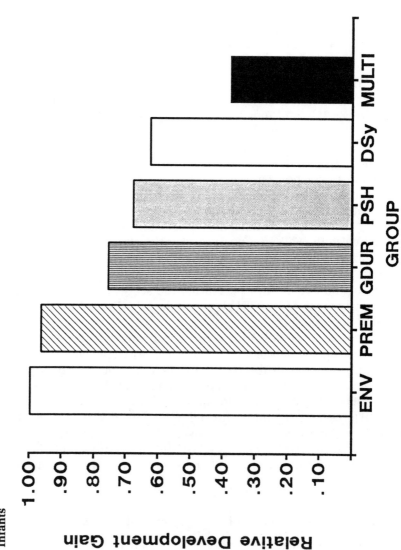

Figure 5.4
Caldwell HOME Inventory Total Scores at Entry and Exit for the Six Subgroups of Infants

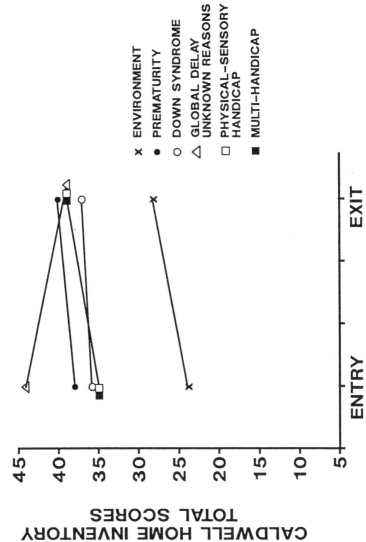

Figure 5.5
Home Maternal Involvement Scores at Entry and Exit for the Six Subgroups of Infants

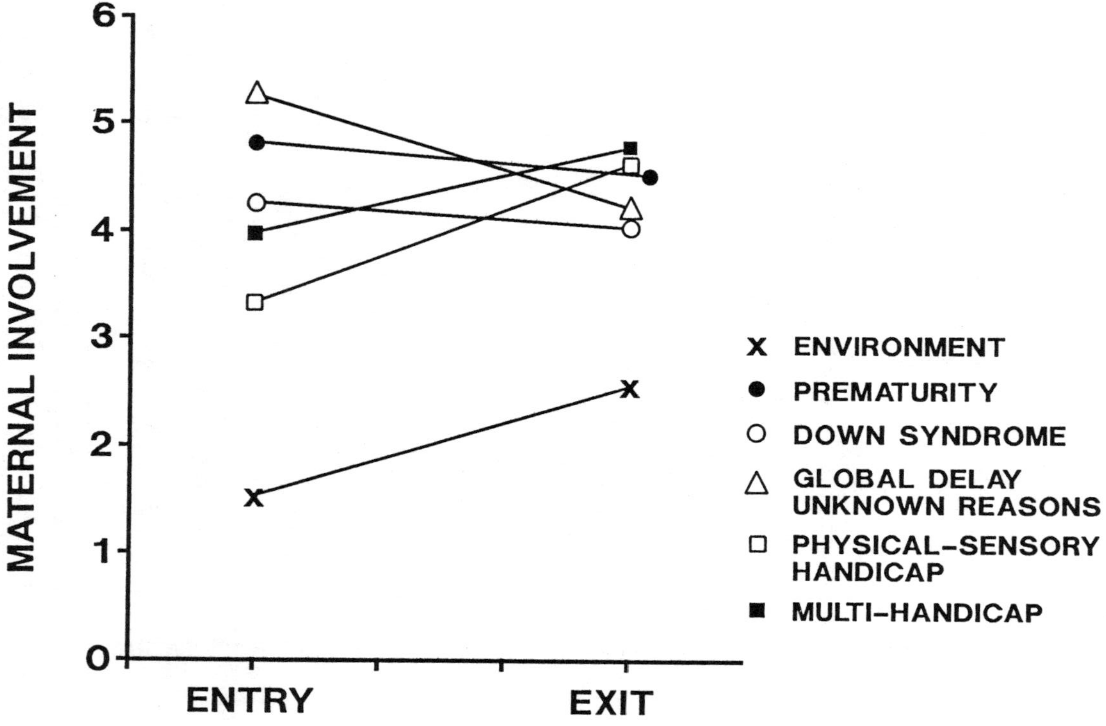

progression from the lowest scores for the infants over twelve months of age at referral to the highest scores for the infants referred at less than six months of age. The main effect for time confirmed an overall increment in the scores, observed in the previous analysis.

The motor scores yielded a significant interaction for age of entry and time of assessment ($F_{(2,116)}$ = 4.88, $p < .009$), which is shown in Figure 5.6. All age groups showed an increment in their scores. However, the PDI scores of infants who started the intervention before six months of age were significantly higher both at entry and at exit than the scores of the infants who enrolled in the program after their first birthday.

Age at Entry and Changes in the HOME Scores

The total HOME scores indicated a significant main effect for time ($F_{(1,116)}$ = 13.94, $p < .001$), suggesting an improvement in the overall home environment. This improvement was confirmed in the subscales of maternal responsivity ($F_{(1,116)}$ = 7.41, $p < .007$), maternal involvement ($F_{(1,116)}$ = 4.72, $p < .03$), provision of opportunities ($F_{(1,116)}$ = 75.87, $p < .0001$), and opportunities for variety of stimulation ($F_{(1,116)}$ = 15.24, $p < .001$). There was also an interaction of age and time of assessment in provision of materials, indicating significant increments ($p < .05$) for the "less-than-six-months" and "between-six-and-twelve months" groups ($F_{(2,116)}$ = 6.65, $p < .002$).

Prediction of Outcomes at Two Years

Two analyses are reported here. In the first, developmental age at exit was the dependent variable, and the following variables served as predictors: developmental age at entry, months of treatment, number of home visits, HOME at entry, HOME at exit, treatment focus (on child, parent, home, or all combined), duration of home visits, and number of agencies involved with the family. In the second analysis, total HOME scores at exit served as the dependent variable, and HOME at entry, developmental age at entry, months of treatment, number of home visits, treatment focus, duration of home visits, and number of agencies served as the predictors.

Developmental age at exit was significantly predicted by developmental age at entry, months of intervention, HOME scores, and number of home visits focusing on parent and child (R^2 = .50, $F_{(12,112)}$ = 8.42, $p < .001$). The HOME scores at exit were significantly predicted by the HOME scores at entry—the major contributor to the variance (21%)— developmental age at entry, number of home visits, and visits with the

Figure 5.6
Bayley Motor (PDI) Scores at Entry and Exit for Infants Enrolled at Less Than 6 Months, Between 6 and 12 Months, and Over 12 Months of Age

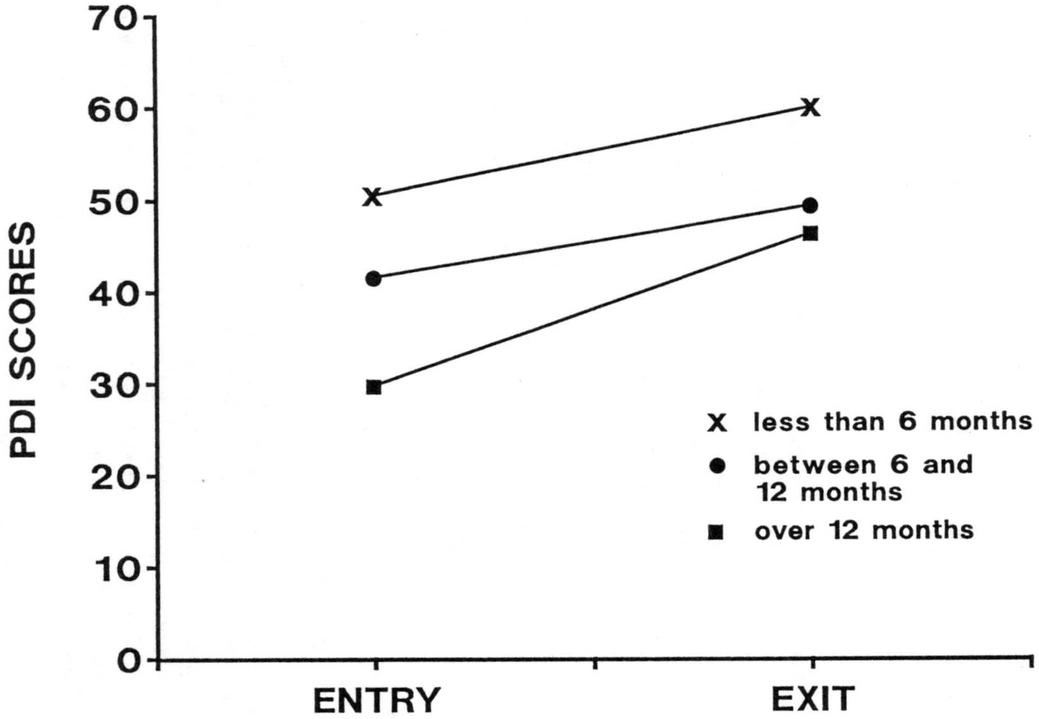

focus on all components of the home environment ($R^2 = .56$, $F_{(11,103)} = 12.17$, $p < .001$).

DISCUSSION AND SUMMARY

In this chapter I have described the transactional model of early home intervention (TMEHI) and the Infant-Parent Program and presented some empirical evidence regarding developmental and caretaking intervention outcomes. This evidence comes from developmentally delayed infants and their families, stratified into six groups based on the primary factor associated with the delay. It represents an example of the implementation of the model and addresses important questions in early intervention research with developmentally delayed infants and their families.

The evidence suggests that the rate of development during intervention varies across the various subgroups of delayed infants, with the environmentally and medically (premature) at-risk infants showing the greatest gain and the multihandicapped infants showing the poorest. The developmental data from the Bayley Mental Scale are presented in the standard MDI scores, as developmental age (DA), and in the RDG ratio, which takes into account one of the treatment variables—months of treatment. Both the MDIs and the PDIs suggest that with the exception of the Down syndrome and the multihandicap groups, children increased their cognitive competence over the intervention period. At first glance the MDI and the DA findings may appear contradictory, but careful examination indicates otherwise. The DA data indicate that all groups improved over the intervention period. However, the discrepancy analysis of developmental and chronological age, shown in Figure 5.2, places this progress into perspective. Although all groups showed improvement after intervention, the discrepancy between developmental age and chronological age became greater in the Down syndrome and multihandicap groups. The latter may reflect both relative degree of severity and differences in developmental patterns across the subgroups of developmentally delayed children.

The RDG ratio also identifies the Down syndrome and the multihandicap groups as showing the lowest developmental gain after intervention. Future research should systematically examine differences in developmental gain during short or long intervention periods with Down syndrome and multihandicapped children in order to ascertain the efficacy of intervention.

Analysis of developmental data by age of entry supports the hypothesis that intervention starting earlier results in greater developmental gains, although the motor performance data suggest that intervention starting around the first birthday may result in greater gains. Because of insufficient numbers, age at entry could not be stratified by subgroup. The question still remains of whether all subgroups of developmentally delayed infants will benefit from earlier enrollment in an early intervention program.

In summary, the developmental analyses described here suggest careful consideration of the various ways of measuring developmental outcome. MDIs and PDIs alone may not be appropriate when groups vary in their age of enrollment and in many other variables. At least with young children, developmental age may be a better developmental outcome measure than MDI, as it reflects different increments of developmental progress. The RDG ratio is useful in determining developmental gain during intervention, as it takes into consideration the duration of treatment. However, given the diversity of factors influencing development, the heterogeneous nature of developmental delay, and the variability in age of enrollment, multiple regression analyses seem more appropriate to determine the contribution of intervention than analyses that imply univariate effects.

The regression analyses described here support the hypothesis that developmental outcome at the end of intervention is predicted mainly by developmental age at entry *and* duration of intervention. Whereas the intervention had some beneficial effect on the child's development, such effect seems to be part of a complex contribution by many factors, particularly the child's own developmental characteristics. Future intervention research must consider the complexity of human development and examine systematically the multiplicity of factors, including intervention factors, that may contribute to developmental outcome.

The findings on the caretaking environment, measured by Caldwell's HOME inventory, revealed a different picture. Not surprising, the caretaking environment of the environmentally at-risk infants was the poorest both at entry and at exit (within the lower twenty-fifth percentile). The scores of the other subgroups were within the fiftieth to the upper twenty-fifth percentiles, suggesting adequate home environments. The maternal involvement subscale indicated significant caretaking environment improvements in the multihandicap and the physical handicap groups. This is an encouraging finding as the literature suggests that parental involvement with physically handicapped children decreases as the child grows older. Shere and Kastenbaum (1966) concluded that physically handicapped children may be in double jeopardy, initially by the organic, nonreversible impairment, and potentially by dysfunctional interactive patterns with parents that might further inhibit development. We are currently examining interaction data that may provide more evidence supporting the positive benefits of the intervention program for the parent-child relationship.

Analyses regarding intervention benefits for the parents and the entire family are in progress. Although there is no conclusive evidence supporting the assumption that for every family with a developmentally delayed child early enrollment is better, clinical wisdom suggests that parents should be offered support and early intervention as soon as the child is identified as being delayed or at risk for developmental delay, to assist them in adapting to the realities of parenting a disabled child.

Finally, this chapter has described the TMEHI as a relationship-focused model, with an ecological, developmental, family systems perspective. The TMEHI identifies the parent-infant dyad within the context of the family as the focus of intervention; it promotes optimal development of parents and infants in healthy families and mutual collaboration between the intervention recipients and intervention staff; it proposes problem-solving strategies as the main vehicle of intervention transactions; and it considers evaluation research an integral part of intervention. The objectives, focus, and implementation of the Infant-Parent Program reflect the components of the TMEHI. In the program, special emphasis is placed on the role of the infant-parent therapist as the frontline staff who works regularly with parents and their children in the setting of their own home. The comprehensive variety of services offered by the program reflects the scope of the TMEHI.

ACKNOWLEDGMENTS

Preparation of this chapter was supported by the Province of Ontario Ministry of Community and Social Services, and by the Chedoke-McMaster Hospitals, Hamilton, Ontario. I thank the staff of the Infant-Parent Program for sharing their experiences with parents and infants. Special thanks are due to Ann Sentpetery for her secretarial assistance, Dr. P. Rosenbaum, Mrs. Linda Hancock, and Mrs. Alayne Langerak for their comments on earlier versions of the manuscript. I also thank my husband, Mr. Kalman Bohus, for his support and understanding throughout my long hours of work.

NOTE

1. Copies of each of the instruments and record forms mentioned in this section are available upon request.

REFERENCES

Abidin, R. R. (1983). *The Parenting Stress Index*. Charlottesville, VA: Pediatric Psychology Press.

Affleck, G., McGrade, B. J., McQueeney, M., & Allen, D. (1982). Relationship-focused early intervention in developmental disabilities. *Exceptional Children, 49,* 259-261.

Allen, D. A. (1987). Measuring rehabilitation outcomes for infants and young children. In M.J. Fuhrer (Ed.), *Rehabilitation outcomes: Analyses and measurement* (pp. 185-195). Baltimore: Paul H. Brookes.

Ballard, J., Maloney, M., Shank, M., & Hollister, L. (1984). Sibling visits to a newborn intensive care unit: Implications for siblings, parents, and infants. *Child Psychiatry and Human Development, 11,* 203-214.

Barrera, M. E., Cunningham, C. C., & Rosenbaum, P. L. (1986). Low birth weight and home intervention strategies: Pre-term infants. *Journal of Developmental and Behavioral Pediatrics, 7*(6), 361-366.

Barrera, M. E., Doucet, D. A., & Kitching, K. J. (1990). Early home intervention and socio-emotional development of pre-term infants. *Infant Mental Health Journal, 11*(2), 142-157.

Barrera, M. E., Lounsbury, B., Toal, C., Miron, A., & Darling, J. (1984). *Curriculum manual of developmental activities for teaching parents and their children.* Hamilton, Ontario: Chedoke-McMaster Hospitals.

Barrera, M. E., & Rosenbaum, P. L. (1986). The transactional model of early home intervention. *Infant Mental Health Journal, 7,* 112-131.

Barrera, M. E., Rosenbaum, P. L., & Cunningham, C. E. (1986). Early home intervention with low birth weight infants and their parents. *Child Development, 57,* 20-33.

Bayley, N. (1969). *Bayley Scales of Infant Development.* New York: The Psychological Corporation.

Beck, A. T. (1976). *Cognitive therapy and the emotional disorders.* New York: International Universities Press.

Bell, R. Q. (1968). A reinterpretation of the direction of effects in studies of socialization. *Psychological Review, 75,* 81-95.

Bell, S. M., & Ainsworth, M.D.S. (1972). Infant crying and maternal responsiveness. *Child Development, 43,* 1171-1190.

Bromwich, R. (1981). *Working with parents and infants: An interactional approach.* Baltimore: University Park Press.

Bromwich, R. M., & Parmelee, A. H. (1979). An intervention program for pre-term infants. In T. M. Field, A. M. Sostek, S. Goldberg, & H. H. Shuman (Eds.), *Infants born at risk: Behavior and development.* (pp. 389-411). New York: Spectrum Publications.

Bronfenbrenner, U. (1975). Is early intervention effective? In M. Guttentag & E. Struening (Eds.), *Handbook of Evaluation Research: Vol. 2* (pp. 852-894). Beverly Hills: Sage.

Bronfenbrenner, U. (1979). *The ecology of human development.* Cambridge, MA.: Harvard University Press.

Caldwell, B. M. (1978). *Home observation for measurement of the environment.* Little Rock: University of Arkansas.

Carey, W. B., & McDevitt, S. C. (1978). Revision of the Infant Temperament Questionnaire. *Pediatrics, 61,* 735-739.

Casto, G., & Mastropieri, M. A. (1986). The efficacy of early intervention programs: A meta-analysis. *Exceptional Children, 52*(5), 417-424.

Dawson, B., de Armas, A., McGrath, M. L., & Kelly, J. A. (1986). Cognitive problem solving training to improve the child-care judgment of child neglectful parents. *Journal of Family Violence, 1,* 209-221.

Denenberg, V. H. (1969). Experimental programming of life histories in the rat. In A. Ambrose (Ed.), *Stimulation in Early Infancy* (pp. 21-43). London: Academic Press.

Denhoff, E. (1981). Current status of infant stimulation or enrichment programs for children with developmental disabilities. *Pediatrics, 67*(1), 32-37.

Dunst, C. J. (1985). Rethinking early intervention. *Analysis and Intervention in Developmental Disabilities, 5,* 165-201.

Dunst, C. J., & Rheingrover, R. M. (1981). An analysis of the efficacy of infant intervention programs with organically handicapped children. *Evaluation and Program Planning, 4,* 287-323.

Dunst, C. J., & Trivette, C. M. (1988). A family systems model of early intervention with handicapped and developmentally at-risk children. In D. R. Powell (Ed.), *Parent education as early childhood intervention: Emerging directions in theory, research, and practice* (pp. 131-179). Norwood, NJ: Ablex Publishing.

Dunst, C. J., Trivette, C. M., & Deal, A. (1988). *Enabling and empowering families.* Cambridge: Brookline Books.

Fraiberg, S. (1975). Intervention in infancy: A program for blind infants. In B. Z. Friedlander, G. M. Sterritt, & G. E. Kirk (Eds.), *Exceptional infant: Assessment and intervention: (Vol. 3)* (pp. 40-61). New York: Brunner/ Mazel.

Fraiberg, S. (1977). *Insight from the blind.* New York: Basic Books.

Guralnick, M. J., & Bricker, D. (1987). The effectiveness of early intervention for children with cognitive and general developmental delays. In M. J. Guralnick & F. C. Bennett (Eds.), *The effectiveness of early intervention for at-risk and handicapped children* (pp. 115-173). New York: Academic Press.

Halpern, R. (1984). Home-based early intervention: Emerging purposes, intervention approaches, and evaluation strategies. *Infant Mental Health Journal, 5*(4), 206-220.

Hamilton, J. D. (1976). The McMaster Curriculum: A critique. *British Medical Journal, 1,* 1191-1196.

Hansen, D. J., Pallota, G. M., Tishelman, A. C., Conway, L. P., & MacMillan, V. M. (1989). Parental problem solving skills and child behavior problems: A comparison of physically abusive, neglectful, clinic and community families. *Journal of Family Violence, 4*(4), 353-368.

Harris, S. (1987). Early intervention for children with motor handicaps. In M. J. Guralnick & F. C. Bennett (Eds.), *The effectiveness of early intervention for at-risk and handicapped children* (pp. 175-212). New York: Academic Press.

Hayden, A. H., & Haring, N. G. (1976). Early intervention with high risk infants and young children: Programs for Down syndrome children. In T. D. Tjossem (Ed.), *Intervention strategies for high risk infants and young children* (pp. 573-607). Baltimore: University Press.

Ireton, H., & Thwing, E. (1974). *Minnesota child development inventory.* Minneapolis: Interpretive Scoring Systems.

Ireton, H., & Thwing, E. (1980). *Minnesota infant development inventory.* Minneapolis: Interpretive Scoring Systems.

Jacobson, N. S., & Gurman, A. S. (Eds.). (1986). *Clinical handbook of marital therapy.* New York: The Guilford Press.

MacMillan, V. M., Guevremont, D. C., & Hansen, D. J. (1988). Problem-solving training with a multiply distressed abusive and neglectful mother: Effects on social insularity, negative affect, and stress. *Journal of Family Violence, 3*(4), 313-326.

Marfo, K. (1990, April). *Correlates and predictors of child developmental progress and parental satisfaction in an early intervention program.* Paper presented at the annual meeting of the American Educational Research Association, Boston.

Marfo, K., Browne, N., Gallant, D., Smyth, R., Corbett, A., & McLennon, D. (1988). *Early intervention with developmentally delayed infants and preschool children in Newfoundland and Labrador.* St. John's: Faculty of Education Publications Committee, Memorial University of Newfoundland, Canada.

Marfo, K., & Kysela, G. M. (1985). Early intervention with mentally handicapped children: A critical appraisal of applied research. *Journal of Pediatric Psychology, 10*(3), 305-324.

McDevitt, S. C., & Carey, W. B. (1978). The measurement of temperament in 3–7 year old children. *Journal of Child Psychology and Psychiatry, 17,* 223-228.

Minuchin, S. (1974). *Families and family therapy.* Cambridge, M.A.: Harvard University Press.

Neufeld, J. R., & Barrows, H. (1974). The "McMaster Philosophy": An approach to medical education. *Journal of Medical Education, 49,* 1040-1050.

Rappaport, J. (1981). In praise of paradox: A social policy of empowerment over prevention. *American Journal of Community Psychology, 9*(1), 1-25.

Sameroff, A., & Chandler, M. S. (1975). Reproductive risk and the continuum of caretaking casuality. In F. D. Horowitz, M. Hetherington, S. Scarr-Salapatek, & G. Siegel (Eds.), *Review of Child Development Research: Vol. 4* (pp. 187-244). Chicago: University of Chicago Press.

Shere, E., & Kastenbaum, R. (1966). Mother-child interaction in cerebral palsy: Environmental and psychosocial obstacles to cognitive development. *Genetic Psychology Monographs, 73,* 255-335.

Shonkoff, J. P., & Hauser-Cram, P. (1987). Early intervention for disabled infants and their families: A quantitative analysis. *Pediatrics, 80*(5), 650-658.

Simeonsson, R. J., Cooper, D. H., & Scheiner, A. P. (1982). A review and analysis of the effectiveness of early intervention programs. *Pediatrics, 69*(5), 635-641.

Spitz, R. A. (1945). Hospitalism. *Psychoanalytic Study of the Child, 1,* 53-74.

Tjossem, T. D. (Ed.). (1976). *Intervention Strategies for High Risk Infants and Young Children.* Baltimore: University Park Press.

6

At the Crossroad: Reviewing and Rethinking Interaction Coaching

Jeanette A. McCollum

Infants with a variety of disabilities and special needs bring to dyadic interactions with their caregivers characteristics and behaviors that may interfere with the pleasure and developmental appropriateness of those interactions. This chapter has two purposes. The first is to review one approach to interaction intervention—interaction coaching—as it has been applied to helping caregivers alter interactions with their infants with special needs. In order to identify and synthesize where we are now with regard to understanding these interventions, available research and project descriptions will be reviewed to extract themes related to goals, foci of intervention, and intervention procedures. The second purpose is to propose some future directions that will ground interaction coaching efforts within a broader family-centered orientation. Preliminary to these two purposes, the wider context of this fairly narrow realm of interaction coaching will be described. The intent is to clarify thinking about related lines of practice and research.

Few self-respecting early interventionists would propose that early intervention services for infants with special needs be delivered outside of the context of the family system. Parents have long been viewed as having essential roles in early intervention efforts, to the extent that strong beliefs regarding active family involvement undergird the whole early intervention movement (Guralnick, 1989). In actuality, however, it has been the case that services often are delivered outside of family environments or with family members playing passive rather than active roles. Due in large part to families themselves, this reality is changing (Turnbull & Summers, 1985): increasingly, families serve not only as supporters of intervention efforts made on behalf of their children (a "family-involvement-with-program" perspective), but rather as central players in these efforts (a "program-involvement-with-family" perspective).

In a recent analysis of early intervention efficacy research, Guralnick (1989) concluded that the one factor which may best differentiate successful from unsuccessful early intervention efforts is the degree to which families are supported in their own development as competent and confident caregivers of their children, as well as in their roles as central players in intervention. Parental competence is viewed increasingly as the most vital link to long-term early intervention effects. In the United States, this changing perspective on service delivery is illustrated most vividly in Public Law 99–457. A family-centered orientation is the heart of this new legislation. In essence, this law provides a framework for developing service delivery systems that support and facilitate each family's own competence in assuring its infant's optimal development. Within this framework, helping relationships in early intervention are, by definition, those that nurture, facilitate, and expand competence and independence in family members and in the family system as a whole. Increasingly, early intervention service delivery will be evaluated from the perspective of its congruence with these values.

Parent-infant interaction as a potentially powerful focus for early intervention with infants with special needs is a new and emerging phenomenon. Intuitively, it would appear that the concept of parent-infant interaction as a direct focus of intervention would fit naturally and easily within the larger movement toward family-centered intervention. Certainly this focus places intervention squarely at the center of each infant's most natural and powerful environment. Instead, the family systems movement and interaction intervention have developed largely in parallel. Consequently, different approaches to interaction intervention must be challenged in terms of their compatibility with the larger perspective of families as competent, able supporters of their infants' development.

In large part, the emerging focus on parent-infant interaction as an important aspect of early intervention reflects a deepening understanding of developmental and learning processes in all children, including children with special needs. Two perspectives on development are of particular relevance. First, early development is organized in such a way that its many different subsystems are inextricably intertwined: no domain of development proceeds without influencing and being influenced by all others (Walker & Crawley, 1983). Early on, different aspects of development are so interwoven that it is not possible to say that any particular behavior is a manifestation of any one area or domain (Hodapp & Mueller, 1982). A second and closely related perspective underlying the emerging emphasis on parent-infant interaction as an intervention focus is that all aspects of early development are embedded within a social context largely defined by social interactions with caregivers (Clarke-Stewart, 1973; Goldberg, 1977; Uzgiris, 1981). As a primary context of early life, social interactions appear to provide powerful underpinnings for the development of emotional systems (Tronick & Gianino, 1986), communication and language (Bricker & Carlson, 1981; Lowe & Dunst, 1985; Ratner & Bruner, 1977), and cognition (Bruner, 1974; Goldberg, 1977; Rogoff, Malkin, & Gilbride, 1984). Social interactions therefore play a central role in mediating the general development of competence (Marfo, 1990). Consequently, interactions are increasingly viewed by interventionists as critical entry points for exerting a positive influence on the infant's early development, both in general and with regard to specific aspects of development.

Successful dyadic interactions are characterized by mutual feelings of effectance, defined as the extent to which the partners perceive themselves as influencing the interactive behaviors of the other (Goldberg, 1977). Undergirding the normal establishment of a mutually reinforcing interactive process is the dyad's ability to capture or hold each other's attention and to reinforce each other. There is now a fairly extensive literature (see reviews by Field, 1980; Mitchell, 1987; Walker, 1982) indicating that infants with special needs bring to the social interactive situation characteristics and behaviors that may present unique challenges to their caregivers' ability to engage them in pleasurable, mutually reinforcing interactions. In general, this literature indicates that infants with various disabilities, as well as those born prematurely or with other conditions placing them at biological risk, may differ in ways that make them more difficult as social partners. Interactions may occur not only less spontaneously but may differ in overall structure (Field, 1980) or in the ways in which interactive modalities are used (McCollum, 1987; McCollum & Stayton, 1988). Infants with disabilities and other biological risk factors have been described as less readable, less responsive, and as taking less initiative during social interaction (Als, 1982; Emde, Katz, & Thorpe, 1978; Fischer, 1987; Fraiberg, 1974; Jones, 1977), making it more difficult for their caregivers to establish or maintain mutually satisfying interactions.

Dunst (1985) has interpreted the general problem posed by the biologically different infant as one of readability, resulting from a certain degree of misinformation that the infant brings to the interactive situation. Given the view of dyadic interaction as a transactional system, differences in the interactive characteristics of the infant's partner might be expected as well. Research has yielded fairly consistent results. In interaction with infants with biologically based differences, parents tend to overstimulate their infants (Field, 1980), to be more directive, and to take more dominant and less balanced roles (Mahoney & Powell, 1988). The structure of these interactions therefore tends to be more one-sided and less closely synchronized. Interactions also have been described as less pleasurable (Bromwich, 1976; Walker, 1982). Under these conditions, infants may have fewer opportunities to expand their interactive roles and repertoires. Further, opportunities for mutual effectance and enjoyment between the two partners may be greatly reduced. At the very least, interactions characterized by these qualities may be exhausting and unsatisfying to one or both partners. It is toward these characteristics that interaction coaching is most immediately directed.

As expected, the view of early interaction as an important process for many areas of development is mirrored by the broad array of intervention approaches that have early interactions as their focus. The link between types of presenting problems, the intervention situation (the parent-infant interaction), and the expected outcomes of intervention may be conceived as an hourglass, with a wide range of reasons for entry into interaction intervention at the top, a variety of developmental and psychological outcomes at the bottom, and interaction intervention at the narrower center. The view of parent-infant interaction as a mediator and integrator of all areas of the infant's development, as well as the point at which coaching occurs, explains the diversity of entry problems that interaction intervention addresses. Any problem that may interfere with the interaction, whether it resides in the infant, the caregiver, or the interaction itself, has the potential to upset the developmentally facilitative functions of the interaction, and possibly any one or more areas of development. It is also clear that a variety of interaction intervention outcomes might be predicted, including changes in the interaction itself, in the functioning in one of the related domains of development, or in the parent-child relationship. Not surprisingly, intervention that considers parent-infant interaction as central to its philosophy and methods has not been confined to any one discipline. Instead, the differing goals of a variety of disciplines have been approached through parent-infant interaction.

CONTEXTS OF INTERACTION COACHING WITH
INFANTS WITH SPECIAL NEEDS

The purpose of this chapter is to examine interaction coaching as one approach to interaction intervention that has been applied to dyads in which the infants manifest biologically based developmental problems or risks. However the contexts of the literature describing interaction coaching with this population are much broader and must inform our analysis and evaluation. First, infant-caregiver interactions beyond those that occur in direct face-to-face situations are also crucially important for development; the quality of ongoing brief encounters within the context of the daily routine, for example, has been linked to developmental outcomes in children (Belsky, Goode, & Most, 1980). Furthermore, although critical, interactions are but one manifestation of the larger parent-child relationship and cannot, in reality, be separated from that relationship or from its familial and cultural contexts (Bromwich, 1981; Dunst & Trivette, 1988; Hodapp, 1988). The interpretation of interactions within a particular dyad at any point in time is meaningless unless it is placed within these perspectives (Marfo, 1990).

   Another important context for this review is the interaction-coaching work with populations other than the one of major interest here. Similar approaches can be found in interventions with somewhat older children with disabilities, particularly those whose primary or secondary disability is language delay (Girolametto, 1988b; MacDonald & Gillette, 1982; Snow, Midkiff-Borunda, Small, & Proctor, 1984). Although this literature will not be addressed here, many of the actual parent behaviors that are the focus of intervention, as well as many of the approaches taken to intervention, are virtually identical to those used with parents of younger infants. In some cases, the same programs have been recommended (MacDonald & Gillette, 1988) or applied across the age span (Girolametto, Ushycky, & Hellman, 1987). Similarities also appear in coaching efforts in which it is the parent (rather than the infant) who brings potentially interfering characteristics to dyadic interaction. A variety of such populations has been studied, including teen parents (Baskin, Umansky, & Sanders, 1987), abusive or potentially abusive parents (Lutzker, Lutzker, Braunling-McMorrow, & Eddleman, 1987; McDonough, 1989), parents who are mentally handicapped (Feldman et al., 1986), and parents who are mentally ill (Ostrov, Dowling, Wesner, & Johnson, 1982). As in the case of language delay, many of the goals and procedures used in interaction intervention with these populations have also been identical to those described here, again illustrating the apparently central role of certain characteristics of parent-child interaction for early development.

   A final and important aspect of the overall context for our examination of interaction coaching is interaction intervention work utilizing other intervention approaches. The way that we approach interaction intervention with parent-infant dyads is determined largely by how we view differences in interactions among dyads (Stern-Bruschweiler & Stern, 1989). In broad terms, current approaches may be distinguished by whether or not observed differences are interpreted as mirroring a deeper perception, or "working model," of the partner in the dyadic relationship. Interventionists who hold this belief have tended to direct their efforts toward changing this internal working model, usually through helping the caregiver examine his or her own individual thoughts and feelings. The assumption here is that meaningful changes in interactive behavior will result only from a healthy and realistic working model. Intervention may or may not occur with the infant present. In contrast, where such a belief is not held, interventionists have been more likely to direct their efforts toward the overt characteristics of the interaction, thereby automatically including both members of the dyad in the intervention process. The assumption here is that the behavior change either will provide a new experience base that may lead to a qualitative difference in the parent-infant relationship, or that it is in itself is a worthy aim. Interaction coaching has exemplified the latter approach.

These two broad approaches to interaction intervention have tended to come from different literatures, with each reflecting its own theoretical underpinnings. However, as pointed out by Stern-Bruschweiler and Stern (1989), all interaction interventions are aimed at the same dyadic system; thus, any approach might be expected to accomplish at least some of the goals of alternative approaches. Most interaction interventionists probably assume that their intervention efforts will have an influence throughout the dyadic system. Seifer and Clark (1985), for example, employed coaching not only to decrease stimulation that is not contingent on infants' behavior but to optimize the family's ability to enjoy and care for the infant during everyday interactions. Conversely, interventions that aim to influence the caregiver's cognitive and emotional representation of the infant (Cardone & Gilkerson, 1989) might also anticipate behavioral differences in the interaction.

INTERACTION COACHING: WHAT AND HOW

In interaction coaching, caregivers are asked to focus on specific aspects of their own interactive behaviors and to consciously alter these behaviors in relation to their infants (Field, 1982; Dunst, 1985). Hence, the caregiver serves as the direct recipient of intervention but assumes the role of vehicle for change within the dyadic unit and potentially within the infant. Interaction coaching offers an intuitively appealing, positive, straightforward approach to dyads in which the infant brings characteristics that may interfere with the interaction.

A relatively small number of interaction-coaching efforts directed toward the population of concern here have been described in published literature or project reports. Those located for review are listed in Table 6.1. To be included, coaching efforts had to fit the following criteria: (a) children were in the infant/toddler period, and had or were at risk for developing biologically related delays or differences; (b) coaching was directed primarily toward affective or structural, rather

Table 6.1
Overview of Interaction Coaching Descriptions

Author/ Project	Diagnostic Category	Age	Length of Intervention	Location	Delivery System
Barrera & Rosenbaum (1986)	Disabled, biological and environmental risk	0-24 mos.	Weekly or monthly, 0-24 months	Home, 1-1	Component of early intervention program
Barrera, Rosenbaum & Cunningham (1986)*	Preterm	0-12 mos.	12 mos., average 13 sessions	Home, 1-1	Parent-infant interaction only
Bromwich (1976,1981)	Variety	0-36 mos.	No info.	Center, 1-1	Component of early intervention program
Field (1977, 1982)*	Preterm	3-5 mos.	1 session	Lab, 1-1	Parent-infant interaction only
Girolametto, Ushycky & Hellman (1986)	Preterm	No info.	Weekly, 5 sessions	Center, group	Component of didactic group presentation/ discussion
Hodapp & Goldfield (1983)	Severe delay (case study)	2-year-old	No info.	Clinic/ center	No info.
Kelly (1982)*	Disabled	2-18 mos	8 sessions	Home	Research adjunct to early intervention program

Table 6.1 (continued)

Author/ Project	Diagnostic Category	Age	Length of Intervention	Location	Delivery System
Klein & Briggs (1987)	Biological and environmental risk	0-12 mos	No info.	Hospital/home plus center choice: 1-1 and group	Component of follow-up program
Mahoney (1988)/ Mahoney & Powell (1988)*	Disabled	0-32 mos., 18 mos. avg.	5-24 mos., 12 mos. avg.	Home	Component of early intervention program
McCollum (1984)/ McCollum & Stayton (1985)*	Variety	0-36 mos.	6-10 sessions	Home	Research adjunct to early intervention program
PAVII Project (n.d.)	Blind infants	0-36 mos.	No info.	No info.	Component of early intervention program
Rosenberg & Robinson (1985)*	Disabled	0-34 mos., 21 mos. avg.	6 sessions average	Center	Component of early intervention program
Seifer & Clark (1985)*	Disabled	1-21 mos.	Up to 6 sessions	Center	Research adjunct to comprehensive early intervention program

* Indicates research as well as description.

than linguistic, aspects of the interaction; and (c) the intervention procedures used fit the definition above. These efforts will be examined with regard to the goals and the interaction strategies that are coached, as well as the settings and procedures used by interventionists. The purpose will be to describe the strengths and limitations of coaching as an interaction intervention procedure, with particular attention to how coaching efforts have measured up to the central criterion of family-centered early intervention—recognizing and supporting the caregiver's independence and competence.

The "Curriculum" of Coaching

Two broad purposes undergird most available descriptions of interaction coaching. The first is to support and facilitate the pleasure that partners in the dyad derive from the interaction and from one another. An implicit assumption underlying this purpose is that pleasurable interactions will provide a healthy and continuing affective basis for attachment and relationship building. The second purpose is to achieve interactive characteristics (e.g., contingency) viewed as basic to further optimal development and learning. Both broad purposes are grounded in the view of social interaction as a primary scaffold for development. Hence, many interaction-coaching efforts have had a third aim as well: to influence developmental outcome in infants with special needs. Even within the context of dyads in which the infant already displays observable interactive differences or where dyadic mismatch is an issue, remediation has taken a back seat to facilitation and prevention goals.

The goals of interaction coaching have derived in large measure from two sources. The first has been characteristics of pleasurable interactions between parents and their normally developing infants, including parental behaviors that appear to facilitate these characteristics. The second has been the differences that research has identified in interactions involving infants with and without biologically based developmental problems.

Field's (1978) "3 Rs" (rhythms, repertoires, and responsivity) provide a useful framework for summarizing both the characteristics of interactions that appear to support dyadic pleasure and synchrony and areas in which interactive differences have been found for infants with special needs. As shown in Table 6.2, they are also useful for categorizing the goals of interaction coaching. Each of these three Rs, and its associated characteristics, has provided targets for various interaction-coaching efforts. For example, at a fairly general level, an increase in responsiveness has been a target (Barrera, Rosenbaum, & Cunningham, 1986), representing a broad characteristic of the caregiver as an interactive partner. At a somewhat finer level, an increase in contingent

Table 6.2
The 3 Rs and Selected Goals as Interaction Coaching Targets

Characteristics	Goal Areas
Responsiveness	Respond to variety of initiations Respond contingently Establish joint attention Provide positive affective envelope
Repertoire	Establish play opportunities Set the stage Vary modalities Vary range, rhythms, intensity Combine theme and variation Play infant games Provide clear cues
Rhythm	Match infant's rhythm and pace Establish turn-taking sequences Balance roles

responding to the infant's initiations has served as a more explicit goal (Rosenberg & Robinson, 1985) that might be expected to contribute to overall responsiveness. An even more specific interactive strategy that might serve to increase contingent responding also could be selected as the target for coaching; for example, the caregiver might be asked to vocalize only in imitation of the infant's vocalizations. In addition to the level of specificity at which the coaching target is geared, different intervention efforts have varied in the number of targets selected for any one coaching effort.

The different ways in which the "curriculum" of interaction coaching has been approached by particular projects may usefully be categorized in terms of how coaching targets for individual dyads have been defined. Three broad approaches have been used: (a) a predetermined set of interaction characteristics is employed with all caregivers, (b) each individual dyad is assessed in relation to a previously defined list of interaction characteristics, and (c) each dyad is assessed clinically from the point of view of features that appear to foster a match between infant and caregiver.

Using predetermined targets. One way of approaching coaching content has been through a predetermined curriculum in which the same goals or targets have been used with all participants. In some reports, one or two qualities or strategies have been identified, and the goal has been to increase (or decrease) these particular aspects of the interaction. In others, broader lists of interaction characteristics have formed the basis of intervention.

Field's (1977, 1982) initial coaching studies illustrate the former. With the aim of decreasing the tendency of mothers to overstimulate infants who had experienced respiratory distress, Field asked mothers to imitate their infants' behaviors, to repeat their own phrases, and otherwise to remain silent. Similarly, Seifer and Clark (1985) selected one aspect of behavior as a focus for coaching, with the goal being to decrease maternal overstimulation in dyads in which the infants had disabilities or delays. It is important to note that where a small number of predetermined targets have been used, they generally have been selected to address some characteristic(s) thought to be especially important or problematic for some particular subgroup of dyads.

Another approach that might be characterized as a predetermined curriculum emphasizing a fairly small number of targets has been to ask the parent to engage the infant in a specific game selected for its interactional qualities. In a case study with a severely delayed two-year-old, Hodapp and Goldfield (1983) analyzed two games (ball rolling and peek-a-boo) for elements of stage setting (face-to-face positioning), attention getting, and providing contextual cues to support the baby's participation. As the mother played with her baby, she was coached to include these features in the game, enabling the baby to take a more active, independent role in the interaction. Interactive strategies thus were embedded within a game context that provided a natural support for mutual participation, enjoyment, and turntaking. The game context was selected specifically by these authors as a way to ensure mutual reinforcement and effectance.

In a second type of predefined curriculum, coaching has been organized around a hierarchically arranged sequence of interactive skills or characteristics, with all dyads proceeding through the same curriculum sequence. The Hanen curriculum (Girolametto, 1988a; 1988b) illustrates this approach. While usually applied as a remediation curriculum for parents of young children who are experiencing language delay, it has also been used as a prevention curriculum for parents of premature infants (Girolametto, Ushycky, & Hellman, 1987), with the goal of establishing a context for later language development. To illustrate the types of coaching targets selected, curriculum topics in this program, in the order in which they are presented to parents, include: (a) observe, wait, and listen; (b) follow the child's lead (including imitation and matching the child's pace); (c) respond so that the child will learn (including mapping language onto the child's focus of attention and routines); (d) keep it going (turntaking and asking for one more turn); and (e) set up times for learning. These strategies closely resemble those already reviewed. Although topics are presented in a class format, coaching is built into a portion of each session so that parents receive individual feedback on their use of the target strategies.

Targets derived from individual assessment. A second way of approaching the curriculum of interaction coaching has been to compare the interactive characteristics or strategies of the individual dyad or caregiver to a predetermined list and then to concentrate coaching on those aspects of the interaction that the parent may be able to employ more effectively. Like the above, these potential targets have been chosen to reflect characteristics of "good" interactions or ways in which dyads with special needs have been found to differ.

Two types of lists have been employed as a basis for individual assessment: those that are seen as representing a hierarchy of strategies or styles, in which the higher levels generally build on the lower (Bromwich, 1981; Klein & Briggs, 1987; Mahoney & Powell, 1984), and those in which no hierarchy is apparent (Barrera & Rosenbaum, 1986; PAVII, 1987; Rosenberg & Robinson, 1985). In each case, dyads are observed during interactive play, using the list as an observation guide, and individual dyadic goals or targets are selected based on the results.

Of the four hierarchical systems reviewed, one (Bromwich, 1981) was developed from a socioemotional perspective, with the hierarchical progression based on the caregiver's increasing ability to create independently pleasurable interactive situations. Characteristics of relationships, rather than of interactions, form the lower levels, with a focus on interaction coming into play only when the lower levels are achieved. The remaining systems were derived primarily from a language development perspective, representing either a broad developmental age progression or a progression from a broad foundation to a more specific strategy. Despite differences in derivation, the majority of items included in these hierarchies again fit within the framework of the three Rs, emphasizing characteristics and strategies identical to those already mentioned. For instance, each of the scales emphasizes pleasurable play interchanges and turntaking. It is only at the higher levels of the hierarchies that different approaches tend to become more closely aligned with a particular diagnostic category, developmental domain, or professional discipline. Language-based coaching efforts thus tend to include conversation as one of the higher levels and to be directed toward one particular discipline (speech and language pathology).

Nonhierarchical rating scales have also been used as a basis for an individually derived coaching curriculum. The PAVII Project (1987), designed for blind infants and their parents, included interaction coaching as one component of a comprehensive early intervention program. Coaching targets were determined through a structured self-observation/discussion guide, with items representing areas such as setting the stage, motivating the infant to participate, and turntaking. A second example has been described by Rosenberg and Robinson (1985). In their project, a fifteen-point rating scale designed to evaluate parents' teaching skills was used to select specific targets for coaching with individual parents. Although called "teaching," constructs and strategies measured in the items were largely the same as those included in other projects: providing clear cues, developmental matching, and contingency. The work of Barrera, Rosenbaum, and Cunningham (1986) has provided yet a third example of interaction intervention based on a nonhierarchical rating scale. What is unique about the latter is the degree to which caregivers were involved in a self-assessment process using the rating scale.

Clinically based curriculum. A final broad approach to defining the coaching curriculum comes from those projects in which targets have been derived based on clinical observation not tied to any particular list of characteristics or strategies (although these same characteristics or strategies may very well guide the clinician's observations). Kelly (1982) conducted a study in which parent and interventionist viewed an initial videotape together, identifying both positive and negative aspects of the interaction. Concerns identified were then used as the targets of coaching. A second project using an open-ended clinical approach was described by McCollum and her colleagues (McCollum, 1984; McCollum & Stayton, 1985). This project differed somewhat from those previously mentioned in that the caregiver strategies chosen as coaching targets were selected and measured within the context of related infant behaviors. In one dyad, for example, it was hypothesized that the severely delayed infant's ability to participate in parent-infant games (a behavior that pleased her mother) was related to the position in which she was held or placed; the latter therefore became the focus of coaching. Similarly, in a second dyad, a link was hypothesized between eye contact in the infant and his mother's exaggeration of face and voice, with these becoming the coaching curriculum for that dyad. Hence, while strategies and behaviors selected were the same as those in other projects, they were selected through more subjective, clinical impressions of hypothesized links between desired child behaviors and related behaviors of the parent. These were, based, however, on a larger theoretical framework.

The Processes of Coaching

Coaching efforts have varied so widely in the intervention processes used that it is difficult to abstract any substantial number of common themes; in general, each report represents a relatively unique combination of elements. For present purposes, different approaches to process will be discussed under the headings of settings and procedures.

Coaching settings. The settings of coaching define the conditions under which coaching has occurred, including where, when, how long, and by whom. Coaching typically has occurred on an individual basis, or on an individual basis within a group context. Home settings (Barrera & Rosenbaum, 1986; Kelly, 1982) and center-based settings (Rosenberg & Robinson, 1985; Seifer & Clark, 1985) seem to have been equally common as sites for individual coaching sessions. The group setting for coaching has been used primarily as an adjunct to more didactic presentations related to a specific curriculum (Girolametto, Ushycky, & Hellman, 1987).

Where and when coaching efforts have begun have been at least partially dependent on the particular diagnostic category of the infants in the dyads. In large measure, however, these differences appear to relate more to mutual access between interventionists and dyads than to dyadic characteristics or needs. For example, coaching projects aimed at premature or low-birth-weight infants and their parents have been more likely initiated while infants were still under medical care and also younger (Barrera, Rosenbaum, & Cunningham, 1986), whereas coaching with dyads in which infants have had identifiable disabilities have more likely begun after the family entered a more comprehensive early intervention program (Mahoney, 1988; Mahoney & Powell, 1988; Seifer & Clark, 1985). Projects with infants displaying delays in development have tended to begin even later (Girolametto, 1988a), at a time when delays have become evident. The predominant discipline of the interventionists involved has varied accordingly. However, these distinctions are by no means clear.

The number of coaching sessions used has varied greatly. Field's coaching study (1982), designed as an experimental study rather than an intervention program, involved only one intervention session. Other projects, particularly those with well-articulated sequential curricula, have lasted for some longer, set number of sessions (e.g., eight sessions in the Hanen program). Those projects embedded within more comprehensive intervention programs have tended to vary in length for different parents. Rosenberg and Robinson (1985), for example, reported an average of six sessions, with a range of up to forty-three sessions for one of their dyads. In that study, the number of sessions was regulated not by time but by the achievement of criterion behaviors. McCollum and Stayton (1985) used three to five sessions for each curriculum target, with two targets per parent, and reported that parents appeared to become bored when targets were not changed fairly frequently. Most coaching efforts reported in available literature appear to have lasted from six to eleven weeks. A final important context variable is whether coaching is the primary or only intervention or whether it is embedded within a larger program. Embedded coaching has taken the form of an adjunct to (McCollum & Stayton, 1985) or a component of (Rosenberg & Robinson, 1985) a comprehensive early intervention program.

Coaching procedures. Coaching is designed to provide caregivers with information and experiences that will enable them to achieve a pleasurable, reciprocal interaction with their infants. By definition, coaching procedures are geared toward caregivers' awareness and conscious application of interaction strategies that will help them to achieve this goal. A variety of different procedures has been employed in coaching. Many projects have utilized videotaped analysis of interactions as a primary vehicle for providing feedback to parents. A major advantage of videotape is that caregivers may examine their own behavior and its effect on their infants. However, direct coaching has also been common. With either approach, specific coaching strategies employed by the interventionist have included providing information, interpreting, reinforcing, demonstrating, guided observation, guided practice, role playing, and structuring the interactive situation. Combining these strategies has been more common than the use of any single procedure.

Reports of different coaching projects have varied widely in the precision with which the actual coaching procedures were described. It is clear that the relationship between interventionist and caregiver may take many forms, ranging from "educator/learner" to "mutual problem solvers." The available literature falls into two distinct groups: those efforts in which primary attention has been given to the content of coaching, and those in which procedures have assumed equal importance with, and were explicitly selected to support, coaching content. In general, the former have tended to rely on fairly direct approaches to coaching, such as providing information, making recommendations, modeling, prompting, and guided practice. In contrast, the latter have adopted more indirect approaches, including self-analysis of videotapes, problem solving, interpreting the infant for the caregiver, "talking for" the infant, and making attributions of competence. The latter have also tended to identify self-efficacy and independence in caregivers as explicit goals. Kelly (1982) selected suggestion and reinforcement over modeling on the grounds that the former were more supportive of the parent's competence. In a similar vein, McCollum and Stayton (1985) used as coaching targets those aspects of intervention viewed as important to the parent. Some projects have emphasized not only the need to reinforce current feelings of competence but to build generalizable problem-solving skills (Klein & Briggs, 1987; McCollum & Stayton, 1985). Projects emphasizing the caregiver's ability to read the infant's cues have tended to select coaching procedures based on this goal, including discussion and reinforcement of the parent's observations of the child. Thus, conscious decisions with regard to broader parent goals, and subsequent delineation of roles of the participants in the coaching process, are features that distinguish these two approaches.

In general, those coaching efforts in which procedures have been extensively described tend to be those in which procedures have been carefully selected to support particular coaching goals or to be congruent with an underlying philosophy. They also tend to take a more clinical, individualized approach to identifying coaching targets. In comparison, those efforts utilizing a predefined curriculum tend to emphasize the interaction strategies outlined in the curriculum, deemphasizing the particular procedures selected for fostering these strategies in caregivers.

Several projects have offered fairly extensive descriptions of procedures. For example, both McCollum (1984) and Barrera and Rosenbaum (1986) emphasized the importance of a "hypothesis orientation." In McCollum's procedure, parent and interventionist used this orientation to problem solve, select potentially beneficial strategies, and then test their hypotheses. Similarly, Barrera and Rosenbaum (1986) recommended a continuum of techniques, ranging from supportive to more directive, to maintain self-motivated learning by the parent. Klein and Briggs (1987) also provided a specific rationale for their choice of strategies (e.g., attributions of competence, supporting current strengths). An important aspect of this latter model is that, within the coaching triad, interventionists explicitly employ with parents the interactive characteristics (e.g., responsiveness) that they are trying to facilitate between parent and child.

Outcomes: What Do We (Not) Know?

This section has reviewed the themes that characterize the relatively small number of available descriptions of interaction/coaching efforts with dyads in which the infant has been characterized as having, or being at risk for, biologically based interactional differences. These have included infants with a variety of disabilities and delays and those who are biologically or medically at risk. The proportion of these coaching efforts yielding research results has been even smaller: only seven articles or conference presentations (noted in Table 6.1) were located. Of these, three used experimental group designs, two used single-subject designs, and two were pre-post.

A number of important assumptions form the theoretical underpinnings of interaction coaching. A transactional model of interaction would predict a number of interrelationships between variables both at specific points in time and across time. Moreover, most interaction-coaching efforts cite broader outcomes as a rationale for behavioral intervention. Optimally, if these various assumptions are to be tested, measures must address: (a) changes or differences in interaction behaviors of caregivers and infants that occur as a result of coaching, as well as any relationships between these; (b) changes or differences in broader developmental and psychological qualities and characteristics of infants and caregivers presumed to be related to or influenced by behavioral changes, as well as any relationships between these; and (c) relationships or influences between various behavioral and broader measures used for the above factors. Furthermore, each of these should be measured on both short-term and long-term bases, with analyses of predicted relationships between different points in time. Few of these linkages have been studied. Most coaching research to date has relied on coding or rating of interaction behavior (usually of the caregiver, somewhat less commonly of the infant) either during or closely following intervention. Very few broader outcome measures have been employed, even on a short-term basis. In addition, few attempts have been made to establish relationships between behavioral and broader outcomes or between results for the two partners at either of these levels.

What may be most surprising is that any patterns emerge at all, given the range not only in design and outcome measures used but also in age of infants, number of sessions, content of sessions, and coaching procedures. Results based on behavioral observations of caregivers indicate that interaction behaviors (e.g., vocalization, gaze) and characteristics (e.g., contingency, responsiveness) have been consistently responsive to interaction coaching. Measures of behavior changes in infants have shown that these, too, are quite responsive to coaching, indicating that behavioral changes in caregivers can bring about changes in their infants. Results are, however, not unequivocal. Mahoney (1988) reported that certain affective characteristics in caregivers (e.g., warmth and enjoyment) were less responsive to coaching, and in addition, mediated other outcomes. Similarly, Kelly (1982) found no changes in affect in infants as a result of coaching, even though McCollum and Stayton (1985) found increases in infant smiling. Studies examining generalization of behavioral changes across situations have found little carry-over (McCollum & Stayton, 1985). Short-term maintenance of behavioral changes across short periods of time (e.g., one month), given the same type of situation, have been more successful (McCollum & Stayton, 1985). These mixed results are important to consider. Overall, however, coaching clearly and consistently results in changes in interactive behaviors of both caregivers and infants, even in those studies with only one intervention session (Field, 1982).

Few coaching studies have included broader outcome measures, but these results also have yielded a mixed picture. Barrera, Rosenbaum, and Cunningham (1986) found no differences between experimental and control groups of preterm infants on Bayley scores. A temperament measure also yielded no differences. However, differences were found in aspects of the home environment for the two groups, as measured on the HOME Scale (Caldwell, 1978). In contrast, Mahoney and Powell (1988) reported significant differences in rate of development prior to and after intervention, as measured on the Bayley Scale. Kelly (1982) also found differences on the Bayley Scale. Measures of broader caregiver outcomes have been limited to the one measure of the home environment already mentioned.

One series of single-subject studies (McCollum & Stayton, 1985) established a relationship between the behaviors of the two partners. This provides some support for one underlying assumption of interaction coaching—that coaching of caregivers can alter the interactive environment that the infant experiences.

No studies have addressed possible relationships between behavioral and broader measures within the same individual. Mahoney's work is unique in that it is the only coaching effort in which observations of behavioral changes in caregivers have been positively related to global measures of outcome in infants. This is an important result, indicating that coaching of caregivers may influence the rate of development in infants with disabilities. However, it should be noted that these results were based on a pre-post design and remain to be replicated experimentally.

Overall, research to date simply has not been sufficient in quantity or complexity to address the larger assumptions and predictions upon which interaction coaching is grounded. Measures have primarily addressed behavioral characteristics of interactions, whereas statements of rationale and intent indicate that the real purposes of interaction coaching are much broader. It appears that coaching can establish the conditions that have been associated with learning and development. What is not yet known is whether learning and development do in fact follow. A study with slightly older infants (Girolametto, 1988b) indicates that this is a critical gap in our knowledge. That study found that changes in interaction and language in mothers and babies were not accompanied by changes in language development as measured by standardized tests. Thus, current results, while promising, are a bare beginning and need clarification through replication. Many questions remain to be addressed. It is clear that the results of coaching interventions must be approached from multiple points of view with the aim of determining effects at different levels, as well as relationships between levels. One result of this examination may be the acceptance of less far-reaching goals—for example, facilitating pleasurable interactions between infant and caregiver may be a desirable aim in and of itself. Another result may be a shift in focus to broader outcome measures that are more closely related theoretically to the mechanisms that are presumed to underlie longer-range influences. These might include, for instance, measures of locus of control in caregivers or of mastery motivation in infants.

Summary and Issues: At a Crossroad

Although the specificity with which coaching targets have been stated has varied considerably, the descriptions of coaching reviewed above have consistently taken as their goals and targets those strategies and characteristics that define the "3 Rs." There are few clear differences in stated goals with regard to the infant's diagnostic category or age; rather, any differences tend to be in emphasis. For example, with younger infants, there has been a somewhat greater emphasis on pleasurable affect, whereas coaching in dyads with older infants has somewhat stressed parent strategies and turntaking roles. In addition, those efforts designed first with slightly older infants and toddlers have placed a bit more emphasis on some particular aspect of development (usually language). Prevention and remediation also have received slightly different emphases at different ages. However, commonalities in goals and specific curriculum targets have far outweighed any differences, regardless of the theoretical bases and disciplines of the interventionists or the subpopulations for whom the curriculum has been developed and used. This is not surprising, given the view of social interaction not only as a context for interrelated development and learning, but as a window to many aspects of development. Perhaps the infant, who draws so much developmental gain from this relationship and from these interactions, has something to tell the array of different professionals who may employ interaction coaching for their own more restricted purposes.

None of the intervention-process variables reviewed clearly differentiates between projects with regard to age of infants, diagnostic category, or the professional discipline of the interventionist. As with coaching content, these differences are in degree or in emphasis. What does differentiate between approaches has been the extent to which targets were individually derived, and the extent to which caregivers were actively involved in selecting their own targets. Furthermore, these differences appear to mirror basic differences in assumptions and philosophy between different coaching efforts.

Research to date is insufficient to judge the effects of variations in curriculum or process, yet these may well have implications for whether outcomes extend beyond observed characteristics of the partners during dyadic interaction. Coaching curricula have varied considerably in terms of which of the "3 Rs" comprised the specific focus of coaching, as well as in how targets were selected for individual dyads. In addition, the level at which targets are stated has varied from quite specific to quite broad. Neither different levels of specificity in stating coaching targets nor different ways of deriving targets have been subjected to extensive scrutiny. Moreover, in some efforts, these targets have been the sole curriculum, whereas in others they have been embedded either within broader relationship-focused efforts or within comprehensive early intervention service systems. Carefully controlled studies are sorely needed to determine whether differential outcomes may be gained from approaching the coaching curriculum in different ways, and whether this may vary for dyads with different characteristics.

Perhaps an even more critical gap in our knowledge lies in the settings and processes through which interaction coaching is delivered. Underlying philosophies and values have been mirrored more in the processes employed in coaching than in the targets selected. The studies reviewed indicated wide variations in context variables such as time and place. It is likely that the optimum number of sessions, as well as where and with whom sessions are conducted may vary for targets at different levels of specificity and for different dyads. Different coaching procedures undoubtedly play a central role. Clear conceptualization and explication of procedures, followed by careful testing, are needed.

A REDEFINITION OF INTERACTION COACHING

Increasingly, parent-infant interaction is viewed as central to early intervention, not only as a mediator of the effectiveness of early intervention efforts but even more significantly as a window through which to gain access to virtually every aspect of early development. This change represents a welcome evolution in the field of early intervention and mirrors emerging recognition of the critical roles that families play as providers and mediators of their infants' social and physical environments.

Some studies have demonstrated that interaction coaching can be an effective approach for bringing about changes in the interactive behaviors of caregivers and their infants. More pleasurable, integrated interactions have been effected, and new interaction patterns believed to provide more optimal scaffolds for development have been achieved. Furthermore, there are some indications that coaching may have beneficial effects beyond the behavioral changes achieved, although these results have been mixed. Coaching also has potential advantages above and beyond its ability to achieve results. Because the focus is on overt behavior, no assumptions need to be made as to whether either partner is to "blame" for interactional differences. Rather, both partners may be viewed as bringing to the interaction behaviors that have the potential to be responded to and enjoyed by the other. The dyadic match, rather than either partner, may be regarded as the central intervention focus. This perspective seems particularly relevant in dyads where infants have biological problems that may make their interactive behaviors more difficult to interpret and match. Coaching provides a positive approach to achieving results immediately observable by the caregiver. Through coaching, caregivers can be supported in trying out new strategies that will enhance their ability to match what may be unique interactive behaviors and styles in their infants, thereby optimizing their infants' and their own participation and enjoyment.

The vantage point offered by the preceding review provides a perspective from which to evaluate the compatibility of previous approaches to interaction coaching with the values of family-centered early intervention. Unfortunately, it is clear from this perspective that coaching has not achieved its full usefulness and richness. First, although a transactional model of interaction lies at the heart of interaction coaching, there has been a tendency to view interactional patterns which deviate from those observed in dyads with nondelayed infants as maladaptive rather than as adaptations made by one or both partners in establishing a transactional interaction. One major challenge to interaction coaching therefore arises from the assumption that the characteristics of interaction found in dyads in which infants are developing normally are necessarily the best intervention targets for dyads to which infants bring biologically based differences. Other research indicates that the issue is not a simple one. In some cases, what works may differ for infants with and without disabilities (Landry & Chapieski, 1989). To add a further level of complexity, an adjustment that a caregiver makes may be adaptive for achieving a specific interaction but may not be adaptive for longer-range purposes. As shown in the study by Landry and Chapieski, the degree of support and direction needed for an infant to accomplish a particular task may differ for infants with and without handicaps. Yet providing greater support for all interactions of infants with certain characteristics, as might be implied from these results, may mean that the infant has fewer opportunities to take the initiative, thereby potentially influencing the development of mastery motivation or sense of efficacy. Clearly, the relationships between caregiver and infant behaviors are far more complex than has been recognized in past interaction-coaching efforts.

The review of interaction coaching presented above indicates that whereas few distinctions could be made between interaction-coaching efforts on the basis of population characteristics or coaching targets, basic differences were apparent in the processes used. Herein lies the second major challenge to interaction coaching. Two different approaches to process were identified. In one, processes were essentially undefined, with the focus being on the coaching targets. In the other, coaching processes were chosen explicitly to support not only the interaction targets but also the caregiver's independence, self-confidence, and competence. Clearly, the latter approach is more family-centered. By expanding upon these themes, interaction coaching may be better defined from the perspective of a family-centered orientation. Simultaneously, it may be contended that by placing the coaching process firmly within the context of the larger caregiver-infant relationship and the family's everyday life, additional and needed complexity not only will be accounted for but will be introduced automatically into research developed to study future coaching efforts.

Guralnick (1989) has called for a "second generation" of early intervention efficacy research, noting that the feature of early intervention that may best separate this new, less simplistic generation from the older one is its focus on the central role of families. The inconsistencies within interaction coaching itself, as well as the mixed results related to the few broader outcomes measured, indicate that our assumptions and employment of coaching may have also been overly simplistic. Coaching has the flexibility to be employed and defined from a number of different perspectives with which it may be equally compatible; to date, however, coaching primarily has been implemented without the benefit of critical examination or definition from any particular perspective. Coaching is clearly at a crossroads in this regard. An atheoretical approach has not been able to account for the mixed results yielded by more complex analyses, nor is it likely to suffice in future research addressing the important gaps in the total framework of critical research questions.

This chapter will not presume to formulate a total road map for such a redefinition. Some thoughts can be offered, drawing in part on past interaction-coaching efforts. If we adopt the basic premise of a family-centered orientation—that is, that families are able, competent supporters of their infants' development—then each component of interaction coaching may be examined from the perspective of its congruence with that premise. First, specific linkages between coaching and a family-centered perspective must be established. Second, implications for practice must be identified.

Three linkages seem especially critical for binding interaction coaching to the values of a family-centered orientation. First, it seems apparent that intervention must acknowledge and begin at the level of the relationship, rather than the interaction. The infant who brings biologically based differences to the interactive dyad automatically will challenge the caregiver's working model; the goal must be to build from this structure, enabling the caregiver to establish a realistic and accurate model that continually changes as the infant grows and develops. Rather than specific changes in behavior, this may provide the framework capable of carrying interactive changes forward to offer a base for continuing development. This linkage implies that interaction coaching must be a very individual matter. One implication of acknowledging the caregiver's perceptions and beliefs may be the decision that coaching is not the most appropriate approach to interaction intervention for any given dyad at any given point in time. A second implication is that rather than viewing individual differences in interaction as maladaptive, we must examine them in terms of the function they serve for that dyad in establishing and maintaining the interaction. An understanding of the caregiver's perceptions, interpretations, and intentions is critical. In addition, however, individual differences must be examined for their development-supporting properties. We would do well to remember that there is not yet a research base sophisticated enough to provide firm support for judgments about what is or is not adaptive. Rather, clinical judgment is essential. Broad differences, such as those found between dyads with different characteristics, can provide a useful framework of knowledge that can aid the interventionist and the parent in understanding and evaluating patterns of behavior.

A second critical linkage for binding interaction coaching to a family-centered perspective is that interaction coaching must address interactions that are meaningful to caregivers and infants in their ongoing, everyday lives. Coaching that ties new interactive behaviors to daily routines of play and caregiving are most likely to be seen as meaningful and used with enough frequency to become familiar, easily employed behavior patterns. Another implication of this linkage is that interactions themselves must be viewed as meaningful by the caregiver. Interaction coaching will be most effective when it is valued by the caregiver as meeting particular needs present at that time in the family's life. A related consideration is whether coaching should be embedded within a larger array of techniques aimed at the dyadic relationship more generally, rather than at behavioral characteristics alone. It is interesting to note that one of the few programs heralded by Guralnick (1989) as exemplifying the "second generation" of efficacy studies used just such an approach (Nurcombe et al., 1984; Rauh et al. 1988).

A final linkage, and perhaps the most important, is that interaction coaching must provide social-interaction tools that caregivers can carry over into the future, enabling them to be independent agents in analyzing and adapting their own continuing interactions with their infants. This goal must be reflected in all components of coaching. The most important coaching targets, from this perspective, are the caregiver's ability to observe, interpret, hypothesize, and adapt independently. Observation and interpretation of infants' cues and signals have been explicit or implicit targets in virtually every interaction-coaching effort. From a family-centered orientation, a "4th R" must be added to the top of the list of curriculum targets provided in Table 6.2. "Readerability" must assume primary importance as an interaction-coaching target.

With regard to the coaching process, those efforts that have delineated a philosophy-based approach to selecting coaching strategies also have provided some guidelines for supporting and building competence and independence in caregivers (Barrera & Rosenbaum, 1986; Klein & Briggs, 1987; McCollum, 1984). What these efforts have in common is that the interventionist mirrors through the coaching process the dyadic relationship, and strategies that provide the goal for the caregiver-infant dyad: accepting, hypothesizing, and collaborating. This relationship is much like scaffolding, in which the amount of support provided is enough, but not too much, leaving the growth process to emerge from within the learner. Like the caregiver, the interventionist, too, must learn to use a continuum of support strategies that can be employed as needed.

This redefinition of interaction coaching as a more clinical approach has moved it closer to those models described by Stern-Bruschweiler and Stern (1989), which focus on changing the working models that caregivers use with their infants. However, important definitional features of interaction coaching have been maintained. As already noted, different approaches to interaction intervention, although grounded in different assumptions, more often than not have overlapping goals. Again, the infant may be speaking: his or her existence cannot be so neatly separated into segments that match the convenience or beliefs of interventionists.

Two factors will contribute to the inevitable increase in the popularity of coaching as an early intervention approach. The first is the recognition of the central importance of the caregiver-infant interaction as an envelope for continuing development. The second is the seeming simplicity of coaching as an approach to influencing the interaction. As these efforts are implemented, a tension between coaching and the increasingly pervasive values of family-centered early intervention will inevitably arise. One major challenge will be to delineate gradually the components of interaction coaching so that they are compatible with, and supportive of, the tenets of a family-centered perspective. A second will be to design and implement research that addresses the complex assumptions and predictions of interaction coaching as redefined.

ACKNOWLEDGEMENT

The author gratefully acknowledges the thoughtful, key contributions made by Dr. Eva Thorp to the development of this chapter.

REFERENCES

Als, H. (1982). The unfolding of behavioral organization in the face of a biological violation. In E. Z. Tronick (Ed.), *Social interchange in infancy: Affect, cognition and communication* (pp. 125-160). Baltimore: University Park Press.

Barrera, M., & Rosenbaum, P. (1986). The transactional model of early home intervention. *Infant Mental Health Journal, 7*(2), 112-131.

Barrera, M., Rosenbaum, P., & Cunningham, C. (1986). Early home intervention with low birth weight infants and their parents. *Child Development, 57,* 20-33.

Baskin, C., Umansky, W., & Sanders, W. (1987). Influencing the responsiveness of adolescent mothers to their infants. *Zero to Three 8*(3), 7-11.

Belsky, J., Goode, M. & Most, R. K. (1980). Maternal stimulation and infant exploratory competence: Cross-sectional, correlational and experimental analyses. *Child Development, 51,* 1168-1178.

Bricker, D. D., & Carlson, L. (1981). Issues in early language intervention. In R. L. Schiefelbusch & D. D. Bricker (Eds.), *Early language: Acquisition and intervention* (pp. 477-515). Baltimore: University Park Press.

Bromwich, R. M. (1976). Focus on maternal behavior in infant intervention. *American Journal of Orthopsychiatry, 46,* 439-446.

Bromwich, R. M. (1981). *Working with parents and infants: An interactional approach.* Baltimore: University Park Press.

Bruner, J. (1974). The organization of early skilled action. In M.P.M. Richards (Ed.), *The integration of the child into a social world* (pp. 167-184). London: Cambridge University Press.

Caldwell, B. M. (1978). *Home Observation for Measurement of the Environment.* Little Rock: University of Arkansas.

Cardone, I. A., & Gilkerson, L. (1989). Family administered neonatal activities: An innovative component of family-centered care. *Zero to Three, 10*(1), 23-28.

Clarke-Stewart, A. (1973). Interactions between mothers and their young children: Characteristics and consequences. *Monographs of the Society for Research in Child Development, 38* (6,7, Serial No. 153).

Dunst, C. J. (1985). Communicative competence and deficits: Effects on early social interactions. In E. T. McDonald & D. L. Gallagher (Eds.), *Facilitating social-emotional development in multiply-handicapped children* (pp. 93-140). Philadelphia: Michael C. Prestegord.

Dunst, C. J. & Trivette, C. M. (1988). Determinants of parent and child interactive behavior. In K. Marfo (Ed.), *Parent-child interaction and developmental disabilities: Theory, research, and intervention* (pp. 3-31). New York: Praeger.

Emde, R., Katz, E., & Thorpe, J. (1978). Emotional expression in infancy: Early deviations in Down syndrome. In M. Lewis & L. Rosenblum (Eds.), *The development of affect* (pp. 351-360). New York: Plenum.

Feldman, M. A., Towns, F., Betel, J., Case, L., Rincover, A., & Rubino, C. A. (1986). Parent education project II: Increasing stimulating interactions of developmentally handicapped mothers. *Journal of Applied Behavior Analysis, 19*(1), 23-37.

Field, T. (1977). Effects of early separation, interaction deficits, and experimental manipulation on infant-mother face-to-face interaction. *Child Development, 48,* 763-772.

Field, T. (1978). The three Rs of infant-adult interactions: Rhythms, repertoires, and responsivity. *Journal of Pediatric Psychology, 3*(3), 131-136.

Field, T. (1980). Interactions of high-risk infants: Quantitative and qualitative differences. In S. B. Sawin, R. C. Hawkins, L. O. Walker, & J. H. Penticuff (Eds.), *Exceptional infant: Psychosocial risks in infant-environment transactions, Vol. 4* (pp. 120-143). New York: Brunner/Mazel.

Field, T. (1982). Interaction coaching for high-risk infants and their parents. *Prevention in Human Services, 1*(4), 4-23.

Fischer, M. A. (1987). Mother-child interaction in preverbal children with Down syndrome. *Journal of Speech and Hearing Disorders, 52,* 179-190.

Fraiberg, S. (1974). Blind infants and their mothers: An examination of the sign system. In M. Bullowa (Ed.), *Before speech: The beginnings of interpersonal communication* (pp. 149-169). Cambridge: Cambridge University Press.

Girolametto, L. E. (1988a). Developing dialogue skills: The effects of a conversational model of language intervention. In K. Marfo (Ed.), *Parent-child interaction and developmental disabilities: Theory, research, and intervention* (pp. 145-162). New York: Praeger.

Girolametto, L. E. (1988b). Improving the social-conversational skills of developmentally delayed children: An intervention study. *Journal of Speech and Hearing Disorders, 53,* 156-167.

Girolametto, L., Ushycky, I., & Hellman, J. (1987). Hanen training program for parents of high-risk infants. *Proceedings of the symposium: High risk infants: Facilitating interaction and communication.* Toronto: Hanen Resource Center.

Goldberg, S. (1977). Social competence in infancy: A model of parent-infant interaction. *Merrill-Palmer Quarterly, 23*(3), 163-177.

Guralnick, M. J. (1989). Recent developments in early intervention efficacy research: Implications for family involvement in Public Law 99-457. *Topics in Early Childhood Special Education, 9*(3), 1-17.

Hodapp, R. M. (1988). The role of maternal emotions and perceptions in interactions with young handicapped children. In K. Marfo (Ed.), *Parent-child interaction and developmental disabilities: Theory, research, and intervention* (pp. 32-46). New York: Praeger.

Hodapp, R. M. & Goldfield, E. C. (1983). The use of mother-infant games as therapy with delayed children. *Early Child Development and Care, 13,* 17-32.

Hodapp, R. M., & Mueller, E. (1982). Early social development. In B. B. Wolman

(Ed.), *Handbook of Developmental Psychology* (pp. 284-300). Englewood Cliffs, NJ: Prentice-Hall.

Jones, O. (1977). Mother-child communication in pre-linguistic Down syndrome and normal infants. In H. Schaffer (Ed.), *Studies in mother-infant interaction* (pp. 379-401). New York: Academic Press.

Kelly, J. F. (1982). Effects of intervention on caregiver-infant interaction when the infant is handicapped. *Journal of the Division for Early Childhood, 5,* 53-63.

Klein, M. D., & Briggs, M. H. (1987). Facilitating mother-infant communicative interaction in mothers of high-risk infants. *Journal of Childhood Communication Disorders, 10*(2), 95-106.

Landry, S. H., & Chapieski, M. L. (1989). Joint attention and infant toy exploration: Effects of Down syndrome and prematurity. *Child Development, 60,* 103-118.

Lowe, L. W., & Dunst, C. J. (1985, October). *Fostering communicative competence in infants: The role of parent-infant interaction.* Paper presented at the Annual Conference of the North Carolina Association for the Education of Young Children, Winston Salem, NC.

Lutzker, S. Z., Lutzker, J. R., Braunling-McMorrow, D., & Eddleman, J. (1987). Prompting to increase mother-baby stimulation with single mothers. *Journal of Child and Adolescent Psychotherapy, 4*(1), 3-12.

MacDonald, J. D., & Gillette, Y. (1982). *ECO: Ecological communication system: A clinical handbook for parents and teachers.* Columbus, The Nisonger Center, Ohio State University.

MacDonald, J. D., & Gillette, Y. (1988). Communicating partners: A conversational model for building parent-child relationships with handicapped children. In K. Marfo (Ed.), *Parent-child interaction and developmental disabilities: Theory, research, and intervention* (pp. 220-241). New York: Praeger.

Mahoney, G. (1988). Enhancing the developmental competence of handicapped infants. In K. Marfo (Ed.), *Parent-child interaction and developmental disabilities: Theory, research and intervention* (pp. 203-219). New York: Praeger.

Mahoney, G. J., & Powell, A. (1984). *The transactional intervention program: Teacher's guide.* Farmington, CT: Pediatric Research and Training Center.

Mahoney, G., & Powell, A. (1988). Modifying parent-child interaction: Enhancing the development of handicapped children. *Journal of Special Education, 22,* 82-96.

Marfo, K. (1990). Maternal directiveness in interactions with mentally handicapped children: An analytical commentary. *Journal of Child Psychology and Psychiatry, 31,* 531-549.

McCollum, J. A. (1984). Social interaction between parents and babies: Validation of an intervention procedure. *Child: Care, Health, and Development, 10,* 301-315.

McCollum, J. A. (1987). Looking patterns of retarded and non-retarded babies in play and instructional situations. *American Journal of Mental Deficiency, 91*(5), 516-522.

McCollum, J. A., & Stayton, V. D. (1985). Infant/parent interaction: Studies and intervention guidelines based on the SIAI model. *Journal of the Division for Early Childhood, 10,* 125-135.

McCollum, J. A., & Stayton, V. (1988). Gaze patterns of mothers and infants as indicators of role integration during play and teaching with toys. In K. Marfo (Ed.), *Parent-child interaction and developmental disabilities: Theory, research, and intervention* (pp. 47-63). New York: Praeger.

McDonough, S. C. (1989, December). *Interaction guidance: Using video feedback for treatment of early relationship disturbances.* Paper presented at the 6th Biennial National Training Institute of the National Center for Clinical Infant Programs, Washington, D.C.

Mitchell, D. R. (1987). Parents' interactions with their developmentally disabled or at-risk infants: A focus for intervention. *Australia and New Zealand Journal of Developmental Disabilities, 13*(2), 73-81.

Nurcombe, B., Howell, D. C., Rauh, V. A., Teti, D. H., Ruoff, P., & Brennan, J. (1984). An intervention program for mothers of low birth-weight infants: Preliminary results. *Journal of the American Academy for Child Psychiatry, 23,* 319-325.

Ostrov, K., Dowling, J., Wesner, D. O., & Johnson, F. K. (1982). Maternal styles in infant psychotherapy: Treatment and research implications. *Infant Mental Health Journal, 3*(3), 162-173.

PAVII Project. (1987). *Parents and visually impaired infants.* San Francisco: PAVII Project.

Ratner, N., & Bruner, J. (1977). Games, social exchange and the acquisition of language. *Journal of Child Language, 5,* 391-401.

Rauh, V. A., Achenbach, T. M., Nurcombe, B., Howell, C. T., & Teti, D. M. (1988). Minimizing adverse effects of low birthweight: Four-year results of an early intervention program. *Child Development, 59,* 544-553.

Rogoff, B., Malkin, C., & Gilbride, K. (1984). Interaction with babies as guidance in development. In B. Rogoff & J. V. Wertsch (Eds.), *Children's learning in the "zone of proximal development"* (pp. 31-43). San Francisco: Jossey-Bass.

Rosenberg, S. A., & Robinson, C. C. (1985). Enhancement of mothers' interactional skills in an infant education program. *Education and Training of the Mentally Retarded, 20,* 163-169.

Seifer, R., & Clark, G. (1985, April). *Mother-infant interaction patterns and effects of coaching in early intervention participants.* Poster presented at Society for Research in Child Development, Toronto, Ontario.

Snow, C., Midkiff-Borunda, S., Small, A., & Proctor, A. (1984). Therapy as social interaction: Analyzing the contexts for language remediation. *Topics in Language Disorders, 4,* 72-85.

Stern-Bruschweiler, N., & Stern, D. N. (1989). A model for conceptualizing the role of the mother's representational world in various mother-infant therapies. *Infant Mental Health Journal, 10*(3), 142-156.

Tronick, E. Z. & Gianino, A. F., Jr. (1986). The transmission of maternal disturbance to the infant. In E. Z. Tronick & T. Field (Eds.), *Maternal depression and infant disturbance* (pp. 5-11). San Francisco: Jossey-Bass.

Turnbull, A. P., & Summers, J. A. (1985, April). *From parent involvement to family support: Evolution to revolution.* Paper presented at the Down syndrome State-of-the-Art Conference, Boston.

Uzgiris, I. C. (1981). Experience in the social context: Imitation and play. In R. L. Schiefelbusch & D. D. Bricker (Eds.), *Early language: Acquisition and intervention* (pp. 477-515). Baltimore: University Park Press.

Walker, J. A. (1982). Social interactions of handicapped infants. In D. Bricker (Ed.), *Intervention with handicapped and at risk infants: From research to application* (pp. 217-232). Baltimore, MD: University Park Press.

Walker, J. A., & Crawley, S. B. (1983). Conceptual and methodological issues in studying the handicapped infant. In S. G. Garwood & R. R. Fewell (Eds.), *Educating handicapped infants: Issues in development and intervention* (pp. 25-68). Rockville, MD: Aspen.

7

The Maternal Directiveness Theme in Mother-Child Interaction Research: Implications for Early Intervention

Kofi Marfo

As the theme of this volume suggests, we are currently witnessing a period of significant transitions in early intervention programming for children with developmental disabilities. In Chapter 1, the shift toward making the parent-child interaction process an intervention target was identified as one of the more dominant transitional themes. The growing prominence of *interaction-focused early intervention* (IFEI) is now widely evident in the literature (Affleck, McGrade, McQueeney, & Allen, 1982; Bailey & Simeonsson, 1988; Bromwich, 1981; Mahoney & Powell, 1988; Marfo, 1990; McCollum, 1984; Rogers, 1988; Rose & Calhoun, 1990; Rosenberg & Robinson, 1988). This chapter, like the one before it, deals with this transitional theme. Unlike McCollum's much broader focus, however, the present chapter addresses one specific dimension of parent-child interaction that has attained considerable popularity in the literature during the last decade—the dimension of maternal directiveness.

Although by no means the only impetus for the shift toward IFEI (see Marfo, 1990, for a discussion of other forces), research comparing mothers' interactions with handicapped and nonhandicapped children is contributing significantly to the IFEI movement. This research, as synthesized in various sources (Barnard & Kelly, 1990; Dunst, 1984; Field,

This chapter draws in part from the author's recent paper, "Maternal directiveness in interactions with mentally handicapped children: An analytic commentary," published in the *Journal of Child Psychology and Psychiatry*, 1990, Vol. 31, No. 4, pp. 531-549.

1980, 1983; Marfo, 1984; Marfo & Kysela, 1988; Maurer & Sherrod, 1987; Rogers, 1988; Tannock, 1988a), suggests that mothers of mentally retarded and developmentally delayed children tend to exhibit excessive amounts of control and directiveness in their interactions. This finding is being used increasingly to rationalize IFEI studies and programs (Seitz, 1975; Weistuch & Lewis, 1985). Even when this literature has not been referred to explicitly as providing the rationale for intervention, the reduction of directive behaviors has served as a major goal for interventions targeting the parent-child interaction process (Cheseldine & McConkey, 1979; Girolametto, 1988; Mahoney, 1988b; Mahoney & Powell, 1988; Price, 1984).

As maternal directiveness continues to be depicted as an aberrant interactional style and as a syndrome associated with parenting a handicapped child, the management or reduction of maternal directive behavior is likely to become a major goal of early intervention programs in the years ahead. The principal position presented in this chapter is that some of the current beliefs about maternal directiveness and its potential role in the development of handicapped children may not have strong theoretical or empirical foundations. Through a critical examination of conceptual and empirical issues related to the maternal directiveness literature, the discussion here is intended to accomplish two principal objectives: (a) to caution early interventionists against a bandwagon rush to rid mothers of handicapped children of their "directiveness syndrome," and (b) to identify some directions for future research on the maternal directiveness theme. The substance of the first objective is not intended to suggest in any way that the management of directive behavior is completely inappropriate or unnecessary in interventions with parents of handicapped children; the point, instead, is that such management, where it is deemed necessary, must be founded on sound, empirically validated principles.

MATERNAL DIRECTIVENESS AS OPERATIONALIZED IN THE MENTAL RETARDATION LITERATURE

Discussions of the incidence and developmental implications of maternal directiveness depict it as a construct with a uniform definition. However, a closer examination of the empirical literature reveals that directiveness has multiple operational definitions. In this section, I examine the variety of operational definitions that exists in the mental retardation literature. At least four different ways of operationalizing maternal directiveness are discernible. Table 7.1 provides a summary of the use of the various definitions in existing investigations. Each of the four classes of directiveness is defined briefly below.

Response Control: This class includes aspects of maternal behavior,

Table 7.1
Summary of Research Studies by Type of Measurement and Definition of Directiveness

	Type of Measurement	Definition of Directiveness			
		RC	TC	TTC	IC
Breiner & Forehand (1982)	BC	X			
Buium, Rynders, & Turnure (1974)	BC	X			
Cardoso-Martins & Mervis (1985)	BC	X	X		
Crawley & Spiker (1983)	RS	X			
Cunningham, Reuler, Blackwell, & Deck (1981)	BC	X	X		
Davis & Oliver (1980)	BC	X	X	X	X
Eheart (1982)	BC	X	X		
Garrard (1989)	BC	X			
Gutmann & Rondal (1979)	BC	X			
Hanzlik & Stevenson (1986)	BC	X			
Herman & Shantz (1983)	BC	X		X	
Jones (1980)	BC		X		
Kogan, Wimberger, & Bobbitt (1969)	BC	X		X	X

Table 7.1 (continued)

	Type of Measurement	Definition of Directiveness			
		RC	TC	TTC	IC
Mahoney (1983)	BC	X	X	X	
Mahoney (1988a)	BC		X		
Mahoney, Finger, & Powell (1985)	RS		X		
Mahoney, Fors, & Wood (1990)	BC and RS	X	X		
Mahoney & Robenalt (1986)	BC	X	X		
Marfo (1991)	BC and RS	X	X	X	X
Marfo & Kysela (1988)	BC	X			
Marshall, Hegrenes, & Goldstein (1973)	BC	X			
Maurer & Sherrod (1987)	BC	X			
Rondal (1977)	BC	X			
Stoneman, Brody, & Abbott (1983)	BC	X		X	
Tannock (1988a, 1988b)	BC	X	X	X	
Terdal, Jackson, & Garner (1976)	BC	X			

Type of Measurement: BC = Behavior Count; RS = Rating Scale
Definition of Directiveness: RC = Response Control; TC = Topic Control; TTC = Turn-Taking Control; IC = Inhibitive Control

mainly verbal, that depict the tendency to issue commands, ask command questions, or make demands on the child to perform a task or respond in a particular manner. As Table 7.1 shows, most of the frequently cited studies in this area of research employed this definition of directiveness either explicitly or implicitly.

Topic Control: This class focuses on the relative role of the mother and child in driving the topics of interaction. It consists mainly of behaviors relating to leadtaking during play or verbal interactions. For example, in addition to mothers' imperative utterances of a demanding nature, Eheart (1982) also coded maternal leadtaking as an index of control, defining it as the extent to which interactions between mothers and their children revolved around child-selected versus mother-selected toys. Jones (1980) defined maternal control in terms of the extent to which mothers tended to direct play activity instead of letting their child take the initiative.

Turntaking Control: Under this class, directiveness is viewed as turn dominance or a drastic imbalance in turntaking. For example, employing a procedure originally developed by Kaye and Charney (1980), several researchers have focused on turntaking as the primary metric for coding parent-child interaction (Girolametto, 1988; Mahoney, 1988a, 1988b; Mahoney & Robenalt, 1986; Tannock, 1988b). The end of a turn is marked by a "pronounced pause in which the partner might or might not take the floor" (Kaye & Charney, 1980, p. 214). Turns are typically classified into four categories—mands, responses, turnabouts (or response-mands), and unlinked turns. Under this system, at least two ways of indexing directiveness are identifiable. The first involves the use of the frequency of mands as an index of directiveness. This index corresponds to the response-control operationalization described above. The second method—which fits the turn dominance or imbalance operationalization—indexes maternal directiveness as the ratio of maternal turns (in any category) to the total number of turns taken by the child (Mahoney & Robenalt, 1986).

Inhibitive Control: Under this class, directiveness is defined in terms of restrictions, terminations, and interferences on the part of the mother. For example, Herman and Shantz (1983) included in their definition of directiveness mothers' tendency to restrict or interfere with the child's activity. Restrictions had to do with mothers' "attempts to reduce the intensity of the child's activity or the manner of its execution," while interference involved "attempts to stop an activity of the child" (p. 220). Similarly, Davis and Oliver (1980) coded prohibitions, along with commands, as instances of directiveness, while Kogan, Wimberger, and Bobbitt (1969) included maternal prohibiting and restraining in their definition of control.

Each of these operational definitions in effect describes a different subtype of directive behavior, and there are several reasons why it is important to delineate the subtypes in this fashion. First, it provides a framework for interpreting the findings of individual investigations, although this task is beyond the scope of the chapter. Second, it forces us to entertain the hypothesis that different patterns of individual or group differences may exist for different subtypes of directiveness, or that developmental sequelae for different populations of children may vary for different subtypes of maternal directive interactional behavior. Third, it reveals limitations in our current understanding of the notion of directiveness. Major conclusions about directiveness have been drawn by investigators, based, in many cases, upon analyses involving only one or two of the subtypes described here. It is important, then, for future researchers to operationalize directiveness in relation to the classification of subtypes presented here, in order to place their findings in a proper perspective.

MATERNAL DIRECTIVENESS: A GENERAL CONCEPTUAL DEFINITION

To better appraise the contributions made to the maternal directiveness literature by researchers in the mental retardation and developmental disabilities field, it is important that the notion of directiveness be examined from a much broader conceptual framework. The seminal works of leading developmental psychologists studying parent-child interaction in the 1960s and 1970s (Bell, 1968, 1974; Lewis & Rosenblum, 1974; Schaffer, 1977) have culminated in the well-established view that the parent-child relationship is a system characterized by mutuality, bidirectionality, and reciprocity. It is strongly acknowledged, however, that this view does not necessarily connote equality of influence or of purposefulness between parent and child, especially during the early years. As Schaffer and Crook (1979) point out, mothers often have "purposes and goals of their own which they need to convey to their children and with which the children are expected to comply" (p. 986). Maternal control is the term used in the developmental literature to refer to all those behaviors—verbal as well as nonverbal—that the mother employs to regulate or direct the ongoing behavior and activity of the child during any given interactive episode. In the words of Schaffer and Crook (1980), the function of control techniques is "to channel behavior in certain directions, inhibiting some tendencies and enhancing others" (p. 54).

As the information in Table 7.1 confirms, in the mental retardation literature, the term "directiveness" has been used to depict not only the incidence of verbal directives, but also the use of all kinds of verbal and nonverbal behaviors to *control* or *direct* the child's actions. From a broader definitional perspective, then, maternal control or directive behavior, as employed in the mental retardation literature, should also be seen as representing an aspect of normative parental or adult behavior toward the child. Furthermore, it should be considered as an inherent attribute of every parent's mediator role of helping the child to select, define, relate to, and internalize relevant aspects of the environment.

Given this definitional framework, one wonders why maternal directiveness has been assigned negative connotations in the mental retardation literature. In the remaining sections of the chapter, I trace the origins of this negative connotation, indicate methodological orientations that have tended to perpetuate it, and review available research that provides empirical support for it.

ORIGINS OF THE NEGATIVE CONNOTATIONS ASSOCIATED WITH DIRECTIVENESS

Maternal directiveness is generally portrayed in the mental retardation literature as an inherently problematic interactional style. The origins of this negative connotation can be traced to research on normal language development, in particular to correlational research examining variation in parental behavior and child linguistic competence. Findings from this line of enquiry, with few exceptions (Barnes, Gutfreund, Satterly, & Wells, 1983), have generally suggested that at least some of the intersubject variation in children's linguistic competence "may be environmentally conditioned to the extent that it reflects differences in parent interaction styles" (Bloom & Lahey, 1978, p. 61).

As an example, Nelson's (1973) classic study of eighteen infants (followed for one year from ages ten to fifteen months) examined the relationship between maternal language teaching style and linguistic development in the child. Children whose mothers were accepting of language productions by the child were found to be better at vocabulary acquisition than children whose mothers were highly directive and often imposed their own agenda on the child. Examining interactions between caregivers and eighteen-month-old children in home and day-care settings, Rubenstein and Howes (1979) also found that in both settings greater caregiver control over the choice and use of play objects was associated with lower levels of play competence in children. Similar findings have been reported in other investigations (Olson-Fulero, 1982; White & Watts, 1973).

In many respects, it is not by accident that the negative connotations associated with maternal directiveness have been accentuated in research involving mentally retarded and other handicapped children. Indeed, some of the earliest parent handicapped child interaction studies addressing the issue of directiveness were concerned specifically with the relationship between the quality of the maternal linguistic environment and the development of linguistic competence in handicapped children (Buckhalt, Rutherford, & Goldberg, 1978; Buium, Rynders, & Turnure, 1974; O'Kelly-Collard, 1978; Rondal, 1977). Since then, the directiveness theme has been picked up in studies in which the relationship between maternal linguistic environment and the development of linguistic competence in children has not necessarily been the primary focus (Breiner & Forehand, 1982; Cook & Culp, 1981; Eheart, 1982; Marfo & Kysela, 1988; Stoneman, Brody, & Abbott, 1983). Essentially, then, the negative connotation associated with directiveness in the mental retardation literature is a carryover from the language development literature.

The primary design for studying directiveness has been to compare the interaction patterns of mothers and their mentally retarded children with those of mothers and their nonhandicapped children. In much of this research, directive behaviors have been shown to occur significantly more often in interactions with mentally retarded children than they do in interactions with nonhandicapped children (Breiner & Forehand, 1982; Cunningham, Reuler, Blackwell, & Deck, 1981; Eheart, 1982; Jones, 1980; Mahoney & Robenalt, 1986; Marshall, Hegrenes, & Goldstein, 1973). Interpretations of the foregoing evidence have largely reflected the following line of reasoning: In the general literature, maternal directive behavior has been found to be negatively related to the development of competence in children; mentally retarded children are exposed to significantly higher amounts of directiveness, and therefore maternal directiveness must account, at least in part, for the poor developmental outcomes (poor language and communication skills) associated with mental retardation. This line of reasoning has led to the conclusion that high occurrences of maternal directive behaviors are not only atypical but inherently problematic.

Critical Appraisal

There are two problems with this conclusion. First, the above implication—that a relationship exists between directiveness and poor developmental outcomes in mentally retarded children—is based largely on speculation. In the mental retardation literature, very few studies (Mahoney, 1988a, 1988b; Mahoney, Finger, & Powell, 1985) have examined this relationship directly. I address this issue in greater detail later in the chapter.

Second, and more pertinent to the present discussion, the conclusion fails to recognize the fact that parents and children are highly adaptive and responsive to each other's signals and characteristics. As suggested earlier, parents in particular are highly purposive and goal-directed in their interactions. The language literature has shown, for example, that mothers tend consistently to modify several linguistic features of their speech when addressing younger children. Specifically, maternal speech to very young children has been characterized as being simpler, shorter, slower, and more redundant (Baldwin & Baldwin, 1973; Broen, 1972; Newport, 1976; Snow, 1977). It can be interpolated from this finding that similar modifications will be made by mothers of mentally retarded children. In fact, observations made by Sorce and Emde (1982) in a study of emotional expressions in Down syndrome infants indicate that this may very well be the case. Mothers of the DS children had recalibrated their responsiveness threshold to such a degree that they were much more likely to react even to very low intensity emotional signals than mothers generally do. Thus, as Schaffer (1984) observes, child pathology does not result inevitably in an aberrant dyadic inter-action, as some mothers learn to compensate for their children's di-minished or deviant capabilities.

Bell's control theory (Bell & Harper, 1977, Chapter 4) would also argue against the view of increased maternal directiveness as an inherently negative interactional phenomenon. According to Bell, both parent and child exert two types of control (upper-limit and lower-limit) on each other's behavior, depending upon "the intensity, frequency, or situa-tional appropriateness of behavior shown by the other" (p. 65). On the part of the parent, upper-limit controls serve to redirect or reduce exces-sive or inappropriate behavior, while lower-limit controls seek to stim-ulate and prime child behavior in situations where it is perceived to be below an acceptable standard. Lower-limit control behaviors are often the same kinds that are indexed by the directiveness label. On the basis of Bell's theory, we would expect parents of mentally retarded children to engage in significantly more lower-limit control (i.e., directive) be-haviors than mothers of nonhandicapped children. This is because mentally retarded children tend to be less active and less responsive in interactive contexts than nonhandicapped children. From this perspec-tive, maternal directiveness is a form of adaptive behavior.

It appears, then, that at least some of the observed differences in the interaction styles of mothers of handicapped and mothers of nonhan-dicapped children may be the result of modifications the former make on the basis of the feedback they receive from their children. Being different, in this case, is not necessarily negative; in fact, some of the obviously different interaction styles, including increased use of di-rectives, may be designed to serve repair and facilitative functions. Whether these adaptive strategies do actually facilitate or inhibit chil-dren's development is a different question altogether, one that will be examined later in the discussion.

THE ROLE OF METHODOLOGY

Methodology has certainly played a significant role in the way in which directiveness has been viewed as a negative interactional phenomenon. Two ways in which methodology has contributed to this characterization of directiveness are examined briefly. The first has to do with the dominance of the between-group contrastive design in this area of research. The second pertains to failure on the part of researchers to examine the role context plays in mothers' use of control strategies.

Between-Group Designs and the Homogeneity Myth

An overwhelming majority of the research consists of studies employing between-group designs to examine differences between dyads with handicapped children and those with nonhandicapped children. Emerging from this research is a pervasive picture of a *maternal directiveness syndrome* to which mentally retarded and other developmentally at-risk children are said to be exposed. Whether we look at discussions of the results of individual investigations or at reviews and summaries of the literature, we are confronted with an implicit but strong depiction of mothers of handicapped and at-risk children as a homogeneous group of individuals who share the common attribute of being overly directive in their interactions. Consistent with this depiction, recommendations for intervention are often offered in a manner that suggests that most mothers of handicapped children need professional assistance to reduce directive interactional behavior.

Evidence in Support of Individual Differences. Between-group designs are based on the assumption of within-group homogeneity of variance. Unfortunately, while research findings have tended to be interpreted as if this assumption has been met, most of the contrastive studies in the directiveness literature generally have not included adequate controls to satisfy the homogeneity of variance assumption. The relatively few studies in the literature that have examined individual differences through correlational and descriptive analyses reveal that far from being a homogeneous group, mothers of handicapped children manifest a wide range of differences not only in the use of directive behaviors but in their overall interactional style (Crawley & Spiker, 1983; Mahoney, 1988a, 1988b).

Crawley and Spiker (1983) found that mothers of children with Down syndrome varied not only in directiveness ratings but also in the manner in which their directive behaviors were integrated into other interactional behaviors (e.g., sensitivity, intrusiveness, and stimulation value). Variations in directiveness, as a function of child interactional behavior, were also observed. For example, as noted later in the discussion, mothers whose children showed less interest during play and those whose children initiated fewer actions with objects were more directive than other parents.

Using cross-sectional data, Mahoney (1988a) found variations in maternal directiveness and communicative responsiveness as a function of increasing child age and cognitive competence. In other work, Mahoney (1988b) found individual differences in maternal use of directives as a function of children's level of participation in the interaction.

Context and Function as Sources of Individual Differences. Examination of the context and functions of maternal directive behavior contributes further to our understanding of individual differences. However, as implied in the preceding section, in much of the research the more central goal has been to establish whether one group of mothers issues more directives than another, rather than to identify factors associated with increased use of directives. The few studies in the literature that have examined directiveness more broadly and in the context of a wider range of maternal and child behaviors (Mahoney, 1988b; Maurer & Sherrod, 1987; Tannock, 1988b) provide useful insights that are counter to the simplistic view of directiveness as an inherently negative interactional phenomenon.

Maurer and Sherrod (1987) examined, among other issues, the influence of context on maternal directiveness when Down syndrome and nonhandicapped children were matched roughly on mental age. Maternal directives were recorded in relation to their immediate antecedents and consequents, yielding conditional probability scores. Among the findings of relevance to the present discussion are the following:

1. Mothers of Down syndrome children were significantly less likely to issue a directive when the child was playing with an object in a functionally appropriate manner (i.e., in a way that the object was designed to be used) than were mothers of nonhandicapped children. However, when the child played in a functionally inappropriate manner with an object, mothers of Down syndrome children were significantly more likely to issue a directive than were mothers of nonhandicapped children.

2. Mothers of Down syndrome children were significantly less likely to issue a directive when they did not have their children's attention, but they were significantly more likely to issue a directive following noncompliance by the child than were mothers of nonhandicapped children.

3. In terms of child behavior, Down syndrome children were significantly more likely to play with an object in a functionally appropriate fashion following a maternal directive than were nonhandicapped children.

These results must be taken cautiously, given that they are based on very small samples of dyads in each group (n = 6 for DS group; n = 4 for nonhandicapped group). Nevertheless, the study is significant for its methods of data analysis. The findings suggest that differences in the use of directives by the two populations of mothers vary as a function of both contextual and child behavior differences. Such analysis of context provides some insight regarding the functions of directives for different categories of mothers. For example, mothers of Down syndrome children appeared to employ directives to promote appropriate use of play objects and to obtain compliance, whereas mothers of nonhandicapped children appeared to employ directives to gain attention and to encourage further exploration. With regard to mothers' use of directives to promote appropriate manipulation of play objects, it is significant to note that the child behavior data confirmed that this strategy was somehow successful, as shown in the third point above.

Aspects of the Maurer and Sherrod (1987) results are corroborated by results obtained by Mahoney and his associates. Mahoney (1988b) observed that directives used by mothers of Down syndrome and nonhandicapped children appeared to serve different purposes. Among mothers of nonhandicapped children, only 25% of all directives took the form of action requests; most of them (53%) were attention requests. The reverse was true of mothers of children with Down syndrome; 51% of all directives issued by these mothers were action requests, while only 26% took the form of attention requests. In fact, Mahoney (1988b) has observed within-group differences in maternal use of directives, as a function of the activity level of the child. He notes:

When Down syndrome children are inactive . . . their mothers' action requests appear to be designed to both engage them in the interaction and encourage them to perform challenging tasks; when Down syndrome children are actively involved in the interaction, their mothers' requests are used primarily to challenge the child. (p. 208)

Finally, Tannock (1988b) reported that both mothers of handicapped and mothers of nonhandicapped children employed certain directives (response control) as a tool to support the child's participation in interaction rather than to override the child's established topic.

These findings not only challenge the homogeneity assumption but, perhaps more important, they also challenge the assumption that the presence of a handicap per se is the sole determinant of maternal directiveness. The evidence shows clearly that beyond the child's handicapping condition, mothers adjust their directive behaviors on the basis of the child's age, developmental competence, and degree of involvement/activity. As well, it appears that both context and purpose influence how much and which types of directive behaviors mothers employ.

EMPIRICAL EVIDENCE ON TWO CENTRAL PROPOSITIONS

Beside the issues discussed in the preceding sections, the view of directiveness as a negative interactional phenomenon is predicated on two central, empirically testable propositions: (a) the inference that directiveness is accompanied by intrusiveness, while precluding sensitivity and responsiveness and (b) the prediction that directiveness will have detrimental effects on handicapped children's development of competence. In many respects, the validity of the view of directiveness as a problematic interactional style may be seen to rest on finding supportive evidence for these two propositions. I turn now to a discussion of the empirical evidence available on these two issues.

Does Directiveness Either Presuppose Intrusiveness or Preclude Responsiveness and Sensitivity?

Parental interactional behaviors such as warmth, sensitivity, contingent responding, and elaboration have generally been regarded as inherently facilitative of child development. Intrusiveness and lack of sensitivity, on the other hand, are deemed to be inherently disruptive to normal development. One of the major shortcomings of the empirical research on directiveness is that instead of analyzing the incidence of directive behaviors in relation to other maternal behaviors, researchers have tended to make inferences about these other behaviors on the basis of observed levels of directiveness. For example, directiveness has tended to be equated with intrusiveness and lack of sensitivity. In this section, I review evidence from several investigations suggesting that there is no basis for this inference.

Crawley and Spiker (1983) examined the relationship between directiveness and other maternal behaviors in a correlational study of eighteen two-year-old Down syndrome children and their mothers. Because this study examined directiveness more elaborately than any of the other studies cited in this chapter, it will be described in greater detail. The study had two stated purposes: to examine individual differences in mother-child interactions, and to determine whether individual differences in patterns of interaction were related to children's cognitive competence.

Six maternal behaviors were rated on multipoint scales: *directiveness* (ranging from use of indirect requests and suggestions to the consistent use of commands, gestures, and physical guidance to demand child compliance); *elaborativeness* (extent to which mother followed up on or elaborated upon the child's behaviors); *sensitivity* (extent to which mother's behavior reflected awareness of child's cues and signals); *stim-*

ulation value (extent to which mother's participation in play provided optimal cognitive stimulation for the child); *mood* (the quality of mother's expressed mood toward the child); and *mother appeal* (mother's overall appeal, from rater's point of view).

Four other variables, considered to be separable components of maternal sensitivity and maternal directiveness, were rated on a dichotomous scale: *pacing* (whether mother allowed child time to perform requested activity); *developmental appropriateness* (whether mother pitched activities within reasonable limits of the child's developmental level); *readability* (whether mother's intentions and directives were clear and made sense in the context of the ongoing interaction); and *intrusiveness* (whether maternal initiations or elaborations were made in a manner that did not interrupt child behavior rather abruptly). One dyadic variable, measuring the degree of harmony between parental and child interactive behavior, was coded on a five-point scale as *mutuality*.

With the exception of one significant negative correlation between directiveness and elaborativeness, Crawley and Spiker's analyses showed no relationship between directiveness and other maternal interactional qualities. On the other hand, strong positive intercorrelations were found among sensitivity, elaborativeness, stimulation value, and mutuality. In the absence of significant negative correlations between directiveness and variables such as sensitivity and stimulation value, Crawley and Spiker concluded that directiveness was not a highly negative feature of dyadic interaction in the sample.

A descriptive analysis of the four components of directiveness and sensitivity showed that most of the mothers in the sample (78–83%) received satisfactory ratings on developmental appropriateness, pacing, and readability, although only 44% of the mothers were found to be consistently appropriate in terms of intrusiveness. The researchers then examined the extent to which subgroups of mothers differing in sensitivity (high, moderate, and low) also differed in directiveness. Interestingly, even within the high-sensitivity group (n = 8), an equal number of directive and nondirective parents was found. All the mothers in the moderate-sensitivity group (n = 4) were classified as directive. In the low-sensitivity group, four directive and two nondirective mothers were identified.

Crawley and Spiker concluded from these and other aspects of their results that directiveness and sensitivity are not necessarily mutually exclusive maternal interactional styles; mothers may be at the same time directive and sensitive. Second, directive mothers are not necessarily intrusive. Support for these conclusions has come from at least four other studies.

In a more recent study involving twenty-five mothers and their developmentally delayed toddlers and preschool children, Marfo (1991) examined, among other issues, the extent to which directiveness varies as a function of variations in other maternal behaviors. In this study, directiveness was measured in two distinct ways, using two independent sets of coders. Through a rating scale, global ratings of directiveness were obtained for each of the mothers in the sample, along with ratings on seven other maternal and six child behaviors. A behavior-count system was also used to obtain frequency counts for the four classes of directiveness described earlier in this chapter and elsewhere (Marfo, 1990): turntaking control, response control, topic control, and inhibitions.

The correlational analysis revealed two clusters of maternal behaviors. The first cluster consisted of five positively intercorrelated behaviors: warmth, sensitivity, responsivity, elaborativeness, and wait time. The second cluster consisted of two positively correlated behaviors—directiveness and intrusion—which were either unrelated to or negatively correlated with behaviors in the first cluster. Directiveness correlated negatively only with wait time and not with any of the first-cluster behaviors, suggesting that while directive mothers may tend to deny children response opportunities, directiveness does not necessarily suppress warmth, sensitivity, responsivity, and elaborativeness.

The significant correlation between the directiveness and intrusiveness ratings was a most intriguing finding, given the evidence and some of the arguments presented in this chapter. However, none of the relationships between the behavior-count measure of intrusiveness and the four behavior count-measures of directiveness was significant. In fact, a tendency for more directive mothers to be less intrusive was detected. Additionally, no relationships were found between the intrusiveness rating and the four behavior-count measures of directiveness.

Although Tannock (1988b) found mothers of mentally retarded children to employ a significantly larger number of topic controls, these mothers were as verbally responsive to their children's turns as mothers of nonhandicapped children. Similarly, Mahoney and Robenalt (1986) reported that while mothers of Down syndrome children were overwhelmingly more directive, they were as responsive to their children's communication as mothers of nonhandicapped children.

Employing a sequential dependency analysis to examine the ongoing relationships between maternal and child behavior, Marfo and Kysela (1988) reported essentially similar findings. Mothers of mentally retarded children issued twice as many instructions to their children as did mothers of both CA- and MA-matched nonhandicapped infants. However, the interactions of both categories of mothers were characterized equally by significant degrees of responsiveness to children's gestures and visual regard, imitation of children's vocalizations, and positive reinforcement of children's compliance.

Clearly, then, regardless of how dominant directiveness may be in the interactions of these mothers, the emerging literature does not support the use of this one dimension of interaction to draw inferences about the general tone or quality of parental interactional style. A noteworthy implication of this conclusion is that the search for the developmental sequelae of maternal directiveness per se may not be as worthwhile an exercise as researchers may have thought in the past. The evidence reviewed here suggests that it may be more worthwhile to search for how directiveness combines with other aspects of parental interactional style to influence the development of competence.

What Long-Term Effects Does Maternal Directiveness Have on the Handicapped Child's Development?

Much of the attention given to directiveness in the mental retardation literature is premised on the strong concern that a maternal interaction style characterized by high levels of directiveness may have a long-term detrimental effect on the handicapped child's development of competence. Admittedly, to the extent that excessive directiveness could inhibit response initiative and suppress response opportunities on the part of the child, maternal directiveness could have profound implications for the child's development. However, until recently (see Crawley & Spiker, 1983; Herman & Shantz, 1983; Mahoney, 1988a; Mahoney, Finger, & Powell, 1985), the relationship between maternal directiveness and mentally retarded children's development had not been investigated directly.

The concern about the potential negative impact of maternal directiveness on handicapped children's development of competence evolved largely from the combined influence of two forces: (a) extrapolations from the general developmental literature linking parental characteristics such as sensitivity, responsiveness, warmth, and enjoyment with enhanced child developmental competence, and (b) findings from contrastive investigations indicating that on the average mothers of mentally retarded children exhibit more directiveness than mothers of nonhandicapped children. The common inference that such "higher levels" of directiveness could contribute to retarded performance or hinder the development of competence, while plausible, is perhaps flawed on the basis that the research has not yet addressed the issue of how much directiveness is developmentally appropriate.

For example, there is evidence to suggest that for younger children, some amount of directiveness may be developmentally appropriate. In their longitudinal study of the relationship between adult speech and children's language development, Barnes, Gutfreund, Satterly, and Wells (1983) found a positive correlation between mothers' directives and children's gain scores. Other studies have found nonhandicapped eighteen- to twenty=four-month-old infants to produce a high frequency of appropriate responses following directive questions (Leifer, 1979; Shatz, 1977). In a study on children's acquisition of conversational response skills, Leifer and Lewis (1984) reported a similar finding on eighteen- to twenty-three-month-old mentally retarded infants. These infants were found to produce relatively more appropriate responses following maternal directive questions.

Thus, there is the need for research to address the questions of how much directiveness is necessary to provide an optimal learning environment and how much constitutes excessive control with potential deleterious effects. In the absence of such research, speculations regarding developmental effects that are based on gross and imprecise characterizations of "high levels" of maternal directiveness can be misleading.

At any rate, a more substantive way to address the developmental sequelae issue is to examine the findings of investigations in which the link between maternal directiveness and mentally retarded children's developmental competence has been examined more directly through correlational and causal designs. So far, causal designs employing longitudinal data to examine developmental sequelae are nonexistent in the literature; however, several correlational studies have been reported (Crawley & Spiker, 1983; Herman & Shantz, 1983; Mahoney, 1988a; Mahoney, Finger, & Powell, 1985). The findings of these studies are examined below.

In a contrastive study involving ten-year-old educable mentally retarded and nonhandicapped children, Herman and Shantz (1983) reported significant correlations between children's social problem-solving behavior and maternal interaction style within the handicapped group. First, handicapped children whose mothers were more directive (during interactions across free play, cooperative task, and teaching situations) performed more poorly on a social problem-solving task. Second, handicapped children whose mothers played interactively and encouraged problem solving across the three interactive situations performed more competently on the social problem-solving task. These relationships remained signficant even after partialling out the effect of IQ differences. Herman and Shantz found no relationship between the two maternal interactive styles. They concluded that for mentally retarded children, maternal directiveness may "serve as a poor elicitor of reflective cognitive activity," when in fact the development of these children's problem-solving ability may require "experiences where reflection and initiation are allowed or directly elicited and rewarded" (p. 224).

The relationship between maternal interaction style and cognitive developmental status was examined in a study of organically impaired mentally retarded children between ages one and three years (Mahoney, Finger, & Powell, 1985). Based on a factor analysis of eighteen maternal behavior categories originally coded, Mahoney and his associates extracted the following three factors:

1. *Child-oriented/maternal pleasure*, made up of behaviors depicting maternal sensitivity to child's state, responsivity, playfulness, and pleasure.
2. *Quantity of stimulation*, consisting of behaviors depicting amount of physical and social stimulation, expressiveness, and degree of inventiveness.
3. *Control*, made up of directiveness and achievement orientation (positive factor loading), sensitivity to child's interests, and permissiveness (negative factor loading).

These three factors significantly predicted children's cognitive competence, accounting for almost one-quarter of the variance in the children's Bayley mental development scores. More related to the focus of the present discussion is the finding that while maternal responsivity, playfulness, and pleasure (Factor 1) correlated positively with children's mental development, the correlations between each of Factors 2 and 3 and the children's mental development were negative. Interpreted in relation to the signs of the loadings on Factor 3, greater directiveness and insensitivity on the part of the mother were associated with lowered cognitive competence in the child.

In a subsequent analysis of the same data, Mahoney (1988a) examined the relationship between mothers' communicative style and their children's current level of communicative competence. Maternal and child data were pooled across the three child age levels (one-, two-, and three-year olds). A factor analysis of the original eighteen maternal behavior categories yielded six factors, three of which predicted children's expressive language competence ($R^2 = .33$). Mothers who were more attentive (Factor 1) and responsive (Factor 2) to their children's communicative behaviors had children with higher expressive language skills, whereas mothers who issued more action requests and less information requests had children with lower expressive language skills.

The final study to be considered in this section (Crawley & Spiker, 1983) did not find the directiveness-child competence relationship reported in the other three studies. Two indices of child developmental competence were used in this study: the Bayley Mental Development Index (MDI) and a cluster of three child interactional behaviors (play maturity, social initiative, and social responsivity). There was no correlation between maternal directiveness and MDI; none of the three child competence interactional variables was related to maternal directiveness either. The only maternal variables that correlated directly with MDI were stimulation value and appeal. However, a set of maternal variables that the authors described as a sensitivity cluster (sensitivity, elaborativeness, and stimulation value) correlated positively with the three competency-related child interactional variables—play maturity, social initiative, and social responsiveness. The only child interactional variables that correlated significantly with maternal directiveness were interest and initiative. Thus, while directiveness did not appear to be related to child developmental competence, children who were less interested in play interactions and initiated fewer actions with objects had more directive parents.

In light of their finding that many mothers combined sensitivity and directiveness, Crawley and Spiker examined, descriptively, differences in child MDI and interest as a function of differences in degrees of maternal sensitivity and directiveness. They reported a tendency for children of high-sensitive/high-directive mothers to have higher MDIs than other subgroups of children. Similarly, higher levels of interest were found among children of high-sensitive/high-directive mothers. These results should be held tentative, as the researchers themselves acknowledge, because of the limitations that sample size placed on statistical analyses of subgroup differences. It is necessary for future research to attempt to replicate the results, employing larger samples to allow the application of statistical tests to examine subgroup differences.

Nevertheless, the results of Crawley and Spiker's descriptive analysis make sense intuitively and are indeed corroborated by the Mahoney, Finger, and Powell, (1985) factor-analytic study. Recall that in the latter study, maternal control (Factor 3) correlated negatively with children's mental development. However, the signs associated with the two variables (directiveness and sensitivity) making up the control factor indicated that it was the *combination* of high directiveness and low sensitivity that was associated with lowered cognitive competence in children. A corollary finding that can be inferred from this data, then, is that highly directive mothers who were also highly or reasonably sensitive did not have children with lowered cognitive competence.

In the absence of studies employing causal designs, these four investigations provide the only data base upon which conjectures about the potential developmental sequelae of maternal directiveness can be made. Unfortunately, these studies have not produced clear-cut results. It appears that the issue of whether directiveness and sensitivity/responsiveness are orthogonal interactional styles remains a major conceptual obstacle to the meaningful interpretation of even correlational studies. While three of the studies (Herman & Shantz, 1983; Mahoney, 1988a; Mahoney, Finger, & Powell, 1985) can be said to have established a siginificant negative relationship between maternal directiveness and mentally retarded children's development of competence, the data from the Crawley and Spiker (1983) and the Mahoney and associates (1985) studies cast doubts on the meaningfulness of this relationship.

IMPLICATIONS FOR EARLY INTERVENTION

The arguments and evidence presented in this chapter underscore the fact that our knowledge of maternal directiveness and its potential effects on the development of competence in mentally retarded children is still very limited, in spite of the remarkable increase in research on the subject in recent years. This conclusion has profound implications for the interaction-focused early intervention movement and for basic and applied researchers as well.

In light of the limitations identified in this chapter, early interventionists need to exercise caution as they attempt to apply the maternal directiveness research in their work with parents of handicapped children. This review has shown that beyond the child's handicap, many factors—including the child's age, developmental competence, degree of involvement, context of interaction, and maternal agenda—have an influence on how much and what type of directive behaviors are employed by the mother of a handicapped child. Thus, the implicit characterization of all mothers of mentally retarded children as being pathologically directive is, indeed, a myth. The review has also shown that the use of directive behaviors is only one dimension of a complex interaction system, and that directiveness and responsiveness or sensitivity are not necessarily orthogonal interactional characteristics. Consequently, directive behavior cannot be meaningfully addressed in isolation from the various sources of individual differences; neither can it be addressed without paying attention to how it is integrated into the total interaction style.

Meaningful interaction-focused early intervention strategies should be based on theoretical formulations that consider specific parental and child behaviors in a broader transactional framework. Fortunately for the field, systematic theory-driven programs with goals that transcend the reduction of maternal directive behaviors are beginning to emerge in the literature. Several of these promising new approaches have been reviewed in various chapters in this volume. In Chapter 1, Marfo and Cook reviewed Mahoney's Transactional Intervention Program, Bromwich's Mutual Enjoyment Model, and McCollum's Social Interaction Assessment and Intervention Model as exemplary approaches in the United States. In Chapter 5, Barrera described how an interaction-focused intervention process based on a transactional view of the parent-child relationship has been incorporated into a comprehensive early intervention program in Canada. Equally demonstrative of this promising trend is the conversational model of interaction-focused early intervention, as exemplified by the Hanen Program in Canada (see Chapter 9) and MacDonald's work in the United States (see MacDonald & Gillette, 1988).

The viability and potential efficacy of intervention-focused early intervention will depend very much on the extent to which intervenors draw from comprehensive theoretical models in which (a) relationships between intervention strategies and anticipated outcomes are clearly specified, and (b) intervention strategies are tailored to the needs of individual parent-child dyads, based on both historical and situational analyses of each dyad's interactional patterns.

IMPLICATIONS FOR FUTURE RESEARCH

To researchers, the analysis undertaken in this chapter underscores the need to go beyond the frequently posed question of whether parents of handicapped and other developmentally at-risk children are significantly more directive in their interactions than other parents. More research is needed on the sources of variation within groups of dyads with handicapped children. Knowledge from such research, while important in its own right, is crucial if interaction-focused interventions are to be designed to suit the unique characteristics of individual dyads. Perhaps the biggest challenge facing researchers in this area lies in finding answers to some of the fundamental questions that this review has raised. Rigorous correlational and causal research is needed to shed light on the relative developmental significance of the various subtypes of directiveness identified here and elsewhere (Marfo, 1990).

Given, the theoretical and intuitive appeal of the view that directiveness may have developmentally counterproductive effects (Mahoney, 1988b; Mahoney & Powell, 1988), there is the need for future research to address the issue of how much directiveness is appropriate for normal development and how much is excessive. Furthermore, any hypothesis that directiveness would have negative long-term developmental consequences must be premised on the assumption that maternal directive behavior occurs at the expense of dimensions of interaction deemed conceptually to facilitate development—such as responsiveness, sensitivity, and enjoyment. As pointed out earlier, evidence reported in several of the investigations reviewed contradicts this assumption (Crawley & Spiker, 1983; Marfo, 1991; Marfo & Kysela, 1988; Tannock, 1988a, 1988b). Future research needs to examine this assumption more closely. The final challenge to researchers is that the unidimensional search for the long-term developmental sequelae of directiveness should give way to an exploration of the complex ways in which directiveness combines or interacts with various other parental interactional behaviors to influence the development of competence in children.

ACKNOWLEDGMENT

This chapter is based on research supported by the Spencer Foundation Small Grants Program (Grant No. SG 044).

REFERENCES

Affleck, G., McGrade, B. J., McQueeney, M., & Allen, D. (1982). Promise of relationship-focused early intervention in developmental disabilities. *Journal of Special Education, 16*, 413-430.

Bailey, D. B., & Simeonsson, R. J. (1988). Home-based early intervention. In S. L. Odom & M. B. Karnes (Eds.), *Early intervention for infants and children with handicaps: An empirical base* (pp. 199-215). Baltimore: Paul H. Brookes.

Baldwin, A. L., & Baldwin, C. P. (1973). The study of mother-child interaction. *American Scientist, 61*, 714-721.

Barnard, K. E., & Kelly, J. F. (1990). Assessment of parent-child interaction. In S. J. Meisels & J. P. Shonkoff (Eds.), *Handbook of early childhood intervention* (pp. 278-302). New York: Cambridge University Press.

Barnes, S., Gutfreund, M., Satterly, D., & Wells, G. (1983). Characteristics of adult speech which predict children's language development. *Journal of Child Language, 10*, 65-84.

Bell, R. Q. (1968). A reinterpretation of the direction of effects in studies of socialization. *Psychological Review, 75*, 81-95.

Bell, R. Q. (1974). Contributions of human infants to caregiving and social interaction. In M. Lewis & L. A. Rosenblum (Eds.), *The effect of the infant on its caregiver* (pp. 1-19). New York: Wiley.

Bell, R. Q., & Harper, L. V. (1977). *Child effects on adults.* Hillsdale, NJ: Erlbaum.

Bloom, L., & Lahey, M. (1978). *Language development and language disorders.* New York: Wiley.

Breiner, J., & Forehand, R. (1982). Mother-child interactions: A comparison of clinic-referred developmentally delayed group and two non-delayed groups. *Applied Research in Mental Retardation, 3*, 175-183.

Broen, P. A. (1972). The verbal environment of the language learning child. *Monographs of the American Speech and Hearing Association, 17*, 1-103.

Bromwich, R. M. (1976). Focus on maternal behavior in infant intervention. *American Journal of Orthopsychiatry, 46*, 439-446.

Bromwich, R. M. (1981). *Working with parents and infants: An interactional approach.* Baltimore: University Park Press.

Brooks-Gunn, J., & Lewis, M. (1984). Maternal responsivity in interactions with handicapped infants. *Child Development, 55,* 782-793.

Buckhalt, J. A., Rutherford, R. B., & Goldberg, K. E. (1978). Verbal and nonverbal interaction of mothers with their Down syndrome and nonretarded infants. *American Journal of Mental Deficiency, 82,* 337-343.

Buium, N., Rynders, J., & Turnure, J. (1974). Early maternal linguistic environment of normal and Down syndrome language learning children. *American Journal of Mental Deficiency, 79,* 52-58.

Cardoso-Martins, C., & Mervis, C. (1985). Maternal speech to prelinguistic children with Down syndrome. *American Journal of Mental Deficiency, 89,* 451-458.

Cheseldine, S., & McConkey, R. (1979). Parental speech to young Down syndrome children: An intervention study. *American Journal of Mental Deficiency, 83,* 612-620.

Cook, A. S., & Culp, R.E. (1981). Mutual play of mothers with Down syndrome and normal infants. *International Journal of Rehabilitation Research, 4,* 542-544.

Crawley, S. B., & Spiker, D. (1983). Mother-child interactions involving two-year-olds with Down syndrome: A look at individual differences. *Child Development, 54,* 1312-1323.

Cunningham, C. E., Reuler, E., Blackwell, J., & Deck, J. (1981). Behavioral and linguistic developments in the interactions of normal and retarded children with their mothers. *Child Development, 52,* 62-70.

Davis, H., & Oliver, B. (1980). A comparison of aspects of the maternal speech environment of retarded and nonretarded children. *Child: Care, Health, and Development, 6,* 135-145.

Dunst, C. J. (1984). Communicative competence and deficits: Effects on early social interactions. In E. McDonald & D. Gallagher (Eds.), *Facilitating social-emotional development in the young multiply handicapped child* (pp.93-140). Philadelphia: HMS Press.

Eheart, B. K. (1982). Mother-child interactions with nonretarded and retarded preschoolers. *American Journal of Mental Deficiency, 87,* 20-25.

Field, T. M. (1980). Interactions of high-risk infants: Quantitative and qualitative differences. In D. B. Sawin, R. C. Hawkins, L. O. Walker, & J. H. Penticuff (Eds.), *Exceptional infant: Vol. 4. Psychosocial risks in infant-environment interactions* (pp. 120-143). New York: Brunner/Mazel.

Field, T. M. (1983). High-risk infants "have less fun" during interactions. *Topics in Early Childhood Special Education, 3,* 77-87.

Garrard, K. R. (1989). Mothers' verbal directives to delayed and nondelayed children. *Mental Retardation, 27*(1), 11-18.

Girolametto, L. E. (1988). Developing dialogue skills: The effects of a conversational model of language intervention. In K. Marfo (Ed.), *Parent-child interaction and developmental disabilities: Theory, research, and intervention* (pp. 145-162). New York: Praeger.

Gutmann, A. J., & Rondal, J. A. (1979). Verbal operants in mothers' speech to nonretarded and Down syndrome children matched for linguistic level. *American Journal of Mental Deficiency, 83,* 446-452.

Hanzlik, J. R., & Stevenson, M. B. (1986). Interaction of mothers with their infants who are mentally retarded, retarded with cerebral palsy, or non-retarded. *American Journal of Mental Deficiency, 90,* 513-520.

Herman, M. S., & Shantz, C. U. (1983). Social problem solving and mother-child interactions of educable mentally retarded children. *Journal of Applied Developmental Psychology, 4,* 217-226.

Jones, O.H.M. (1980). Prelinguistic communication skills in Down syndrome and normal infants. In T.M. Field, S. Goldberg, D. Stern, & A.M. Sostek (Eds.), *High-risk infants and children: Adult and peer interactions* (pp. 205-225). New York: Academic Press.

Kaye, K., & Charney, R. (1980). How mothers maintain "dialogue" with two-year-olds. In D. R. Olson (Ed.), *The social foundations of language and thought: Essays in honour of Jerome S. Bruner* (pp. 211-230). New York: Norton.

Kogan, K. L., Wimberger, H. C., & Bobbitt, R. A. (1969). An analysis of mother-child interactions in young mental retardates. *Child Development, 40,* 799-812.

Kysela, G. M., & Marfo, K. (1983). Mother-child interactions and early intervention programs for handicapped infants and young children. *Educational Psychology, 3/4,* 201-212.

Leifer, J. (1979). *The interrogative episode in mother-child conversation.* Unpublished doctoral dissertation, Princeton University, Princeton, NJ.

Leifer, J. S., & Lewis, M. (1984). Acquisition of conversational response skills by young Down syndrome and nonretarded young children. *American Journal of Mental Deficiency, 88,* 610-618.

Lewis, M., & Rosenblum, L. A. (Eds.). (1974). *The effect of the infant on its caregiver.* New York: Wiley.

MacDonald, J. D., & Gillette, Y. (1984). Conversation engineering: A pragmatic approach to early social competence. *Seminars in Speech and Language, 5*(13), 171-183.

MacDonald, J., & Gillette, Y. (1988). Communicating partners: A conversational model for building parent-child relationships with handicapped children. In K. Marfo (Ed.), *Parent-child interaction and developmental disabilities: Theory, research, and intervention* (pp. 220-239). New York: Praeger.

Mahoney, G. (1983). A developmental analysis of communication between mothers and infants with Down syndrome. *Topics in Early Childhood Special Education, 3,* 63-76.

Mahoney, G. (1988a). Maternal communication style with mentally retarded children. *American Journal on Mental Retardation, 92,* 352-359.

Mahoney, G. (1988b). Enhancing the developmental competence of handicapped infants. In K. Marfo (Ed.), *Parent-child interaction and developmental disabilities: Theory, research, and intervention* (pp. 203-219). New York: Praeger.

Mahoney, G., Finger, I., & Powell, A. (1985). The relationship between maternal behavioral style and the developmental status of mentally retarded infants. *American Journal of Mental Deficiency, 90,* 350-355.

Mahoney, G., Fors, S., & Wood, S. (1990). Maternal directive behavior revisited. *American Journal on Mental Retardation, 94,* 398-406.

Mahoney, G., & Powell, A. (1988). Modifying parent-child interaction: Enhancing the development of handicapped children. *Journal of Special Education, 22*, 82-96.

Mahoney, G., & Robenalt, K. (1986). A comparison of conversational patterns between mothers and their Down syndrome and normal infants. *Journal of the Division for Early Childhood, 10*, 171-180.

Marfo, K. (1984). Interactions between mothers and their mentally retarded children: Integration of research findings. *Journal of Applied Developmental Psychology, 5*, 45-69.

Marfo, K. (1988). Enhancing interactions between parents and their developmentally disabled children: A missing link in early intervention? In E. R. Boersma, H. J. Huisjes, & H.M.C. Poortman (Eds.), *A holistic approach to perinatal care and prevention of handicap* (pp. 231-239). Groningen, The Netherlands: Erven B. van der Kamp Publishers.

Marfo, K. (1990). Maternal directiveness in interactions with mentally handicapped children: An analytical commentary. *Journal of Child Psychology and Psychiatry, 31*, 531-549.

Marfo, K. (1991, April). *Maternal directiveness in interactions with developmentally delayed children: A correlational analysis.* Paper presented at the Biennial Meeting of the Society for Research in Child Development, Seattle, Washington.

Marfo, K., & Kysela, G. (1988). Frequency and sequential patterns in mothers' interactions with mentally handicapped and nonhandicapped children. In K. Marfo (Ed.), *Parent-child interaction and developmental disabilities: Theory, research, and intervention* (pp. 64-89). New York: Praeger.

Marshall, N. R., Hegrenes, J. R., & Goldstein, S. (1973). Verbal interactions: Mothers and their retarded children vs. mothers and their nonretarded children. *American Journal of Mental Deficiency, 77*, 415-419.

Maurer, H., & Sherrod, K. B. (1987). Context of directives given to young children with Down syndrome and nonretarded children: Development over two years. *American Journal of Mental Deficiency, 91*, 579-590.

McCollum, J. A. (1984). Social interaction between parents and their babies: Validation of an intervention procedure. *Child: Care, Health, and Development, 10*, 301-315.

Nelson, K. (1973). Structure and strategy in learning to talk. *Monographs of the Society for Research in Child Development, 38* (Serial No. 149).

Newport, E. L. (1976). Motherese: The speech of mothers to young children. In N.J. Castellan, D. B. Pisoni, & A. R. Potts (Eds.), *Cognitive theory: Vol. II* (pp. 177-217). Hillsdale, NJ: Erlbaum.

O'Kelly-Collard, M. (1978). Maternal linguistic environment of Down syndrome children. *Australian Journal of Mental Retardation, 5*(4), 121-125.

Olson-Fulero, L. (1982). Style and stability in mother conversational behavior: A study of individual differences. *Journal of Child Language, 9*, 543-564.

Price, P. (1984). A study of mother-child verbal interaction strategies with mothers of young developmentally delayed children. In J. M. Berg (Ed.), *Perspectives and progress in mental retardation: Vol. 1. Social, psycho-*

logical, and educational aspects (pp, 189-199). Baltimore: University Park Press.

Richards, N. (1986). Interaction between mothers and infants with Down syndrome: Infant characteristics. *Topics in Early Childhood Special Education, 6*(3), 54-71.

Rogers, S. J. (1988). Characteristics of social interactions between mothers and their disabled infants: A review. *Child: Care, Health, and Development, 14,* 301-317.

Rondal, J. A. (1977). Maternal speech in normal and Down syndrome children. In P. Mittler (Ed.), *Research to practice in mental retardation: Vol. II. Education and training* (pp. 239-243). Baltimore: University Park Press.

Rose, T. L., & Calhoun, M. L. (1990). The Charlotte Circle Project: A program for infants and toddlers with severe/profound disabilities. *Journal of Early Intervention, 14,* 175-185.

Rosenberg, S. A., & Robinson, C. C. (1988). Interactions of parents with their young handicapped children. In S. L. Odom & M. B. Karnes (Eds.), *Early intervention for infants and children with handicaps: An empirical base* (pp. 159-176). Baltimore: Paul H. Brookes.

Rubenstein, J. L., & Howes, C. (1979). Caregiving and infant behavior in day care and in homes. *Developmental Psychology, 15,* 1-24.

Schaffer, H. R. (Ed.). (1977). *Studies in mother-infant interaction.* London: Academic Press.

Schaffer, H. R. (1984). *The child's entry into a social world.* London: Academic Press.

Schaffer, H. R., & Crook, C. K. (1979). Maternal control techniques in a directed play situation. *Child Development, 50,* 989-996.

Schaffer, H. R., & Crook, C. K. (1980). Child compliance and maternal control techniques. *Developmental Psychology, 16,* 54-61.

Seitz, S. (1975). Language intervention: Changing the language environment of the retarded child. In R. Koch & F. de la Cruz (Eds.), *Down syndrome (Mongolism): Research, prevention, and management* (157-179). New York: Brunner/Mazel.

Shatz, M. (1977). On the development of communicative understandings: An early strategy for interpreting and responding to messages. In J. Glick & A. Clarke-Stewart (Eds.), *Studies in social and communicative development* (pp. 24-65). New York: Gardner.

Snow, C. E. (1977). The development of conversations between mothers and babies. *Journal of Child Language, 4,* 1-22.

Sorce, J., & Emde, R. (1982). The meaning of infant emotional expressions: Regularities in normal and Down syndrome infants. *Journal of Child Psychology and Psychiatry, 23,* 145-158.

Stoneman, Z., Brody, G. H., & Abbott, D. (1983). In-home observations of young Down syndrome children with their mothers and fathers. *American Journal of Mental Deficiency, 87,* 591-600.

Tannock, R. (1988a). Mothers' directiveness in their interactions with their children with and without Down syndrome. *American Journal on Mental Retardation, 93,* 154-165.

Tannock, R. (1988b). Control and reciprocity in mothers' interactions with

Down syndrome and normal children. In K. Marfo (Ed.), *Parent-child interaction and developmental disabilities: Theory, research, and intervention* (pp. 162-180). New York: Praeger.

Terdal, L. E., Jackson, R. H., & Garner, A. M. (1976). Mother-child interactions: A comparison between normal and developmentally delayed groups. In E. J. Mash, L. A. Hamerlynck, & L. C. Handy (Eds.), *Behavior modification and families* (pp. 249-264). New York: Brunner/Mazel.

Weistuch, L., & Lewis, M. (1985). The language interaction project. *Analysis and Intervention in Developmental Disabilities, 5,* 97-106.

White, B. J., & Watts, J. C. (1973). *Experience and environment: Major influences on the development of the young child.* Englewood Cliffs, NJ: Prentice Hall.

II

INTERNATIONAL PERSPECTIVES

8

Early Intervention in the United States

Marcia Summers and Mark S. Innocenti

The development and implementation of early intervention activities for young children who have a delay or who are at risk for future delays are relatively recent phenomena in the United States. Early intervention as an applied and academic field has developed primarily within the specialty area of early childhood special education (ECSE), a field comprised of professionals from many disciplines. The genesis of ECSE in the United States may be traced to the formation, in 1968, of the Handicapped Children's Early Education Program (HCEEP) branch within the United States Department of Education. Although other work had occurred in early intervention prior to this time, the establishment of HCEEP provided national recognition and federal funds to address early intervention issues.

Since 1968, rapid changes have occurred in the field of early intervention. The most significant event impacting on early intervention was the passage of Public Law 99–457 (P.L. hereafter) in 1986. This law mandates education for handicapped children aged three to five years and provides both impetus and funding for early intervention for children younger than age three.

From the viewpoint of an outside observer, the passage of only eighteen years from the establishment of a specialty area to that specialty area demonstrating efficacy such that its tenets become law is admirable. However, these tenets, and the practices derived from them, are based on research that has recently received negative reviews (Casto & Mastropieri, 1986; Dunst, 1986; Dunst, Snyder, & Mankinen, 1987). It is clear that ECSE has done well, but many challenges remain to be met (Bricker, 1988; Odom & Warren, 1988). Failure to conquer these challenges could result in a loss of valuable ground that many have worked hard to achieve.

To confront the future adequately, it is necessary to understand the past and present. This chapter will (a) provide a history of early intervention in the United States with an emphasis on federally funded projects, (b) discuss some current contentious issues, (c) outline current practice, and (d) make suggestions for future directions. Consistent with the scope of this volume, the chapter will focus primarily on early intervention for young children with handicaps. This group includes children with biologically established handicapping conditions (e.g., Down syndrome) and those who display significant delays of unknown etiology.

HISTORY

The history of early intervention in the United States is a blending of influences from such diverse fields as philosophy, psychology, special education, early childhood education, and medicine. Particularly influential have been advances in special education and early childhood education practices.

Special Education

The humane treatment of the physically and mentally handicapped is less than 150 years old (Kaufman, 1980). Prior to 1800, churches generally provided the only organized benevolent treatment of retarded persons. By the nineteenth century, developments in science and in philosophical appraisals of human nature started to change views toward handicapped persons. John Locke, who regarded the mind as a blank slate (tabula rasa) at birth, argued that people learned through sensory experience and that knowledge came from experience, not from God. Darwin's *Origin of Species* attacked the notion of divine creation and further helped to change thinking that handicapped individuals were suffering the wrath of God (Garwood, 1979). It was during this period that attempts to educate handicapped persons in the United States began with the establishment of schools such as the American Asylum for the Education and Instruction of the Deaf and Dumb (1817), the New England Asylum for the Blind (1829), and the Experimental School for Teaching and Training Idiotic Children (1848).

Extremely influential in this field were the achievements of Jean-Marc Gaspard Itard, a Frenchman. Itard was the first physician/educator to use a clinical method to study, observe, and educate an exceptional child (Kaufman, 1980)—a boy who had been abandoned when small and grew up as an animal. Itard's successes with the child, while mixed, demonstrated that it was possible to change the behavior of severely retarded individuals through education and training.

It was a student of Itard's, Edward Segun, who brought the idea of the residential school to the United States around 1850. Segun used a physiological approach that emphasized educating the muscular system first, the auditory sense next, and finally the visual abilities. Many of the first schools for retarded children in the United States were begun in an attempt to experiment with Segun's methods and theories. Admission was refused to the severely retarded, the very young, and the very old, who were not thought to profit by these methods and theories. However, these early schools did lay the foundation for the state residential schools of the future. Segun was also instrumental in organizing the original chapter of what is known today as the American Association on Mental Retardation (Dexter, 1987).

By the turn of the century, education for the handicapped was still a sporadic business. Not until education became compulsory in the United States did teaching of the handicapped truly become a public issue. With the advent of compulsory education laws passed by the individual states (from 1852 to 1918), a number of children with handicaps were forced for the first time to attend school. Many handicaps (such as mild retardation or learning disabilities) were not noticeable at a time when few individuals could read and write, and it was only when mass general education became widely accepted that the retarded stood out (Pritchard, 1963, in Sigmon, 1987). Special classes for the handicapped came about, not for humanitarian reasons but because exceptional children were unwanted in the regular public-school classroom (Chaves, 1977, in Sigmon, 1987). Still, many school-aged children with handicaps did not receive an education. It was common to exclude the wheelchair bound, those not toilet trained, and those considered uneducable, because of the problems schooling them would entail. The institutionalization model was still prevalent, and children were generally required to leave their families.

In 1911 New Jersey became the first state in the nation to mandate the establishment of special classes for the deaf, the blind, and the mentally retarded (Sigmon, 1987). From 1915 to 1930, the number of special classes in public schools increased dramatically, but between 1930 and 1940, a sharp reversal in this trend occurred. The financial burdens of the Depression, dissatisfaction with the premature establishment of inadequately planned special classes with untrained teachers, and misinterpretation of the assumptions of progressive education combined to dampen public enthusiasm for special education (Robinson & Robinson, 1965, in Sigmon, 1987.)

After World War II, special education once again began to prosper.

Two factors have been noted as especially significant in this expansion. The first resulted from the IQ testing movement. During the war, nearly one million men were excluded from military service on the basis of some type of mental incompetency. Yet many of these men were sufficiently competent to return home and lead visibly productive and useful lives. This helped to reduce some of the stigma associated with mental handicaps. Second, among the returning war veterans were many thousands of men who were physically damaged, intellectually impaired, or emotionally disturbed. Now that handicapped persons comprised a visible minority, attitudes toward them began to change. These men were considered heroes who deserved their country's thanks, and being handicapped was therefore seen in a less negative light. Taking this cue, parents of children with handicaps started to organize advocacy groups on behalf of their children and were joined by special education professional groups (e.g., the Council for Exceptional Children).

An event that significantly impacted education for handicapped children was based on civil rights issues. This event was the U.S. Supreme Court case of *Brown vs. Board of Education of Topeka* of 1954. The outcome of this case was that state laws that permitted or required racially segregated public schools were held in violation of the fourteenth Amendment of the U.S. Constitution. Advocacy groups for handicapped children recognized that rights afforded to one minority group applied to all minority groups. Thus began a movement that eventually culminated in a guaranteed free and public education for school-aged children with handicaps (P.L. 94–142).

Early Childhood Education

Concurrent with the development of education for handicapped children was the development of early childhood education. Early childhood education in the United States has its origins in the writings of Rousseau, Pestalozzi, and Locke. These writers stressed that a child's education begins at birth and that children should be treated with compassion. These ideas were incorporated into Froebel's view of the "child as seed," and as a result Froebel developed the first kindergarten in Germany in the 1830s.

Margarette Shurz, a German who emigrated to America, had been influenced by Froebel and established the first kindergarten in Wisconsin in 1856. Although this was the first kindergarten in the United States, it was for German-speaking children. In 1860, Elizabeth Palmer Peabody opened the first English-speaking kindergarten in Boston. The first public-school kindergarten in the United States was opened in St. Louis in 1873, partly due to the influence of Peabody. Although kindergarten has subsequently become established within the American educational system, kindergarten is not mandatory in some parts of the United States.

Early childhood education in the United States remained relatively unchanged from the nineteenth-century Froebelian view until the 1950s and 1960s. The primary changes that occurred were societal in nature. For example, child-labor laws were established to prevent the abuse of children in the work place, and school became mandatory for children. It was not until the 1950s that the work of Jean Piaget and Maria Montessori became accepted in the United States (although the work of both occurred early in the twentieth century). Preschool programs based on these approaches began to emerge, and attention began to focus on the potential of young children.

In the early 1960s, J. McVicker Hunt's *Intelligence and Experience* (1961) and Benjamin Bloom's *Stability and Change in Human Characteristics* (1964) provided evidence of the importance of the early years to later development and stimulated early intervention research and program development (Garwood & Sheehan, 1989). Bloom estimated that about 80% of the development of intelligence takes place between conception and eight years of age. Implicit in this continuity view is that predictions of adult status can be made for some important psychological characteristics in the preschool years (Kaufman, 1980). The early years of a child's life thus came to be viewed as a "critical period" during which intervention would yield greater benefit than later treatment.

These influences on early childhood education resulted in the field gaining momentum in the early 1960s. Early childhood programs currently enjoy wide public acceptance, as increasing numbers of children take part in them. More important, one impact of early childhood education on children with handicaps has been the growing recognition that early help may be more effective than later treatment for these children. Several key influences provided impetus for this notion, and these are described in the next section.

Early Evidence for Early Intervention

As the fields of special education and early childhood education evolved, evidence was accumulating that early intervention could be effective. In a classic study, Skeels and Dye (1939; cf., Skeels, 1942) examined the effects of environmental stimulation on two comparable groups of infants. Mentally retarded females acted as surrogate mothers for one group (n = 13), providing these children with attention and stimulation. Twelve infants with average IQs remained in a non-stimulating orphanage environment. Eighteen months later, the stimulated infants gained an average 27.5 IQ points while the control group dropped 26.2 points.

Twenty-one years later, Skeels (1966) continued to find differences between those who were placed in the enriched environment and those who were not. Of those in the experimental group, all were found to be self-supporting as adults. Four of these adults had completed college and, as a group, had a median high-school education. Of those in the control group, four adults had been institutionalized. The median education for these adults was at the third-grade level.

Additional evidence came from the work of Kirk (1958, 1965), who studied handicapped preschoolers. He compared institutionalized mentally handicapped preschoolers who received a preschool program with a comparable group who remained on the wards and received no intervention services. Children in the experimental program showed significant gains on intellectual measures. Six of the fifteen-experimental group children were able to leave the institution by age eight, while none of the children in the control group left the institution.

Work by Bidder, Bryant, and Gray (1975); Gray and Klaus (1965); Schweinhart and Weikart (1981); Stedman and Eichorn (1964); Weiss (1981); and others provided additional evidence for the value of early intervention. The work of Bloom (1964) and Hunt (1961), discussed earlier, also provided affirmation of the value of early intervention activities. Based upon these studies, the consensus emerged that children's cognitive skills develop early in life and very rapidly, and that early enrichment can have profound influences on a child's future functioning. Although this consensus is no longer accepted without question, this philosophy, nevertheless, played a major role in the acceptance of early intervention and helped to create a social climate for legislation favoring handicapped children.

Legislative Activities

Both research and societal factors converged to provide momentum for the early intervention movement in the 1960s. The changing social climate in the United States in the 1960s led to the passage of favorable legislation for several groups. Litigative and legislative activities occurred in the areas of civil rights, rights for the disadvantaged, and rights for the handicapped. Table 8.1 presents a summary of legislation relevant to disadvantaged and handicapped children. A breakthrough for early intervention, focusing on disadvantaged children, was the Economic Opportunity Act of 1964. Part of this act was directed at the establishment of Project Head Start. This program was designed to provide early intervention for disadvantaged preschool children in the

Table 8.1
Legislative Activity Affecting Early Intervention

Legislation	Description
Disadvantaged:	
Public Law 85-568 (1964) Economic Opportunity Act	Created the Office of Economic Opportunity that developed and began administration of Project Head Start during the Summer of 1965.
Public Law 92-424 (1972) Economic Opportunity Act Amendments	Established a preschool mandate that required that not less than 10% of the total number of Head Start placements be reserved for handicapped children.
Handicapped:	
Public Law 90-538 (1968) Handicapped Children's Early Education Assistance Act	Significant to the education of handicapped preschool children; established experimental early education programs throughout the country (HCEEP).
Public Law 94-142 (1975) Education of All Handicapped Children Act	Revised and expanded P.L. 93-380 (1974) which established a total federal commitment to the education of the handicapped. Provided a free, appropriate public education with related services to all handicapped children between ages 3 and 21, although states were given the option of not serving children ages 3-5.
Public Law 98-199 (1983) The Education of the Handicapped Act Amendments of 1983	Provided financial incentives for states to extend service levels down to birth.
Public Law 99-457 (1986) The Education of the Handicapped Act Amendments of 1986	Reauthorized P.L. 98-199; authorized states to establish early intervention systems for children 0-3 and their families; increased funding for states to serve all eligible 3-5 years olds. Laws to be fully implemented by 1991.

hopes that it would place them on an equal cognitive and social footing with their nondisadvantaged peers once they began public school.

The initial research on Head Start was favorable, demonstrating significant gains in Head Start children. Unfortunately, early follow-up research found that these IQ gains disappeared after the children entered school (Westinghouse Learning Corporation, 1969). Based on societal and political pressures, Head Start continued despite the negative research findings. Arguments by researchers who questioned the findings and suggested that unmeasurable gains were being made (Gotts, 1973; Zigler & Trickett, 1978) bolstered the pro-Head Start forces.

The results of a nineteen-year longitudinal study on children who participated in Head Start (the Perry Pre-school Project) found a number of positive results (Berrueta-Clement et al., 1984). These benefits included: (a) less need for special education, (b) more positive school attitudes, (c) less arrests, (d) less teen pregnancy, and (e) better employment histories. Other research has supported these findings (Lazar & Darlington, 1982).

As an early intervention program, Head Start is the most well-known in the United States and has served over eight million preschoolers. Additionally, Head Start has had a major impact on early intervention for children with handicaps. The Economic Opportunity Acts Amendments of 1972 mandated that at least 10% of the total population served by Head Start be children with handicaps, giving Head Start the status of the first mandated, mainstreamed early intervention program in the United States. This occurred well before the concept of mainstreaming became popular in special education.

One of the most important pieces of legislation regarding young children with handicaps was the Handicapped Children's Early Education Assistance Act of 1968. This act established the Handicapped Children's Early Education Program of the Department of Education, which has been responsible for funding the majority of innovative service projects in early intervention that occurred in the United States. This legislation may be viewed as the formal beginning of the field of early intervention for the handicapped. HCEEP programs will be discussed more fully later in this chapter in the section on current practices.

The next major legislation to affect early intervention activities was an act that impacted significantly on educational practices for all handicapped children—the Education of All Handicapped Children Act of 1975 (P.L. 94–142). P.L. 94–142 provided for a free, appropriate public education with related services to all children with handicaps between the ages of three and twenty-one years. This act has been called the "Bill of Rights" for children with handicaps. The overall impact of this act on educational practice has been discussed in other places (Turnbull & Turnbull, 1986). While this act documented acceptance of the need for early intervention by the federal government, it also provided individual states with the option not to serve these young children. Unfortunately, this was an option many states adopted. In 1985, only twenty-four of the fifty states had mandated services for handicapped children under age five and only eight states had mandated services for handicapped children under age three (Fraas, 1986).

Although P.L. 94–142 had a major impact on such intervention, supporters of early intervention were aware of the implementation problems involved in serving young children. As a result of successes with preschool early intervention, the need for services for even younger children was being heralded (Hayden & McGinness, 1978; Palmer, 1977). Congress responded to these calls for early intervention in 1983 by passing the Amendments to the Education of the Handicapped Act (P.L. 98–199). These amendments provided financial incentives for states to extend early intervention service levels down to birth. Unfortunately, funding remained dependent upon the number of children served between the ages of three and five, and the act, in effect, diluted the funding available for the three- to five-year-old children. Also, incentives built into these amendments to encourage individual state participation were weak and ineffectual.

Lobbying groups for early intervention continued their activities to push through a law mandating early intervention for all young children with handicaps (cf., Fraas, 1986). In 1986, Congress responded by passing P.L. 99–457 (Amendments to the Education of the Handicapped Act). P.L. 99–457 mandated that all preschool-aged children with handicaps receive a free and appropriate education by 1991. This law provided penalties for states that did not conform to the law. In addition, P.L. 99–457 created a new state grant program for infants and toddlers with handicaps.

The passage of P.L. 99–457 has signaled a new era for early intervention. The federal government has recognized the need for early intervention (at least at the preschool level) and has provided funds to support it. P.L. 99–457 is also significant in other ways. Children need not be classified into narrowly defined categories to receive services. The importance of the family in development has been heavily emphasized, especially for those children under age three years. For infants and toddlers, the definition of what constitutes intervention services has been broadened. For all children, a wide variety of possible intervention options has been acknowledged.

It is clear that the passage of P.L. 99–457 is not the final stop for advocates of early intervention. Concerns regarding how states will implement preschool services and how service policies will be defined remain. Questions regarding services for infants and toddlers are just beginning to be addressed. Many problems still exist (cf., Bricker, 1988), but Public Law 99–457 represents a major accomplishment for advocates of early intervention and a benefit for the children and families who will receive services.

PROBLEMS IN THE PRESENT

The history of early intervention demonstrates admirable advances. Currently, early intervention activities regarding the development of and research on "best practices" are occurring (McDonnell & Hardman, 1988; Decker, 1989). However, there is a growing tendency to question some of what has been accomplished by early intervention. Questions have arisen concerning the research on which early intervention activities are based and on the data from which costs have been obtained. These particular areas—research and costs—have traditionally provided a foundation for early intervention (Bricker & Dow, 1980; Palmer, 1977; Wood, 1981). The next sections will briefly review concerns regarding knowledge of costs and the research base of early intervention (see Chapter 1 in this volume for a more extensive coverage of issues pertaining to the research base of early intervention).

Early Intervention Research

In a "review of reviews," White, Bush, and Casto (1985-86) found overwhelming agreement that early intervention is effective (94% of fifty-two studies). Unfortunately, they also found that a number of these reviews based this assertion primarily or solely on studies done with disadvantaged children. The benefits of early intervention for disadvantaged children is not a major issue of contention (Berrueta-Clement et al., 1984; Lazar & Darlington, 1982; White & Casto, 1985). Controversy ensues when these findings are overgeneralized to children with handicaps.

A number of well-conducted reviews of early intervention for handicapped children has been completed (Casto & Mastropieri, 1986; Dunst, 1986; Dunst & Rheingrover, 1981; Dunst, Snyder & Mankinen, 1987; Simeonsson, Cooper, & Scheiner, 1982). These reviews have been cautious with their conclusions, but overall the findings have been quite negative, particularly regarding the validity of the studies. Dunst and Rheingrover (1981) found that 71% of the forty-nine studies they reviewed used methods that made the results scientifically uninterpretable. Simeonsson, Cooper, and Scheiner (1982) essentially agreed with the Dunst and Rheingrover (1981) findings. They then attempted to argue that the lack of effectiveness found for early intervention programs was a result of the nature of studies in early intervention. Casto and Mastropieri (1986) used meta-analytic techniques to examine a number of common assumptions made regarding early intervention programs and found little empirical support for those assumptions.

An extremely comprehensive review by Dunst, Snyder, and Mankinen (1987), which examined 105 studies by degree of causality and by type of child served, was no more positive for the early intervention movement. These authors stated that any conclusions regarding the efficacy of early intervention must be considered tentative and conditional. They noted that "there is insufficient evidence at this time to conclude that there are cause-effect relationships between the interventions and outcomes observed" (p. 285). Dunst and associates further stated, in agreement with Casto and Mastropieri (1986), that children in early intervention programs do make positive developmental and behavioral changes across time but that "the extent to which the interventions are responsible for observed effects is difficult to ascertain" (p. 285).

Some researchers have been critical of reviews of early intervention because they tend to exclude single-subject methodology research (Strain & Smith, 1986). Many of the problems in reviewing this literature base are related to the subjective nature of comparing this research, as no standard metric is employed across studies (Scruggs, Mastropieri, & Casto, 1987). Reviews of the single-subject literature in early intervention have been conducted and are favorable but have not significantly refuted other reviews (Dunst, Snyder, & Mankinen, 1987; Scruggs, Mastropieri, & McEwen, 1988). Single-subject studies do show strong evidence for a functional relationship between dependent and independent variables. These single-subject studies usually focus on a narrow, well-defined objective. Although this is useful for demonstrating functional relationships, it represents only parts of the whole of an early intervention program. Also, these studies are usually conducted under rigorous investigative control, a feature not available in most early intervention programs. Successful programs frequently have problems when disseminated for use by a wider audience (Kamps et al., 1989). Also, many single-subject studies do not sufficiently address generalization and maintenance issues. Scruggs, Mastropieri, and McEwen (1988) provide suggestions for single-subject research in early intervention, many of which are identical to those that need to be addressed by group research.

Costs of Early Intervention

While expert opinion and studies supporting the concept of early intervention have been enormously influential on legislative activity, perhaps most convincing to politicians and administrators has been the perceived cost effectiveness of early intervention. Several analyses have been conducted in this realm. In an often cited study, Wood (1981) compiled an extensive review of the relative costs of special education in the United States, based upon age of entry into intervention programs. Using the work of Kakalik, Furry, Thomas, and Carney (1981), who determined the cost of special education to be 2.17 times the cost of regular education, Wood developed a cost model based upon the following assumptions: (a) early intervention results in proportional attrition rates from special education into regular education from one educational level to another, and (b) those going into regular education will remain there. Wood's review resulted in the calculation of the following costs for the provision of special education intervention per child to age eighteen years, at various entry ages:

Intervention at birth: $37,273

Intervention at age 2 years: $37,600

Intervention at age 6 years (with attrition and entrance into regular education): $48,816

Intervention at age 6 years (without attrition and no eventual movement to regular education): $53,340

These data have frequently been cited in support of the notion that the delay of early intervention services results in more costly special services, and the greater the delay, the larger the costs.

In a similar vein, Schweinhart and Weikart (1981) conducted a benefit-cost economic analysis of the Perry Pre-school Project (cf., Barnett, 1985). They calculated that the program resulted in a 348% return on the original investments. Weiss (1981) also calculated the benefit-cost of the INREAL pre-school project. Over a three-year period, a cost savings of $1,283.76 per pupil resulted due to reduced need for special-education services and fewer retention-in-grade placements. The consensus has been that substantial savings to taxpayers can be gained by beginning educational intervention prior to age 6 years. Early childhood intervention seems to be a sound investment that provides financial benefits for society.

The exact nature of these benefits are now being questioned. Barnett and Escobar (1988) reviewed the studies mentioned above and a number of other early intervention studies that examined cost data. These authors found the cost data fragmentary and problematic and undeserving of the strong conclusions that have been made regarding cost efficacy or cost benefits. In another article, Barnett (1988) provides suggestions for research and policy that need to be addressed in relation to costs; the interested reader is referred to that article for further information.

The need for more methodologically sound studies of the cost and effectiveness of early intervention is apparent. These are areas of great importance to the continued development of the field.

CURRENT PRACTICE

Ideally, early intervention practices should react to criticism and concerns regarding early intervention research. Unfortunately, no data base is available to clearly gauge how practice reflects current knowledge (Dunst, Snyder, & Mankinen, 1987). In a recent synthesis of best practices in early intervention, McDonnell and Hardman (1988) note many important accomplishments. These authors point out that most of these accomplishments are the result of successful demonstration projects rather than the result of standardized, replicable models (i.e, research-based models). Dunst, Snyder, and Mankinen (1987) are even more critical of the development of practice, stating, "What evidence we do have would suggest that state of practice is not keeping pace with our ever expanding knowledge base" (p. 286).

One approach to focusing on trends in best practice that may address the practice versus knowledge issue would be through an examination of model/demonstration programs. Although a number of agencies fund these types of programs (e.g., the Office of Maternal and Child Health, the National Center for Clinical Infant Programs, etc.), the agency funding the majority of these programs is the HCEEP branch of the Office of Special Education Programs within the Department of Education. Therefore, this survey of practices will be based on HCEEP-funded model/demonstration programs.

All HCEEP-funded programs have been formally evaluated twice before (Roy Littlejohn Associates, 1982; Stock et. al., 1976). (Another evaluation of early intervention effectiveness—that of Abt Associates in 1973—included many HCEEP projects but was not specifically directed at HCEEP.) The results of both of these reports have been favorable toward HCEEP programs. A summary of major findings from these reports suggests that:

1. Children enrolled in HCEEP projects make 1.5 to 2 times the progress they would be expected to make without intervention.

2. More than half the children who leave HCEEP projects are placed in classrooms for nonhandicapped children. Of these children, many perform in the average range.

3. Almost all parents perceive positive changes in their children.

4. HCEEP projects have an impressive record of continuing past their federal-funding stage.

5. HCEEP projects have had major impact through replication and product dissemination activities.

6. HCEEP dollars expended for programming have generated an 18 to 1 return in programming dollars spent.

These evaluations have been in clear agreement regarding the benefits of HCEEP projects. The positive impact of HCEEP projects on early intervention practice cannot be disputed, but the data regarding costs and benefits to children must be viewed skeptically, based on information presented earlier in this chapter. The highest status that a federally funded program can achieve is JDRP (Joint Dissemination Review Panel) approval. To obtain JDRP approval, a project must demonstrate product fidelity and provide evaluation data demonstrating effectiveness. JDRP standards are considered rigorous (Datta, 1977; Odom & Fewell, 1983; Tallmadge, 1977). Twenty-three HCEEP projects have obtained JDRP approval.

White, Mastropieri, and Casto (1984) reviewed twenty-one JDRP/approved projects originally funded by HCEEP. They concluded that these projects had made a substantial contribution to the field of early intervention in terms of intervention, assessment, and dissemination activities. This conclusion was similar to that expressed by Odom and Fewell (1983) in an earlier review. However, White Mastropieri, and Casto (1984) found serious weaknesses in the evaluation methodologies of these projects and concluded that little about the efficacy of early intervention could be gleaned from them.

A review conducted for this chapter looked at HCEEP projects from 1978-79 to 1988-89 for types of handicaps served, goals of the program, program focus, and service delivery methods. The source of these data was the annually published HCEEP reviews of funded projects. The goal of this review was to examine trends in the types of projects funded. No clear pattern emerged as to type of handicapping condition most often served (see Table 8.2). Typically, programs aimed to serve children with all types of handicaps. There did appear to be a slight trend toward more programs aimed at medically/physically at-risk children over the decade studied. Otherwise, there was great variability from year to year in terms of type of handicap served.

Clearly, the most common goal of HCEEP projects was direct service and parent involvement (see Table 8.3). Increases may also be noted in information dissemination and professional training, while mainstreaming appears to rise slightly and then fall. When secondary goals were examined, the pattern was extremely similar to that for the major goal, with the exception that an increasing tendency to serve families was noted. Most programs would appear, then, to be aimed fairly clearly at providing service for children with handicaps and systematically involving parents.

Not surprisingly, the focus of most programs over the years has been the child and the parent, although programs aimed solely at the child have declined (see Table 8.4). Concurrently, there has been a shift toward projects emphasizing an interagency focus. Finally, Table 8.5

Table 8.2
HCEEP Review: Handicapping Conditions

	1978-79 (33)*	1979-80 (53)	1980-81 (39)	1981-82 (36)	1982-83 (25)	1983-84 (27)	1985-86 (52)	1986-87 (30)	1987-88 (20)	1988-89 (29)
Biologically at-risk	12%	9%	10%	17%	16%	7%	6%	13%	10%	10%
Environmentally at-risk	6%	6%	8%	17%	12%	15%	21%	17%	5%	21%
Medically/physically at-risk	0	2%	3%	6%	4%	0	8%	7%	20%	14%
D.D.	15%	15%	18%	14%	8%	15%	15%	33%	5%	7%
All types	58%	58%	41%	39%	48%	48%	46%	23%	50%	41%
Other	9%	9%	21%	8%	12%	15%	4%	3%	10%	7%

* Number of projects.

Table 8.3
HCEEP Review: Primary Goal of Projects

	1978-79 (33)*	1979-80 (53)	1980-81 (39)	1981-82 (36)	1982-83 (25)	1983-84 (27)	1985-86 (52)	1986-87 (30)	1987-88 (20)	1988-89 (29)
Mainstreaming	0	2%	0	3%	8%	15%	4%	13%	0	0
Direct service	91%	79%	92%	75%	48%	56%	67%	30%	40%	41%
Parent training	9%	19%	5%	14%	32%	26%	25%	23%	50%	21%
Professional training	0	0	0	3%	0	0	0	3%	5%	21%
Information dissemination	0	0	0	0	4%	4%	2%	10%	5%	0
Product development	0	0	0	0	0	0	0	7%	0	14%
Transition	0	0	0	0	0	0	0	7%	0	0
Assessment	0	0	3%	3%	0	0	0	0	0	0
Serve families	0	0	0	0	4%	0	0	7%	0	3%
Other	0	0	0	0	0	0	2%	0	0	0

* Number of projects

Table 8.4
HCEEP Review: Primary Recipient of Project Services

	1978-79 (33)*	1979-80 (53)	1980-81 (39)	1981-82 (36)	1982-83 (25)	1983-84 (27)	1985-86 (52)	1986-87 (30)	1987-88 (20)	1988-89 (29)
Child	94%	89%	92%	86%	60%	78%	83%	57%	50%	52%
Parent	6%	11%	5%	11%	28%	15%	13%	20%	40%	10%
Family	0	0	0	0	12%	4%	2%	13%	0	3%
Agencies	0	0	0	3%	0	4%	2%	10%	5%	31%
Other	0	0	3%	0	0	0	0	0	5%	3%

* Number of projects.

Table 8.5
HCEEP Review: Primary Setting for Delivery of Project Services

	1978-79 (33)*	1979-80 (53)	1980-81 (39)	1981-82 (36)	1982-83 (25)	1983-84 (27)	1985-86 (52)	1986-87 (30)	1987-88 (20)	1988-89 (29)
Home	6%	17%	3%	11%	8%	19%	19%	23%	15%	21%
Center	15%	9%	31%	25%	20%	30%	17%	37%	5%	21%
Public school	0	6%	8%	6%	4%	0	6%	3%	10%	0
Head Start	0	0	0	0	4%	0	0	0	5%	0
Hospital	0	0	3%	6%	8%	0	2%	7%	0	3%
Day care	0	0	3%	0	4%	0	0	10%	5%	0
Home/Center	73%	66%	51%	42%	36%	44%	50%	17%	45%	14%
Other	6%	2%	3%	8%	16%	7%	6%	0	15%	41%

* Number of projects.

shows that the home/center setting has been the most commonly used means of service delivery, although this approach appears to be declining slightly as use of other settings increases.

This review of HCEEP projects is limited in many respects. It is limited because the source of information (project abstracts) did not provide comprehensive information about the projects. There were many projects with which the authors were familiar, yet descriptions did not detail aspects of the projects that made them unique. Also, the format of these abstracts was not identical for each year information was published. We were not able to contact individual projects for greater description or to analyze final reports.

From an information perspective, on the surface these data are of little utility. Trends in funding preference are shown—funding preferences that may have been partly the result of announced priorities based on political factors rather than on research. At a deeper level, these data may reflect the activities of the field over those years—great effort without a clear unifying objective. The practices that these data reflect were criticized by others (Dunst, Snyder, & Mankinen 1987; McDonnell & Hardman, 1988) as needing more research direction. These practices and programs were, at that time, appropriate. The goal of HCEEP was to fund projects that would enhance the practice of early intervention. Early reviews indicate that HCEEP projects were meeting this goal (Roy Littlejohn Associates, 1982; Stock et al., 1976).

HCEEP continues to be responsive to the changing needs of the field, as indicated in the literature. Research institutes have been funded since 1977. These institutes have been addressing issues over which concerns have been raised. During 1988-89, three HCEEP research institutes were being funded (Decker, 1989). These research institutes were focused on transition practices (Kansas Early Childhood Research Institute, University of Kansas); infant personnel preparation (Carolina Institute for Research on Infant Personnel Preparation, University of North Carolina); and the cost and immediate and long-term effects of early intervention (Early Intervention Research Institute, Utah State University).

In addition, the focus of HCEEP funding has shifted. Although the majority of HCEEP funds goes to demonstration and outreach projects, six experimental and nine research projects were funded during 1988-89 (Decker, 1989), representing 13% of funded projects. Other divisions in the Office of Special Education Programs (OSEP) are also increasing their emphasis on issues in early childhood. In 1988-89, the OSEP Division of Innovation and Development funded twenty-four research projects focused on early childhood (Decker, 1989).

The emphasis of research combined with practice is a positive step. These changes in emphasis are only first steps though. Federal funding has a strong influence on what types of projects exist. If the field of early childhood special education is to address the contentious issues that have been raised, then HCEEP should continue to make changes that facilitate addressing these issues. More stringent evaluation activities should be mandatory in demonstration projects. Methodologically sound data from research on early intervention practice could be maintained at a single site to facilitate their availability and use. Catalogs of products from all HCEEP projects could be kept so that practitioners do not have to "reinvent the wheel" with each project, allowing for a greater focus on adaptation with evaluation. These suggestions do not encompass all possibilities for changes, but combined with other changes in HCEEP, they would signal to those in the field the critical role that sound evaluation must play.

DIRECTIONS FOR THE FUTURE

It is hoped that the reader of this chapter will not conclude that early intervention in the United States, or in general, is in a state of decline. Such a supposition is far from true. In many respects, early intervention is at an apogee. The passage of P.L. 99–457 has forced many in education and other fields, who may otherwise have had only a peripheral view of the area, to focus on young children with handicaps. This focusing process emphasizes the importance of early experiences on the development of children and on societal obligations to help young children with handicaps and their parents. Additionally, P.L. 99–457 has provided an influx of funds to establish and operate early intervention programs and has offered an impetus for increased funding from other sources for intervention, demonstration, and research programs.

The contentious issues that have been raised have not occurred as a result of P.L. 99–457 but rather concurrently with it, as the field of early intervention has moved into a transitional phase—one that will ultimately result in a clearer understanding of how to intervene with young children with handicaps. The view that early intervention is effective has survived criticism (cf., Casto & Mastropieri, 1986; Dunst, Snyder, & Mankinen, 1987). What has been criticized is the lack of quality research that enables the field to answer specific questions about the interventions being used or about the populations that benefit most from specific interventions. These are questions of refinement.

The concurrent occurrence of exposure for early intervention because of P.L. 99–457 and this transitional phase has a potential negative impact (cf., Odom & Warren, 1988). Supporters of early intervention must actively compete for federal and state funds in a climate where funds for social and educational programs are not always available or are so at less than optimal levels. The increased exposure and funding of early intervention will force advocates to maintain funds more actively and to seek additional funds that other interests may desire. In such a competitive climate, intrafield criticisms must not negatively affect the image that early intervention presents to the public. Yet, early intervention must realistically present the benefits that children with handicaps can derive.

Odom and Warren (1988) express two concerns regarding this issue of how early intervention presents itself. One concern is that early intervention may not be able to meet the expectations that society currently holds for it. For example, is it truly reasonable to expect early intervention to result in substantially less need for future special education? Are early intervention advocates inadvertently leading society to believe that children with handicaps can be cured?

A second concern expressed by Odom and Warren is that P.L. 99–457 may force early intervention to become "institutionalized." Early intervention has long been known for its creativity and acceptance of diverse means (interventions) for meeting ends (child and family outcomes). Will this flexibility and innovativeness be stifled as early intervention becomes part of the public education system? It has been pointed out that public education in the United States is bureaucratic and conservative and not open to innovation (Haas, 1986). Related to this issue of flexibility are costs. Barnett (1988) has stated that different types of programs could vary the national costs of early intervention from two billion to ten billion dollars.

The goal for many in early childhood special education is that all children with handicaps, from birth to age five years, will be served in the most appropriate manner. In ideal circumstances, the following recommendations would be met (cf., Dunst, Snyder, & Mankinen, 1987):

1. Services are proactive, building on strengths rather than deficits.
2. Parents are involved based on individual needs rather than preselected activities.
3. The program uses a systems approach (Dunst, 1986), examining all environments in which the child and family participate.
4. Children are served based on individual needs rather than placed into an activity-based program.

Unfortunately, present trends indicate that these goals may not be realized. Funds for infants and toddlers are limited, creating restrictions in the services that may be offered to these children. Intervention geared to preschool children has often utilized the IEP exactly as stated in P.L. 94–142, thus implying a deficit model. Districts within a number of states are implementing activity-based classrooms rather than gearing programs to meet individual needs. Parent involvement in preschool programs often revolve around the IEP process. Is the "institutionalization" aspect of Odom and Warren's (1988) prophecy coming true?

A brief return to the history of special education may be illustrative. Between 1915 and 1930, there was a dramatic rise in the number and variety of special-education programs in the public schools. However, between 1930 and 1940, there was a sharp reversal in this upward trend due to dissatisfaction with the premature establishment of inadequately planned classes with untrained teachers and the misinterpretation of the assumptions of special education (i.e., cure). Conditions similar to those in the past now exist in early childhood special education. While it is unlikely that reversals in the field, if they occur, will be as dramatic as they were previously, professionals should still exercise caution. Care should be taken that the challenges facing the field currently are adequately addressed. The field cannot be allowed to become complacent or self-satisfied lest it ends up moving backward rather than forward. As Yule (cited in Hayden & McGinness, 1978) has noted, "Responsibility implies always asking whether one is justified in intervening, and considering what value the goal has for both the individual and society" (p. 159). Ultimately, early intervention serves not only the handicapped child and his or her family but also the society in which the child lives.

Responsibility for the field of early childhood special education implies a need for quality efficacy research. This research must try to overcome the methodological problems that have plagued past research (Casto & Mastropieri, 1986; Dunst, Snyder & Mankinen, 1987). The questions addressed by research must focus more on the conditions under which different interventions are effective and for whom they are effective (Dunst et al., 1987; Guralnick, 1988; Meisels, 1984). Research must address issues related to cost (Barnett, 1988; Odom & Warren, 1988). The long-term effects of early intervention need to be examined (Odom & Warren, 1988); longitudinal research has benefited early intervention for disadvantaged children (Berrueta-Clement et al., 1984).

From a practitioner's perspective, studies should occur less in tightly controlled settings using highly trained personnel and more in settings where intervention is typically provided by personnel who are continuously engaged in such activities. Research conducted by the Early Intervention Research Institute (White, 1989) provides examples of studies that address all of these issues with group experimental research designs.

In addition to refinements in current approaches to research, the examination of alternative research approaches must be considered (Gallagher, 1988; Odom, 1988; Odom & Warren, 1988). These alternative approaches are not really new, but they address the way in which interventions are developed and the types of questions that are addressed by the research. One promising approach to the development of interventions is the ecobehavioral model (Carta, Sainato, & Greenwood, 1988). This approach attempts to identify environmental factors, and student and teacher behaviors that result in desired outcomes. Once identified, interventions can be developed around these "contexts." This approach has the advantage of increased practitioner use because it is based on events that already occur in the natural environment. Approaches that focus on the questions addressed by research include studies guided by systems theory (Dunst, 1986), studies that utilize indicators of social validity (Reid et al., 1985; Van Houten, 1979; Wolf, 1978), and studies using an ethnographic approach (Jordan, 1985; Tharp, 1989). These alternative approaches can prove beneficial to our understanding of the effects of early intervention.

The responsibility of professionals in the field to build a strong research base from which to implement sound practices is clear. It behoves us as researchers and as practitioners to examine our ideas and beliefs both regularly and carefully. As early childhood special education reflects the influences of a number of disparate disciplines and is comprised of individuals from a variety of fields, so, too, does early childhood special education have the power to positively influence other areas of study. To accomplish this, we must demonstrate what the best of early intervention can be. Much has been accomplished already; there is every reason to believe that the challenges of the present can be met and that the future will be bright.

REFERENCES

Abt Associates. (1973). *Exemplary programs for the handicapped.* Cambridge, MA: Abt Associates. (Contract # OEC-0-72-5182).

Barnett, W. S. (1985). Benefit-cost analysis of the Perry Pre-school Program and its long-term effects. *Educational Evaluation and Policy Analysis, 7,* 333-342.

Barnett, W. S. (1988). The economics of pre-school special education under Public Law 99-457. *Topics in Early Childhood Special Education, 8,* 12-23.

Barnett, W. S., & Escobar, C. M. (1988). The economics of early intervention for handicapped children: What do we really know? *Journal of the Division for Early Childhood, 12,* 169-181.

Berrueta-Clement, J. R., Schweinhart, L. J., Barnett, W. S., Epstein A. S., & Weikart, D. P. (1984). *Changed lives: The effects of the Perry Pre-school Program on youths through age 19.* Ypsilanti, MI: High/Scope.

Bidder, R., Bryant, G., & Gray, D. (1975). Benefits to Down syndrome children through training their mothers. *Archives of Diseases in Childhood, 50,* 383-386.

Bloom, B. S. (1964). *Stability and change in human characteristics*. New York: Wiley.

Bricker, D. (1988). Commentary: The future of early childhood special education. *Journal of the Division for Early Childhood, 12*, 276-278.

Bricker, D., & Dow, M. (1980). Early intervention with the young severely handicapped child. *Journal of the Association for the Severely Handicapped, 5*, 130-142.

Carta, J. J., Sainato, D. M., & Greenwood, C. R. (1988). Advances in the ecological assessment of classroom instruction for young children with handicaps. In S. L. Odom & M. B. Karnes (Eds.), *Early intervention for infants and young children with handicaps: An empirical base* (pp. 217-239). Baltimore: Paul H. Brookes.

Casto, G., & Mastropieri, M. A. (1986). The efficacy of early intervention programs: A meta-analysis. *Exceptional Children, 52*, 417-424.

Datta, L. (1977). The external implications of an internal review of effectiveness: The DHEW Education Division's Joint Dissemination Review Panel. In *Education Division's Joint Dissemination Review Panel: Three Papers*. New York: EPIE Institute. (ERIC Document Reproduction Service No. ED 156 217).

Decker, M. J. (1989). *1988–1989 directory of selected early childhood programs*. Chapel Hill: National Early Childhood Technical Assistance System, University of North Carolina.

Dexter, B. L. (1987). A brief historical background of special education ... in the beginning. In B. L. Dexter (Ed.), *Special education and the classroom teacher: Concepts, perspectives, and strategies* (pp. 3-29). Springfield, IL: Charles C. Thomas.

Dunst, C. J. (1986). Overview of the efficacy of early intervention programs: Methodological and conceptual considerations. In L. Bickman & D. Weatherford (Eds.), *Evaluating early intervention programs for severely handicapped children and their families* (pp. 79-147). Austin, TX: Pro-Ed.

Dunst, C. J., & Rheingrover, R. M. (1981). Analysis of the efficacy of infant intervention programs for handicapped children. *Evaluation and Program Planning, 4*, 287-323.

Dunst, C. J., Snyder, S. W., & Mankinen, M. (1987). Efficacy of early intervention. In M. C. Wang, M. C. Reynolds, & H. J. Walberg (Eds.), *Handbook of Special Education, Vol. 3* (pp. 259-294). New York: Pergamon.

Fraas, C. J. (1986). *Pre-school programs for the education of handicapped children: Background, issues, and federal policy options*. Washington, D.C.: Library of Congress, Congressional Research Service. (Report No. 86–55 EPW).

Gallagher, J. J. (1988). Comments on "Early Childhood Special Education in the Year 2000" by Samuel Odom & Steven Warren. *Journal of the Division for Early Childhood, 12*, 274-275.

Garwood, S. G. (1979). Special education and child development: A new perspective. In S. G. Garwood (Ed.), *Educating young handicapped children: A developmental approach* (pp. 3-21). Germantown, MD: Aspen Systems Corporation.

Garwood, S. G., & Sheehan, R. (1989). *Designing a comprehensive early intervention system: The challenge of Public Law 99–457.* Austin, TX: Pro-Ed.

Gotts, E. E. (1973). Head Start research, development, and evaluation. In J. L. Frost (Ed.), *Revisiting early childhood education* (pp. 409-420). New York: Holt, Rinehart, and Winston.

Gray, S. W., & Klaus, R. A. (1965). An experimental pre-school program for culturally deprived children. *Child Development, 36,* 887-898.

Guralnick, M. J. (1988). Efficacy research in early childhood intervention programs. In S. L. Odom & M. B. Karnes (Eds.), *Early intervention for infants and young children with handicaps: An empirical base* (pp. 75-88). Baltimore: Paul H. Brookes.

Haas, J. D. (1986). Educational futures: Six scenarios. *Future Research Quarterly, 6,* 15-30.

Hayden, A. H., & McGinness, G. D. (1978). Bases for early intervention. In E. Sontag, G. Smith, & N. Certo (Eds.), *Educational programming for the severely and profoundly handicapped* (pp. 153-165). Reston, VA: Council for Exceptional Children.

Hunt, J. M. (1961). *Intelligence and experience.* New York: The Ronald Press Company.

Jordan, C. (1985). Translating culture: From ethnographic information to educational program. *Anthropology and Education Quarterly, 16,* 105-123.

Kakalik, J. S., Furry, W. S., Thomas, M. A., & Carney, M. F. (1981). *The cost of special education: Summary of study findings.* Santa Monica, CA: Rand Corporation.

Kamps, D. M., Carta, J. J., Delquadri, J. C., Arreaga-Mayer, C., Terry, B., & Greenwood, C. R. (1989). School-based research and intervention. *Education and Treatment of Children, 12,* 359-390.

Kaufman, B. A. (1980). Early childhood education and special education: A study in conflict. *Volta Review, 82,* 15-24.

Kirk, S. A. (1958). *Early education of the mentally retarded.* Urbana: University of Illinois Press.

Kirk, S. A. (1965). Diagnostic, cultural, and remedial factors in mental retardation. In S. F. Osler & R. E. Cooke (Eds.), *The bio-social basis of mental retardation* (pp. 129-145). Baltimore: Johns Hopkins University Press.

Lazar, I., & Darlington, R. (1982). Lasting effects of early education: A report from the consortium for longitudinal studies. *Monographs of the Society for Research in Child Development, 47* (2, Serial No. 195).

McDonnell, A., & Hardman, M. (1988). A synthesis of "best practice" guidelines for early childhood services. *Journal of the Division for Early Childhood, 12,* 328-341.

Meisels, S. J. (1984). The efficacy of early intervention: Why are we still asking this question? *Topics in Early Childhood Special Education, 5,* 1-12.

Odom, S. L. (1988). Research in early childhood special education. In S. L. Odom & M. B. Karnes (Eds.), *Early intervention for infants and young children with handicaps: An empirical base* (pp. 1-21). Baltimore: Paul H. Brookes.

Odom, S. L., & Fewell, R. R. (1983). Program evaluation in early childhood special education: A meta-evaluation. *Educational Evaluation and Policy Analysis, 5,* 445-460.

Odom, S. L., & Warren, S. F. (1988). Early childhood special education in the year 2000. *Journal of the Division for Early Childhood, 12,* 263-273.

Palmer, F. A. (1977). *The effects of early childhood educational intervention on school performance.* Paper prepared for the President's Commission on Mental Health, U.S. Government Printing Office, Washington, D.C.

Reid, O. H., Parsons, M. B., McCarn, J. E., Green, C. W., Phillips, J. F., & Schepis, M. M. (1985). Providing a more appropriate education for severely handicapped persons: Increasing and validating functional classroom tasks. *Journal of Applied Behavior Analysis, 18,* 289-302.

Roy Littlejohn Associates. (1982). *An analysis of the impact of the handicapped children's early education program.* Washington: Roy Littlejohn Associates. (Contract # 300–81–0661).

Schweinhart, L. J., & Weikart, D. P. (1981). Effects of the Perry Pre-school Program on youth through age 15. *Journal of the Division for Early Childhood, 4,* 29-39.

Scruggs, T. E., Mastropieri, M. A., & Casto, G. (1987). The quantitative synthesis of single-subject research: Methodology and validation. *Remedial and Special Education, 8,* 24-33.

Scruggs, T. E., Mastropieri, M. A., & McEwen, I. (1988). Early intervention for developmental functioning: A quantitative synthesis of single-subject research. *Journal of the Division for Early Childhood, 12,* 359-367.

Sigmon, S. B. (1987). Historical foundations of American special education: A new interpretation of the roots and development. In S. B. Sigmon (Ed.), *Radical analysis of special education: Focus on historical development and learning disabilities* (pp. 19-34). London: Farmer.

Simeonsson, R. J., Cooper, D. H., & Scheiner, A. P. (1982). A review and analysis of the effectiveness of early intervention programs. *Pediatrics, 69,* 635-641.

Skeels, H. (1942). A study of the effects of differential stimulation on mentally retarded children: A follow-up study. *American Journal of Mental Deficiency, 46,* 340-350.

Skeels, H. M. (1966). Adult status of children with contrasting early life experiences. *Monographs of the Society for Research in Child Development, 31,* 1-57.

Skeels, H. M., & Dye, H. B. (1939). A study of the effects of differential stimulation on mentally retarded children. *Proceedings and Addresses of the 63rd Annual Session of the American Association of Mental Deficiency, 44,* 114-130.

Stedman, D. J., & Eichorn, D. H. (1964). A comparison of the growth and development of institutionalized and home-reared mongoloids during infancy and early childhood. *American Journal of Mental Deficiency, 69,* 391-401.

Stock, J. R., Wnek, L. L., Newborg, J. A., Schenck, E. A., Gabel, J. R., Spurgeon, M. S., & Ray, H. W. (1976). *Evaluation of the Handicapped Children's Early Education Program.* Columbus, OH: Battelle Memorial Institute.

Strain, P. S., & Smith, B. J. (1986). A counter-interpretation of early intervention effects: A response. *Exceptional Children*, 53, 259-294.

Tallmadge, G. K. (1977). *Ideabook: The Joint Dissemination Review Panel*. Washington, D.C.: U.S. Office of Education.

Tharp, R. G. (1989). Psychocultural variables and constants: Effects on teaching and learning in schools. *American Psychologist*, 44, 1-11.

Turnbull, A. P., & Turnbull, H. R. (1986). *Families, professionals, and exceptionality: A special partnership*. Columbus, OH: Merrill Publishing.

Van Houten, R. (1979). Social validation: The evolution of standards of competency for target behaviors. *Journal of Applied Behavior Analysis*, 12, 581-592.

Weiss, R. (1981). INREAL intervention for language handicapped and bilingual children. *Journal of the Division for Early Childhood*, 4, 40-51.

Westinghouse Learning Corporation. (1969). *The impact of Head Start: An evaluation of the Head Start experience on children's cognitive and affective development*. Athens: Ohio University Press.

White, K. R. (1989). *1988–89 annual report of the longitudinal studies of the effects and costs of early intervention for handicapped children*. Logan: Early Intervention Research Institute, Affiliated Developmental Center for Handicapped Persons, Utah State University.

White, K. R., Bush, D. W., & Casto, G. C. (1985-86). Learning from reviews of early intervention. *Journal of Special Education*, 19, 417-428.

White, K., & Casto, G. (1985). An integrative review of early intervention efficacy studies with at-risk children: Implications for the handicapped. *Analysis and Intervention in Developmental Disabilities*, 5, 177-201.

White, K. R., Mastropieri, M., & Casto, G. (1984). An analysis of special education early childhood projects approved by the Joint Dissemination Review Panel. *Journal of the Division for Early Childhood*, 7, 11-26.

Wolf, M. M. (1978). Social validity: The case for subjective measurement or how applied behavior analysis is finding its heart. *Journal of Applied Behavior Analysis*, 11, 203-214.

Wood, M. E. (1981). Costs of intervention programs. In C. Garland, N. W. Stone, J. Swanson, & G. Woodruff (Eds.), *Early intervention for children with special needs and their families: Findings and recommendations* (pp. 15-25). Seattle: University of Washington. (WESTAR Series Paper No. 11.)

Zigler, E., & Trickett, P. (1978). IQ, social competence, and evaluation of early childhood intervention programs. *American Psychologist*, 33, 789-798.

9

The Evolution and Current Status of Early Intervention in Canada

Kofi Marfo

Canada's proximity to the United States is both a blessing and a curse to the Canadian special education scene—a blessing because progressive legislation and other developments and practices with potentially beneficial impact on Canadian education often cross the border, duty-free, and are assimilated into provincial and district-level policies. It is a curse because this assimilation process tends to breed a false sense of complacency and security. A case in point is the frequency with which U.S. Public Law 94–142 has been cited by Canadian advocates for handicapped children's rights to education, particularly before Section 15 of the Canadian constitution became law. Indeed, many school districts across the country, including even ones in provinces without mandatory special-education legislation, have developed mainstreaming policies and practices, drawing liberally from the *least restrictive environment* provisions of Public Law 94–142, as if the latter were a piece of Canadian legislation. While these derived policies and practices are desirable—perhaps even laudable—the obvious danger is that unless they are entrenched in indigenous legislation, there is no guarantee that they would stand up in court when litigated.

As a branch of special education (i.e., early childhood special education), the early intervention field in Canada mirrors the picture painted above for its parent field. Indeed, so strong is the influence from across the border that there are some who would even question the wisdom of devoting two separate chapters to early intervention in Canada and the United States in the same volume. Remarkably, however, Canada's proximity to the United States has produced a situation whereby the current levels and status of early intervention services have been achieved largely through a *passive import model* rather than through concerted governmental effort with financial and legislative backing, as is the case in the United States. Thus, there are distinct and interesting differences in the way early intervention services have evolved in the two countries, making a focused study of the Canadian context an interesting and legitimate exercise in its own right. This chapter attempts to present such a focused study.

The chapter begins with an overview of developments and issues at the national level that have shaped the evolution of services. This is followed by a selective chronicling of the emergence of early intervention programs in the provinces. Some exemplary program development initiatives are then presented to illustrate the presence of indigenous leadership in the field. A fourth section provides a brief description of the current status of services. Next, two classes of early intervention research across the country are described, with summaries of some of the key findings generated through this research. The final section identifies some of the trends occurring in the field within Canada and raises a number of critical issues that need to be addressed to advance the field and maximize benefits to the families and children who stand to gain from such advances.

Consistent with the overall focus of this volume, this chapter examines early intervention services and research mainly in relation to infants and young children with established handicaps or developmental disabilities. Thus, although the target population of many programs may include environmentally disadvantaged and medically at-risk children (e.g., premature infants), the criterion for selecting programs and research for review was that they have as their primary target group children with established handicaps.

THE NATIONAL SCENE IN HISTORICAL PERSPECTIVE

Experience throughout the major industrialized countries shows that rapid expansions in innovative services occur frequently as a function of governmental support, especially if such support is enshrined in some form of legislation. This scenario is certainly true of early intervention services. In the United States, even the earliest university-based research/program development and demonstration activities were spurred by and supported through legislative action. For example, several of the model programs that set the stage for the proliferation of services in the 1970s were funded under the Handicapped Children's Early Education Assistance Act (Public Law 91–230, Title VI, Part C, Sec. 623). The passage of the popular Public Law 94–142 (the Education for All Handicapped Children Act of 1975) provided a major impetus for early intervention services for preschool handicapped children, through the establishment of financial incentives to encourage all states to develop programs to serve three- to five-year-old handicapped children. Subsequent revisions of Public Law 94–142 have increased the per-child funding allocation available to states from the federal government. Perhaps the most profound development since Public Law 94–142, as far as early intervention services are concerned, is the passage in 1986 of Public Law 99–457, which goes into effect in 1991. This law now extends federal support for early intervention services to handicapped children in the birth to two-year age group.

In Britain, legislative support and encouragement for early intervention services came with the passage of the Education Act of 1981, based on the 1978 report of the Committee of Enquiry into the Education of Handicapped Children and Young People (Warnock, 1978). One of the major recommendations of the Warnock Report was that provision be made for all exceptional children under five years of age to receive services. As Sturmey (Chapter 11) points out, the United Kingdom has witnessed a massive expansion of a wide range of services, including early psychoeducational intervention for preschool handicapped children, since the passing of the Education Act of 1981.

Unlike its neighbor to the south, or Britain, with which it has had a long history of constitutional ties, Canada does not have institutional structures or legislative provisions at the national level to coordinate and give direction to the development and delivery of early intervention services. One of the features that sets Canada's federal system of government apart from that of the United States is that, constitutionally, Canada has much more limited jurisdiction over matters pertaining to education, health, and social welfare in the provinces. In fact, Canada does not have a national department of education; the British North America Act delegated the responsibility for education to the provinces, and although the federal government provides grants in support of education to all provinces, the setting of educational policy and standards is solely the prerogative of provincial governments.

Although Canada has a national department of health and welfare (Health and Welfare Canada), this department has no national agenda on early intervention. In the absence of national mandatory legislation and funding allocations, it is not surprising that the provision of early intervention services around the country remains uneven. Commenting on the status of federal support for special-education services in Canada a decade ago, Perkins (1979) had this to say:

Canada has no national center for the study of special education. As a result, we are very dependent on American research and curriculum development and American teaching materials.... We still suffer from a frontier mentality both at the federal and provincial level when it comes to making a full commitment to handicapped children and to ensuring comprehensive and quality services based on social planning, research, and management. (p. 33)

Ten years have elapsed since Perkins made his observation, but research, curriculum development efforts, and teaching materials from the United States remain the king-pins driving early intervention programs in Canada today. Another significant void is the absence of a national clearinghouse on early intervention and generic early childhood services for handicapped children.

The difficulties noted above make the task of trying to construct a composite national picture on the evolution and status of early intervention services a rather onerous one. Fortunately, however, I did not have to start from scratch. Dana Brynelsen (1990) generously shared with me a paper she had recently prepared for presentation at the Atlantic Conference on Early Intervention, in which she reviewed the history of early intervention services in Canada. In addition, through the writings of Barbara Bloom and her associates at the University of Saskatchewan (Bloom, 1976; Bloom & Glazer, 1985), I acquainted myself with a rather well documented history of services in the province of Saskatchewan. The historical perspective that I have attempted to provide in this chapter is based largely on these sources and on my ten years of experience conducting and participating in early intervention research in two provinces: Alberta and the province of Newfoundland and Labrador.

The Role of the Parent Movement

The parent movement in mental retardation, which emerged and began to sweep across North America shortly after World War II, is credited as the single most important force behind the development of services for children and adults with disabilities in Canada (Brynelsen, 1990; National Institute on Mental Retardation, 1981). Between 1947 (when the first local association for persons with mental handicap was formed in Ontario) and 1958 (when the Canadian Association for the Mentally Retarded was formed), as many as 130 local associations sprang up across the country (Brynelsen, 1990).[1] Brynelsen notes that "the majority of infant development programs that have developed in Canada are a direct result of efforts by local and provincial associations for the mentally handicapped" (p. 2).

The Influence of International Developments

Generally, it is a matter of fact that many developments in the fields of education and social services in Canada have been shaped by those occurring in the United States. Several events in the United States and elsewhere in the 1960s served to catalyze the developing emphasis on services for young handicapped children in Canada. First was President Kennedy's appointment, in 1962, of the President's Committee on Mental Retardation. The influence of the committee's many recommendations—including its emphasis on the need for early diagnosis, home support, early education, and community-centered services—seemed to have crossed the border to Canada. As Brynelsen (1990) notes:

In 1964, two years after the creation of the President's Committee on Mental Retardation, Ottawa sponsored the first Canadian federal-provincial conference on mental retardation.... Throughout the conference, participants reiterated the need for early education, including home visiting programs staffed by trained persons to establish adaptive programs of home care early in the child's life. (p. 7)

A second influence came through a number of major publications— for example, J. McVicker Hunt's *Intelligence and Experience* (1961) and Benjamin Bloom's *Stability and Change in Human Characteristics* (1964)—and specific research findings, such as the longitudinal results from the Iowa environmental studies (Skeels & Dye, 1939; Skeels, 1966). While these works have been criticized for a variety of reasons in more recent years, they drew attention to the growing belief that the early childhood years were of critical importance to later development, underscored the phenomenal role of environmental enrichment in children's development, ushered in new hopes regarding the malleability of intellectual functioning, and enegerized the fledgling early intervention movement beyond the borders of the United States.

Third, a movement occurring contemporaneously in Scandinavia provided additional impetus to the early intervention movement in both Canada and the United States. The normalization movement, which stemmed from the work of Bank-Mikkelson (1969) in Denmark, spurred the deinstitutionalization process significantly. As more and more handicapped children were kept at home, the need for home- and community-based support services came to be increasingly acknowledged. In Canada, as in the United States, the concept of normalization found very strong acceptance. The Canadian Association for the Mentally Retarded adopted it as one of the central pillars of its service delivery philosophy. The doctrinaire status that normalization attained in Canada is still evident across the country in preambles to many major documents on community-based services for handicapped persons.

Early National Initiatives

Four early national initiatives, three at the federal government level and one by a nongovernmental national organization, are worth noting. Reference has already been made to the conference of 1964 organized under the sponsorship of the Federal Department of National Health and Welfare, the purpose of which was to identify ways to coordinate and improve services for persons with mental handicap. Although this appears to be the only national conference on mental retardation convened by a federal department, it also appears that its timing and partial emphasis on home-based services in the early years of development contributed, if indirectly, to the development of early intervention services.

The second noteworthy event is the federal government's appointment in 1966 of the Commission on Emotional and Learning Disorders in Children (CELDIC). The CELDIC Report (Lazure, 1970) made a total of 144 recommendations, several of which were supportive of a broadly conceived notion of early intervention. For example, the report stressed the need for comprehensive services, the need for immediate help at the earliest sign of difficulty, and the delivery of services at the local community level. As Brynelsen (1990) notes, the report "awakened a very strong interest in improving services for children with special needs in this country" (p. 8).

Third, some funding initiatives on the part of the federal government in the early 1970s may have helped to translate many of the ideals engendered by the foregoing developments into real action in the form of programs and services. A new federal-provincial cost-sharing funding formula was introduced under the Canada Assistance Plan (see Brynelsen, 1990) to fund community-based programs solely. These funds were made available only to provincial social-service agencies. According to Brynelsen (1990), parent groups and professionals in the field of mental retardation took advantage of this funding arrangement to develop noninstitutional alternatives to the care and education of handicapped persons.

It appears however, that the impact of the Canada Assistance Plan on the early intervention movement was rather minimal and perhaps indirect. Despite this source of funding, most early intervention programs in the country started with nongovernment funds. The cost-sharing feature of the Canada Assistance Plan meant that a provincial government had to make a commitment to early intervention and be prepared to provide funding that the federal government would match. An episode recorded by Brynelsen (1990) illustrates how difficult it was for initiators of early intervention programs to take advantage of the Canada Assistance Plan. An early intervention project proposal submitted to the Canada Assistance Plan by the Geoff Humphrey Center for Mental Retardation at Brandon University was deemed to have met the objectives of the plan but could not be funded because the Manitoba government could not be persuaded to participate in the funding arrangement.

Finally, while the earliest programs were still springing up, the National Institute on Mental Retardation organized a conference on early intervention at Banff, Alberta, in 1976. By providing the opportunity for some of the earliest workers in the field across the country to share experiences, this conference—coming at the time that it did—may have been one of the most significant developments in the founding era. Unfortunately, as Brynelsen (1990) laments, there has not been a national conference on early intervention since then.

The historical events chronicled in this section suggest that while the primary impetus and scientific base for the early intervention movement in Canada came from other nations, the rapid proliferation of services across the country was aided significantly by a Canadian response to international trends, even if this response was uncoordinated.

EVOLUTION OF PROGRAMS AT THE PROVINCIAL LEVEL

Most of the earliest programs emerged in the mid-1970s. Three demonstration programs in the United States seemed to have had a significant influence on Canadian programs. Two of these—the Portage Project, based in Wisconsin, and the Multidisciplinary Preschool Program for Down Syndrome Children at the University of Washington in Seattle—were initiated in 1969 with funding from the U.S. Bureau of Education for the Handicapped (now the Office of Special Education) under the Handicapped Children's Early Education Assistance Act (Public Law 91–230, Title VI, Part C, Sec. 623). The principal developers of these two programs were Alice Hayden, Norris Haring, and Valentine Dmitriev for the Seattle program and David Shearer and Marsha Shearer for the Portage program. The Infant, Toddler, and Preschool Research and Intervention Project by William Bricker and Diane Bricker (then at the University of Miami's Mailman Center for Child Development) also had some influence on Canadian programs. By far, however, the Portage Project had the most profound inflence on early intervention services in Canada, and indeed in the United Kingdom—as Chapter 11 illustrates so vividly.

Two Case Studies of Early Efforts: British Columbia and Saskatchewan

Even if equally detailed information on the history of early intervention in all Canadian provinces and territories were available, it would be impossible to document it thoroughly in this chapter because of space limitations. In this section, I present a brief historical overview of service development in two provinces. Bits and pieces of the history of services in several other provinces can be gleaned from the sections on exemplary program development initiatives and current status of services.

British Columbia. In 1972, the mother of a child with Down syndrome, through the Home Care Committee of the Vancouver-Richmond Association for the Mentally Retarded, spearheaded the founding of the first home-based early intervention program in this province (Brynelsen, 1990). That year, a number of parents from the association visited Alice Hayden's Down Syndrome Program at the University of Washington's Model Preschool Center for Handicapped Children. On their return, they opted not for a center-based program but for one that would serve families and their handicapped children in their own homes.

In 1973, the Home Care Committee hired a professional supervisor, Dana Brynelsen. A primary-school teacher by profession, Ms. Brynelsen has remained in the early intervention field since 1973 and has provided strong leadership not only at the provincial level but also at the national level. Writing on her memories of this first year, she notes:

I had a caseload of around 15 families and the majority of those families were referred by public health nurses. All the children had diagnosed handicaps or severe developmental delay. There were few tools available. I had Kathryn Barnard's book *Teaching the Mentally Retarded Child*, an early edition of *Portage*, materials developed by institutions, such as *A Guide to Early Developmental Training*, and a D.D.S.T. I was an instant convert to this field and very excited. . . . Within six months, I was in regular communication with people in the States and materials started flooding in. (Brynelsen, 1990, p. 11)

When the Ministry of Social Services and Housing appointed Ms. Brynelsen provincial coordinator of infant development programs in 1975, there were five programs in the province. Now, in 1990, there are thirty-seven programs operating around the province. As many as 1,400 children are referred annually, and it is estimated that over 13,000 infants and their families have been served by these programs since their inception in 1972 (Brynelsen, 1990).

The B.C. Infant Development Program has several unique features. It has a longer history of coordination at the provincial level; since 1975, it has had a provincial steering committee with a membership of parents as well as professionals (which reports directly to the Deputy Minister of Social Services and Housing), and it has a policy and procedures manual (Brynelsen, 1988) providing guidelines for administration, for hiring, training, and monitoring staff, and for starting new programs.

At the local level, staff report to a local advisory committee comprised of parents and health, education, and social services professionals.

Saskatchewan. Bloom and Glazer (1985) trace the origins of early intervention services in the province of Saskatchewan to the 1960s, when home-based intervention services—delivered by a small number of social workers and public-health nurses—were made available to parents who, despite the social pressures of the times, had chosen to keep their handicapped children at home rather than institutionalize them. It appears from the writings of Bloom and her associates (Bloom, 1976; Bloom & Glazer, 1985) and the Provincial Council of Saskatchewan's early intervention program (Saskatchewan ECIP, 1985) that the founding in 1967 of the Alvin Buckwold Center—a diagnostic, teaching, and research center for the prevention and treatment of mental retardation—was perhaps the most important milestone in the history of early intervention services in that province.

Attached to the Department of Pediatrics and the University Hospital, the Buckwold Center had a medical perspective; however, many of its functions and goals depicted a significant psychoeducational emphasis. The following four specific programs of the center described by Bloom (1976) illustrate this psychoeducational mission.

1. A comprehensive assessment and educational program for children with multiple handicaps (birth to twelve years of age) living within a 160-kilometer radius of Saskatoon.

2. A parent training program offering instructional services to parents living within a 120-kilometer radius of Saskatoon.

3. A center-based infant stimulation program for handicapped children under 2.5 years of age. This program was open to all families across the province who wished to and could afford to take their child to the center.

4. A preschool program providing early identification and short-term intervention (two to six months) services for developmentally disabled children between ages two and six.

Today, the Buckwold Center, in collaboration with the Saskatchewan Association for Community Living, continues to provide outreach and consultative services to families and intervention programs throughout the province (Saskatchewan ECIP, 1985a, 1985b). Its traveling clinics program, designed to carry out diagnostic assessment, remediation, and counseling in remote communities (Zaleski, 1983), remains one of its significant contributions to the care of exceptional children in the province.

A second major stimulant of early intervention services in Saskatchewan was the launching in 1976 of a preschool project by the Institute of Child Guidance and Development at the University of Saskatchewan.

The SEECC Preschool Project (Bloom, 1978; Bloom, Braun, & Glazer, 1980; Bloom & Hnatiuk, 1982), as the name suggests, appears to have been part of a larger research program initiated in response to the Standards for Educators of Exceptional Children in Canada (SEECC) Report (see Hardy et al., 1971). This project will be discussed in a bit more detail in the section on program development initiatives. For now, it will suffice to point out that the positive findings reported by the.investigators in their final report (Bloom, 1978) and in a follow-up study (Bloom & Hnatiuk, 1982) were instrumental in courting the support and involvement of the Saskatchewan Association for the Mentally Retarded (SAMR) and the provincial government.

With the view to facilitating the further development of home-based early intervention programs across the province, the SAMR established a project in the spring of 1980 to "provide information and assistance to local parent and citizen groups who were interested in setting up a home-based program" (Saskatchewan ECIP, 1985b, p. 5). In addition, the association began to provide initial seed monies for the setting up of programs by local groups. Fortunately, it did not have to do this for too long, for later that same year, the Rehabilitation Services Division (known in those days as Core Services) of the Department of Social Services began to fund programs through community/parent-operated boards.

In September 1982, the Early Childhood Intervention Program Provincial Council, with representation from local boards and staff, was inaugurated to give direction to programs across the province. That same year, the council quickly drew up Saskatchewan's first provincial guidelines and standards; they were essentially an adoption of aspects of British Columbia's guidelines. In 1985, a revised standards and guidelines document (Saskatchewan ECIP, 1985a), reflecting the changing needs and new realities of programs in Saskatchewan, was published.

Saskatchewan currently has sixteen programs with forty-five workers serving 400 children and their families across the province (Saskatchewan ECIP, 1988a, 1988b, 1988c). It is significant to note that at the time of the national early intervention survey by Kendall, Brynelsen, and Lapierre (1985), the province reported fifteen programs and thirty-five workers. Thus, there was a remarkable 29% increase in staff size between 1985 and 1988.

SOME EXEMPLARY PROGRAM DEVELOPMENT INITIATIVES

Although early intervention services in Canada have been shaped remarkably by legislative actions as well as research and development activity in the United States, as pointed out at the beginning of this chapter, Canada can boast of a good number of program development initiatives in the early years; indeed some of the chief architects of these initiatives continue to extend and refine their early contributions. In this section, four distinct program development initiatives, which took place in three provinces, will be described briefly.

The Alberta Early Education Project

In 1975, the Planning and Research Division of Alberta Education awarded a research contract to Dr. Gerard M. Kysela of the University of Alberta to develop and evaluate a model early intervention service for young handicapped children. Over the next two years, Dr. Kysela and his associates developed two programs for moderately and severely handicapped children: a school-based program for toddlers and pre-school children, housed at a local elementary school, and a home-based program for children under 2.5 years of age. In all, twenty-two children (thirteen boys and nine girls) and their parents participated in the home-based program, while twenty-three children (fourteen boys and nine girls) and their parents were enrolled in the school program.

While the project drew a great deal from research and demonstration projects in the United States (for example, the curriculum was an adaptation of Portage), its principal objective was to innovatively extend, rather than merely adopt, existing knowledge and curricula. Founded on behavioral principles and teaching techniques, the project revolved around a developmental curriculum targeting five domains: cognition, self-help, motor, language, and socialization. Some of the key features of this project were: (a) refinement of a test-teach method of criterion-referenced assessment; (b) implementation and evaluation of two instructional models—the direct and incidental teaching models; (c) development of a staff training program; (d) development of a parent training program; and (e) systematic data collection over the period of the intervention. According to Kysela, this project was the first instance of the conjoint use of the incidental and direct teaching approaches with infants and young children (Kysela, 1978, p. 149).

Findings from the empirical data were reported in relation to normative assessments and observed functional behavioral skills. According to the final report on the project, "the normative data indicated that the children's rate of development was significantly accelerated in mental development and language areas for the school program and in the area of mental development for the home program," while the functional behavior data showed "profound and rapid increases in knowledge and skills" (Kysela, 1978, p. 140).

This project made a major impact on the development of early intervention services in Alberta. The two programs that were established through the project are still in existence today.

The SEECC Preschool Project

As indicated in an earlier section, this project was initiated by the Institute of Child Guidance and Development at the University of Saskatchewan as part of a larger, school-based project. It had the following twofold objective: "(a) to provide educational intervention in the home at the point of parent-child interaction; (b) to provide cognitive and emotional support for parents to enhance their parenting skills and satisfaction in parenting their exceptional children" (Bloom, 1978, p. 5). During the course of the two-year project, fifty-four children were served.

The project was based on the philosophy that "any approach to educational intervention with handicapped preschool children must be based on a true partnership between parents and professionals" (Bloom, 1978, p. 4). To control potential "overwhelming of the parents" by the professionals, the program utilized community-based paraprofessionals, referred to as *parent partners*. In addition to working directly with parents, the partners served as liaisons between parents and a wide range of professionals. Parent partners received a nine-day preservice training program, described in an extensive manual (Bloom, Braun, & Glazer, 1980; see also Bloom, 1981).

This project was unique for several reasons. First, although there was no control group against which to judge changes in the intervention children, the researchers used simple but innovative statistical techniques to get around the internal validity question. For example, program effects were inferred not from straight pretest/posttest change scores but from an index of developmental progress that compared the rate of development during an intervention phase with the pre-intervention rate of development. Second, the researchers conducted a follow-up study of eleven of the project children after their enrollment in school (Bloom & Hnatiuk, 1982), thus providing evidence regarding longer-term program impact. In both the original and the follow-up analyses, the researchers reported evidence in support of the program's effectiveness. Finally, the researchers included in their original report a cost analysis of the intervention program.

It is clear from the documentation available from the provincial program council that it was the findings of this project, coupled with the work of the Alvin Buckwold Center, that encouraged the Saskatchewan Association for the Mentally Retarded to give its support to early intervention services in 1980 (Saskatchewan ECIP, 1985a, 1985b).

The Transactional Model of Early Home Intervention

One of Ontario's established early intervention programs is the Infant-Parent Program, an outpatient, home-based service of the Child and Family Center at Chedoke-McMaster Hospital in Hamilton. Supported by provincial government funding, the Infant-Parent Program has as its mission the provision of early intervention services to families with environmentally and biologically at-risk children from birth to age two years (Barrera, Chapter 5; Barrera & Rosenbaum, 1986).

The transactional model of early home intervention (TMEHI) was first developed as the basis for the Infant-Parent Program some ten years ago. The early stages of the model emphasized child developmental competencies, parent-child interaction, and the application of behavior analysis and other educational strategies. However, over the past few years, the model has been extended and refined to incorporate the contributions of the ecological and family/social systems perspectives on human development (Chapter 5). From this perspective, the TMEHI, in its present form, provides a good Canadian example of some of the transitions currently taking place in the early intervention field.

In the TMEHI program, the infant-parent dyad, rather than the child or parent, is considered the target of intervention. One objective of the program is to optimize reciprocal and mutually satisfying parent-infant interactions. Reflecting a family/social systems perspective, a second objective of the program is to assist parents in mobilizing resources from within and outside of the family in their efforts to cope with their child's handicap and provide developmentally enhancing experiences. The professional who works directly with infants and their parents is the Infant-Parent Therapist (IPT).

Because of the program's status as part of a university-affiliated center, it has personnel resources that are rare to most other programs—a multidisciplinary team consisting of a psychologist, a pediatrician, a psychometrist, a social worker, and a speech pathologist. Evaluative research is another strong feature of this program. The effectiveness of the program has already been assessed in relation to medically at-risk infants and their families (Barrera, Rosenbaum, & Cunningham, 1986) and has been assessed in this volume in relation to families of infants with established developmental disabilities (Chapter 5).

The Hanen Early Language Program

The origin of the Hanen Program dates back to 1974, at the Lakeshore Baldwin-Cartier School Board, Montreal. Faced with the challenge of providing effective speech-therapy services to a class of eight "educably mentally retarded" children at Dorset School, Ayala Manolson (currently Hanen's executive director) initiated a pilot project to involve parents. The program that evolved from this pilot project was designed along the lines of MacDonald's conversational model of language intervention, then in its early stages of development at Ohio State University's Nisonger Center (Manolson, 1984). With time, the original model was refined and extended through the introduction of group programming, the involvement of fathers, and the use of videotapes for evaluative feedback (Manolson, 1984).

The event that gave the program its name and thrust it into a new era of research and development activity occurred in 1977. That year, the Hanen Early Language Resource Center was established at McGill University's School for Human Communication Disorders with funding from the estates of Sam and Lena Hanen. In February 1981, the resource center moved to Toronto, where it is currently located at the Ontario Institute for Studies in Education. Having established the center, the executive director and her associates sought and obtained funding from the Ontario Ministry of Community and Social Services to provide a service program for parents (the Hanen Early Language Parent Program). This funding enables the program to provide services to forty families a year in the metro-Toronto area.

Central to the program's philosophy and practice are several principles. First, children learn language through dialogue/conversation, and therefore the promotion of dialogue skills must be at the heart of language intervention. Second, the didactic (or *trainer-oriented*) approach to language intervention must give way to a *child-focused* approach in which parents and significant other adults are helped to promote dialogue skills in the child. Third, the etiology of language delay is irrelevant for treatment purposes. "Successful therapy can be built without consideration for diagnosis, for it is the behavioral aspect of the condition, not the biological or neurological aspects, that requires the modification of the language training procedures" (Manolson, 1985, p. 1).

It appears that during the development phase, Hanen's emphasis on research was minimal, compared to the other initiatives presented in this section. However, in recent years, empirical validations of the Hanen approach have begun to appear in the literature (Girolametto, Greenberg, & Manolson, 1986; Girolametto, 1988; Tannock, Girolametto, & Siegel, 1988). The designs employed in these studies are, on the whole, superior to those employed in the other initiatives. The evidence generated so far attests to the program's effectiveness in equipping parents with conversational styles that facilitate appreciably high levels of responsiveness, topic initiation, and turntaking in children (Girolametto, Greenberg, & Manolson, 1986). However, the extent to which improved child interactional skills translate into linguistic competencies, as measured with standard language assessments, is yet to be demonstrated (Girolametto, 1988).

In 1988, Hanen received additional funding from the Ontario Ministry of Community and Social Services to participate in the preparation of child-care staff for integrated preschool settings. The training program is offered by Hanen through evening sessions, with site visits to the participating child-care centers. The focus of training is to provide child-care staff with the competencies they need to facilitate emerging language development in young children, while preventing the occurrence of language delays in at/risk children. Through another grant received in 1990 from Health and Welfare Canada under the Child Care Initiatives Fund, Hanen is developing resource materials (a resource manual and videotapes) on the development of communication for child-care workers.

Beside having one of the longest histories of service and development, Hanen is remarkably unique in the extent of its influence beyond the two provinces (Quebec and Ontario) where it has been based during the past sixteen years. The Hanen program is used by some 167 certified speech-language pathologists across Canada, the United States, and in several countries abroad—for example Australia, Israel, and Portugal. Key program materials appear in four languages (English, French, Hebrew, and Portuguese), and Spanish translations are currently underway by an independent researcher. Some of the more basic resources, such as program posters, now have Chinese versions (Manolson, personal communication May, 1990).

CURRENT STATUS OF SERVICES

Even in the absence of federal-level institutional support, funding, and direction, there has been a remarkable expansion of early intervention services during the past decade. According to Brynelsen (1990), the most rapid expansion has taken place in Ontario. While acknowledging the contributions of many committed parents and professionals, Brynelsen attributes the rate of expansion in Ontario largely to the early involvement and commitment of the provincial government. She writes:

By 1976, Ontario had developed draft guidelines...with funding from the Ministry of Community and Social Services. Their recently formed Mental Retardation Community Resource Branches at regional levels were available to assist individuals or agencies in Ontario to develop briefs to request funds. (p. 12)

Across the country, expansion in services has occurred as a function of increased provincial government involvement. In 1985, Nova Scotia

Table 9.1

Number of Early Intervention Programs and Workers in the Ten Provinces
and Yukon as of 1985

Province/ Territory	Number of programs	Number of workers
Alberta	12	31
British Columbia	27	54
Manitoba	3	5
Newfoundland	1*	23
New Brunswick	4	11
Nova Scotia	4	4
Ontario	50	222
Prince Edward Island	1	1
Quebec	20	--
Saskatchewan	15	35
Yukon	1	1
TOTAL	**138**	**387**

The information in this table is based on data presented by Kendall, Brynelsen, and
   Lapierre (1985).
* Newfoundland has a centralized program.

was the only province where early intervention services were yet to
receive government funding (Brynelsen, 1990; Kendall, Brynelsen, &
Lapierre, 1985). Results from the only nationwide survey of early intervention services on record (Kendall, Brynelsen, & Lapierre, 1985),
and its currently ongoing follow-up (Brynelsen, 1990), provide a
glimpse of the growth of services. The survey gathered the following
types of data from all ten provinces and the Yukon: number of programs
operating in the province/territory, number of staff, availability of services for rural communities, availability of provincial funding, required
background training for intervention staff, and remuneration. Kendall
and his associates reported the existence of 138 programs with 410
intervention staff, broken down provincially, as shown in Table 9.1.

With follow-up responses from half of the provinces yet to come in,
Brynelsen (1990) has updated the number of programs and staff, as of
spring 1990, to 189 and 517, respectively. The figures suggest that even
if the other five provinces do not report any changes, the last five years
would have witnessed at least a 37% increase in the number of programs
and a 26% increase in program staff. While the above statistics depict

a seemingly more rapid growth in the number of programs than in program staff, this picture is not uniform across the country. As mentioned earlier on, in the three-year period of 1985 to 1988, the number of intervention workers in Saskatchewan increased by 29%, compared to a 7% increase in the number of programs in that province. There are no available statistics on how many children and families are being served nationwide, but my hunch is that an analysis of actual numbers of families served would show an even more dramatic rate of expansion.

Organization and Delivery of Services: A National Picture

The national norm in the organization and delivery of early intervention services is depicted by the numbers in the second column of Table 9.1: most provinces have several to many independently run programs, although the bulk of the funding for most programs in a province comes from the provincial government. In some provinces (e.g., British Columbia, Ontario, and Saskatchewan), most of the programs are operated by nonprofit parent/community groups—often local chapters of a provincial or national association operating on behalf of persons with disabilities. In other provinces (e.g., Alberta and Newfoundland and Labrador), services are delivered more directly under the auspices of governmental structures. For example, ten of the seventeen programs in Alberta, as of 1990 (Ludvigsen, personal communication), are operated by health units within the provincial department of health. Of the remaining seven, two are offered through schools, four by associations, and one by an assessment and treatment center (D. Ludvigsen, personal communication, June 7, 1990). In Newfoundland and Labrador, all early intervention services are provided through the Mental Retardation Services Division of the Department of Social Services. Because of its organizational attribute, the Newfoundland and Labrador program is described in a bit more detail later in this section.

The multiple organizational approach to service delivery presents some real challenges with regard to provincial coordination and the maintenance of provincial data bases. In their survey of 1985, Kendall and his associates found that only British Columbia and Newfoundland had full-time provincial coordinators of intervention services. Alberta and Saskatchewan had part-time coordinators at that time. Alberta, Nova Scotia, and Prince Edward Island now have full-time coordinators. The following observation about the Ontario situation sums up the kinds of difficulties that arise in the absence of provincial coordination:

Although government funding was forthcoming, unfortunately, as with most provinces in Canada, programs in Ontario developed in isolation of each other without provincial coordination. Ontario did at least have guidelines prepared but they were not disseminated well and there were no provincial staff available to assist in program/staff development or interpretation of the guidelines at the local level. In 1982 the Ontario government commissioned a study of their infant development programmes. It found that a number of program directors were unaware that guidelines had been established by the Ministry in 1977. (Brynelsen, 1990, p. 13)

The absence of provincial coordination has meant also that standards and guidelines for the development, delivery, and administration of programs are nonexistent in many provinces. For many years, British Columbia was unique in terms of having not only a document on guidelines and procedures but also a provincial steering committee. In 1988, a new policy and procedures manual for British Columbia was published (Brynelsen, 1988). In 1985, Saskatchewan—which has had a provincial coordinating council since 1982—revised the guidelines it adopted from the British Columbia program three years earlier (Saskatchewan ECIP, 1985a). In 1986, Ontario began a new effort to develop new guidelines (Ontario Community Services Division, 1986). Although Alberta now has a provincial steering committee, it is yet to develop comprehensive policies and guidelines. The program standards document from 1980, which continues to be used and is currently being revised, is highly inadequate. Brynelsen (1990) reports that New Brunswick has submitted proposals for the setting up of a steering committee to the provincial government.

Newfoundland and Labrador: A Unique Tradition

The province of Newfoundland and Labrador offers a system of early intervention service delivery that is unique across the country. The province has the only truly centralized, publicly funded program in Canada. Established in 1975, and supported completely by the Department of Social Services, the Direct Home Services Program (DHSP) provides services to all families of developmentally delayed children across the entire province. Child Management Specialists (CMS), the intervention workers in this province, are based in nineteen centers in the province's five regions. As of 1988, there were twenty-one full-time and five part-time CMSs and four EIWs (Early Intervention Workers).

The minimum educational qualification for a full- or part-time CMS position is a bachelor's degree in psychology or related fields. The EIW position requires a minimum of two years of college preparation, with course work in psychology, education, or a related human-service field, and considerable experience in working with children. The EIW position is part of innovative strategies implemented to ensure that services reach even the most remote rural areas of the province. Most EIWs are recruited from the local community, to reduce rapid staff turnover and thus provide greater continuity of services.

The program is run by a coordinator and an assistant coordinator. The coordinator's position is one of management within the Department of Social Services. Officially, it requires a master's or doctoral degree in developmental psychology or a related field. The coordinator reports to the assistant director of the Division of Mental Retardation Services.

There are obvious advantages to this centralized system of service delivery. Although remote regions of the province may not receive the same level of services as the relatively urban centers, the system nevertheless ensures greater equity in the distribution of services around the province. For example, the EIW position described above was established in connection with a policy of providing services in areas that would otherwise have difficulty attracting CMSs. Plans are currently afoot to put in place a specialized training program and delivery system that will better meet the needs of the province's native populations.

For the sake of accountability, there is also an advantage to having the same program administration with uniform practices across the province. It is much easier to build a provincial data base—something that is sorely missing in most provinces—and thus easier to monitor progress and plan for future expansions in services. Additionally, large-scale evaluative studies employing the same variables regardless of the regional distribution of the sample are easier to carry out, whether they are done by program staff or by independent researchers.

THE STATUS OF EARLY INTERVENTION RESEARCH

A respectable amount of research activity has been carried out since the mid-1970s, and there are several studies currently in progress in several parts of the country. In this section, I review intervention research focusing specifically on handicapped and developmentally delayed children. Studies focusing primarily on premature and other medically at-risk children carried out in neonatal intensive care units (Piper et al., 1986; Piper, Mazer, Hardy, & Doucette, 1986; Piper, Mazer, Silver, & Ramsay, 1988) are not included. The research reviewed is grouped into two categories: province-wide evaluative investigations and individual early intervention studies.

Province-wide Evaluative Investigations

The criterion for including a study in this category was that the primary purpose of the investigation be to evaluate early intervention services across a province. Table 9.2 summarizes the characteristics of

Table 9.2
Summary of Province-wide Evaluative Studies

Study	Province	No. of Programs and Sample Size	Design	Measures Included
Bloom & Glazer (1985)	Saskatchewan	12 programs; 391 families.	Longitudinal; Noncontrolled	**Child:** Alpern-Boll Developmental profile.
Kysela (1982)	Alberta	5 programs; control group from waiting lists in 2 health units; 19 families in each group.	Longitudinal; Experimental	**Child:** Bayley, Reynell language scales; criterion-referenced tests. **Other:** parent-child interaction; HOME scale; family adjustment interview; home caregiver questionnaire; intervention worker questionnaire; community caregiver questionnaire.
Marfo, Browne, Gallant, Smyth, Corbett, & McLennon (1988)	Newfoundland and Labrador	Centralized program; 200 families.	Partly longitudinal; Noncontrolled	**Child:** Alpern-Boll. **Other:** parental satisfaction; parental knowledge gain; worker competence; quality of home environment; expectations about child's future; family resources; parent-child interaction.
Musselman, Wilson, & Lindsay (1988)	Ontario (hearing-impaired children only)	Exact number of programs unknown; 118 children in all	Longitudinal; Noncontrolled	**Child:** social development receptive language; expressive language.

four investigations that met this criterion in varying ways. The New-foundland and Saskatchewan studies best satisfied the criterion. There were twelve programs in Saskatchewan at the time of the Bloom and Glazer (1985) study and all of them were included in the evaluation. Similarly, the study by Marfo and his associates (1988) evaluated one centralized program serving the entire province from nineteen centers. Although the Kysela (1982) study was funded specifically to evaluate early intervention programs across Alberta, a range of difficulties—including problems in getting some health units to participate—drastically reduced the size of the study. Finally, although the study by Musselman and her associates (Mussleman, Lindsay, & Wilson, 1988; Musselman, Wilson, & Lindsay, 1988) was truly province-wide, its focus was on hearing-impaired children only.

The Alberta Evaluation Study. The Alberta evaluation study (Kysela, 1982) is significant not so much for its findings or recommendations but for its objectives and design. Through an experimental comparison of families in intervention with waiting list families, the research sought to accomplish the following objectives: (a) to assess program effects on the handicapped child's development, (b) to assess program effects on the well-being of the family, (c) to evaluate the effectiveness of the EIW's role as parent educator and family support/resource person, (d) to analyze the attitudes of health professionals toward the early intervention program, (e) to analyze the costs of early intervention in relation to its benefits and outcomes, and (f) to develop an ongoing system of evaluation to assist in local and provincial planning.

Had this study been a success, it would have been one of the most comprehensive evaluation studies in the early intervention field. However, while it was originally intended to follow participants for a period of twelve to eighteen months (with assessments occurring at six-month intervals), the study was terminated after only six months. Participation by intervention staff in the various health units was extremely low, resulting in a highly small and unrepresentative sample of nineteen intervention and nineteen control families. At the time the study was terminated, however, two data points had been covered and the investigator was able to make several recommendations regarding the need for provincial standards and coordination, personnel preparation programs, and awareness campaigns to educate community caregivers about early intervention programs.

The Descriptive Study of Early Intervention Programs in Saskatch-ewan. The Saskatchewan evaluation study (Bloom & Glazer, 1985) was initiated at the request of the ECIP Provincial Council, the Department of Social Services, and the Saskatchewan Association for the Mentally Retarded. Intended as the first step in a multilevel evaluation process, the study had the following goals: (a) to describe the twelve existing intervention programs, (b) to describe the children being served by the programs, (c) to ascertain whether there had been improvements in the children's rates of development since enrollment, and (d) to gather longitudinal data in order to more effectively plan for and meet future needs. The study included a total of 391 children.

The study identified that 62% of the children receiving services fell into the following five broad categories: developmental delay; speech or language delay; physical disabilities, including cerebral palsy; environmentally at-risk; and Down syndrome. Because this research was conducted in part because of future planning, more fine-grained tabular descriptions of the distribution of children by primary, secondary, and tertiary disabilities and by centers were provided.

The principal analysis, however, centered on the charting of developmental progress over the period of participation in intervention. The statistic used for this purpose was the proportional change index (PCI), which compares children's rates of development at pretesting to their rates of development during intervention. The children in the study were subdivided into several groups, as a function of how many data points they had (data points were roughly five to seven months apart). Bloom and Glazer found a trend suggesting that the very early stages of intervention were associated with dramatic increases in the rate of development, followed by a levelling off of changes in the rate of development.

The Ontario Study of the Effects of Early Intervention on Hearing-Impaired Children. This study, which is reported in two sources (Musselman, Lindsay, & Wilson, 1988; Musselman, Wilson, & Lindsay, 1988), was based on a large-scale provincial investigation of the linguistic and social development of preschool hearing-impaired children in the province (Musselman, Lindsay, & Wilson, 1985). The purpose of the 1988 study was "to investigate the effects of age of intervention, program intensity, and direct parent instruction on the language and social development of children with severe and profound hearing losses" (Musselman, Wilson, & Lindsay, 1988, p. 222).

The study included 118 prelingually hearing-impaired children with hearing parents, ranging in age from three to five years at the beginning of the longitudinal study. Children were either in school programs or in one of several specialized programs: hospital-based, home-visiting, or itinerant. The results of the regression analyses performed on the data suggested that, by and large, early entry into intervention, intensive programming, and direct instruction by parents produced no sustained gains in children's social development or in their receptive and expressive language.

To place the findings of this study in a proper perspective, it is important to comment briefly on how each of the three independent measures (age of intervention, program intensity, and parent instruction) was measured. Almost all the children (91%) were enrolled in a program by age three, so the "age of intervention" variable actually was limited to subgroups of children, all of whom could be said to have entered intervention early in life. The assessment of program intensity was based on the number of hours spent in a program and not or how much intervention activity actually occurred. Parent instruction was measured in terms of hours of instruction per week, through a rating of the content of an in-depth interview with parents. Thus, as the investigators rightly point out, because qualitative aspects of programming intensity and parent instruction were not considered, the results should be taken as reflecting "the effectiveness of general educational practice, rather than the effects of best practice" (Musselman, Wilson, & Lindsay, 1988, p. 228).

The Newfoundland and Labrador Study. The Newfoundland and Labrador early intervention study (Marfo et al., 1988; in press) was designed on the premise that thorough analyses of parental attributes and family ecological variables that impinged on the intervention process were necessary if the then-eleven-year-old program was to be adapted to better serve the needs of all families. Among the key objectives of the investigation were the following: (a) to examine parents' early experiences pertaining to the detection of the child's problem, access to early intervention services, and contact with support groups; (b) to assess parental satisfaction with the intervention program, including perceptions about the intervention workers' competence and professional skills; (c) to ascertain the program's effectiveness relative to child developmental progress; and (d) to examine the relative role that child, family ecological, and early intervention variables played in the intervention process.

The study included 200 families served by the Direct Home Services Program across the province and employed the following three classes of measures to address the goals outlined above: (a) child developmental variables (chronological age, entry-level developmental age, current developmental age, severity of delay, rate of development during intervention); (b) program variables (time spent in intervention, parental satisfaction with intervention, parental perception of worker competence, parental perceived knowledge gain); and (c) family ecological variables (quality of the home environment, parental expectations about the child's future, family resources, family income, parental education).

The detailed findings from descriptive, zero-order correlational, and regression analyses of the data have been published in a monograph (Marfo et al., 1988) and in several subsequent papers (Marfo, 1990a; Marfo et al., 1989; in press). According to the investigators, the most significant finding of the study was that intervention outcomes, both in terms of children's development and parental satisfaction, were predicted not by program variables alone or by any one class of variables but by a combination of child, program, and family ecological variables. This finding underscores the need for intervention researchers to recognize that the intervention program is only one of many variables that impinge on intervention outcomes in general and children's development in particular.

One weakness must be borne in mind in any interpretation of this study. While the child developmental data were longitudinal, and included entry-level scores and posttest scores, all the family ecological variables were gathered post-hoc. Thus, while parental expectations and the quality of the home environment turned out to be powerful correlates or predictors of developmental progress, the scores on these variables may themselves have been influenced by parental perceptions of the child's progress over the period of the intervention.

Individual Early Intervention Studies

Table 9.3 provides a summary of six studies reported by researchers working in various parts of Canada. With the exception of the study by Tannock, Giralometto, and Siegel (1988) which is a conference presentation, all the studies have been published in major sources. Although the interventions described are relatively brief in duration, it is remarkable that three of the studies employed experimental designs to test program effectiveness. The studies by Girolametto (1988), Holdgrafer, Kysela, and McCarthy (1989), and Tannock, Girolametto, and Siegel (1988) had a more specialized focus (language) and targeted the parent-child interaction process as the vehicle of change, while the other studies were more didactic and were diffused in their focus on skill development in a variety of developmental domains.

The results of Girolametto's (1988) intervention study were mixed. Although the intervention produced some observable differences in the interactional skills of experimental and control dyads, the improved quality of interaction in the experimental families did not produce corresponding increases in children's linguistic competence as measured by mean length of utterance or by receptive and expressive language skills. The Tannock, Girolametto, and Siegel (1988) study produced somewhat similar results: greater responsiveness and reduced directiveness on the part of experimental mothers were not accompanied by superior linguistic skills in their children. In contrast, the descriptive study of four mother-child dyads by Holdgrafer, Kysela, and McCarthy (1989) reported improvements in mother-child interaction and an increase in the size of the children's vocabulary.

The Piper and Pless (1980) study has gained notoriety in the inter-

Table 9.3
Summary of Individual Early Intervention Studies

Study	Sample Characteristics	Nature of Intervention	Design	Outcome Measures Included
Girolametto (1988)	20 preschool DD children and their mothers. Treatment n = 9 (mean age = 39 mth). Control n = 11 (mean age = 36 mth)	Conversational language program based on Hanen. 11-week parent training: 8 group sessions and 3 individual home sessions.	Experimental	**Child:** MLU; receptive language; expressive language. **Other:** contingent responsiveness by mother and child; topic control by mother and child; uninvolved behavior on the part of child.
Holdgrafer, Kysela, & McCarthy (1989)	4 DD children (including one with DS) and their mothers. Mean age of children = 29.3 mth.	Language intervention focusing on joint action and turntaking with communication. 90-minute weekly sessions over 10 weeks.	Pre/post-test design with emphasis on descriptive case	**Child:** vocabulary size; socio-communicative usage of target words. **Dyadic:** turntaking exchanges; imitation of actions.
*Kysela, Hillyard, McDonald, & Ahlsten-Taylor (1981)	29 children and their families in two programs: home-based (n = 21, mean age at Test 1 = 13.5 mth); school-based (n = 8, mean age at Test 1 = 28.4 mth)	Didactic intervention program with teaching staff and parents employing direct and incidental teaching techniques to foster skill development in 5 domains.	Longitudinal; Uncontrolled, except for comparison of home- and school-based children's normative gains.	**Child:** mental development (Bayley or Stanford-Binet); receptive & expressive language (Reynell).

Table 9.3 (continued)

Study	Sample Characteristics	Nature of Intervention	Design	Outcome Measures Included
Piper & Pless (1980)	37 DS children; Treatment: n=21 (mean age=9.3 mth); Control: n=16 (mean age=8.4 mth)	Six-month, bi-weekly therapy sessions of 1 hr duration, designed to stimulate normal development + written instructions for parents to follow up between sessions.	Experimental	**Child:** Griffiths total DQ, and DQs on each of the five subscales: locomotor; personal-social; hand-eye; performance; hearing and speech.
Piper, Gosselin, & Mazer (1986)	32 DS children, birth to age 24 months.	Home-based weekly program in which parents taught activities to facilitate the normal sequence of development	Longitudinal cum cross-sectional; non-controlled. Chn assessed at 6, 12, 18, 24 mth.	**Child:** Griffiths total DQ, and DQs on each of the five subscales: locomotor; personal-social; hand-eye; performance; hearing and speech.
Tannock & Girolametto (1988)	32 children and their mothers. Treatment n=16 (mean age=35 mth) Control n=16 (mean age =32 mth)	Conversational language program based on Hanen. 12-week training (9 group sessions and 3 individual sessions at home	Experimental	**Child:** social communication; receptive language on SICD; measures of lexical development. **Other:** parent evaluation of program effectiveness; changes in parental interactive behavior; parent and child behavior at 3-mth follow-up.

* Only the normative evaluation components of this study are included in this summary.

national literature for its negative findings. Over the intervention period, the experimental group manifested a more dramatic decline in developmental quotients (in four out of six domains) than the control group, leading the investigators to conclude, "There is no statistical evidence to support the notion that early intervention, as provided in this trial, was efficacious in remediating retardation in infants with Down syndrome" (pp. 465-466). In retrospect, the bitter criticisms of these findings from the early intervention research community were unwarranted, given its generally good quality design; but, as Gibson and Fields (1984) have rightly observed, these reactions reflected the highly vested nature of the early intervention movement.

Piper and her colleagues (1986), on the other hand, did not address the issue of efficacy—although their findings have significant implications for early intervention programming. The study sought to chart the development of DS children in intervention over a two-year period. The findings revealed the following: (a) the children manifested the most profound degree of retardation in the area of language acquisition; (b) in addition to being the second most retarded for children at age two, motor skills showed the most dramatic overall decline during the first two years; (c) the personal-social, hand-eye, and performance domains portrayed either minimal increases or a levelling off of the decline over time. Piper and her associates concluded from these findings that these last three domains (personal-social, hand-eye, and performance) "may represent those developmental areas that are most responsive to early programming" (p. 192).

Finally, Kysela, Hillyard, McDonald, and Alsten-Taylor (1981) employed developmental ratios (the ratio of mental age or language age to chronological age) to assess over-time gains in development, and to compare the relative effectiveness of home versus school-based programming. For both the home and the school program children, the researchers reported a generally consistent over-time acceleration of mental and language (receptive and expressive) development. A comparison of ratios for the home group at the last data point with ratios for the school group at the first data point (a comparison that equated the two groups on chronological age) indicated that at a comparable chronological age, the home group was superior in mental and linguistic development. It must be borne in mind, however, that the question of whether these reported changes were intervention-induced cannot be answered, given the design of the study.

TRENDS, ISSUES, AND FUTURE CHALLENGES

In this concluding section, I undertake two tasks. First, I present and comment on the implications of two key trends occurring in the early intervention field in Canada: the trend toward increased provincial coordination of services, and the trend toward a broader focus on the family as the target of intervention. Second, I present a shopping list of needs that must be met to advance the status of early intervention in the country. The list includes increased research activity, greater involvement of universities in both research and manpower training, and a national clearinghouse to facilitate knowledge dissemination.

Coordination of Programs within the Provinces

There is a clear trend toward bringing individual programs within the provinces under some form of provincial coordination. In the last few years, several provinces have established provincial coordinating councils and, in some cases, steering committees, which report to the government department with funding responsibility for early intervention services. This certainly is a move in the right direction, because coordination gives rise to greater regard for better standards and for equity in the distribution of services and resources across the population. Coordination also makes it easier to build the much needed data bases necessary for effective future planning and expansion.

Above all, the structures that are put in place to facilitate coordination have the potential ripple effect of also creating a unified and strong political voice for early intervention. For example, in 1988, Saskatchewan's Provincial Council submitted briefs to three provincial ministers whose jurisdictions affect early intervention services in some way: education, health, and social services (Saskatchewan ECIP, 1988a, 1988b, 1988c). The briefs to the ministers of health and social services contained five recommendations each, while the education brief had three recommendations. It is instructive to note that one of the recommendations to the minister of education called for "a revision to the Education Act to mandate the education of 3- and 4-year old children with developmental disabilities or mild to severe handicaps, in order that their right to a free and appropriate public education is met" (Saskatchewan ECIP, 1988b, p. 2). The end result of a favorable response to the thirteen recommendations would, without doubt, be massive expansion and improvement in the quality of services. It is going to take this kind of organization in all provinces to get early intervention higher on the agenda of respective provincial governments. Looking further ahead into the future, it is conceivable that it will take the concerted effort of a national organization of all provincial coordinating councils to move early intervention services up on the agenda of the federal government as well.

Beyond Skill Teaching: The Trend Toward Family-Focused Intervention

The traditional skill-teaching model has been criticized for turning parents into teachers, and for having the potential to erode parents' natural parenting skills and thereby jeopardize the normal child developmental mechanisms that are so much a part of the day-to-day parent-child interaction process. Some programs already depart significantly from the traditional skill-teaching model. For example, the Hanen Program takes the approach of not teaching language-delayed children the mechanics of language (e.g., form and content) but of facilitating language acquisition and use by fostering effective parent-child conversational skills. While the parent receives training, the purpose of such training is not to make him or her a *teacher* of the child. Barrera's transactional model of early intervention targets the ongoing interactions within the parent-child dyad and within the family as a whole as the vehicle of developmental change. This emerging shift is partly a reflection of a North American trend toward interaction-focused early intervention (see Bromwich, 1981; Mahoney, 1988; Mahoney & Powell, 1988; Marfo, 1988, 1990b; McCollum, 1984, and Chapter 6).

At the provincial programming level, there is demonstrable recognition in Canada of the need to extend the focus of early intervention services beyond the traditional *infant curriculum* model with its dominant emphasis on *skill teaching*. The increasing recognition that sound family functioning is essential for providing a supportive and developmentally appropriate environment for the child is making interventionists more and more sensitive to the importance of family coping strategies and other family resources, such as social networks and supports (Piper, 1988). Brynelsen (1990) has described the transition from a focus solely on the child to a family focus in the British Columbia program. In Alberta, four of the eight statements of philosophy that will drive future services are family-focused. Similarly, four of Saskatchewan's five goals mention the family, and one of them specifically refers to providing "opportunities for families to develop mutual support networks within their communities" (Saskatchewan ECIP, 1985b, p. 3). Ontario's new guidelines highlight both the child's and the family's developmental needs. Two goals reflecting the new family focus are: "to assist parents . . . to develop their abilities to plan, problem solve and advocate for their children's ongoing developmental and special needs" and "to assist families . . . in the ongoing development of their family unit" (Ontario Community Services Division, 1986; cited in Brynelsen, 1990, p. 43). Earlier on, we saw how recognition of the need to target intervention toward the child's broader family ecology led the

Newfoundland program to carry out a major research study into the role of child, program, and family ecological variables in intervention (see Marfo et al., 1989; in press).

While this shifting focus is, again, in tandem with trends in the United States and elsewhere, the operationalization of the family focus into specific intervention strategies and activities will remain a major challenge for some time. Will *direct skill instruction* continue to have a place in family-focused intervention? If skill teaching is sacrificed for a more diffused focus, will the developmental needs of every handicapped child be met, and how? Do intervention programs, as currently constituted, have what it will take to strengthen or empower families? What kind of skills will intervention workers need to function effectively within the new framework? How will intervention programs handle the needs of diverse groups of families in an increasingly multicultural society? These are only a few of the many questions that must be asked and answered by early interventionists in Canada as the new era of early intervention dawns.

The Research Imperative

The need for increased research activity in the field becomes even more critical when we consider some of the transitions and the programming questions raised above. It is time for all levels of government to recognize that there are limits to the benefits of universal research knowledge. While we have to be careful not to keep reinventing the wheel, we cannot lose sight of the fact that Canadian research is the most valuable source in determining how best to develop, deliver, or improve services for handicapped children and their families in Canada.

The onus for raising the profile of early intervention research lies on governments, universities, and individual researchers. Through its major funding channels, the federal government should provide leadership by establishing grants for early intervention research across the country. In the same vein, provincial governments should set up grants to stimulate research that addresses provincial needs. But, as the saying goes, it takes two to tango! Researchers based in universities and elsewhere also have a significant role to play if the profile of early intervention research is to be raised. Beside lobbying for special grants to be established, researchers in the early intervention field need to take greater advantage of existing funding sources to pursue both basic and applied research. More important, perhaps, researchers need to team up with early intervention program personnel at the community level to develop the kinds of research programs that will strengthen programs at the local level, while generating new knowledge for universal consumption.

The Role of Universities

Leadership is needed from Canadian universities on at least two fronts. On the research front, universities can influence levels of funding by developing program priorities and seeking funding for centers of excellence in early intervention. Beside research, however, universities have a major role to play in the training of personnel for the early intervention field. Canadian universities are significantly behind their U.S. counterparts in the development of early childhood special-education program concentrations. It appears that the University of British Columbia (Brynelsen, 1990) and the University of Alberta (Kysela & McDonald, 1989) are in the process of introducing courses on early intervention in their undergraduate programs. The University of British Columbia now has a one-year graduate diploma program in infant development and early intervention. Much more initiative is needed across the country to train personnel at both the undergraduate and graduate levels.

The Need for a National Clearinghouse

Finally, the need for a national clearinghouse on early childhood educational and welfare services cannot be overemphasized. Knowledge dissemination is as important as knowledge production. In a large country like Canada, where there is little, if any, coordination among the provinces, a national outfit for the dissemination of knowledge should lead to overall improvement of services and research by making developments in any part of the country accessible nationwide. The initiative to establish such an outfit can come from a variety of sources. Although it makes sense to expect Health and Welfare Canada to initiate it, any of the universities or a national organization of the provincial coordinating councils can take such an initiative and seek funding support from Health and Welfare Canada.

ACKNOWLEDGEMENTS

I wish to express my gratitude to the following individuals for providing valuable information on the topic: Dana Brynelsen of British Columbia; Donna Ludvigsen of Alberta; Barbara Bloom and Carol Glazer of Saskatchewan; Ayala Manolson, Luigi Girolametto, and Rosemary Tannock of Ontario. I owe a second debt of gratitude to Dana Brynelsen for her thoughtful comments on an earlier draft of the chapter.

NOTE

1. According to Brynelsen, the Canadian Association for Community Living (formerly Canadian Association for the Mentally Retarded) now consists of 423 member associations across the country.

REFERENCES

Bank-Mikkelsen, N. E. (1969). A metropolitan area in Denmark: Copenhagen. In R. Kugel & W. Wolfensberger (Eds.), *Changing patterns in residential services for the mentally retarded* (pp. 227-254). Washington, D.C.: President's Committee on Mental Retardation.

Barrera, M., & Rosenbaum, P. (1986). The transactional model of early home intervention. *Infant Mental Health Journal, 7*(2), 112-131.

Barrera, M., Rosenbaum, P., & Cunningham, C. (1986). Home intervention with very small birth weight infants and their parents. *Child Development, 57,* 20-33.

Bloom, B. J. (1976, November). *How to maximize participation of parents in the education/habilitation of their mentally retarded child.* Paper presented at the American Association of Mental Deficiency (Region IV) Conference, Tucson, Arizona.

Bloom, B. J. (1978, October). *Final report of the SEECC preschool project: Early intervention through parent-professional partnership.* Paper presented at the Canadian Council for Exceptional Children Conference, Winnepeg, Manitoba.

Bloom, B. J. (1981, October). *Preparing professionals for work with families of preschool exceptional children.* Paper presented at the Fourth Congress of the Canadian Council for Exceptional Children, Halifax, Nova Scotia.

Bloom, B. J., Braun, E., & Glazer, C. (1980). *The SEECC pre-school project: Parent partner training program.* Unpublished manuscript, Institute of Child Guidance and Development, University of Saskatchewan, Saskatoon.

Bloom, B. J., & Glazer, C. (1985). *A descriptive study of early childhood intervention programs in Saskatchewan: Final report for the year 1984–85.* Unpublished report, Department for the Education of Exceptional Children, University of Saskatchewan, Saskatoon.

Bloom, B. J., & Hnatiuk, R. (1982). *A follow-up study of some SEECC pre-school children now in school.* Unpublished manuscript, Department for the Education of Exceptional Children, University of Saskatchewan, Saskatoon.

Bloom, B. S. (1964). *Stability and change in human characteristics.* New York: Wiley.

Bromwich, R. M. (1981). *Working with parents and infants: An interactional approach.* Baltimore: University Park Press.

Brynelsen, D. (1988). *British Columbia infant development program policy and procedures manual.* Vancouver: Infant Development Program of British Columbia.

Brynelsen, D. (1990, May). Historical perspective on infant development programs in Canada. In Proceedings of the Atlantic Conference on *Early Intervention: Current Issues and Future Directions* (pp. 29-60). Department of Child Study, Mount Saint Vincent University, Halifax, Nova Scotia.

Gibson, D., & Fields, D. L. (1984). Early infant stimulation programs for children with Down syndrome: A review of effectiveness. In M. L. Wolraich & D. K. Routh (Eds.), *Advances in developmental and behavioral pediatrics—Vol. 5* (pp. 331-371). Greenwich, CT: JAI Press.

Gibson, D., & Harris, A. (1988). Aggregated early intervention effects for Down syndrome persons: Patterning and longevity of benefits. *Journal of Mental Deficiency Research, 32*, 1-17.

Girolametto, L. E. (1988). Developing dialogue skills: The effects of a conversational model of language intervention. In K. Marfo (Ed.), *Parent-child interaction and developmental disabilities: Theory, research, and intervention* (pp. 145-162). New York: Praeger.

Girolametto, L. E., Greenberg, J., & Manolson, A. (1986). Developing dialogue skills: The Hanen early language parent program. *Seminars in Speech and Language, 7*, 367-382.

Hardy, M., McLeod, J., Minto, H., Perkins, S., & Quance, W. (1971). *Standards for educators of exceptional children in Canada.* Toronto: Canadian Committee, Council for Exceptional Children.

Holdgrafer, G., Kysela, G. M., & McCarthy, C. (1989). Joint action intervention and child language skills: A research note. *First Language, 9*, 299-305.

Hunt, J. M. (1961). *Intelligence and experience.* New York: Ronald Press.

Kendall, D., Brynelsen, D., & Lapierre, J. (1985). *Survey of infant development programs in Canada.* Unpublished report, Faculty of Education, University of British Columbia.

Kysela, G. M. (1978). *The early education project.* Edmonton, Alberta: Planning and Research Division, Alberta Education.

Kysela, G. M. (1982). *An evaluation of early intervention programs in Alberta.* Unpublished report, Department of Educational Psychology, University of Alberta.

Kysela, G., Hillyard, A., McDonald, L., & Alsten-Taylor, J. (1981). Early intervention: Design and evaluation. In R. L. Schiefelbusch & D. D. Bricker (Eds.), *Early language: Acquisition and intervention* (pp. 341-388). Baltimore: University Park Press.

Kysela, G. M., & McDonald, L. (1989). Early intervention within the Canadian context. In M. Csapo & L. Goguen (Eds.), *Special education across Canada: Issues and concerns for the 90s* (pp. 167-178). Vancouver: Center for Human Development and Research.

Lazure, D. (Ed.) (1970). *One million children: The CELDIC report.* Toronto: Crainford.

Mahoney, G. (1988). Enhancing the developmental competence of handicapped infants. In K. Marfo (Ed.), *Parent-child interaction and developmental disabilities: Theory, research, and intervention* (pp. 203-219). New York: Praeger.

Mahoney, G., & Powell, A. (1988). Modifying parent-child interaction: Enhancing the development of handicapped children. *Journal of Special Education*, 22, 82-96.

Manolson, A. (1984). In celebration of communication: Hanen's tenth anniversary. *Wig Wag (Hanen Early Language Resource Center Newsletter)*, 1, 3.

Manolson, A. (1985). Breakthrough for language-delayed children: Parents and teachers play key roles. *Orbit*, 16(1), 1-4.

Marfo, K. (1988). Enhancing interactions between mothers and their developmentally disabled children: A missing link in early intervention? In E. R. Boersma, H. J. Huisjes, & H. M. C. Poortman (Eds.), *A holistic approach to perinatal care and prevention of handicap* (pp. 231-239). Groningen, Netherlands: Erven van der Kamp.

Marfo, K. (1990a, April). *Correlates and predictors of child developmental progress and parental satisfaction in an early intervention program*. Paper presented at the Annual Meeting of the American Educational Research Association, Boston.

Marfo, K. (1990b). Maternal directiveness in interactions with mentally handicapped children: An anlytical commentary. *Journal of Child Psychology and Psychiatry*, 31, 531-549.

Marfo, K., Browne, N., Gallant, D., Smyth, R., & Corbett, A. (in press). Issues in early intervention: Insights from the Newfoundland and Labrador evaluation project. *Developmental Disabilities Bulletin*.

Marfo, K., Browne, N., Gallant, D., Smyth, R., Corbett, A., & McLennon, D. (1988). *Early intervention with developmentally delayed infants and preschool children in Newfoundland and Labrador*. Faculty of Education Publications Committee, Memorial University of Newfoundland (ERIC Document Reproduction # ED 313 132).

Marfo, K., Browne, N., Gallant, D., Smyth, R., & Corbett, A. (1989). *Child, program, and family ecological variables in early intervention*. Unpublished paper, Department of Educational Psychology and Leadership Studies, Kent State University.

Marfo, K., & Kysela, G. (1985). Early intervention with mentally handicapped children: A critical appraisal of applied research. *Journal of Pediatric Psychology*, 10, 305-324.

McCollum, J. A. (1984). Social interaction between parents and babies: Validation of an intervention procedure. *Child: Care, Health, and Development*, 10, 301-315.

Musselman, C. R., Lindsay, P. H., & Wilson, A. K. (1985). *Linguistic and social development in preschool deaf children*. Toronto: Ontario Ministry of Education.

Musselman, C. R., Lindsay, P. H., & Wilson, A. K. (1988). An evaluation of recent trends in preschool programming for hearing-impaired children. *Journal of Speech and Hearing Disorders*, 53, 71-88.

Musselman, C. R., Wilson, A. K., & Lindsay, P. H. (1988). Effects of early intervention on hearing impaired children. *Exceptional Children*, 55, 222-228.

National Institute on Mental Retardation. (1981). *Orientation manual on mental retardation*. Toronto: NIMR.

Ontario Community Services Division. (1986). *Consultation paper on proposed guidelines for infant development services*. Toronto: Ministry of Community and Social Services.

Perkins, S. A. (1979). Problems and issues in special education. *Education Canada, 19*(3), 32-37, 43.

Piper, M. C. (1988). Infant stimulation: Who needs it? *Pediatric Division Newsletter (Canadian Physiotherapy Association)*. Summer, 1-5.

Piper, M. C., Kunos, V. I., Willis, D. M., Mazer, B. L., Ramsay, M., & Silver, K. M. (1986). Early physical therapy effects on the high-risk infant: A randomized controlled trial. *Pediatrics, 78*, 216-224.

Piper, M. C., Mazer, B. L., Hardy, S., & Doucette, C. (1986). Monitoring the effects of early physical therapy on the high-risk infant: Preliminary results. In M. Schwebel & C. A. Maher (Eds.), *Facilitating cognitive development: Principles, practices, and programs* (pp. 303-318). New York: Haworth Press.

Piper, M. C., Mazer, B., Silver, K. M., & Ramsay, M. (1988). Resolution of neurological symptoms in high-risk infants during the first two years of life. *Developmental Medicine and Child Neurology, 30*, 26-35.

Piper, M. C., & Pless, I. B. (1980). Early intervention for infants with Down syndrome: A controlled trial. *Pediatrics, 65*, 463-468.

Saskatchewan ECIP. (1985a). *Saskatchewan's Early Childhood Home-Based Intervention Program (ECIP) standards and guidelines*. Saskatoon, Saskatchewan: The ECIP Provincial Council and the Saskatchewan Association for the Mentally Retarded.

Saskatchewan ECIP. (1985b). *Saskatchewan's Early Childhood Home-Based Intervention Program (ECIP): Procedures manual*. Saskatoon, Saskatchewan: The ECIP Provincial Council and the Saskatchewan Association for the Mentally Retarded.

Saskatchewan ECIP. (1988a). *Proposal to the minister of health*. Saskatoon, Saskatchewan: The ECIP Provincial Council and the Saskatchewan Association for the Mentally Retarded.

Saskatchewan ECIP. (1988b). *Brief to the minister of education*. Saskatoon, Saskatchewan: The ECIP Provincial Council and the Saskatchewan Association for the Mentally Retarded.

Saskatchewan ECIP. (1988c). *Brief to the minister of social services*. Saskatoon, Saskatchewan: The ECIP Provincial Council and the Saskatchewan Association for the Mentally Retarded.

Saskatchewan ECIP. (1988d). *Saskatchewan's Early Childhood Home-Based Intervention Program (ECIP): Board orientation package*. Saskatoon, Saskatchewan: The ECIP Provincial Council and the Saskatchewan Association for the Mentally Retarded.

Skeels, H. M. (1966). Adult status of children with contrasting early life experiences: A follow-up study. *Monographs of the Society for Research in Child Development, 31*(3).

Skeels, H. M., & Dye, H. B. (1939). A study of the effects of differential stimulation of children. *Proceedings of the Annual Convention of the American Association on Mental Deficiency, 44*, 114.

Tannock, R., Girolametto, L., & Siegel, L. (1988, August). *Efficacy of a conver-*

sational model of language intervention: Preliminary findings. Paper presented at the eighth Congress of the International Association for the Scientific Study of Mental Deficiency, Dublin, Ireland.

Warnock, H. M. (1978). Special Educational Needs: Report of a Committee of Enquiry into the Education of Handicapped Children and Young People. London: HMSO.

Zaleski, W. (1983). Traveling clinics in Saskatchewan—Diagnostic assessment and counseling. In G. Schwartz (Ed.), Advances in research and services for children with special needs (pp. 13-17). Vancouver, B.C.: University of British Columbia Press.

10

The Changing Face of Early Intervention in Australia: Following Fads and Fashions?

Alan Hayes

SOME BACKGROUND

Scope of the Chapter

It is a difficult assignment to analyze the state of play in an area as complex as early intervention within a country as geographically large and culturally diverse as Australia. Early intervention is an evolving field with much heterogeneity that makes it difficult for any overview to match the changing reality "on the ground." But equally, it may be difficult to appreciate trends when confronted with the mass of specific information that any comprehensive survey generates.

The present chapter does not attempt to provide a comprehensive mapping of current programs. Rather, it analyzes some of the broad trends in early intervention in Australia and examines their intellectual ancestry, focusing particularly on programs for children with intellectual disabilities or general developmental delays. As such, it (a) briefly traces the development of the field, (b) identifies the main approaches to early intervention in Australia, (c) illustrates the discussion of approaches with reference to lighthouse programs, (d) describes some innovations in service provisions in isolated parts of the country, and (e) discusses the further development of early intervention in Australia. Before turning to the topic of early intervention, however, I want to put the discussion in context by considering some of the key characteristics of contemporary Australia.

Contemporary Australia in Overview: A Small Nation in a Large Continent

It may seem absurd now but for some years after Australia was settled, in 1788, most of the soldiers and convicts had little idea of where they were. It was not at all unusual, for example, for the first unwilling settlers to dream of escape to China, which they firmly believed would be found just to the west of their settlements perched along the East Coast (Hughes, 1988). While such basic geographical errors may not be as common these days, in the minds of many who have not visited the country, it may still represent little more than a land of stockmen (ranchers), aboriginals, dingoes, koala bears, kangaroos and untold millions of sheep and cattle, coexisting contentedly on the shores of Sydney Harbour, in the shadows of those solitary symbols of modernity—the Sydney Harbour Bridge and the Opera House. The most popular examples of the recent Australian film genre do little to dispel these misconceptions.

Contemporary Australia, however, is a diverse, multicultural society of 16,747,600 people, occupying a continent with a land area only slightly smaller than the coterminous states of the United States (2.98 versus 3.02 million square miles, respectively). The 1986 census (Australian Bureau of Statistics, 1988) shows that the majority of Australians live in cities of 100,000 or more inhabitants (62.9%), or towns of 1,000 or more inhabitants (22.4%). Only 14.6% still live in rural settings. Like the United States, the population tends to cluster in large cities and conurbations along the coasts.

The proportion of black Australians is quite small—1.5%—in contrast to the U.S. figure of 12.2% (U.S. Department of Commerce, Bureau of Census, 1989). Increasingly, however, Australia is home to a rich melange of people from many lands. Instead of the integrationist "melting pot," Australia has increasingly embraced a policy of multiculturalism, with the members of each ethnic group retaining much of their cultural distinctiveness and thereby contributing to the diversity of the nation. While this policy is not without its critics (see, for example, Blainey, 1984), it represents an advance over the exclusionist policies prior to the 1950s.

Australians enjoy a relatively high standard of living, and while there is poverty (Hollingworth, 1979), it tends not to be the extensive *ghetto-based* phenomenon present in Europe or the United States. Australia is a democracy, with a federal government based on the Westminster system and led by a prime minister. While Elizabeth II is queen of Australia, her representative in Australia is the governor general. Under the Constitution, citizens elect members to the House of Representatives and the Senate. The six states and two territories vary in size and population as well as in their specific democratic systems.

Education is administered by each state or territory, although with a bulk of funding provided by the federal government. There is an increasing move toward decentralization of the administration of education, with regionalization of the once monolithic state education departments and greater community involvement. Even so, education systems are far less diverse than in the United States, where staffing, resources, policies, and curricula vary considerably across local school districts. Another major area of difference between the two countries is in the area of policy development. It is much less likely in Australia that federal legislation provides the impetus for policy development in the states (Safran, in press). In fact, the Australian Constitution enshrines the rights of the states to exercise sovereignty in the area of education. Policy is much more likely to develop as a result of initiatives from within the education departments, in response to administrative and community concerns.

Distance and the Transportation of Ideas to Australia

Distance sets the metaphor for much of Australia's character as a place where transportation looms large in many issues. However as Blainey (1982) observed, while distance has exacted a tyrannous cost in terms of the transport of people or goods, "for ideas the freight has often been cheap. In the history of this land, ideas have usually leapt with relative ease across the ocean and even across the inland" (p. i). This chapter, as much as anything, is about the transportation and transplantation of ideas concerning early intervention.

One of the distinct advantages for Australian educators and policy makers is their ability to draw on the international pool of educational ideas and to apply innovations elsewhere to the development of services in the country. Clearly, this represents a benefit for the country in reducing research and development costs. By the same token, it can also be a source of potential problems, as ideas developed in one context are rapidly, and at times hastily, applied to very different contexts of Australian society.

In the early days of the colony, the sources of ideas and influence were inescapably British, and the key thinkers in Australian education tended either to be British or, if born in Australia, to be educated in British universities. While ideas from Britain and Europe still exert powerful influences, increasingly the stamp of U.S. thinking is clear in many areas of the educational systems of Australia. American television, movies, and "commercial culture" have had a considerable impact on Australian life, as they have throughout the world.

One unfortunate legacy of all the years of material, cultural, and psychological dependence on Britian and Europe has been called the "cultural cringe" (Hughes, 1988). This is a tendency in Australians to evaluate anything from outside as inherently better than home-grown products. Education has suffered from this problem as much as any area of Australian life, as is shown by a review of the development of early intervention.

EARLY INTERVENTION: A HISTORICAL OVERVIEW

The emergence of early intervention is one of the major educational innovations of this century. It represents the confluence of ideas in developmental psychology, early childhood education, and special education, as well as some fundamental shifts in philosophy and policy in relation to persons with disabilities. Following the United States and Europe, movements for normalization, deinstitutionalization, and provision of community-based services gained momentum in Australia throughout the 1970s. The same decade also saw a rapid increase in the movement for provision of early intervention services for young children with disabilities.

The present historical overview is based on the two major reviews of early intervention in Australia. The first, by Watts, Elkins, and associates (1981), covered the period to the beginning of the 1980s and was based on a comprehensive national survey. The second, representing an update, was provided by invited reviewers in the volume edited by Pieterse, Bochner, and Bettison (1988).

The Australian Scene: The First Phase

The first phase of development of early intervention services was marked by the emergence of a small number of programs, starting in the 1950s and predominantly involving categorical programs for children with clearly identified disabilities, such as cerebral palsy and hearing or visual impairment (Watts, Elkins et al., 1981). In the main, these programs were sponsored by voluntary organizations and operated with a combination of funds from charitable organizations and government subsidies.

The Second Phase

The national survey conducted by staff of the Schonell Educational Research Center documented the rapid rise of early intervention services in the second phase of service development, particularly from 1975 onwards (Watts, Hayes, & Apelt, 1981). To summarize the results briefly, 82% of programs were established between 1970 and 1979, with most of these commencing after 1975. At the time of the survey, the majority of the children (78%) attending early intervention programs in Australia ranged from age one to six years, with 60% of the children aged three years, or more.

A major feature of the second phase was the move to adopt "noncategorical" approaches to early intervention (Ashby, Cliffe, Culbert, & Miller, 1979). Only a third of the programs surveyed by Watts and associates (1981) catered to children with a single disability, such as intellectual handicap or hearing impairment. Most now had a heterogeneous clientele, including children with multiple handicaps, although over 75% of programs involved some children with intellectual handicaps.

While the staff of most programs reported that children and their families were the clients of the early intervention, Watts, Elkins, and colleagues (1981) found that programs differed considerably in their approach to service delivery. Almost half the programs identified (46%) were entirely center-based, while 49% involved some combination of home- and center-based elements. Only 5% were entirely home-based. Service delivery patterns varied from a single professional working with limited support from other professions to multi-, inter-, and occasionally trans-disciplinary teams. While most programs also included some combination of therapists, medical personnel, social workers, psychologists, and school guidance staff, teachers had the most extensive involvement in program delivery. In addition to teachers, teachers' aides also played a very important role in the provision of early intervention services.

The pattern of service provision across the states and territories revealed considerable diversity in the development of early intervention in Australia at the beginning of the 1980s. For example, in New South Wales, while forty programs were identified, there were no government-sponsored programs for children under five, except in the area of hearing impairment (Conrad, Willis, Hayes, & Shepherd, 1981). The most populous state in the nation had very limited coordination of services, and no government department accepted responsibility for early intervention (Conrad, Willis, Hayes & Shepherd, 1981). While the remaining states had a combination of voluntary agency and government involvement in early intervention, fragmentation and problems in coordination characterized the second phase (Conrad, Willis, Hayes, & Shepherd, 1981).

To summarize, at the time of the survey by Watts, Elkins and associates (1981), the picture was one of recent expansion of services, showing considerable diversity in program philosophies, location, and sponsorship. Key problems were evident in coordination of services, training of personnel, funding, and provision of services in the more isolated rural areas of the country. A critical feature of the second phase of development of early intervention was the emergence of some *lighthouse* programs that will be reviewed in greater detail below.

The Third Phase

The third phase in the development of early intervention in Australia has been marked by the rapid expansion of services in each of the states and territories, with increased involvement of state and federal governments (Bettison, 1988). While there is evidence of greater coordination of services in some states, there is still a lack of policy coordination for the area. As Bettison observed, these policies have led to "a proliferation of small, self-contained projects and a preponderance of center-based rather than home-based programs focusing on particular categories of disability" (p. 3).

There has, however, been a focus on increased parent involvement, a greater emphasis on integration and normalization, and a continuing shift in the focus from therapy-oriented programs to educationally based intervention approaches (Bettison, 1988). Identification and needs evaluation remain a major problem in some states and result in a lack of clear data base for service planning (Bettison, 1988). Funding seems a perennial problem, exacerbated by government policies of providing pilot funding, with little security of continued funding once service has been established.

States that had limited evidence of agency-based early intervention, such as New South Wales, Tasmania, and the Northern Territory, now have active programs. Western Australia and Queensland had developed comprehensive networks of services. In Queensland and Tasmania, a single government department has assumed responsibility for early intervention. Some interesting innovations in delivery of services in isolated communities will be discussed in detail in a section to follow.

Table 10.1 provides a summary of the current problems confronting early intervention services across the nation in this third phase of early intervention development. Importantly, many of the problems identified by recent reviewers remain essentially similar to those identified in the Schonell Center survey of the second phase of development (Watts et al., 1981). The reviews presented in the volume edited by Pieterse and associates (1988) will now be used to summarize, briefly, the situation in each of the states and the Northern Territory, up to the second half of the 1980s.

Table 10.1
Problems Reported in the Reviews of Early Intervention in the States of Australia

State	Clientele	Coordination	Staffing	Funding	Isolation
New South Wales	X	X	X	X	X
Victoria	X	X	X		X
Queensland			X		X
South Australia			X		X
Western Australia	X		X	X	X
Tasmania			X		X
Northern Territory		X	X		X

In New South Wales, there was a marked transition from the categorical programs of the first phase of early intervention to programs with more diverse clientele (Goodfellow, 1988). Community management of programs is a feature of early intervention in New South Wales, and Goodfellow concluded that, in light of this move to community management, caution needs to be exercised to avoid increasing the burden on families. The services provided by the Health Department remained focused on therapy, and the Education Department continued to play a limited role, albeit fragmented and lacking in coordination, in the area.

Victoria witnessed a considerable expansion of services in the years following the publication of the Schonell Center survey (Moore, 1988), characterized by greater parent participation and the impact of the philosophy of normalization. However, lack of coordinated, comprehensive services, and difficulties in providing services for those with general developmental delays, were noted by Moore. A major problem identified by Moore was the lack of a coordinated state-wide screening program. In the absence of such a program, the exact scale of need in the state was difficult to evaluate. A further problem arose from the passage of the Intellectually Disabled Persons Act of 1986, which prohibits registration of children as intellectually disabled until the age of six years. Finally, the absence of appropriate training programs and gaps in service delivery in rural areas were additional problems in Victoria.

The review of programs in Queensland, by Ashby and Taylor (1988), highlighted the emergence of a coordinated set of early intervention programs administered by the Queensland Department of Education. Problems of communication and coordination identified in the report on the first two years of operation of the pilot intervention programs commenced in 1978 (Hayes et al., 1981) had been addressed by the development of a network of interdepartmental coordinating committees. Increasingly, the Education Department has emerged as the primary provider of early intervention service in the state, a process facilitated by the amendment of the Education Act to remove reference to a lower age for provision of special education services. The impact of the integration movement had increased over the years, with the development of a cascade of service options, ranging from the monitoring of progress in the regular preschool to full-time placement in an early intervention center. In addition, the Isolated Children's Special Education Unit and the Isolated Severely Handicapped Children Support Program had led to improved services for young children living in the remote parts of the state. A major resource, the Handbook of Early Intervention, was produced in 1985 by staff of the Education Department's Division of Special Education.

Services in South Australia had been marked by the impact of moves to regionalization and implementation of a policy of normalization. In reviewing services, Bottroff (1988) commented on the lack of effective supports for the integration program and the lack of coordination of services. Other problems included provision of services to isolated communities, emphasis on center-based services, and the lack of trained staff.

There has been a considerable expansion of services in Western Australia, although in a climate of static resources (Cocks, 1988). Some problems of fragmentation also have occurred recently as a result of regionalization. Cocks concluded that there is a need for increased services to meet family needs, greater parental involvement in policy development, and new forms of service delivery for isolated parts of the state.

As a result of its smaller size and population, and the central role of the Education Department in early intervention, Tasmania has experienced fewer problems of coordination than the other states (Jacob, 1988). Typically, referrals are made from screening clinics operated by Child Health Services to a network of assessment centers jointly staffed by the Health and Education Departments. Intervention programs that emphasize family support are offered either in a center or at home, according to parental preference. Continuing problems include a lack of training programs and difficulties in delivering services to the more isolated areas of the state.

The review of early intervention in the Northern Territory describes the recency of service development there, and the problems arising from the vastness of the territory and the diversity of the needs of its sparsely distributed population (Rouse, 1988). Among the particular problems identified were the lack of staff, the transience of the clients, the lack of extended family support for those who move to the territory for employment, and the difficulties in delivering services to the aboriginal population. Itinerant consultants had used video recording in the homes of isolated families to link them to city-based specialists and had given a high priority to the development of local community support networks.

The development of services in each of the states has been influenced by the lighthouse programs commenced in the 1970s. While these programs share many goals and features in common, they can be categorized broadly as exemplifying different approaches to early intervention. Two broad approaches to early intervention can be identified in Australia: the *direct instruction* and the *milieu* approaches. Each approach has its origins in ideas from overseas, although over the years considerable adaptation has occurred.

LIGHTHOUSE PROJECTS: CONTRASTING APPROACHES

The Direct Instruction Approach

The direct instruction approach, which is based on behavior theory and the field of applied behavior analysis, "emphasizes direct intervention to bring about selected learning skills in young children" (Lerner, Mardell-Czudnowski, & Goldenberg, 1987, p. 136). For any skill area, normal developmental sequences are produced by using task analysis, a process that involves breaking a long-term behavioral objective, such as using a spoon for feeding, into a series of subordinate behaviors, arranged sequentially in order of increasing difficulty (Gagne, 1970). The key assumption is that the process of development is essentially the same for all children; thus, those with disabilities go through the same developmental stages but in a manner and at a rate dependent on environmental experiences (Pieterse, 1988).

The two most salient Australian examples of lighthouse programs based on direct instructional approaches are the Down Syndrome Program, at Macquarie University, which commenced in 1975 (Pieterse, 1988), and the Education Program for Infants and Young Children (EPIC), at the Preston Institute of Technology, which started in 1976 (Clunies-Ross, 1976, 1979, 1988; Hudson & Clunies-Ross, 1984). For the purposes of this discussion, the Macquarie Program will be used as the example.

The Macquarie University Down Syndrome Program. The Down Syndrome Program is based on a program developed at the Experimental Education Unit in Seattle and exemplifies the following principles and practices (Pieterse, 1988, p. 86):

1. education available to child and parent from the time of diagnosis of the child's impairment;
2. an individualized educational program designed for each child and family and therefore individual assessment and programming;
3. a data-based program in which the child's responses are graphed daily and teaching decisions are based on the child's performance to ensure progress;
4. application of theoretically justified intervention strategies;
5. emphasis on language and communication skills;
6. parental involvement, support, and training; and
7. normalization principles applied at all levels of programming, methods, and outcomes.

The program usually involves twenty-one children with Down syndrome, aged between two months and five years, assessed initially on the "Developmental Skills Inventory (DSI) of the Macquarie Program for Developmentally Delayed Children, and T.E.L.L., the communication program" (Pieterse, 1988, p. 86). An individualized, structured program is constructed for each child, on the basis of the assessment data.

Attendance patterns and program elements vary across age groups. Infants, aged between two and eighteen months, are brought to the center weekly for an individualized program involving teacher, therapist, and parent. Toddlers, aged between eighteen and thirty-six months, visit the center for two sessions that are each 2.5 hours long. The toddlers participate in individual and group programming. Half of each session is devoted to parent training in interactional skills related to play and communication. Preschoolers, aged between three and five years, have three morning sessions at the center per week that are each 2.5 hours, and attend regular preschool on the other days. The intervention program for preschool children focuses on play, communication, and preacademic skills.

The guiding assumptions for the Macquarie Down Syndrome Program are, that (a) analysis of "normal" development provides the most appropriate basis for the design of task sequences for children with disabilities and (b) the optimal goal of intervention is to facilitate the integration of each child in a regular school (Pieterse, 1988). The curriculum was constructed from analyses of norm-referenced tests by Cohen and Gross (1979), and adapted by Pieterse to derive program steps that were sufficiently fine-grained to detect performance improvement (1988). Additional items, focused on the skills required for successful integration, were derived from surveys of teachers in the regular preschool and school systems.

Several studies by Pieterse and her colleagues have examined issues of program effectiveness. She reports significant differences in performance on the Denver Developmental Screening Test between children who had been in the program for a year and a "matched" set of control children, who had received basic therapy services but no structured early intervention (Pieterse, 1988). A second study presented data for a six-year period that show that children in the program attained, on average, 80 to 100% of the skills expected for their chronological age on the Uniform Performance Assessment Scale (Pieterse, 1988).

The third set of studies focuses on integration. Pieterse and Center (1984) presented data for eight children integrated in kindergarten or first, second, or third grade in regular schools, with itinerant specialist support. The children ranged in IQ on the Stanford Binet from 47 to 67 (M = 59; SD = 7.7). Data are reported for a battery of tests of word knowledge, reading comprehension, and mathematics, as well as scales for assessing social adjustment. On standardized tests, word knowledge ranged from the fourth to the twenty-fifth percentile, with a mean percentile rank of 10.9. In mathematics, however, all but one child ranked in the lowest percentile. With ongoing support in the lower primary grades, Pieterse and her coworkers concluded that children who had attended the early intervention program for a number of years could be successfully integrated, academically and socially. In the upper primary grades, however, without ongoing specialist support, the children could not be maintained in the regular school (Pieterse, 1988).

The procedures for recruitment of children to the program may limit the generalization of Pieterse's results. While she suggests that selection is randomized, the procedure "has been to offer a place to the first parent who makes enquiries about admission to the program whose infant is under four months of age, has regular Trismony 21 and lives within commuting distance" (Pieterse, 1988, p. 85). Some sample bias may inadvertently result from this procedure. The children of better-informed parents, who are part of a network of parents of children with Down syndrome, may be more likely to be recruited.

Although some questions remain concerning effectiveness of the program, in the long term, it has had a considerable impact on the development of Australian early intervention services. Program staff have trained many of the personnel to work in centers across the state (Pieterse, 1988), and it has been the model for programs such as the Early Education Clinic in Sydney, which caters to 300 families (Pieterse, 1988). In addition, print and videotape resources for parents and teachers have been prepared by program staff and disseminated widely. It will be interesting to see the results of a long-term follow-up of children who attended the program.

The Macquarie Down Syndrome Program, together with the EPIC program, has set some of the characteristics of the field, particularly the emphasis on center-based intervention using direct instruction. At the same time, an alternative perspective, building on the strong traditions of early childhood education that have evolved in Australia, has also developed.

Programs Based on the Milieu Approach

The second set of approaches to early intervention can be labelled milieu approaches, because they attempt to facilitate development by modifying or supporting the developmental milieu. The milieu approach has its origins in regular early childhood education and development, and emphasizes the developmental importance of interaction, exploration, and play. Informal, incidental opportunities for learning are encouraged, and programs aim to make the intervention program enjoyable (Lerner, Mardell-Czudnowski, & Goldenberg, 1987). As such, they reflect an increasing recognition of the importance of "the ecology of human development" (Bronfenbrenner, 1977). Originally applied to a set of approaches to language intervention most associated with Hart and Risley (1980) and MacDonald (1985), among others, the term can be widened to include many of the compensatory education programs that were developed in the late 1960s and 1970s. One example is the use of home visits by Toy Demonstrators to modify the verbal exchanges between mothers and their toddlers who live in disadvantaged circumstances (Levenstein, 1988; Madden, Levenstein, & Levenstein, 1976). Slaughter (1983, 1988), an advocate of milieu approaches to intervention for black families living in poverty, compared and contrasted Levenstein's approach with a discussion-based program. While both approaches led to short-term benefits, Slaughter (1983) concluded that the discussion group was the more culturally congruent approach for disadvantaged black families living in the United States. In the area of intervention with children with intellectual handicaps, Ludlow and Allen (1979) demonstrated the effectiveness of both home rearing and center-based intervention, as opposed to residential care, in facilitating the development of children with Down syndrome.

In Australia, milieu-based approaches have been used with both disadvantaged and handicapped children. For example, the Home Base Program for children of disadvantaged families living in the Mt. Druitt area of Sydney was founded on ideas from the Head Start, Homestart, and Weikart's Ypsilanti programs (Healey, 1988). Examples of programs for children with disabilities include the Language Intervention Project at Macquarie University, based in part on the milieu approach of MacDonald (Price & Bochner, 1988); the Communication Camps for children with Down syndrome (Parsons, Smith, & Bowman, 1988); the Parents as Educational Partners Program (PEPS: Leach, Swerissen, & Leach, 1988); and the Irrabeena Program (Cocks, 1979, 1982, 1988).

The Noah's Ark Toy Library. One area where the milieu approach has been prominent in Australia is in the toy libraries providing early intervention programs as part of their wider set of services to families with young disabled children. The toy library movement was developed in the 1940s in the United States predominantly to cater to the needs of culturally disadvantaged children (Elkins et al., 1980). Families that were too poor to buy toys could borrow them from the library. In Sweden during the 1960s the toy library concept was adapted to the needs of children with disabilities (Forell & Glue, 1988). The idea spread quickly throughout Europe and the United States with 350 toy libraries operating in England by 1977 (Elkins et al., 1980).

The Australian survey by Elkins and associates (1980) identified forty-five toy libraries providing special services for children with disabilities, including consultative services and reference libraries for parents, as well as assessment of clients, activities for parents and children, and resource support for professionals. Most reported that they served children with diverse disabilities and over half served children ranging from birth to twelve years of age. In many of the libraries advice for parents was also available from therapists (Elkins et al., 1980). For example, the Noah's Ark Toy Library in Melbourne incorporated the services of a team of physio-, occupational, and speech therapists, in addition to a teacher and a nurse. Others, such as the Noah's Ark Toy Library in Cheltenham (North Sydney), used therapists as consultants to ensure that toys lent to children with disabilities were suitable and safe.

The Noah's Ark Toy Library network has emerged as the major community-based organization promoting the importance of parent-child interaction and play for development of children with disabilities (Forell & Glue, 1988). The aims and objectives of the movement (see Forell & Glue, 1988, p. 254) are to:

1. provide for parents a center of guidance with professional help and advice on choosing and using toys and equipment;

2. provide a supply of therapeutic, creative, and sense-stimulating toys to help disabled children overcome their physical, mental, emotional, and perceptual disabilities;

3. help disabled persons and their families overcome the isolation and overprotection to which they are subjected;

4. provide locations where disabled persons and others can meet, play, and develop social confidence, imagination, and speech;

5. provide a program of recreational activities for disabled persons;

6. provide a service for the distribution of toys and equipment (anywhere in the geographic area served) to disabled persons who, due to their handicap or distance, are unable to attend the toy library; and

7. integrate the toy library into the overall network of community services for the disabled.

In summary, toy libraries strive to build on the importance of play by providing equipment and advice to the families of children with disabilities. As such, they focus on play and family involvement, with considerable scope to tailor services flexibly to meet the varied needs of families. They also provide respite care, through the provision of weekend and school holiday activity programs. Noah's Ark Toy Libraries provide a flexible, comprehensive service, available across a wide geographic area with continuity beyond early childhood. Thus, they have been exemplary in solving some of the problems of both disability and distance.

INNOVATIVE SOLUTIONS TO PROBLEMS OF ISOLATION

Distance, as Geoffrey Blainey (1982) put it, has been a tyrannous element in Australia's history since European settlement. Provision of services in rural areas in a country as large as Australia presents some particularly difficult problems, especially in the domain of low incidence disabilities (Barrie & Tomlinson, 1985). Distance, lack of transportation, difficult terrain, and weather are among the factors that make participation in specialized intervention difficult for those living in the more isolated parts of Australia (Batchler & Shaddock, 1988). Often, the only alternatives available to families are placement of their child in a facility in a larger town or city, relocation to a town or city offering the services needed by their child, or provision of rudimentary services in the local community (Hayes & Livingstone, 1986; Hayes, 1988). Values within rural communities, such as emphasis of the rural ethos on self-sufficiency and caring for one's own, also may exacerbate the situation (Helge, 1984).

On the basis of the first national survey of the families of children with disabilities living in isolation, conducted by the Uniting Church National Frontier Mission (Brentall & Dunlop, 1985), it was estimated that over 5,000 young children with disabilities were living in isolated areas of the country at the time of the survey. The survey by Watts, Elkins and associates (1981) had identified only fifteen programs in towns with populations of 10,000 to 30,000 and only five programs in towns with populations of less than 10,000 residents. The Annual Report of the Commonwealth Schools Commission (1984) concluded that the needs of young children with handicaps represented one of the most urgent areas for service delivery. In recent years, however, there have been several interesting initiatives to overcome the problem of rural isolation. These initiatives form a basis for future service development.

The Child and Parent Support Project (CAPS)

This project represents an example of community initiative in a rural location. A detailed description of the project is available in the report by Bramley, Hayes, and Elkins (1985) and in Hayes (1988). To summarize, the project was undertaken in Gympie, a provincial city in the state of Queensland, with a population of 22,000. In the absence of specialized services, families were forced to travel to the state capital, Brisbane, to receive service.

Members of the community formed a coalition with the staff of the education, health, and family welfare agencies and obtained funding for the first year of operation under a federal government scheme for the unemployed—the Community Employment Program (CEP)—and received sponsorship from the Uniting Church Child Care Association. These resources enabled employment of three early intervention specialists, an administrative assistant, a research assistant, and a cleaner. Six types of services were provided by the scheme: home visits for the initial screening and parent support; home programs to be implemented by the parents; programs in the child's regular preschool; center-based individual and group programs; a play group for the children with disabilities and their siblings; and information for parents and family day-care providers to increase their awareness and knowledge of disability.

Problems encountered in implementing the CAPS Project included some initial lack of consensus on the nature and direction of the project; difficulties in developing an effective management structure for the project (given the other demands on the committee members' time); and uncertainties about the funding of the project after its first year.

The achievements of the CAPS Project included positive evaluations by the participating families and agency personnel, and an increase in community awareness of the needs of families with children with disabilities. The project also acted as a stimulus for the Queensland Department of Education establishing a full-time early intervention program in the city.

The Tenterfeild Project

This project arose from recognition of two major problems facing services for young children with disabilities in the rural North West of New South Wales (Batchler & Shaddock, 1988). The first was the problem of inefficient use of specialist staff time in traveling long distances to deliver services on a relatively infrequent basis. The second was the relative inexperience of professionals, especially in relation to providing services for children with low incidence or more severe disabling conditions. One of the characteristics of rural Australia is that services often depend on younger, relatively inexperienced professional staff who, after "paying their dues" in country service, move to a more desirable city or coastal placement. In some states, country service is either mandatory or an unwritten prerequisite for promotion.

The novel feature of the Tenterfeild Project was the use of teleconferencing to supplement an intervention program for young children with disabilities in the small rural town of Tenterfeild (population 2,000), New South Wales. Like the CAPS Project, the project built on existing community services and a team of local volunteer tutors. Five children, four with moderate developmental delays and one with a language disorder and suspected "hyperactivity," participated in the program. The Teaching Research Curriculum of Fredericks was the core program for the children, and three children also had programs based on the DISTAR Language I program (Batchler & Shaddock, 1988).

The project ran for a period of ten months. A two-day intensive training program for the project personnel in Tenterfeild was conducted by a team of specialists, who also provided regular program updates by mail and organized weekly teleconferences. Content analysis of the teleconferences indicated that much of the total time (40%) was spent in using the resource team as a sounding board, while requests for direct assistance occupied a very small proportion (2%) of the time (Shaddock & Batchler, 1986). The teleconferences were regarded as a valuable aspect of the project, and while they offered limited scope for individual counseling or family support, they represented a "relatively inexpensive" alternative to road or air travel.

Qualitative evaluation showed that all the children made satisfactory progress, with three children leaving the program after three months to resume regular education. By the end of the project, only one child remained in a special-education program. Staff and volunteers viewed the project very favorably, although some concerns were expressed about the lack of time to hire staff, organize materials, and update programs, and about the degree of structure involved in the program. Like the CAPS Project, the Tenterfeild Project also extended the base of awareness, knowledge, and skill in the community.

Some Technological Innovations to Overcome the Tyranny of Distance

From the rapid adoption of the telegraph, telephone, and radiophone to the development of the flying-doctor aerial medical service to the outback, Australians have demonstrated a particular skill in finding innovative ways of using technology to reduce the impact of isolation. The Australian Telecommunication Satellite (Aussat) has brought a new set of opportunities for developing innovative approaches to service delivery in the outback. For example, in medicine, the North West Telemedicine Project has broken new ground in the use of high-resolution television signals to allow consultants in Brisbane to read X-rays, ultrasound scans, and electrocardiographs, and rapidly provide an opinion on treatment to a doctor or a nurse in a hospital that is remote from any major center. The satellite has also been used for in-service training of doctors and therapists working in isolated areas. In terms of education, the Queensland Department of Education has conducted pilot programs of interactive televised instruction by teachers in Brisbane for children living on isolated cattle stations in the far North West of the state. It seems only a matter of time before the technology will be applied to early childhood special education, under the aegis of organizations such as the Isolated Children's Special Education Unit.

TOWARD THE FUTURE

The first phases in the development of early intervention in Australia have been marked by considerable expansion of programs and the establishment of a solid base for the further development of the field. Like any new enterprise, however, the process has been a mix of exciting new developments and some challenging problems.

The Prospects and Pitfalls of Following Fads and Fashions

Webster's Dictionary (1989) defines a fad as "a temporary fashion" or "manner of conduct," especially "one followed enthusiastically by a group" (p. 510) and a fashion as "a prevailing custom or style of dress, etiquette, procedure" (p. 517). The positive aspect of fad and fashion is that they reflect processes of creativity, change, and reorientation. The negative aspect is that while fashion prevails, its enthusiastic followers may lose sight of other possibilities. Ironically, fashion may gradually induce conformity and reduce the scope for diversity. Given the time scale for educational change, it is perhaps inappropriate to talk of fads, but it may be appropriate to consider education as an area subject to fashion. Changes in fashion may assist in the process of reform but at the cost of a restriction of focus on alternatives, an uncritical acceptance of the assumptions underpinning the new approach, and a failure to recognize the extent of decontextualization involved in transporting trends across cultures.

For example, the factors and forces that led to early intervention in the United States are not the same as those that led to the emergence of programs for young handicapped children in Australia. The sociopolitical context of the civil rights movement and the war against poverty have no exact parallels in Australia, and compensatory education programs for young disadvantaged children have not been given the priority they received in the United States during the 1960s and 1970s. It is also rather ironic that much of the recent policy in Australian special education reflects the influence of U.S. legislation, particularly the passage of Public Law 94–192—the Education of All Handicapped Children Act (Bailey & Wolery, 1984). As stated earlier, legislative mandate does not have the same influence in Australian policy reform in areas such as special education as it has in the United States. The recognition of the needs of young children with disabilities by parents, professionals, and policy makers, as well as the work of researchers, such as Pieterse and Clunies-Ross, were the driving forces for early intervention in Australia, onto which innovations and trends elsewhere were mapped.

There were many positive effects of adopting direct instructional approaches that ensured their endurance. These included the role of such approaches in breaking down some of the destructive myths of ineducability of persons with disabilities and providing the information required to move beyond the dehumanizing practices of institutionalization, segregation, and denial of access to opportunities. One enduring contribution has been to show that the realms of possibility for children with disabilities are wider than they were once thought to be (Pieterse, 1988). In Australian early intervention, the direct instruction approaches embodied in the Macquarie Down Syndrome Program (Pieterse, 1988) and EPIC (Clunies-Ross, 1988), for example, have contributed greatly to the rapid development of the field and to attitude changes among educators, health professionals, and the community at large.

Direct instruction approaches have set some directions however, that may now require some reconsideration. The focus on center-based intervention (Bettison, 1988) is, in part, one of the results of emulating these lighthouse approaches. A second result is the search for a general model of intervention, based on a single, comprehensive, structured curriculum, framed within a simple "developmental" model, and using a single approach to intervention. The key assumption of the *developmental model*—that task analysis of "normal" developmental sequences can be applied to children with disabilities, irrespective of the nature of their disorders or the degree of severity of the disability—needs to be critically considered (Cherkes-Julkowski & Gertner, 1989). This assumption, which is at the heart of the *delay versus difference* debate, is increasingly open to question, on the basis of data that show some fundamental differences in information processing by persons with intellectual handicaps (Cherkes-Julkowski & Gertner, 1989).

Similarly, assumptions about the course of development for persons with disabilities are open to contention. Given that there are few long-term prospective studies of groups of children with disabilities living at home and in the community, the knowledge base still may not be adequate to permit the design of broad/spectrum early intervention programs. It is only in recent years, for example, that the extent of variation among people with Down syndrome has been widely acknowledged (Gunn & Hayes, 1988). There has, however, been scant consideration of the heterogeneity involved in complex social systems, such as families or peer groups that include children with disabilities (Senapati & Hayes, 1988).

Approaches to programming will require some fundamental reorientations once the heterogeneity and variability of clientele are recognized. For example, highly structured approaches may not be the method of choice for all children. There is now some evidence that structured approaches may be no more effective than less formal enrichment programs (Casto & Mastropieri, 1986) and that they may place demands on young children with disabilities that actually are inappropriate for their age. In emphasizing the need to teach play skills to children with intellectual handicaps, there is a risk that play may lose its spontaneity and become just another form of adult-directed therapy (Jobling, 1988), with the result that the enjoyment of "normal" play is lost (Mogford, 1977).

The research by Skeels and Dye in the 1930s highlighted the importance of a close, caring relationship in facilitating development (Skeels, 1966). It is an irony that in the intervening fifty years this basic message has been somewhat ignored as educators have focused on structured behavioral approaches to intervention. The marriage of early childhood education and special education has been advocated increasingly as one way to refocus the field of early intervention on the importance of considering the emotional characteristics of young children, as well as the influential role of family relationships and activities, such as age-appropriate play, in the development of children (Fewell & Kaminski, 1988; Lerner, Mardell-Czudnowski, & Goldenberg, 1987; McConkey, 1985). One of the strengths of the milieu approach, as exemplified in Australia by the Noah's Ark network, is its emphasis on promoting enjoyable processes of interaction as the central feature of an intervention program. A second strength is the focus on the family, both as an agent of developmental change and as the recipient of support from program staff.

In presenting the contributions of the milieu approach, there is also a danger of falling prey to the same problems of oversimplification that were discussed in relation to the direct instruction approach. For example, Sigafoos and Reichle (in press) have recently highlighted the problems inherent in assuming that milieu-based approaches are the method of choice for addressing the language problems of children and adolescents with severe or profound disabilities. The problem again stems from the assumption of a uniform developmental process—in this case, the key role of "normal" interaction processes in the development of language in all children, irrespective of their type or degree of disability.

FROM A VIEW OF THE PRESENT TO A GLIMPSE OF THE FUTURE

With all dichotomies, there is the danger of exaggerating the differences between approaches and overlooking some of the commonalities or complementarities. Essentially, I am arguing for a plurality of approaches, tailored more sensitively to the diverse needs of a very varied clientele. Additionally, some assumptions of current models of development in early life may need to be reconsidered (Ramey and Suarez, 1985). The impact of early experiences on later development, for example, may not be as simple as the first generation of early interveners thought. It may be too simplistic to see early experience in terms of what happens in the first six years of life, because human development evolves over a longer period of time than the development of other species. Similarly, the relationship of early experience to later development may be much more complex than first thought, being subject to considerable plasticity and multiple determinants over time (Ramey and Suarez, 1985). One implication of this view is that the timing of intervention, and its place in a continuing system of developmental supports, may need some rethinking. Finally, the extent of expected variation in characteristics, and their variability over development, imply that the search for single processes of development may be as futile as the search for the optimal approach to intervention.

Toward Solving Some Perennial Australian Problems

The refocusing of early intervention has some clear implications for the framing of policy and practice in the next phase of early intervention development in Australia. It is now possible to view, in a new light, some of the perennial problems discussed in reviewing the development of early intervention.

Clientele. Making the heterogeneity of clients' needs a central consideration in the design of programs requires consideration of the specialized needs of subgroups, and the framing of a wider range of programs, with greater flexibility to blend structured elements and enrichment to meet the needs of each child and family. Additionally, screening and assessment services need to take greater account of the scope of variability and change in children with disabilities.

Coordination. Developing a more diverse set of services carries the risk of exacerbating the perennial difficulties in communication and coordination. There is some evidence, however, that these problems can be overcome when early intervention services are the responsibility of a single government agency, such as in Queensland and Tasmania. Central coordination of policy with scope for local diversity of practice is needed. The need for development of coordinated federal and state government policy is overdue in this area.

Staffing. The problem of staffing, and particularly the lack of programs for training specialists who work in early childhood special education, has been recognized by all of the 1988 reviews. A shift in emphasis to early childhood education highlights the need for an increased focus on early childhood special education and development in the preparation of teachers to work in early intervention. Again, this should be part of a coordinated set of federal and state government policy reforms.

Funding. The reviewers of development in early intervention in Australia also highlighted tenuous funding as a continuing theme. It is difficult to sustain or disseminate innovations when funding is so uncertain, and there are ethical problems involved when children who start in a program are left, after one or two years, without appropriate services. Funding problems are another symptom of the lack of coherent policies.

Isolation. For early intervention, a major problem has been in translating approaches developed in the large cities of the United States or adapted in the urban centers of Australia, to meet the needs of families with children with disabilities living in smaller, geographically isolated centers. Increasingly, attention has turned to addressing the problems that result from isolation, and, as argued above, a distinct feature of early intervention has been the recent development of innovative solutions to the problem of isolation. The hallmark of these innovations has been the ability of their designers to move away from the more limiting features of the prevailing fashions.

Directions for Research

In parallel with shifts in policy, there is a need to strengthen Australian research efforts in developmental psychology and early childhood special education in order to address the key issues identified above. First, longitudinal studies are required of specific groups of children with disabilities to provide basic data on their developmental trajectories and to inform the development of intervention programs that are more sensitively tailored to children's characteristics and needs than existing program models based on "normal developmental progressions." Second, in such studies, there is a need to focus more directly on issues of between-child differences (variation) and within-child changes (variability) in order to explore the extent of heterogeneity of client characteristics. Third, greater attention should be paid to the importance of contextual factors in the development of young children with disabilities. Specifically, the differences across families, and within families across time, need to be given greater emphasis, as do issues of the extent of match between family and program contexts. Additionally, systematic analyses are required of the legislative and social contexts of Australian society, against which policies and practices imported from other nations might be evaluated. Finally, questions of efficacy require much more sophisticated consideration. As Marfo (1990) has argued, there is a need to move beyond general questions such as "Does early intervention work?" to focus on the match between child characteristics and home and program contexts, and thus address the more detailed question of "What works with whom, under which circumstances and in which setting?" (see also Marfo & Dinero, in press).

Conclusion

Involved in the refocusing of early intervention in Australia is a recognition that disabled children are children first and foremost and that they, and their families, require the respect and dignity afforded to the "nondisabled" members of our society. Recognition of their individuality lies at the heart of this process. The conformity and oversimplification that may accompany an overly enthusiastic adoption of any fashion are the antithesis of individuality. The price of uncritical adoption of fads and fashions may be higher than expected.

SUMMARY

This chapter has examined the development of early intervention in Australia, focusing on (a) the influence of uniquely Australian characteristics, such as the combination of geographical remoteness, small population, and uneven population distribution, (b) the phases in the development of early intervention in the country, (c) the translation of international approaches to early intervention into Australian policy and practice, and (d) the emerging awareness of the need for a shift in the philosophy of early intervention to account for the heterogeneity of clients and the variability in their development throughout life. Key problems—such as client identification, needs evaluation, coordination and communication, personnel and training, funding, and isolation— were identified from reviews of the national scene up to the beginning of the 1980s, and since then. Two approaches, the direct instruction-based and the milieu-based, were defined and illustrated with reference to Australian "lighthouse" programs. In addition, an area of Australian innovation, provision of services in rural and isolated communities, was described. In synthesizing the review of early intervention in Australia, the perennial tendency to import ideas and approaches, and the attendant risk of decontextualzation, were highlighted. The chapter ends with some sketches of future direction for the field, based on the recognition of the need for (a) a diversity of service models to cater to the heterogeneity of the clientele, (b) a more coordinated approach to policy and funding, and (c) a concerted effort to develop training programs with a more balanced blend of early childhood education and early intervention.

ACKNOWLEDGMENTS

The preparation of this chapter would not have been possible without the assistance of several organizations and individuals. First, the University of Queensland and my colleagues at the Fred and Eleanor Schonell Educational Research Center, who enabled me to take study leave to devote myself single-mindedly to research—a rare privilege indeed; second, the Australian Research Council, for providing funding for my research program in the area of disability, including the preparation of this review; third, the Pennsylvania State University, for making available the resources I required to work on my research throughout my period as a visiting professor in the Department of Human Development and Family Studies; and fourth, the staff of the Penn State Nutrition Center, for so generously making available their computer facilities. Finally, I would like to thank Karen Hayes for her support, encouragement, critical comments, and cheerful adoption of the role of research associate and editorial assistant, all of which added greatly to the fun and enjoyment of the task.

REFERENCES

Ashby, G., & Taylor, J. (1988). Early intervention in Queensland. In M. Pieterse, S. Bochner, & S. Bettison (Eds.), *Early intervention for children with disabilities: The Australian experience* (pp. 33-42). North Ryde: Special Education Center, Macquarie University.

Ashby, G. F., Cliffe, S. J., Culbert, N. R., & Miller, S. F. (1979). *Information statement: Early educational intervention programs for children with special needs.* Brisbane: Division of Special Education, Queensland Department of Education.

Australian Bureau of Statistics. (1988). *Australia in profile: Census of 1986.* Canberra: Australian Government Publishing Service.

Bailey, D. B., & Wolery, M. (1984). *Teaching infants and preschoolers with handicaps.* Columbus, OH: Merrill.

Barrie, J., & Tomlinson, D. (1985). *Handicapped children in rural areas: A pilot study of the Eastern Goldfields region.* Perth: The National Center for Research on Rural Education, University of Western Australia.

Batchler, M. W., & Shaddock, A. J. (1988). An approach to early intervention in a rural community. In M. Pieterse, S. Bochner, & S. Bettison (Eds.), *Early intervention for children with disabilities: The Australian experience* (pp. 199-205). North Ryde: Special Education Center, Macquarie University.

Bettison, S. (1988). Overview of early intervention in Australia: 1986. In M. Pieterse, S. Bochner, & S. Bettison (Eds.) *Early intervention for children with disabilities: The Australian experience* (pp 3-5). North Ryde: Special Education Center, Macquarie University.

Blainey, G. (1982). *The tyranny of distance* (2nd ed.). South Melbourne: MacMillan.

Blainey, G. (1984). *All for Australia.* North Ryde: Methuen Haynes.

Bottroff, V. (1988). Early intervention programs in South Australia. In M. Pieterse, S. Bochner, & S. Bettison (Eds.), *Early intervention for children with disabilities: The Australian experience* (pp. 43-53). North Ryde: Special Education Center, Macquarie University.

Bramley, J., Hayes, A., & Elkins, J. (1985). *Monitoring the Child and Parent Support Project, Gympie: Final report.* St Lucia: Fred and Eleanor Schonell Educational Research Center, University of Queensland.

Brentall, B., & Dunlop, M. (1985). *Distance and disability: A survey of children with disabilities in isolated areas of Australia.* Sydney: Uniting Church National Mission Frontier Services.

Bronfenbrenner, U. (1977). Toward an experimental ecology of human development. *American Psychologist, 32,* 513-531.

Casto, G., & Mastropieri, M. A. (1986). The efficacy of early intervention programs for handicapped children: A meta-analysis. *Exceptional Children, 52* (5), 417-424.

Cherkes-Julkowski, M., & Gertner, N. (1989). *Spontaneous cognitive processes in handicapped children.* New York: Springer-Verlag.

Clunies-Ross, G. (1976). A model of early intervention with developmentally handicapped preschoolers: The children's center at Preston Institute of Technology. *Australian Journal of Mental Retardation, 4* (4), 23-27.

Clunies-Ross, G. (1979). Accelerating the development of Down syndrome infants and young children. *Journal of Special Education, 13*(2), 169-177.

Clunies-Ross, G. G. (1988). Early education and integration for children with intellectual disabilities. In M. Pieterse, S. Bochner, & S. Bettison (Eds.), *Early intervention for children with disabilities: The Australian experience* (pp. 97-104). North Ryde: Special Education Center, Macquarie University.

Cocks, E. (1979). Process evaluation of service provision for preschool intellectually handicapped children. *Australian and New Zealand Journal of Mental Retardation, 5*(8), 322-324.

Cocks, E. (1982). Measures of outcome in an early intervention program. *Australian and New Zealand Journal of Developmental Disabilities, 8*(1), 15-20.

Cocks, E. (1988). Early intervention in Western Australia. In M. Pieterse, S. Bochner, & S. Bettison (Eds.), *Early intervention for children with disabilities: The Australian experience* (pp. 55-62). North Ryde: Special Education Center, Macquarie University

Cohen, M., & Gross, P. (1979). *The developmental resource: Behavioral sequences for assessment and program planning, Vol. 1.* New York: Grune and Stratton.

Commonwealth Schools' Commission. (1984). *Report for 1984: Response to government guidelines.* Canberra: Commonwealth Schools' Commission.

Conrad, L. M., Willis, M., Hayes, A., & Shepherd, J. (1981). Overviews of early intervention in the states and territories of Australia. In B. H. Watts, J. Elkins, L. M. Conrad, W. C. Apelt, A. Hayes, J. Calder, A. J. Coulston, & M. Willis (Eds.), *Early intervention programs for young handicapped children in Australia, 1979-1980* (pp. 29-81). Canberra: Australian Government Publishing Service.

Elkins, J., Calder J., Conrad, L., Shepard, J., Clouston, A., & Willis, M. (1980). *Toy libraries in Australia: A report with special attention to their role in service for young handicapped children and their families.* St Lucia: Fred and Eleanor Schonell Educational Research Center, University of Queensland.

Fewell, R. R., & Kaminski, R. (1988). Play skills development and instruction for young children with handicaps. In S. L. Odom & M. B. Karnes (Eds), *Early intervention for infants and children with handicaps: An empirical base* (pp. 145-158). Baltimore: Paul H. Brookes.

Forell, A., & Glue, M. (1988). Noah's ark toy library. In M. Pieterse, S. Bochner, & S. Bettison (Eds.), *Early intervention for children with disabilities: The Australian experience* (pp. 251-261). North Ryde: Special Education Center, Macquarie University.

Gagne, R. M. (1970). *The conditions of learning* (2nd ed.). New York: Holt, Rinehart and Winston.

Goodfellow, J. (1988). Early intervention in New South Wales. In M. Pieterse, S. Bochner, & S. Bettison (Eds.), *Early intervention for children with* disabilities: The Australian experience (pp. 7-20). North Ryde: Special Education Center, Macquarie University.

Gunn, P., & Hayes, A. (1988, August). Down syndrome and developmental mythology. Paper presented at the Australian Developmental Psychology Conference, Sydney.

Hart, B., & Risley, T. R. (1980). In vivo language training: Unanticipated and general effects. Journal of Applied Behavior Analysis, 12, 407-432.

Hayes, A. (1988). The child and family support project: Community initiative in a rural location. In M. Pieterse, S. Bochner, and S. Bettison (Eds.), Early intervention for children with disabilities: The Australian experience (pp. 74-80). North Ryde: Special Education Center, Macquarie University.

Hayes, A. (1990). Families and disability. In A. Ashman & J. Elkins (Eds.), Educating children with special needs (pp. 394-419). Sydney: Prentice-Hall.

Hayes, A., & Livingstone, S. (1986). Mainstreaming in rural communities: An analysis of case studies in Queensland schools. The Exceptional Child, 33, 35-48.

Hayes, A., Steinberg, M., Cooksley, E., Jobling, A., Best, D., & Clouston, A. (1981). Special pre-schools: Monitoring a pilot project, Vol. 1: Project Report. St Lucia: Fred and Eleanor Schonell Educational Research Center, University of Queensland.

Healey, M. (1988). Home-based teaching in Mount Druitt. In M. Pieterse, S. Bochner, & S. Bettison (Eds.), Early intervention for children with disabilities: The Australian experience (pp. 207-217). North Ryde: Special Education Center, Macquarie University.

Helge, D. (1984). The state of the art of rural special education. Exceptional Children, 50, 294-305.

Holingworth, P. (1979). Australians in poverty. Melbourne: Thomas Nelson Australia.

Hudson, A., & Clunies-Ross, G. (1984). A study of the integration of children with intellectual handicaps into regular schools. Australian and New Zealand Journal of Developmental Disabilities, 10(3), 165-177.

Hughes, R. (1988). The fatal shore: The epic of Australia's founding. New York: Vintage Books.

Jacob, A. (1988). Early intervention for the developmentally disabled: Tasmania. In M. Pieterse, S. Bochner, & S. Bettison (Eds.), Early intervention for children with disabilities: The Australian experience (pp. 63-66). North Ryde: Special Education Center, Macquarie University.

Jobling, A. (1988). The 'play' focus in early intervention: Children with intellectual disabilities. The Exceptional Child, 35(2), 119-124.

Leach, D. J., Swerissen, H., & Leach, P. D. (1988). Teaching parents to be direct instructors and child advocates: The Parents as Educational Partners (PEPS) course for parents of intellectually handicapped pre-school children. In M. Pieterse, S. Bochner, & S. Bettison (Eds.), Early intervention for children with disabilities: The Australian experience (pp. 283-304). North Ryde: Special Education Center, Macquarie University.

Lerner, J., Mardell-Czudnowski, C., & Goldenberg, D. (1987). Special education *for the early childhood years* (2nd ed). Englewood Cliffs, NJ: Prentice-Hall.

Levenstein, P. (1988). *Messages from home.* Columbus: Ohio State University Press.

Ludlow, J. R., & Allen, L. M. (1979). The effect of early intervention and preschool stimulus on the development of the Down syndrome child. *Journal of Mental Deficiency Research, 23,* 29-43.

MacDonald, J. D. (1985). Language through conversation: A model of intervention with language delayed persons. In S. F. Warren & A. K. Rogers-Warren (Eds.), *Teaching functional language: Generalization and maintenance of language* (pp. 89-122). Austin, TX: Pro-Ed.

Madden, J., Levenstein, P., & Levenstein, S. (1976). Longitudinal IQ outcomes of the mother-child home program. *Child Development, 47,* 1015-1025.

Marfo, K. (1990, April). *Correlates and predictors of child developmental progress and parental satisfaction in an early intervention program.* Paper presented at the Annual Meeting of the American Educational Research Association, Boston.

Marfo, K., & Dinero, T. E. (in press). Assessing early intervention outcomes: Beyond program variables. *International Journal of Disability, Development and Education.*

McConkey, R. (1985). Play. In D. Lane & B. Stratford (Eds.), *Current approaches to Down syndrome* (pp. 282-314). London: Holt, Rinehart and Winston.

Mogford, K. (1977). The play of handicapped children. In B. Tizard & D. Harvey (Eds.), *Biology of play* (pp. 170-184). London: Heinemann/Spastics International Medical Publications.

Moore, T. G. (1988). Early intervention services in Victoria. In M. Pieterse, S. Bochner, & S. Bettison (Eds.), *Early intervention for children with disabilities: The Australian experience* (pp. 21-32). North Ryde: Special Education Center, Macquarie University.

Parsons, C. L., Smith, I., & Bowman, S. N. (1988). Communication camps: An alternative form of service delivery. In M. Pieterse, S. Bochner, & S. Bettison (Eds.), *Early intervention for children with disabilities: The Australian experience* (pp. 155-172). North Ryde: Special Education Center, Macquarie University.

Pieterse, M. (1988). The Down syndrome program at Macquarie University: A model early intervention program. In M. Pieterse, S. Bochner, & S. Bettison (Eds.,) *Early intervention for children with disabilities: The Australian experience* (pp. 81-96). North Ryde: Special Education Center, Macquarie University.

Pieterse, M., Bochner, S., & Bettison, S. (Eds.). (1988). *Early intervention for children with disabilities: The Australian experience.* North Ryde: Special Education Center, Macquarie University.

Pieterse, M., & Center, Y. (1984). The integration of eight Down syndrome children into regular schools. *Australia and New Zealand Journal of Developmental Disabilities, 10*(1), 11-20.

Price, P., & Bochner, S. (1988). The handicapped child and early language intervention programs. In M. Pieterse, S. Bochner, & S. Bettison (Eds.), *Early intervention for children with disabilities: The Australian expe-*

rience (pp. 147-154). North Ryde: Special Education Center, Macquarie University.

Ramey, C., & Suarez, T. M. (1985). Early intervention and the early experience paradigm: Toward a better framework for social policy. *Journal of Children in Contemporary Society, 17*(1), 3-13.

Rouse, J. (1988). Early intervention in the Northern Territory. In M. Pieterse, S. Bochner, & S. Bettison (Eds.), *Early intervention for children with disabilities: The Australian experience* (pp. 67-73). North Ryde: Special Education Center, Macquarie University.

Safran, S. (in press). Special education in Australia and in the United States: A cross-cultural analysis. *The Exceptional Child*.

Senapati, R., & Hayes, A. (1988). Sibling relationships of handicapped children: A review of conceptual and methodological issues. *International Journal Behavioral Development 11*, 89-115.

Shaddock, A., & Batchler, M. (1986). An analysis of the use of teleconferencing to support a rural early intervention program. *The Exceptional Child, 33*(3), 215-219.

Sigafoos, J., & Reichle, J. (in press). The facilitation of spontaneous verbal behavior. In S. F. Warren (Ed.), *Advances in mental retardation and developmental disabilities, Vol. 5: Research bases of instruction.* Greenwich, CT: JAI Press.

Skeels, H. M. (1966). Adult status of children with contrasting early life experiences. *Monographs of the Society for Research in Child Development, 31* (3, Serial No. 105).

Slaughter, D. T. (1983). Early intervention and its effects upon maternal and child development. *Monographs of the Society for Research in Child Development, 48* (4, Serial No. 202).

Slaughter, D. T. (1988). Black children, schooling, and educational interventions. In D. T. Slaughter (Ed.), *Black children and poverty: A developmental perspective* (pp. 109-116). San Francisco: Jossey-Bass.

U.S. Department of Commerce, Bureau of Census. (1989). *National data book and guide to resources: Statistical abstract of the United States.* Washington, D.C.: U.S. Government Printing Office.

Watts, B. H., Elkins, J., Conrad, J. M., Apelt, W. C., Hayes, A., Calder, J., Clouston, A. J., & Willis, M. (1981). *Early intervention programs for young handicapped children in Australia, 1970-1980.* Canberra: Australian Government Publishing Service.

Watts, B. H., Hayes, A., Apelt, W. C. (1981). Critical issues in early intervention. In B. H. Watts et al. (Eds), *Early intervention programs for young handicapped children in Australia, 1979-1980* (pp. 181-203). Canberra: Australian Government Publishing Service.

Webster's Encyclopedic Dictionary, Unabridged, of the English Language. (1989) New York: Portland House.

11

Early Intervention in the United Kingdom: Historical Perspectives and Current Provision

Peter Sturmey

In this chapter I provide an overview of early intervention efforts within the United Kingdom (UK) over the last twenty years. In order to provide a context for specific issues, a historical overview charts the major legislative and service milestones. Important demographic and social changes are also described. In the next two sections, the two major forms of services are described and critically reviewed: educational and counseling approaches. The educational approach has attempted to prevent or ameliorate handicap by training parents to teach specific skills to their children. This is now an established approach in the UK and is part of many services. Counseling approaches have emphasized working with parents to enable them to reduce distress, solve problems more effectively, gain and use information, and explore their own feelings in relation to having a child with developmental delay. Counseling, although often acknowledged as a subsidiary element in skills-based approaches, is a relatively recent development in the UK. This reflects a broadening of interest, both in services and research, beyond the child to the family and social ecology in which the child is located. In the penultimate section, other approaches, such as nursery provision, preschool play groups, financial support, respite services, perinatal services, and health surveillance, are reviewed. Finally, trends in current services are highlighted, and areas for future research and service development are suggested.

HISTORICAL OVERVIEW

Legislative and Service Milestones

Special provision within the British school system for children with special needs is nearly as old as statutory education itself. Similarly, early institutional provision was aimed specifically at children who were deemed able to benefit from educational efforts (Tomlinson, 1982). However, preschool provision for children with developmental delays is a historically recent phenomenon. Prior to the Education (Handicapped Children) Act of 1971, "severely subnormal" children were excluded from education in England and Wales, and their enrollment in the education system in Scotland and Northern Ireland took even longer to establish. Thus, only when developmentally delayed children were seen as educable and placed in the school system were preschool educational services legitimized. Studies suggesting that hospital provision might handicap children further emerged throughout the 1960s and 1970s (Lyle, 1959; King, Raynes, & Tizard, 1971). These studies, the early promise of behavioral methods, and reports of hospital scandals prompted increased interest in nonhospital provision for all handicapped persons, including young children.

In the mid-1970s the first Portage services were set up (Revill & Blunden, 1979; Smith, Kushlick, & Glossop, 1977) and the Manchester Down Syndrome Cohort study was begun (Cunningham, 1986a). At this time interest in preschool provision was stimulated by the publication of the Court Report (Court, 1976). This report made numerous recommendations concerning handicapped children and adolescents, including preschool children. These recommendations included the establishment of routine local epidemiology, the establishment of multidisciplinary handicap teams, and the expansion of numbers and training of professionals to work in this area. It also recommended that children with mild delays should be provided for by generic, rather than specialist, services. Two years later the report on special educational needs (Warnock, 1978) made explicit recommendations concerning children under age five years. Importantly, it recommended that there be no lower age limits for the education of handicapped children. Like the Court Report, Warnock recommended that parents should have access to a multidisciplinary team that would provide assessment and support for parents. Support was to include information concerning voluntary agencies and other services, as well as the training of parents in methods of teaching their child. Indeed, Warnock (1978) specifically mentioned and recommended the then-recent work on Portage and other work being done with preschool handicapped children at the Hester Adrian Research Centre. However, Warnock (1978) also supported the use of a wide range of other services, including toy libraries, preschool play groups and nurseries, and parent workshops. In order to facilitate parents' use of this range of services, Warnock (1978) recommended that they have access to a named person to co-ordinate their use of services. The style of recommendations made by the Warnock Report was clearly influenced by those of the Court Report. These recommendations subsequently formed the basis of the Education Act of 1981. The major development here was the introduction of a *statement of need* for each child with special education needs, including preschool children. Such a statement was to include an assessment of the child, a statement of identified needs, and ways in which they were to be met. This was to be carried out with full liaison with parents as equal partners.

Nearly ten years later, the impact of this legislation has worked its way through to services on a large scale. Goacher, Evans, Welton, and Wedell (1988) report a major increase in preschool provision for children with special needs within many local education authorities. This includes increases in parent advisory services, opportunity play groups, pediatric assessment centres, and special nurseries. Meltzer, Smyth, and Robus (1989) also report an increase in contact with psychological and other services for preschool handicapped children. Swann (1988) estimates that between 1972 and 1982, this increase in preschool services led to a rise in the placement of five- to ten-year-old children in segregated special schools, from fifty-two to sixty-two places per 10,000 children.

Social and Demographic Changes

Changes in legislation and services have taken place against the backdrop of unprecedented demographic changes in the UK, with subsequent changes in the structure of families and accompanying social attitudes. These changes are not often made explicit in the literature on early intervention. Yet, they highlight a number of issues fundamental to various kinds of early intervention, principally relating to the family and the roles that each family member is expected to fulfill. Since World War II, population fertility has declined substantially. This has led to smaller families and a stable or slightly declining population. Marriage now occurs later and less frequently. It is often preceded by cohabitation, and divorce continues to occur more frequently and earlier. Extramarital births are common; nearly 20% of all births and nearly 30% of all first-time births in the UK in 1985 were to unmarried parents. Reconstituted families, single adults, and childless couples are now more common. The population pyramid has narrowed, with over 15% of the British population being over sixty-five (Clarke et al. 1980).

There is also evidence of massive changes in population mobility. Migration to major urban areas, especially London and the South East, has escalated with concomitant rural depopulation. Migration out of inner-city areas has also led to a decrease in inner-city populations. Migration has tended to be by younger, economically active groups, although migration of elderly people to certain coastal, retirement areas is an exception to this. This has led to increased concentration of older, poorer, more handicapped people in some areas. Since World War II, immigration from commonwealth countries, in particular India, Pakistan, Bangladesh, and the Caribbean, has occurred. Many immigrants have settled in London and the larger cities of the north and Midlands. Thus, the ethnic composition of localities has become highly variable (Clarke et al., 1980), and, services now have to meet the needs of children within a multicultural society.

Recently, the Office of Population Censuses and Surveys (OPCS) published three related reports on disabilities in children. These include a large-scale survey and epidemiological report (Bone & Meltzer, 1989); a report on the financial circumstances of families of disabled children (Smyth & Robus 1989); and a report on the use of services, transport, and education (Meltzer, Smyth, &, Robus 1989). The OPCS surveys are based on a representative sample of 100,000 addresses in the UK. They are based in the World Health Organization classification of impairments (losses of a physical or psychological function), disabilities (restrictions in functioning that result from an impairment), and handicaps (which refer to social disadvantage related to impairments and disabilities). Thus, the OCPS surveys do not refer specifically to handicapped children but rather to childhood disabilities as a whole. Approximately, 40% of the sample were children with mental handicaps. Instead of making a dichotomous distinction of disabled versus non-disabled children, the surveys reported data on the severity of disabilities (graded from one to ten).

Bone and Meltzer (1989) report that the prevalence of disability in children under five years is 21 per 1,000, that is, approximately 74,000 children in the U.K. Most children were found to have milder disabilities. Families of disabled children face numerous additional financial hardships. Eighteen percent were single-parent families, which is about the expected figure given the high base rates. Families of disabled children were less likely to be homeowners and less likely to be employed (both fathers and mothers). These differences in financial status were reflected in the pattern of spending on household goods and leisure items. Thus, they were most apparent in families of lower socioeconomic status (Smyth & Robus, 1989).

The implications of these sociodemographic changes for early intervention are numerous but rarely made explicit. Over half of these families receive state benefits. Many forms of early intervention have assumed the presence of a parent (often, implicitly, a *mother*) at home. Child-care arrangements have become more diverse, with grandparents, neighbors, child-minders, and nurseries also caring for children under five years of age. Higher rates of unemployment among mothers of children with developmental delays have been reported (Pahl & Quine, 1984; Smyth & Robus, 1989), and divorce rates and marital distress may be higher in families with delayed children (Byrne & Cunningham, 1985). These demographic and social trends form the backdrop of all early intervention efforts in the UK.

EDUCATIONAL APPROACHES

Educational approaches to working with delayed or at-risk children have become an established method in the UK. Such approaches were established on an experimental basis in the early 1970s (Revill & Blunden, 1979; Cunningham, 1985). Currently, the style of service delivery associated with these approaches is available in some form in many local areas of the UK (Cameron, 1982; Goacher, Evans, Welton, & Wedell, 1988). Most publications in this area have attempted to evaluate treatment efficacy or some element of treatment. In particular, the Portage Guide to Early Education (Shearer & Shearer, 1972; Shearer 1976) and the Manchester Down Syndrome Cohort (Cunningham, 1986b) have been prominent. Other examples of this style of early intervention are discussed below. Certain fundamental aspects of this manner of working with parents have received less attention—for example, the effects of parents' spontaneous style of teaching upon prescribed teaching styles (McConachie & Mitchell, 1985). Cunningham (1985) provides a useful review of this literature from a British perspective.

Sometimes skills-based approaches to early intervention are criticized for being theoretically impoverished or *atheoretical* (Davis, 1985). Indeed, many authors are not explicit concerning a theoretical model. However, Bijou's (1989) interbehavioral model of developmental retardation is often implicit in many skills-teaching early intervention efforts. Bijou (1977) links this model to early intervention practice. Using other work on the development of nonretarded children as a basis, Bijou applied the notions of an interbehavioral model of development to retarded development. In this model, all development, including retarded development, is seen as the result of continuous and ongoing interaction between the organism and the environment. Three primary classes of independent variables are identified. First, there are biological pathologies that may limit the organism's ability to respond to or perceive internal and external stimuli. Second, the interaction of biological pathologies with social practices may result in retarded development—for example, parents treating a child with cerebral palsy as chronically ill. Third, there are sociocultural handicapping conditions that restrict environmental opportunities for the child. These include material restrictions associated with poverty; limiting, indifferent, or abusive child-rearing practices; and lack of support for valued cultural practices. From this perspective there are four main implications for early intervention (Bijou, 1977). The first is that intervention should be individualized. This can be reflected in the selection of goals and teaching materials and in the organization of teaching. The second is that carefully developed sequences of teaching materials and goals are needed. Third, teaching should involve behavioral principles, since it is the learning of passive-dependent behaviors that may contribute to developmental retardation. Finally, individual programs should be evaluated and modified accordingly. This perspective on retarded development has been most explicit in skills-based approaches to early intervention. However, its relevance extends to other forms of early intervention, such as counseling-based approaches, which attempt to modify the kind of home environment that might potentially limit the child's development through its social or material aspects.

It is important to recognize that many early interventionists have failed to attend to the theoretical basis of their own work. While Bijou's work is often incorporated, it is rarely cited. However, it should be noted that handicapping conditions are highly variable in their etiology. Consequently, a variety of different theoretical models should be explored, each appropriate to different etiological conditions and different patterns of maintenance of developmental delay. We would expect radically different explanations for mental handicap arising from perinatal asphyxia and sociocultural factors. Each theory might give rise to rather different implications for early intervention with different groups of children. Such theoretical sophistication has yet to be developed.

Portage Guide to Early Education

Detailed reviews of the Portage Guide to Early Education are available elsewhere (Sturmey, 1990; Sturmey & Crisp, 1986); hence, only major findings will be highlighted here. There are now over 200 services in the UK. A National Portage Association holds annual conferences and promotes Portage (Copley, Bishop, & Porter, 1986; Cameron, 1982; Dessent, 1984; Hedderley & Jennings, 1987). The main features of a typical Portage service include weekly home visits from a trained home visitor. During this visit the previous week's goals are reviewed, the next teaching goals for the child are negotiated, an activity chart is completed, the teaching method is modeled, and the parent is observed teaching the child. A developmental checklist (Bluma, Shearer, Frohman, & Hilliard, 1976) is used to assess the child at referral, to select goals and to monitor progress.

The service is organized using a pyramidal or cascade model of service delivery (Bernstein, 1982). The entire service is monitored by a management committee that meets only quarterly. Supervisors, who are typically educational or clinical psychologists, monitor home visitors through weekly meetings. Two or three home visitors pass on skills to a still larger number of parents who teach their own children on a daily basis. A package of materials is available that includes a developmental checklist (Bluma, Shearer, Frohman, & Hilliard, 1976), a set of parent readings (Boyd & Bluma, 1977), an instructor's manual for the home visitor (Boyd, Stauber, & Bluma, 1977), and an inventory of parents' teaching behavior (Boyd & Stauber, 1977).

Outcome studies can be categorized as those assessing the number of goals set and achieved, those assessing IQ-like changes, and those that have assessed consumer satisfaction (Sturmey & Crisp, 1986). Broadly speaking, the following findings have been made. A wide range of proportion of goals achieved within one week has been reported, varying from 58% (Clements et al., 1982) to 91% (Cole, 1982; Shearer & Shearer, 1972). Many of these studies are highly unsatisfactory because they rarely include comparison groups to control for naturally occurring development and nonspecific effects of early intervention. At least one study included data relating to goals set for the *mother* rather than the child (Daly, 1980). Also, in this study, the rate at which goals were achieved—over 50% in the first three days after the goal was set—suggests that the criteria used for achievement were rather liberal. Revill & Blunden (1979) partly overcame some of these problems by using a multiple-baseline design across two groups of children. During baselines the two groups of children gained 4.3 and 3.7 skills per month, and during the intervention period when they received Portage, they gained an average of 11.1 and 9.5 skills per month. Although the average rate of skill acquisition increased, inspection of the data from individual children shows that not all children gained skills following the introduction of Portage; in addition, individual differences were large. Thus, the effects of Portage on the rate of goal attainment were not replicable across individuals. Almost all of these studies consider the number of goals set and achieved as a measure of outcome. However, we have argued that this measure would be better regarded as a measure of treatment integrity (Peterson, Homer, & Wonderlich, 1982) since a key element in Portage is to select individual goals small enough to be achieved each week.

Several studies have attempted to demonstrate changes in IQ or DQ following the introduction of Portage. In the original evaluation by

Shearer and Shearer (1972), they showed that a group of seventy-five handicapped and at-risk children with a mean initial IQ of seventy-five gained an average of thirteen months of mental development during an eight-month period. Several studies that have included children with mild handicaps and language delays have found similar results (Cochrane & Shearer, 1984). Other studies of children with established biological handicap have found more modest or no statistically significant pre-post changes in IQ (Clements et al., 1982; Sandow, Clarke, Cox, & Stewart, 1981). Thus, although substantial changes in IQ, which may endure for a number of years, have been shown in some early intervention programs (Gray, Ramsey, & Klaus, 1982; Lazar & Darlington, 1982), there are no consistent data of this nature on the Portage Program. Indeed, to date, no follow-up data on Portage Programs have been published.

A third form of evaluation has been to investigate measures of consumer satisfaction. Studies have found high rates of expressed consumer satisfaction on pencil and paper measures (Daly, 1980; Smith, Kushlick, & Glassop, 1977) and low rates of complaints expressed in meetings with parents (Cameron, 1987). However, measures used were psychometrically unsophisticated and failed to control for response acquiescence on the part of parents (Atkeson & Forehand, 1978).

Although a number of evaluative studies of Portage has been published, many of them have yielded only equivocal data. Two major omissions are noteworthy. First, there is a lack of follow-up data. It is worth noting here the speculations from Swann (1988) that the proliferation of early intervention services might be related to the higher rates of segregated placement in special education. Follow-up data are essential to evaluate the maintenance of any developmental gains and the possibility of washout effects (see Cunningham, 1986a, and Lorenz, 1985, discussed below). Second, the range of outcome measures has been rather narrow, focusing mainly on changes in the child. Effects on other family members and measures other than IQ and behavioral skills should be explored in future research. Finally, all the research carried out failed to attend to potentially important mediating variables such as family characteristics, social class, and maternal factors—including social isolation, depression and anxiety—which may influence the course of outcome for any single treatment.

In the initial review of Portage (Sturmey & Crisp, 1986), we found that the materials were written in language difficult for many people to understand. This is typical of such manuals (Sturmey, 1990). McGaw and Sturmey (1989) showed that this set of parent readings could be rewritten to reduce average sentence and word length. This led to a significant increase in parental knowledge of behavior therapy applied to their children. Similarly, changing the design of activity charts can increase compliance in writing clear goals (Sturmey, Newton, & Crisp, 1988). Future research on materials should focus on (a) compliance with good practice in completing activity charts and (b) the design of materials for parents whose first language is not English.

Although parents receive some training in behavioral methods through modeling and feedback from their Home Visitor, outcomes pertaining to parents and home visitors have been surprisingly neglected until recently. Bidder, Hewitt, and Gray (1982) showed that completing activity charts led to greater child gains compared with simply setting a goal or giving general advice. Recently, Hardy and Sturmey (1990) have shown that parents who received Portage services for six to eighteen months did appear to be substantially more skilled than would be expected of untrained parents. However, they did not have highly sophisticated behavioral skills. Subsequently, the introduction of brief parent training (information, modeling, and verbal feedback given during one home visit), combined with weekly monitoring and positive feedback to parents (cf. Ivancic et al., 1981), led to a rapid and clinically significant increase in parental skill. These gains were maintained at one-month follow-up.

An important issue within Portage services has been the inclusion of service elements other than skills teaching. Among these elements are strategies such as problem-solving, counseling (Cameron, 1989) and bereavement counseling (LePoivedin & Cameron 1985) for parents. Indeed, it is likely that many Portage home visitors act as parents' main source of information, support, and liaison with a wide range of other services.

Portage now has been established as the prototypical example of skills-teaching approaches to early intervention in the UK. Its emphasis on service provision has not been matched by research (Sturmey & Crisp, 1986). In particular, the lack of any follow-up studies, the rather narrow range of outcomes used, and the lack of attention to differential outcomes—specifically, those relating to family characteristics—are areas yet to be explored by research. Finally, the role of Portage services, as one element in a complex, multi-agency matrix of available services, has yet to be fully assessed.

The Manchester Down Syndrome Cohort

Spanning the period of 1973 to 1983, Cunningham and his colleagues built up a longitudinal data base on 181 children with chromosomally confirmed Down syndrome. This represented approximately 90% of children with Down syndrome born during that time period in the catchment area. This research program is notable for the size of the sample, the longitudinal data it has produced, the inclusion of several experimental studies, a final set of multivariate analyses (Cunningham, 1983), and two follow-up studies of large samples (Lorenz, 1985; Cunningham, 1986a).

A summary of the various groups in the cohort is found in Table 11.1. The various groups differ with respect to the presence or absence of intervention; the types of intervention received (e.g., whether or not written advice was given); the kinds of targets trained (general developmental targets, stimulation of sitting and reaching, or intensive training of object permanence skills); the age at which intervention began (six, twelve, or twenty-four weeks); and frequency of visits (every two, three, or six weeks). Although various publications are available on particular phases of the study (see Table 11.1), the overall results reported here are based on the multivariate analyses of the entire cohort (Cunningham, 1983) and the two follow-up studies (Lorenz, 1985; Cunningham, 1986a).

No evidence was found to suggest that age of commencement, frequency of visits, or program intensity were related to long-term outcome on Bayley mental or motor age scales. Although initial acceleration in development was found for groups that received earlier intervention, groups that began later caught up by the age of twelve to eighteen months. Indeed, as time went on, parents tended to express a preference for less frequent, less formal intervention. This may reflect the increasing amount of time that parents and children begin to spend engaging in play activities, as the child matures and becomes more mobile (Cunningham, 1983a). However, it is important to note that parents very often expect and prefer some form of intervention early on (see the section below relating to counseling). Multivariate analysis revealed that the only consistent predictor of Bayley motor age over the ages six to thirty-six months was the presence of medical problems, while Bayley mental age was best predicted by training variables (age of commencement, treatment intensity, etc.) for the first twelve months only. Subsequently, these effects washed out. Bayley mental age during the period of two to five years of age was best predicted by parental variables, mainly the level of parental education, and to a lesser extent by socioeconomic variables, such as place of residence and social class (Cunningham, 1986).

Two studies have reported follow-ups at ages five to ten years, by comparing children who received intervention with matched control children who were not part of the Manchester Down Syndrome Cohort. Both of these studies confirm the failure of early intervention to produce long-term intellectual gains (Lorenz, 1985; Cunningham, 1986a). Also, short-term differences in problem behaviors were found (Cunningham, 1986a). However, the number of children without chronic health problems was greater in the treatment group as compared with the control

Table 11.1
A Summary of the Manchester Down Syndrome Cohort, 1973–1983 (Cunningham, 1983a)

Sub-sample	Group	N	Formal Inter-vention	Description of Intervention(s), If Any, and Examples of Publications
1	1	13	NO	Received visits every 2 weeks during the first year of life and every 6 weeks during the second year of life. Some participated in experiments on visually directed reading and early signalling behavior.
	2	19	YES	Both Groups 2 and 3 received visits every 6 weeks for 2 years. Group 2 was enrolled by age of 12 weeks and Group 3 was enrolled at 24 weeks. (Cunningham & Sloper, 1978; Cunningham & Mittler, 1981).
	3	14	YES	
2	4	34	YES	Both Groups 4 and 5 received visits from a Health Visitor every 6 weeks for 2 years. Like Groups 2 and 3 all received a written set of ideas. Group 4 was enrolled by 12 weeks and Group 5 by 24 weeks. Replicates and extends findings with Groups 3 and 4 (Cunningham, Aumonier, & Sloper, 1982).
	5	24	YES	
3	6	10	YES	All received 2 weekly visits for the first year and 6 weekly visits for the second year. Groups 6 and 7 were matched. Group 6 received intensive stimulation of sitting and reaching and Group 7 acted as a control group. Group 8 represents dropouts (Arnaljotsdottir, 1980).
	7	10	NO	
	8	6	NO	
4	9	12	YES	Groups 9 and 10 received a formal, intensive intervention for 9 months. All groups received visits every 3 weeks from 12th week to 18th month of life. Twelve began treatment before 6 weeks and 12 began treatment between 6 and 12 weeks. Group 10 received intensive training on object permanence and Group 9 acted as a control. Group 11 represents dropouts (Hasraldsdottir, 1983).
Other Groups	12	9	YES	Both groups received visits, Group 12 by Health Visitors who were not members of the research team but were trained by the team and Group 13 received visits from the Health Visitor from the research team.
	13	8	YES	

group (75% versus 55%). Children in the intervention group were also likely to be hospitalized more frequently but for shorter periods than the control group. Parents of children in the experimental group were also more likely to be aware of hearing and sight difficulties in their children. Children in the experimental group were more likely to attend an integrated or semi-integrated class, and their mothers were more likely to return to work and to report feeling able to leave their children alone. Further, these effects were more likely to be found in parents from social classes three, four, and five (semiskilled and nonskilled).

The findings from these studies are both impressive and consonant with those of several other studies that provide long-term follow-up (Lazar & Darlington, 1982; Gray, Ramsey, & Klauss, 1982). They suggest that the effects of early intervention on IQ are relatively circumscribed, but long-term effects may be found on socially important outcomes such as school placement. Other long-term studies have hitherto failed to attend to important outcomes such as health status (perhaps because many of these have studied children without organic impairments) and parents' social functioning. Cunningham (1986b) and Lorenz (1985) suggest that parents in the intervention group may be better informed as to the health needs of their children and the services that are available, and thus may be more assertive with service providers. These outcomes become especially valuable in light of (a) demographic changes in the UK and the implied change in social values discussed at the beginning of the chapter, (b) changes in ideology toward parents as consumers of services, and (c) the commitment toward integrated school services for children with disabilities (Warnock, 1978).

Emerging Issues

Throughout the literature there are numerous case studies and evaluations of particular services and staff training programs. One trend has been the development of staff training centres to support generic community staff who are not part of a broader early intervention service. Among such support staff are health visitors, who often may deal with individual, one-time referrals that may include clients with developmental delays. The trend to integrate skills-teaching approaches into broader-based services is now very marked but rarely made explicit in narrow reports of such approaches.

Although most parents who are skill-trained receive services that make allowances for individual differences in styles of parent-child interaction (PCI), the literature on both Portage and the Manchester Down Syndrome Cohort makes no explicit provision for this. Some studies have compared mothers and fathers teaching their developmentally delayed children. These studies indicate that fathers talk more than mothers and are more inhibiting but consistent, whereas mothers are more flexible (Brachfeld-Child, 1986). Furthermore, mothers believe that teaching is most closely associated with PCI, whereas fathers believe it to be most closely associated with helping and control (McConachie & Mitchell, 1985).

Direct observation of PCI during teaching situations has also revealed stable patterns of individual differences (Mitchell, 1982). There is a tendency for mothers and fathers of the same child to be similar in some aspects of their style of PCI, although some couples may differ more markedly (McConachie & Mitchell, 1985). Studies of PCI during teaching situations have found that parents may show several features that are not consonant with a behavioral method of teaching. These include low rates of consequences and moderately high rates of errors (McConachie & Mitchell, 1985). They suggest that some parents may deliberately choose this style of PCI to foster exploration of rather than success at a particular response (Moss & Hogg, 1982). Such individual differences in styles of PCI during teaching have been taken into account in some skills-teaching approaches to early intervention (Beveridge, Flanagan, McConachie, & Sebba, 1982). To date, no experimental study exists that has compared the match between two or more styles of PCI, such as directive-behavioral versus exploratory-spontaneous, and parents' natural style of teaching.

Almost all the studies discussed so far have not been influenced by Piagetian perspectives, although some of the Manchester Down Syndrome Cohort studies include training of sensorimotor skills. Piagetian research in mental handicap has been carried out for thirty years in the UK (Woodward, 1959), and interest continues to be expressed (MacPherson & Butterworth, 1988). However, its impact on services has been rather circumscribed and appears to be mainly supported from a research context.

COUNSELING APPROACHES

General Counseling Issues

Social policy and behavioral/educational approaches to early intervention have become relatively well established in the UK, both at the level of services and at the level of research. However, only more recently has interest begun to develop in counseling approaches to early intervention. This trend can be seen as part of a general theoretical and practical expansion of interest beyond the child. Research in this area has recently been reviewed by Cunningham and Jupp (1989). Cunningham and Jupp (1989) analyzed over 100 published papers on counseling and found that the issues covered in this work fell into the following areas: disclosure of diagnosis; genetic counseling, prenatal screening, and termination; still birth and bereavement; ethical and legal issues; multidisciplinary teams; evaluation; fostering and adoption; and ethnic minorities. They note that up to the mid-1970s the literature emphasized genetic counseling and allied medical aspects of care; only more recently have psychological aspects received extensive attention.

The most extensive program of research in this area in the UK comes from a series of studies of the Parent Advisor Scheme (PAS) (Buchan, Clemerson, & Davis, 1988; Davis 1985; Davis, Rushton & Choudhury, 1988). The focus of the PAS is the *parent* rather than the child. The aim is for parents to develop their own strengths and resources, enhance their own self-esteem, and explore their understanding of themselves, their children, and their problems. This counseling is done in order for parents to set realistic goals for themselves, plan and take action to achieve these goals, and evaluate their efficacy in attaining them.

These aims are achieved by training *parent advisors* in counseling skills within the frameworks of Egan (1982) and Kelly (1955). The work of Egan emphasized the development of a counselor-client relationship, based upon mutual respect and trust, to facilitate negotiation during counseling. Davis (1985) contrasts this with other models for working with parents. In the *export model* professionals assume responsibility for decision-making and action. In the *transplant model* professionals inject expertise (e.g., skills training) into parents at the risk of neglecting family issues other than those relating to the child. However, the skilled helper, using personal construct theory (Kelly, 1955), tries to discover and respect the frameworks of *constructs* that the client uses to perceive the world; the client is seen as an active scientist making hypotheses about the world.

Parent advisors need training to acquire these skills, and a ten-week, sixty-hour course is described in a manual designed for this purpose (Davis, Buchan, & Clemerson, 1987). An evaluation of this course (Davis, Rushton, & Choudhury, 1988) indicated that members of various professional groups with extensive experience in working with families (e.g., health visitors, physiotherapists, nursery nurses, social workers, and teachers) had poor knowledge and skills relating to this method of counseling. In at least one study the parent advisor also received regular supervision during the service (Davis, Rushton, & Choudhury, 1988).

There have been several evaluations of the PAS. Davis and Choudhury (1987) worked with twenty-eight Bangladeshi families allocated to the PAS or to a control group receiving routing services. The families were described as "almost all extremely poor". The children had moderate to severe delays, and their ages ranged from eighteen months to ten years. Results indicated that parents who received the PAS reported better social and professional support, felt more competent and less stressed, and perceived more positive characteristics and fewer behavior problems in their child. Interestingly, the children whose parents received PAS made significantly greater IQ gains than children in the control group. In a replication study with English-speaking families (Davis, Rushton, & Choudhury, 1988), broadly similar results were found, although the effects were less marked.

It would appear from these studies that a counseling-based approach to early intervention has considerable potential to enhance the lives of parents and the development of their children. The magnitude of these effects may be greatest in families with *greater* levels of deprivation. It is important to note that changes in parental mood, anxiety, and social isolation have important implications for parents' perceptions and use of services (Affleck, McGrade, Allen, & McQueeney, 1985), their interactions with their children, and their compliance with other services such as skills-based approaches (Dumas & Wahler, 1983; Greist, Forehand, & Wells, 1981).

Through the use of the PAS manual the number of trained counselors has gradually increased; Buchan, Clemerson, and Davis, (1988) report that after five courses, forty-one people had been trained. Although the need for training in counseling is emphasized in many early intervention services most staff who work with families do not yet have such training. As with staff training in other skills, the issue of maintenance of staff skills must receive attention.

Counseling Near the Time of Birth

The birth of a child with a developmental delay has long been recognized as a major source of distress for parents (Cunningham & Jupp, 1989). Yet, although staff are clearly sensitive to the issue (Standing Conference of Voluntary Organizations for People with a Mental Handicap in Wales [SCOVO], 1989a, 1989b), parental dissatisfaction with the disclosure of the diagnosis and subsequent services is widespread (Quine & Pahl, 1987). Parental dissatisfaction may arise from lack of information (e.g., undue delay of disclosure), failure to disclose the diagnosis, or lack of information concerning the child's condition. Greater dissatisfaction may be associated with the degree of handicap and an unfamiliar diagnosis (Pahl & Quine, 1984). However, other important aspects of the disclosure procedure may affect parental satisfaction, and possibly other important outcomes, such as whether the parents will take the child home (Cunningham, Morgan, & McGucken, 1984). It has been repeatedly reported that parental satisfaction is greater when (a) parents are told together as soon as possible, in a private place, without interruptions, and (b) the informing is done by a person who shows warmth and understanding, tells the parents directly and honestly, and allows them some time alone together. Further, parents typically wish for further appointments to seek clarification, informa- tion, and support (Cunningham & Jupp, 1989). Cunningham, Morgan, and McGucken (1984) developed a model service for the disclosure of the diagnosis and subsequent services for parents of infants with Down syndrome based upon these guidelines. Approximately six months later, a follow-up carried out by an independent interviewer found high levels of satisfaction and no expression of dissatisfaction by parents in the model service. In contrast, only 20% of parents who received routine disclosure expressed no dissatisfaction. Guidelines for model services for disclosure are now available (Cunningham, Morgan, & McGucken, 1984; Association for Professionals for the Mentally Handicapped, 1981; Independent Council for People with a Mental Handicap, 1982; SCOVO, 1989a, 1989b).

Although these findings have been widely known for many years, compliance by service agencies continued to be poor (Hogg, Lambe, Cowie, & Coxen, 1987). Why is this so? Some studies have shown that nursing and medical staff may find the birth of a handicapped infant difficult and see it as a failure of medical services. This may be shown in avoidant behavior and use of euphemistic language to which parents may be highly sensitive prior to diagnosis (MacKeith, 1973; Jupp, 1987). The birth of a handicapped infant may also highlight to staff their own ignorance of the implications for the child and of the services that are available. Recently, Elliott (1989) examined the beliefs of hospital nurs- ing and administration staff and of community staff who worked with infants and young children with developmental delays. In general, hos- pital staff were more likely to report "don't know" to questions relating to community services (e.g., the availability of play groups, toy libraries, social workers, district Children's Team, and so on), and community staff were more likely to report "don't know" to questions related to disclosure of the diagnosis to parents (e.g., how parents are told). Al- though the sample of administration staff was small (n = 7), they were more likely to present an idealized picture of services. Approximately 50% of the nursing staff sample (n = 73) did not know if there were guidelines within the service concerning developmentally delayed chil- dren. In response to these findings, staff training should not only dis- seminate guidelines and information to all staff but also give staff specific strategies to deal with their own embarrassment and anxiety in dealing with parents who have just had a handicapped infant (see Jupp, 1987, for an example).

Emerging Issues

Counseling services for parents who have a handicapped infant have developed more recently than those based on skills training. Thus, the literature is somewhat thinner, and services are less well developed. However, it should be noted that many services that are primarily oriented to skills-teaching do mention counseling of parents as an element of these services. Future developments are likely to be in the area of dissemination of research findings and good practice (SCOVO, 1989a, 1989b; Davis, Buchan, & Clemerson, 1987; Buchan, Clemerson, & Davis, 1988) and in the area of staff compliance with guidelines and policies. Future developments in counseling should also attend to the important issues raised by particular groups of parents, such as those belonging to ethnic minorities (Davis & Choudhury, 1987), those with multiple social and other problems, and those who themselves have mild mental handicaps. It is notable that recent research in the UK has neglected the role of family doctors, who are often keystones in services for families with developmentally delayed children. Future research should attend to their role, too.

The literature on counseling has been dominated by services for families whose children are identified at an early age or who are easily identified. Thus, most of the literature reviewed by Cunningham and Jupp (1989) refers to families whose children have established, organic handicaps. It is important to recognize that families and their developmentally delayed children are not only highly varied but also that there are implications for the kind of counseling they require and the kinds of issues that need to be addressed as a function of the type of handicap the child has. Clarke and Clarke (1986) estimate that only approximately 25% of developmentally delayed children have established, organic handicaps. Even within families whose children have organic handicaps, the issues to be addressed in counseling will be varied. For example, families who had an organically intact child at birth, but whose child subsequently suffers a major trauma resulting in severe handicap, face the loss of an actual rather than imagined normal child after a period of "normal parenthood." For families whose children have mild delays and who do not have any known organic impairment, the issues are again different. Typically, such children come to the attention of services in the early school years (Swann, 1988), although parents may suspect a problem for some years beforehand. Thus, parents may have faced several years of uncertainty and failure of services to provide an accurate diagnosis. Even when a problem is formally recognized, parents may have no familiar label, such as "Down syndrome," to use (Quine & Pahl, 1987).

Finally, although the problems of stress, social isolation, anxiety, and depression have been recognized as especially important for a minority of parents (Byrne & Cunningham 1985; Dumas & Wahler, 1983; Greist, Forehand, & Wells, 1981; Wilton & Renault, 1986), the literature on counseling in the UK has not yet explicitly addressed those groups of parents for whom these problems are especially prominent. Examples of evaluations of stress-management groups for parents (Scaife & Frith, 1988) and interventions to increase social support (Kirkham, Schilling, Norelius, & Schinke, 1986) exist elsewhere. These kinds of problems are potentially tackled by some parent counseling services described above; however, future research should address these parental needs explicitly.

OTHER APPROACHES

The two preceding sections have emphasized skills-teaching and parent counseling as the two major forms of early intervention in the UK. However, to suggest that these are the only services relevant to early intervention would be a mistake. Rather, they are the two major forms of services that are explicitly described in terms of early intervention and that have received the greatest attention from researchers. As noted previously, various kinds of preschool nurseries and play groups are now more commonly available. Some are specifically for children with developmental delay; some explicitly set up to integrate children with developmental delay; and some preschool groups simply happen to accept such children. These services may provide important respite services during the day for parents, while offering additional educational and social opportunities to children. In many localities, respite services are available on a small scale to offer parents a break, either on a planned or on an emergency basis during evenings, holidays, and weekends. These services have now largely replaced hospitals that frequently made admissions for social reasons in the past. This is consonant with the established, and almost completely achieved, priority of keeping children out of long-stay hospitals unless they require medical care.

Parents of children with developmental delays often face additional financial burdens. These may be either direct—such as additional costs of clothing, washing, aides, and transport—or indirect—for example, costs arising out of later return of mothers to work (Pahl & Quine, 1984; Smyth & Robus, 1989) or reduced family mobility (Meltzer, Smyth, & Robus, 1989). Various forms of financial benefits are available, mainly relating to the additional time parents must attend to their children or to difficulties relating to their children's mobility (Meltzer, Smyth, & Robus, 1989). Although in the past the accessing of these benefits has been patchy, a greater proportion of eligible parents now are aware of and claim these benefits (Cooke, Bradshaw, & Lawton, 1983).

Other services that are as often as not explicitly related to early intervention—but that are part of broader health and social services—also form important elements in prevention and amelioration of developmental delay. These include perinatal care, in particular the health of women during pregnancy (Wynn & Wynn, 1975), compliance with vaccination programs, and the quality of health and surveillance of young children and mothers (Court, 1976). Although services to particular at-risk groups, such as low-birth-weight babies (Lloyd, Wheldall, & Perks, 1988), are pertinent to early intervention, the importance of these services is often ignored; rarely are they evaluated with respect to early intervention.

CURRENT TRENDS AND IMPLICATIONS FOR THE FUTURE

Early intervention services have expanded considerably in the last twenty years from virtual nonexistence to a complex labyrinth of preschool services. Early efforts were primarily concerned with the implementation of behavioral programs at home where the parents merely acted as the vehicles of change. The broadening focus of early intervention efforts is shown (a) by the more recently developed parent-focused, nonbehavioral services, such as counseling, and (b) by the widening range of outcome variables, such as those illustrated by Lorenz (1985) and Cunningham (1986a). This trend is also illustrated by recent descriptive reports of family therapy (Goodyer, 1986). Despite these trends, major omissions still exist. The virtual exclusion of the father from such research is to be deplored (however, see McConachie, 1982, for a review).

As yet, demographic changes and the changing patterns of family life are only indirectly hinted at. Although research on families from ethnic minorities is a welcome example of this (Davis & Choudhury, 1987; Bardsley & Perkins, 1985), many other issues have yet to be explored. The possible diversification of caregivers is one example of an important issue that requires further exploration, as are the problems faced by single, poor parents. It is anticipated that current trends in research in the areas of social networks of parents (Dunst, Trivette, & Cross, 1986) and the possible implications for both intervention practice and outcome research will continue. Although established elsewhere (Affleck, McGrade, McQueeney, & Allen, 1982), no report of relationship-based approaches to early intervention in the UK were identified. Research and the development of services in this area are important future challenges for the field.

One welcome trend has been the gradual increase in attention to staff training and support. This has led to the development of new staff training materials (Davis, Buchan, & Clemerson, 1987); the evaluation of alternative formats of staff training (McGaw & Sturmey, 1989); and increased emphasis on the operationalization of staff and parent performances and their subsequent monitoring and maintenance (Hardy

& Sturmey, 1990). This trend should be continued; in particular, the skills that staff require to work effectively in multi-agency services need further attention (Elliott, 1989).

Almost all research to date has been rather narrowly focused, often using a single dependent variable closely related to the treatment being evaluated. Almost all studies have continued to compare one treatment with no treatment. This approach has established that most forms of treatment can produce some change on selected variables. Future research should attend to comparisons of alternative, viable, credible treatments on multiple outcomes. In this way the possibility exists of matching intervention to child and family characteristics in a more rational way than has hitherto been possible.

ACKNOWLEDGMENTS

I should like to thank various colleagues who have contributed to some of the work reported in this chapter. In particular, I should like to thank Tony Crisp, Sue McGaw, Amanda Gatherer, Liz Elliott, and Sandy Bering, who have all stimulated my interest in early intervention.

REFERENCES

Affleck, G., McGrade, B. J., Allen, D. A., & McQueeney, M. (1985). Factors associated with parents' perceptions of infants in an early intervention program. *Journal of Pediatric Psychology, 10,* 305-316.

Affleck, G., McGrade, B., McQueeney, M., & Allen, D. (1982). Promise of relationship-focused early intervention in developmental disabilities. *Journal of Special Education, 16,* 413-430.

Association of Professionals for the Mentally Handicapped. (1981). *Mental handicap—the first twelve months.* London: APMH.

Atkeson, B. M., & Forehand, R. (1978). Parental behavioral training for problem children: An examination of studies using multiple outcome measures. *Journal of Abnormal Child Psychology, 6,* 449-460.

Bardsley, J., & Perkins, E. (1985). Portage with Asian families in central Birmingham. In B. Daly, J. Addington, S. Kerfoot, & A. Sigston (Eds.), *Portage: The importance of parents* (pp. 109-118). London: NFER-Nelson.

Bernstein, G. S. (1982). Training behavior change agents: A conceptual review. *Behavior Therapy, 13,* 1-23.

Beveridge, S., Flanagan, R., McConachie, H., & Sebba, J. (1982). *Parent involvement in Anson House.* Anson House Project Paper No. 3. Barkingside, England: Barnardo's.

Bidder, R. T., Hewitt, K. E., & Gray, O. P. (1982). Evaluation of teaching methods in a home-based training scheme for developmentally delayed pre-school children. *Child: Care, Health, and Development, 9,* 1-12.

Bijou, S. W. (1977). Practical implications of an interactional model of child development. *Exceptional Children, 44,* 6-14.

Bijou, S. W. (1989). Behavior analysis. *Annals of Child Development, 6,* 61-83.

Bluma, S., Shearer, M., Frohman, A., & Hilliard, J. (1976). *Portage guide to early education manual* (Revised edition). Portage, WI: CESA–12.

Bone, M., & Meltzer, H. (1989). *OPCS surveys of disability in Great Britain: The prevalence of disability among children.* London: HMSO.

Boyd, R. D., & Stauber, K. A. (1977). Parental behavior inventory. In R. D. Boyd, K. A. Stauber, & S. M. Bluma (Eds.), *Instructor's manual: Portage parent program* (pp. 79-87). Portage, WI: CESA–12.

Boyd, R. D., Stauber, K. A., & Bluma, S. M. (1977). *Instructor's manual: Portage parent program.* Portage, WI: CESA–12.

Boyd, S., & Bluma, S. M. (1977). *Parent readings: Portage parent program.* Portage, WI: CESA–12.

Brachfeld-Child, S. (1986). Parents as teachers: Comparison of mothers' and fathers' instructional interactions with infants. *Infant Behavior and Development, 9,* 127-131.

Buchan, L., Clemerson, J., & Davis, H. (1988). Working with families of children with special needs: The parent advisor scheme. *Child: Care, Health, and Development, 14,* 81-91.

Byrne, E. A., & Cunningham, C. C. (1985). The effects of mentally handicapped children on families: A conceptual review. *Journal of Child Psychology and Psychiatry, 26,* 847-864.

Cameron, R. J. (1982). *Working together: Portage in the U.K.* Windsor, England: NFER-Nelson.

Cameron, S. (1987). They can't mean us: Criticism and comments about Portage. In R. Heddersley & C. Jennings (Eds.), *Extending and developing Portage* (pp. 46-56). Windsor, England: NFER-Nelson.

Cameron, S. (1989). *Parents, professionals and preschool children with special needs: Towards a partnership model of problem solving.* Unpublished doctoral dissertation, University of Southampton, England.

Clarke, A. M., & Clarke, A. D. B. (1986). Thirty years of child psychology: A selective review. *Journal of Child Psychology and Psychiatry, 27,* 719-759.

Clarke, J. I., Dewdney, J. C., Evans, I. S., Rhind, D. W., & Visvalingham, M. (1980). *People in Britain. A census atlas.* London: HMSO.

Clements, J., Evans, C., Jones, C., Osborne, K., & Upton, G. (1982). Evaluation of a home-based language training programe with severely mentally handicapped children. *Behavior Research and Therapy, 20,* 243-249.

Cochrane, D. C., & Shearer, D. E. (1984). The Portage model for home teaching. In Bellamy, C. T., Daine, S. C., & Wilcox, B. (Eds.), *Human services that work: From innovation to standard practice* (pp. 86-104). Baltimore: Paul H. Brookes.

Cole, D. (1982). Essential record-keeping and administration. In R. J. Cameron (Ed.), *Working together: Portage in the U.K.* (pp. 1-12). Windsor, England: NFER-Nelson.

Cooke, K., Bradshaw, J., & Lawton, D. (1983). Take-up of benefits of families with disabled children. *Child: Care, Health, and Development, 9,* 145-156.

Copley, M., Bishop, M., & Porter, J. (1986). *Portage: More than a teaching program?* Windsor, England: NFER-Nelson.

Court, S.D.M. (1976). *Fit for the future. Report of the Committee on Child Health Services, Vol. 1.* London: HMSO.

Cunningham, C. C. (1975). Parents as educators and therapists. In C. C. Kiernan, & F. P. Woodford (Eds.), *Mental retardation and behavior research* (pp. 75-88). IRMMH Study Group 8. New York: Associated Scientific Publishers.

Cunningham, C. C. (1983). *Early intervention and its facilitation in infants with Down syndrome. A DHSS funded project. Final report, Part I, October 1983: Summary.* University of Manchester, U.K.: Hester Adrian Research Centre.

Cunningham, C. C. (1985). Training and education approaches for parents of children with special needs. *British Journal of Medical Psychology, 58,* 285-305.

Cunningham, C. C. (1986a). *Abstract summary of final report. The effects of early intervention on the occurrence and nature of behavior problems in children with Down syndrome.* University of Manchester, U.K.: Hester Adrian Research Centre.

Cunningham, C. C. (1986b). Early intervention: Some findings from the Manchester cohort of children with Down syndrome. In M. Copley, M. Bishop, & J. Porter (Eds.), *Portage: More than a teaching program?* (pp. 89-106). Windsor, England: NFER-Nelson.

Cunningham, C. C., Aumonier, M. E., & Sloper, P . (1982). Health visitor support for families with Down syndrome infants. *Child: Care, Health, and Development, 8,* 1–19.

Cunningham, C. C., & Jupp, S. (1989). Literature review. Key areas in early counseling. In Standing Conference of Voluntary Organisations for People with a Mental Handicap in Wales, *Parents deserve better: A review on early counseling in Wales* (pp. 36-74). Cardiff, U.K.: Fingerprints.

Cunningham, C. C., & Mittler, P. J. (1981). Maturation, development and mental handicap. In K. J. Connolly, & H. R. F. Prechtl (Eds.), *Motivation and development: Biological and psychological perspectives* (pp. 24-36). London: Spastics Society International Medical Publications and William Heinemann Medical Books Ltd.

Cunningham, C. C., Morgan, P., & McGucken, R. B. (1984). Down syndrome: Is dissatisfaction with disclosure of diagnosis inevitable? *Developmental Medicine and Child Neurology, 26,* 33-39.

Cunningham, C. C., & Sloper, P. (1978). *Helping your handicapped baby.* London: Souvenir Press.

Daly, B. (1980). Evaluation: Portage home teaching project for prenatal handicapped children, June, 1979-80. A summary of report P/S 02. Available from Barling and Dagenham School Psychological Service, U.K.

Davis, H. (1985). Counseling of parents of children who have intellectual disabilities. *Early Childhood Development and Care, 22,* 19-35.

Davis, H., Booth, A., & Rushton, R. (1988, September). *Parent Counseling and Support.* Paper presented at DHSS/DES/VCHS Joint Seminar on Early Intervention, Castle Priory, Wallingford, U.K.

Davis, H., Buchan, L., & Clemerson, J. (1987). *The parent advisor scheme: Manual for training counsellors to work with families of children with special needs.* London: London Hospital Medical College.

Davis, H., & Choudhury, A. P. (1987). Helping Bangladeshi families: Tower hamlets parent advisory scheme. *Mental Handicap, 16,* 48-51.

Davis, H., Rushton, R., & Choudhury, P. A. (1988). *Supporting families of children with intellectual disabilities: Evaluation of counseling.* Unpublished manuscript. Academic-Department of Psychiatry, London Hospital Medical College, England.

Dessent, T. (1984). *What is important about Portage?* Windsor, England NFER-Nelson.

Dumas, J. E., & Wahler, R. G. (1983). Prediction of treatment outcome in parent training: Mother insularity and socioeconomic disadvantage. *Behavioral Assessment, 5,* 301-313.

Dunst, C. J., Trivette, C. M., & Cross, A. H. (1986). Mediating influences of social support: Personal, family and child outcomes. *American Journal of Mental Deficiency, 90,* 403-417.

Egan, G. (1982). *The skilled helper.* Monterey, CA: Brooks/Cole.

Elliott, E. (1989). *Post-natal service provision following the birth of a baby with special needs.* Unpublished master's thesis, University of Birmingham, U.K.

Goacher, B., Evans, J., Welton, J., & Wedell, K. (1988). *Policy and provision for special education needs: Implementing the 1981 Education Act.* London: Cassell.

Goodyer, I. (1986). Family therapy and the handicapped child. *Developmental Medicine and Child Neurology, 28,* 244-250.

Gray, S. W., Ramsey, B. K., & Klaus, R. A. (1982). *From three to twenty.* Baltimore, University Park Press.

Greist, D. L., Forehand, R., & Wells, K. C. (1981). Follow-up assessment of parental behavioral training: An analysis of who will participate. *Child Study Journal, 11,* 221-229.

Haraldsdottir, G. (1983). *Early stimulation of reflexes in Down syndrome infants.* Unpublished doctoral thesis, University of Manchester, U.K.

Hardy, N., & Sturmey, P. (1990). *Portage guide to early education. III: A rapid training and feedback system to teach and maintain mothers' teaching skills.* Unpublished Manuscript, University of Birmingham, U.K.

Hedderley, R., & Jennings, K. (1987). *Extending and developing Portage.* Windsor, England: NFER-Nelson.

Hogg, J., Lambe, L., Cowie, J., & Coxen, J. (1987). *People with profound retardation and multiple handicaps attending schools or social education centres.* Piper Hill School, Manchester, U.K.: Mencap PRMH Project.

Independent Council for People with a Mental Handicap. (1982). *Elements of a comprehensive local service for people with a mental handicap.* London: King's Fund Centre.

Ivancic, M. T., Reid, D. H., Iwata, B. A., Faw, G. D., & Page, T. J. (1981). Evaluating a supervision program for developing and maintaining therapeutic staff-self-resident interactions during institutional care routines. *Journal of Applied Behavior Analysis, 14,* 95-107.

Jupp, S. (1987). Breaking the news. *Mental Handicap, 15*, 8-11.

Kelly, G. (1955). *The psychology of personal constructs.* New York: Norton.

King, R. D., Raynes, N. V., & Tizard, J. (1971). *Patterns of residential care: Sociological studies in institutions for handicapped children.* London: Routledge & Kegan Paul.

Kirkham, M. A., Schilling, R. F., Norelius, K., & Schinke, S. P. (1986). Developing coping styles and social support networks: An intervention outcome study with mothers of handicapped children. *Child: Care, Health, and Development, 12*, 313-323.

Lazar, I., & Darlington, R. (1982). Lasting effects of early education: A report from the consortium for longitudinal studies. *Monographs of the Society for Research in Child Development, 47* (2-3, Serial No. 195).

LePoivedin, S., & Cameron, S. (1985). Is there more to Portage than education? In B. Daly, J. Addington, S. Kerfoot, & A. Sigston (Eds.), *Portage: The importance of parents* (pp. 69-77). Windsor, England: NFER-Nelson.

Lloyd, B. W., Wheldall, K., & Perks, D. (1988). Controlled study of intelligence and school performance of very low birth weight children from a defined geographical area. *Developmental Medicine and Child Neurology, 30*, 36-42.

Lorenz, S. (1985). *Long-term effects of early intervention on the occurrence and nature of behavior problems in children with Down syndrome.* Unpublished master's thesis, University of Manchester, U.K.

Lyle, J. G. (1959). The effect of an institution environment upon the verbal development of imbecile children. I: Verbal intelligence. *Journal of Mental Deficiency Research, 3*, 122-128.

MacKeith, R. (1973). The feelings and behavior of parents of handicapped children. *Developmental Medicine and Child Neurology, 15*, 524-527.

MacPherson, F., & Butterworth, G. (1988). Sensorimotor intelligence in severely mentally handicapped children. *Journal of Mental Deficiency Research, 32*, 465-478.

McConachie, H. (1982). Fathers of mentally handicapped children. In N. Beall & J. McGuire (Eds.), *Psychological aspects of fatherhood* (pp. 120-143). London: Junction Books.

McConachie, H., & Mitchell, D. R. (1985). Parents teaching their young mentally handicapped children. *Journal of Child Psychology and Psychiatry, 26*, 389-405.

McGaw, S., & Sturmey, P. (1989). The effects of text readability and summary exercises and parental knowledge of behavior therapy: The Portage parent readings. *Educational Psychology, 9*, 127-132.

Meltzer, H., Smyth, M., & Robus, N. (1989). *Disabled child: Services, transport and education.* London: HMSO.

Mitchell, D. R. (1982). Down syndrome children in structured dyadic communication situations with their parents. In J. Hogg & P. J. Mittler (Eds.), *Advances in mental handicap research, Volume I* (pp. 161-194). New York: Wiley.

Moss, S., & Hogg, J. (1982). The development and integration of fine motor sequences in twelve to eighteen-month-old children: A test of the modular theory of motor skill acquisition. *Genetic Psychology Monographs,* *107*, 145-187.

Pahl, I., & Quine, L. (1984). *Families with mentally handicapped children: A study of stress and service response.* Canterbury, U.K.: Health Services Research Unit.

Peterson, L., Homer, A. L., & Wonderlich, S. A. (1982). The integrity of independent variables in behavior analysis. *Journal of Applied Behavior Analysis, 15*, 477-492.

Quine, J., & Pahl, L. (1987). Parental reactions to diagnosis of severe handicap. *Developmental Medicine and Childhood Neurology, 29*, 232-242.

Revill, S., & Blunden, R. (1979). A home-training service for pre-school developmentally handicapped children. *Behavior Research and Therapy, 17*, 204-214.

Sandow, S. A., Clarke, A. D. B., Cox, M. V., & Stewart, F. L. (1981). Home intervention with parents of severely subnormal pre-school children: A final report. *Child: Care, Health, and Development, 7*, 135-144.

Scaife, J., & Frith, S. (1988). A behavior management and life stress course for a group of mothers incorporating training for health visitors. *Child: Care, Health, and Development, 14*, 25-50.

Shearer, D. E., & Loftin, C. R. (1984). The Portage project: Teaching parents to teach their preschool children in the home. In R. F. Dangel & R. A. Polster (Eds.), *Parent training: Foundations of research and practice* (pp. 98-112). London: Guildford.

Shearer, M. S. (1976). A home-based parent training model. In D. L. Lillie, P. L. Trohanis, & K. W. Goin (Eds.), *Teaching parents to teach: A guide for working with the special child* (pp. 49-66). New York: Walker.

Shearer, M. S., & Shearer, D. E. (1972). The Portage project: A model for early childhood education. *Exceptional Children, 36*, 210-217.

Smith, J., Kushlick, A., & Glossop, C. (1977). The Wessex Portage project: A home teaching service for families with a pre-school mentally handicapped child. University of Southampton Health Care Evaluation Research Team, U.K.

Smyth, M., & Robus, N. (1989). *OPCS surveys of disability in Great Britain: The financial circumstances of families with disabled children living in private households.* London: HMSO.

Standing Conference of Voluntary Organizations for People with a Mental Handicap in Wales. (1989a). *Parents deserve better: A review of early counseling in Wales.* Cardiff, U.K.: Fingerprints.

Standing Conference of Voluntary Organizations for People with a Mental Handicap in Wales. (1989b). *Practical steps to better practice. Better early counseling in Wales.* Cardiff, U.K.: Fingerprints.

Sturmey, P. (1990). Portage guide to early education: Partnership with parents and cross-cultural aspects. In P. L. Evans & R. Clarke (Eds.), *Combating mental handicap: A multidisciplinary approach* (pp. 89–100). London: AB Academic Publisher.

Sturmey, P., & Crisp, A. G. (1986). Portage guide to early education: A review of research. *Educational Psychology, 6*, 139–157.

Sturmey, P., Newton, T., & Crisp, A. G. (1988). Writing behavioral objectives:

An evaluation of a simple, inexpensive method. *Journal of Advanced Nursing, 13,* 496-500.

Swann, W. (1988). Trends in special school placement to 1986: Measuring, assessing and explaining segregation. *Oxford Review of Education, 14,* 139-161.

Tomlinson, S. (1982). *A sociology of special education.* London: Routledge & Kegan Paul.

Warnock, H. M. (1978). *Special educational needs: Report of a committee of enquiry into the education of handicapped children and young people.* London: HMSO.

Wilton, K., & Renault, J. (1986). Stress levels in families with intellectually handicapped preschool children and families with non-handicapped preschool children. *Journal of Mental Deficiency Research, 30,* 163-169.

Woodward, M. (1959). The behavior of idiots interpreted by Piaget's theory of sensory development. *British Journal of Educational Psychology, 29,* 65-71.

Wynn, M., & Wynn, A. (1975). *Prevention of handicap and the health of women.* London: Routledge & Kegan Paul.

Author Index

Subject Index

CONTRIBUTORS

DONALD B. BAILEY, JR., Frank Porter Graham Child Development Center, University of North Carolina at Chapel Hill, 105 Smith Level Road, Chapel Hill, NC 27599–8180.

MARIA E. BARRERA, Infant-Parent Program, Chedoke-McMaster Hospital, 1200 Main Street West, Hamilton, Ontario, Canada L8N 3Z5.

CHRISTINE COOK, Early Childhood Special Education Program, Department of Teacher Development and Curriculum Studies, Kent State University, Kent, OH 44242.

ELISABETH M. DYKENS, Child Study Center, Yale Medical School, 213 South Frontage Road, P.O. Box 3333, New Haven, CT 06510.

DAVID GIBSON, Department of Psychology, University of Calgary, 2500 University Drive, N.W., Calgary, Alberta, Canada T2N 1N4.

ALAN HAYES, Fred and Eleanor Schonell Special Education Research Center, University of Queensland, St. Lucia, Queensland 4072, Australia.

ROBERT M. HODAPP, Department of Psychology and Yale Child Study Center, Yale University, Box 11A Yale Station, New Haven CT 06520.

MARK S. INNOCENTI, Early Intervention Research Institute, Utah State University, Logan, UT 84322.

KOFI MARFO, Department of Educational Psychology and Leadership Studies, 405 White Hall, Kent State University, Kent, OH 44242.

JEANETTE A. McCOLLUM, Department of Special Education, 288 Education Building, University of Illinois at Urbana-Champaign, 1310 South Sixth Street, Champaign, IL 61820.

RUNE J. SIMEONSSON, Special Education and School Psychology Programs, School of Education, Peabody Hall 037A, University of North Carolina at Chapel Hill, Chapel Hill, NC 27514.

PETER STURMEY, School of Psychology, University of Birmingham, P. O. Box 363, Birmingham, United Kingdom B15 2TT.

MARCIA SUMMERS, Department of Educational Psychology, Teachers College, Ball State University, Muncie, IN 47306.